OPEN WORLD EMPIRE

POSTMILLENNIAL POP

General Editors: Karen Tongson and Henry Jenkins

Open World Empire

Race, Erotics, and the Global Rise of Video Games

Christopher B. Patterson

NEW YORK UNIVERSITY PRESS
New York

NEW YORK UNIVERSITY PRESS
New York
www.nyupress.org

References to internet websites (URLs) were accurate at the time of writing. Neither the author nor New York University Press is responsible for URLs that may have expired or changed since the manuscript was prepared.

Library of Congress Cataloging-in-Publication Data
Names: Patterson, Christopher B., author.
Title: Open world empire : race, erotics, and the global rise of video games /
Christopher B. Patterson.
Description: New York : New York University Press, [2020] | Series: Postmillennial pop |
Includes bibliographical references and index. |
Identifiers: LCCN 2019030785 | ISBN 9781479802043 (cloth) | ISBN 9781479895908
(paperback) | ISBN 9781479886029 (ebook) | ISBN 9781479886364 (ebook)
Subjects: LCSH: Video games—Social aspects. | Video games—Political aspects.
Classification: LCC GV1469.34.S52 P375 2020 | DDC 794.8—dc23
LC record available at https://lccn.loc.gov/2019030785

New York University Press books are printed on acid-free paper, and their binding materials are chosen for strength and durability. We strive to use environmentally responsible suppliers and materials to the greatest extent possible in publishing our books.

Manufactured in the United States of America

10 9 8 7 6 5 4 3 2 1

Also available as an ebook

For Y-Dang and Kai

In loving memory of Donald Goellnicht,

who played and slipped away.

CONTENTS

LIST OF FIGURES

Introduction

Touching Empire, Playing Theory

If literature was the artistic expression of empire throughout the age of colonization, and cinema was empire's main force of ideological reshaping throughout the era of American military dominance (with its Hollywood endings and its Anglo-American standards of beauty and heroism), then video games are the main artistic expression of empire today, the open world empire. But in order to apprehend games as such, we must be able to play them erotically. That is, not as ideological narratives or as subconscious infiltration devices à la an episode of *Black Mirror*, but to understand games as players do—as mere playthings that afford new passions, pleasures, desires, and attachments, that place grave attention on our own positions in the world and make us conscious of our power over others.

Video games vastly outpace all other entertainment media in revenue and global reach.[1] On the surface, games do not appear ideological, nor are they categorized as national products, yet their very existence has been conditioned upon the spread of militarized technology, the exploitation of racial and gendered labor hierarchies in their manufacture, and the techno-utopian associations of the digital. Games thus reflect the routes and power of information technology (IT). Like Europe's East India Companies that pursued trade with Asia, IT companies are corporate harbingers of empire that create transnational circuits and produce systems of exploitation that do not seem explicitly tied to nationalist projects, even as they increasingly take on more of the sovereign state's roles of surveillance, tracking, identifying, surveying, and censorship. Video games function as the artistic expression of this phenomenon, as products of it, and as attempts to stage discussions concerning how designers and digital cultures relate to the material processes that make games possible as network devices and as cutting-edge hardware. Games discern how war and imperial violence proceed today under the signs of openness, transparency, and digital utopia.

The open world empire is our contemporary empire of information technology, drone warfare, permanent war, and massacres that occur with little scandal or protest. Most often, information technology companies are branded by images of idealistic white leaders who appear too pure and naive to enact the same imperial designs as the rampant bankers, factory owners, and colonial architects who came before them. Yet, games carry production chains that also include the slavery, rape, and violence that comes with gathering raw materials[2] as well as the exploitation, bodily fatigue, environmental degradation, and suicide associated with Asian female sweatshop work.[3] Following Mimi Nguyen's casting of the US empire as an "Empire of Freedom" that instrumentalizes freedom as a universal value "to reinforce a politics of war, terror, and occupation,"[4] video games train us to perceive a transnational, capitalist, and industrial form of empire, an "Open World Empire" where truth, openness, and transparency become elastic terms deployed within networks of forgetting and red herring scandals. Our enduring faith in transparency and scandal has a troubling history in the transpacific, particularly in American wars wherein exposures of the Pentagon papers during Vietnam and the Abu Ghraib scandal in Iraq did not end war (though they are often credited as doing so) but shifted the methods of waging war from a traditional "boots on the ground" strategy to one relying more on militarized technologies, which include massive aerial bombings in the case of Vietnam and drone warfare in the case of the War on Terror. In too many cases, exposure has yielded only calls for greater safety for "our boys," resulting in reforms to replace the methods of warfare with even more distanced forms of killing and remote surveillance so that would-be scandals like the 7.6 million tons of explosives dropped on Indochina or the destruction of orphanages, hospitals, and wedding parties by drones can pass by as transparent already exposed events that evade the nature of scandal, keeping us well adjusted to our own injustices.

Openness brings to mind the technology of a flashlight refusing opacity, erasing the limitless capacity of the darkness, the sublime fear of the unknown, to reveal order, identity, and culpability. As Nguyen writes, the presumption of transparency reiterates "metaphysical fantasies of otherness as authentic resistance, *or* of sameness as common humanity."[5] The universal application of transparency and openness harbors forms of racism ("racializing surveillance"[6]) and suppresses the techniques of racialized peoples to present race as a form of technology that "one uses, even as one is used by it."[7] Yet in the academy, calls by IT industries for greater openness and transparency have been met lockstep by digital humanities disciplines that advance orthodoxies of openness by championing modes of research and teaching that are committed to open, public knowledge and that rely upon the collection of social media and big data. Since the incorporation of digital humanities into the Modern Language Association in 2011, its critics have become more outspoken, claiming that the field "prides itself as all-inclusive [and] interdisciplinary, but really only highlights certain perspectives."[8] While these critiques have pushed the field toward more critical studies that include greater awareness and accountability for gendered, racial, and sexual difference, they have also overlooked the field's imperial dimensions. Though only three of the 188 digital humanities centers in the world reside in Asia, Asia has long functioned as the crucial transit point for the manufacture, engineering, development, and consumption of digital technology. The point here is not to refuse forms of transparency and open access but to ask to what extent imperial violence today hides not in darkness but in plain sight.

Gamers will recognize the "open world" not as an imperial strategy but as a meta-genre of AAA (blockbuster) video games like the *Elder Scrolls* series, the *Fallout* series, and the *Grand Theft Auto* series. These games emphasize the common values of the open world empire inaugurated by information technologies that reimagine the world as a space of openness and new frontiers. Open world video games, too, attempt to give players freedom, yet their freedom is defined not by capitalism (the freedom to own, buy, or sell) or by state rights (the freedom to live, to vote, to believe) but by a child's freedom from the masters of control, a freedom to reinvent and experiment within a "magic circle" of play. Infamously, this open world freedom has revealed the perversity of the gamer, as games like *Grand Theft Auto* conjure a very different type of freedom than digital utopia suggests: the freedom to jack a taxi, to kill a cop, to have sex with prostitutes. This open world vision of freedom reiterates the desire to conquer and dominate foreign spaces and in many ways circles back to an old definition of freedom as travel and dominance, a freedom that is imagined today by comparing the West with the "unfreedoms" that characterize Asian technology (China's "great firewall"; production lines at assembling plants and microprocessor factories; the cyberpunk dystopia of Japan and Hong Kong; the e-waste in toxic rivers and garbage patches; the deaths of Asian gamers who are hopelessly addicted to video games)[9]. However, this "open" form of freedom also carries the potential to counteract neoliberal notions of freedom defined through the freedom to choose one's own route of self-optimization. If the open world of information technology suggests the freedom of transparency and utopic futures, freedom in open world video games alludes to perverse, erotic forms of freedom, a sense of transforming the *well* adjusted into the *mal*adjusted.

Gamers are well aware that the freedom in video games carries limits greater than the sweeping order of information technology would let on. Many games seek to dissolve notions of freedom and choice by expressing "player agency" as an easily susceptible fantasy, a fanciful disobedience that can only be experienced by deviating from the directed path. In the game *The Stanley Parable* (2011), the player takes the role of an office worker, Stanley, whose journey is narrated by a storyteller (voiced by Kevan Brighting) who reacts to the player's seemingly free decisions with irritation and comical antipathy. In my playthrough, I meandered through an office building following instructions by the storyteller: "This is Stanley . . . Stanley left his office."[10] Obeying, I left the office. And I kept obeying, until I came to a set of two doors (see Figure I.1). "When Stanley came to a set of two open doors," the narrator said, "he entered the door on his left."

Of course, I knew what was happening. The narrator, the designer, whoever was behind the curtain, wanted me to go to the door on my right. The left door was a command, a clear-cut progression into someone else's story. I, the open world gamer, wanted my own story. And, it must be said, I wanted to get a rise out of the narrator. Either way, it meant disobedience. The game, too, was in on the ruse, nudging me to the right in the most convincing way a game can: by telling me to go left. So I obeyed by disobeying, blindly following the crumb trails of disobedience by going right. The narrator burst into hysterics, prodding me to go back, to get on track for his story, but the more he pleaded in his

When Stanley came to a set of two open doors, he entered the door on his left.

Figure I.1. A set of doors in *The Stanley Parable*. Screenshot by author.

panicked and authoritative British accent, the more I refused. At some point I fell off a cargo lift and died.

I restarted the game, again went through the door on the right, leaped out of a window, and again died. I restarted again, went right again, perished again. Every new playthrough, I did the opposite of what the storyteller wanted. I walked up stairs when he wanted me to go down. I sat staring at a key combination even as he screamed the code at me. I spent twenty minutes standing still in a broom closet, just to hear him squirm. When I saw no new routes of disobedience left, I leaped down a six-story stairwell. "Feel really powerful now?" the narrator said as I bled out, dead.

The Stanley Parable captures the gamer's strange desire to lash out, a desire that games yank out of otherwise motionless bodies. Open world gamers push buttons for no other reason than to see what nonsense they can conjure. Within every boundary is the desire to transgress that boundary, to leap from a window, to break the game. Games thus summon a definition of openness not as transparency and imperial claim over the foreign but as an openness akin to Michel Foucault's sense of the "open game" of gay sex in volume 2 of *The History of Sexuality*. In contrast to the "closed" game of heterosexual marriage—with clearly defined rules, boundaries, and legal consequences—the open game of gay relationships was open spatially (played in the open), open in attachment (not monogamous by default), open legally (beyond the law), and open metaphorically (as a feeling that anything can happen, as signs without clear meanings).[11] Foucault considered these relationships as "open" games because they were outside traditional sexual boundaries, and therefore they tested one's own self-perceptions as an ethical being capable of moral reasoning. Outside of the constraints of state and religious institutions, gay sex involved an openness that put weight and responsibility upon every action. As in *The Stanley Parable*, openness can form uncertain pathways, often resulting in wastes of time, in trolling those in authority for no other reason than personal pleasure. Yet the game forces us to question our own motives. The "open game" recasts openness not as transparency and the freedom to collect data but as an openness of opacity, of uncertainty, of risk, and of the consistent vexing of our relationships with others, which are not clearly defined and thus ask for more ethical and moral pondering.

Open World Empire takes up play as a form of erotics and applies it to an understanding of open imperial violence in our information-choked era of permanent war. As Chen Kuan-Hsing has argued, imperialization takes place not only in the colonies but within the empire itself, where national subjects must continuously be "imperialized" to think of themselves as endowed with the responsibilities deserving of empire.[12] Like gamers, subjects of this empire are not really supposed to follow the instructions but to practice a form of freedom based on a meaningless gesture of adolescent rebellion, a disobedience where risk is deferred into distant places (in the imperial provinces), distant times (the slow warming of the Earth), and unlikely scenarios (the election of a reality television clown to US president). In misbehaving, subjects are not resisting a system but helping it thrive—a system that provides avatar personalities, each characterized by their own marginalization, alterity, and mode of resistance, where even the rich, powerful, and privileged are made to feel like victims. Video games participate within this thorny context by reinventing concepts of freedom and power through game-based interpretations of openness and erotic play.

Situated within the critical humanities fields of American studies, Asian American studies, critical game studies, and queer theory, *Open*

World Empire explores how games enact playful protests against the power, identity, and order of information technology. While the open world empire relies on forms of self-administration manifested in rigorously calculated self-depictions on social media (where one's value is measurable in likes and friends), the gaming open world evokes an anarchic self—unrestrained, messy, contradictory, not reliant upon political self-depictions but on bodily sensations and erotic engagements. "Erotics" thus distinguishes my understanding of games from dominant perspectives of "gamification," which emphasize play as a type of progress and development, a notion "that most Westerners cherish" but is "more often assumed than demonstrated."[13] Erotics, as I will argue, preserves "some of the wondrous anarchy of childhood" and does not let our strange, addictive mischief go.[14] More importantly, erotics opens us to other forms of disobedience: speaking truth to power; being queer in the face of a culture where power from both the authorities and the pulpit is aligned against queers; sticking up for migrants, refugees, and people of color, even if it means breaking the law or punching a Nazi in the face (there's a game for that). At the heart of *Open World Empire* is an attempt to comprehend these gamer-like strains of disobedience within play; to trace how they flourish from the erotic sensations of a game to our opaque and distanced relationships to others; and to ask how, if we dare, we can be really, really, disobedient.

Games of Catch

The estimated 2.2 billion gamers around the world are not kids (they hold a mean age of thirty-one), nor are they male (men and women game near equally), nor are they American (the Asia-Pacific takes up 47 percent of revenue, led by mainland Chinese players, while Americans only make up 13 percent of revenue), nor are they interpolated into militaristic killing machines (shooting games make up only 25 percent of the US market).[15] Despite these facts, games are still characterized as mere prosthetics of empire that train players in military tactics and whose designers are in league with US military recruiters. While this is undeniably true for a few games, the game industry's flirtation with empire is in fact a much more dispersed story: the material resources for game hardware are often derived from African mines, where minerals like coltan ore in the PlayStation 2 have been categorized as a conflict mate-rial that has propelled parts of the Republic of the Congo into civil war; game hardware is manufactured and processed in Asian sites like the Pearl River Delta, where workers labor under brutal conditions—stuffed into small dormitories, immured within company "campuses"—and work twelve-hour shifts; the most recognizably American game genre is militarized shooting games, many of which have been funded by the US military explicitly for recruitment and propaganda; the controls for com-bat drones or unmanned aerial vehicles (UAVs) are made to mimic video game controllers. These are troubling facts, none of which make games any more or less imperial than literature, music, or film. Still, games are unique in tracing these imperial contexts through the racial, gendered, and sexual norms associated with information technology and in their transpacific routes of circulation.

Despite the troubling violences that make games possible, games are rarely discussed as products of imperial routes.[16] Instead, many game studies scholars continue to discuss games within a pure "ludic" language focused on existential questions of games and being (What is a game? What does it mean to play? Is a game more narrative or more game?).[17] Perhaps the most common example of what it means to play a game comes from Markku Eskelinen in the first ever issue of *Game Studies* (2004), where he insisted that video games cannot be analyzed within national/racial/structural contexts because narrative and representation are only incidental. "If I throw a ball at you," Eskelinen writes, "I don't expect you to drop it and wait until it starts telling stories."[18] Perhaps by focusing on the existential nature of "the game," one misses the obvious narrative and contextual elements of "catching": if I catch the ball, I am strong, fertile, straight, manly; if I stumble, I am childish, queer, a fail-ure, a sissy. "Dropping the ball," a common colloquialism for fucking up, conjures normative aspects of success, heterosexuality, and nationalism (our national sport), just like any game.[19]

The decontextualizing methods of much game studies scholarship has obscured what video games are: commodities routed in transpa-cific processes of labor and resource extraction. *Open World Empire* di-verges from a formalist tradition of game studies to see their transpacific networks as a rich site for fathoming the varied impact of information technology, from the routes of microprocessor factories and assembling plants in Malaysia and China to the routes of intellectual property from Japan to the West. Games do not merely shape how we see empire in Asia but have facilitated its growth and formation through Cold War presumptions of technological ability (techno-Orientalism) and labor availability (colonial-era racial structures). By seeking to understand interactive gameplay experiences alongside the discourses of information technology that envelop them, I hope to unwedge the imperial attitudes within games discourses that see Asia as a space of manufacture/production and America as a site of development/design. Against the discursive ambit of games that presume their universality, *Open World Empire* explores how acts of play are made possible by a vast transpacific network of global exchange that partitions Asia into an open frontier of technological advancement.

While some games discourses have remained mired in questions of game being, others have contributed to the wider belief that games are to blame for much of society's ills—from providing military training to creating capitalist drones.[20] Such studies permit the American war industry to claim games as their own and ignore the various meanings that players themselves give to games, so that the true meaning of a game resides with the theorist, not the players. The pleasure that players take from games can then be reduced to mere ideological conditioning so that, as Richard Dyer wrote, "pleasure remains a forbidden term of reference, particularly on the left."[21] This "leftist" discourse permits the ideology of the war industry to frame an entire medium. Claiming games (and the pleasure received from them) as conduits for violence, capitalism, and misogyny ignores the nuances of game genres, some of which, like horror movies, westerns, superhero movies, etc., contain various depictions of violence no matter their political orientation. Attuned to these nuances, gamers themselves play within their own interpretive context, relying on no institutional authority to interpret a game's meaning for them, permitting games to remain, as Alexander Galloway writes, a "lowbrow" medium, a "beautifully undisturbed processing of contemporary life, as yet unmarred by bourgeois exegeses of the format."[22] Games, unlike literature or a good French wine, demand no refinement, and thus their meanings are, for gamers, radically plural.[23] Both formalist game studies discourses and "leftist" discourses of games as mere ideology fall into what Anna Anthropy calls "a dangerous trap" because both "cede the right to decide the value of games to an authority that has nothing to do with games."[24] Fortunately, these discourses have so far remained irrelevant to most gamers, alongside dated stereotypes of gamers as zombielike addicts to capitalism, patriarchy, and militarism. Most game cultures refuse the mystification of so-called experts who would interpret the meanings of an otherwise pleasurable and erotic activity.[25]

Open World Empire makes no attempt to posit games as serious art— time itself will do that for us. Instead, this book seeks to take advantage of what will ultimately be a very brief and capacious period of gaming history before games are purged of their mercurial ardor and claimed by pedigreed experts as meaningful and artistic "works." For now, we can still play with games as merely perverse objects. To do so, this book practices a "low theory"[26] that collaborates with gamer cultures by apprehending how games work on the body and recognizes a game's various meanings across a spectrum of contexts and audiences.[27] Its research archive puts academic scholarship in dialogue with a range of user-created content that reveals discarded local knowledges and experiential insights from gamers themselves, from "Let's Play" and *Twitch* videos, where gamers record themselves playing and commenting on games, to fan-based archives like online encyclopedias, YouTube comments, and forum posts, to popular magazines like *Kotaku* and *Eurogamer*. Whereas in literature courses one can presume that the teacher has read more than the students, no such presumption can be made in the world of gaming. Even after playing over fifty hours of a single game, a games researcher could then be expected to wade through an ocean of secondary reading/watching/listening in online forums, podcasts, game guides, YouTube channels, etc. Gamer expertise has been widely acknowledged by game companies, who solicit fan participation as a form of "playbour" that informs design decisions and program modification.[28] Where a scholar might interpret video game representations as racist, violent, and misogynist, gamers well versed in reading the nuances of games and game discourses may interpret them as hyperbolic or self-parodying.[29] When gamers are excluded from the archives, scholars miss the fact that their arguments concerning gamers as "interpolated" and subconsciously influenced by games are all too common topics of debate within gamer cultures, and they are often more elaborate within these cultures because they come from a deep well of gameplay experiences. Gamer discourses can even be more sophisticated than academic discourses, since many gamer cultures are not allergic to debates about sexuality, diversity, gender, and racism in video games. Gamers are consistently "in the know" about a world that is altogether inaccessible to many scholars simply due to the lack of time.

There is one games discourse that gamers themselves do not stray very far from: that games are silly, frivolous, jocular, and erotic. As Anna Anthropy aptly writes, games are "an experience created by rules," meaning that "the rules themselves aren't the game, the interaction is!"[30] Interactive experiences can be deeply personal and subjective, from experiences of erotic fulfillment to merely ways of killing time.[31] Rather than try to justify these experiences to others by seeing them as progressive or educational, gamers are often the first to adopt frivolous and erotic sensibilities toward games. Anna Anthropy's own game *Mighty Jill Off* incorporates the already erotic forms of gameplay and makes them explicitly, inescapably sexual. *Mighty Jill Off* inserts the basic "masocore" form of platform gameplay—where one is subjected to frequent deaths and extremely difficult jumping/timing—into a narrative about punishment between a leather-clad domme and her boot-fetish submissive (see Figure I.2). As a queering of the 1986 game *Mighty Bomb Jack*, Anthropy's *Mighty Jill Off* pushes us to reimagine the entire genre of platform games, from *Super Mario Bros.* on, as games that have always carried dimensions of the erotic, the kinky, and the masochistic.

As Brendan Keogh writes, video games' reputation as a form of "low" culture aligns them not with "creative works that engage the mind (literature, classic music, painting)," but with "'lowly' forms that evoke the body (pulp films, pop music, romance novels, pornography)."[32] To get ahold of this 'lowly' form, I join Jack Halberstam and Lauren Berlant in treating a silly archive, what Berlant calls the materials that "frequently use the silliest, most banal and erratic logic imaginable to describe important things, like what constitutes intimate relations, political personhood, and national life."[33] Jack Halberstam would later refer to this archive as the materials that "do not make us better people or liberate us," but "offer strange and anticapitalistic ways of being and acting and knowing" and that "harbor covert and overt

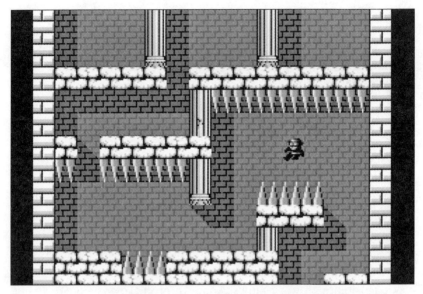

Figure 1.2. Jill proving herself to the Queen in *Mighty Jill Off*. Screenshot by author.

queer worlds."[34] I hope to conceive of games as sensational artistic media that can ignite a sense of new possibilities. This begins by dissecting the silly, the fun, and the pleasurable and treating play sensibly as play. "Play," whether from a cat biting its young or a lover biting an ear, radically shifts the meanings of every act. This does not mean that violence or prejudice in a game are excusable or should be tolerated as mere parody, but that interactivity cannot be well understood without attending to the "open world" freedom play affords to test boundaries and to experiment with and against power in an environment where play remains inescapably playful.

In 2010, Adrienne Shaw criticized games studies for its lack of critical engagement and argued for a "critical cultural study of games" that compelled game scholars to adopt cultural studies modes of critical engagement and reflexivity.[35] Thanks to work from Shaw and many others (Anna Anthropy, Anna Everett, Kishonna L. Gray, Soraya Murray, Lisa Nakamura, Bonnie Ruberg), the landscape of game studies is considerably more open to critical work than ever before, with many works having performed transformative critiques across the field (*Games of Empire, Gaming at the Edge, Queer Game Studies, Gaming*

Representation). Following these giants, *Open World Empire* strives to understand interactive media in relation to discourses of information technology and the commodity routes that they create across the transpacific. In our current context, seeing gameplay as totally apolitical or as totally ideological buttresses discourses of information technology as godlike creators and erases the experiences of those who actually play these games. Video games shed light on the hierarchies built by information technology across the globe while also creatively reimagining spaces in Asia and North America through a frivolous style of playful protest, an "erotics of play," wherein social meanings are construed through pleasure, passion, and intimacy.

Playing Sex

The place where queer subjects and games meet is also
a space of erotic play.
—Bonnie Ruberg, "Queerness and Video Games: Queer
Game Studies and New Perspectives through Play"

In the past decade, game studies has broadened to make room for works by and about minorities and queer folk, yet many of the presumptions of game studies has remained steadfast through the persistent idealization of play itself. Terms like "immersion," "magic circle," and "agency," so commonly invoked in game studies, were conceived as direct refusals of what I am calling the erotic, or what Janet Murray, in her oft-cited book *Hamlet on the Holodeck,* called the fallible methods of poststructural theory and "postmodern critics," who Murray repudiated for their "stylistic (equi)vocation and philosophical detachment."[36] As one of game studies' most cited texts, *Hamlet on the Holodeck* rejected a language of the body, intimacy, and opacity to instead rely on "rational" logics found in the positivistic discourses of cognitive psychology, analytical philosophy, and phenomenology. Murray enjoined values of transparency and openness to game studies by framing games as antithetical to the "postmodern" and its thinkers who use "jargon" (like the word "problematization") for whom "confusion is not a bug but a feature."[37] Though many have faulted Murray's work on games for privileging narrative, overstating player agency, or creating an "immersive fallacy,"[38] few have pointed out how her outright rejection of "the postmodern" has nothing to do with the experience of playing video games and in fact bounds the very act of play within serious forms of the rational and the philosophical.[39] Her polemic against "the postmodern" follows not gamer experience but an open world paradigm that sees interactive media as providing the utopic freedom of "player agency."[40] To focus on erotics, pleasure, race, and empire are indeed antithetical to any project that seeks to shape the user as an agent of freedom and in turn disparages any who would limit that sense of freedom or reveal its structural underpinnings.

Murray's wholesale rejection of "the postmodern" followed a logic of games as providing player agency. In turn, the pleasures, desires, and erotic drives of gameplay have haunted game studies as frivolous subjects for analysis.[41] Another heavily cited text in the field, Bernard Suits's *The Grasshopper* (1978), defined "a game" by naming erotics as its negation. "Playing games," Suits wrote, "is different from sexual activity" because sex has no obvious winner and loser (said no queer person ever!).[42] Yes, games deal in pleasures, passions, and desires, but *sexual* pleasures and *erotic* desires remain excluded from the definition of a game, reconstituting games, game culture, and developers as male "geeks" who remain pure, innocent, and innovative.[43] Erotics has thus suffered in game studies because of such "stereotypes about gaming, masculinity, and sex, evoking an immature, furtive, frustrated, and comically grotesque form of male sexuality."[44] Since its inception, game studies has hesitated to discuss sex except as a "risk" that goes to characterize the perversity of Asian (particularly Japanese) cultures or as an "awkward" element that disrupts their main methodology.[45] Game platforms themselves, like Steam and the Apple digital store, often purge their catalogs of sexually explicit material, even as obscenely violent games remain bestsellers.[46] In the face of this open world paradigm against sex, erotics, and the postmodern, I ask: What if we changed our methodology to account for frivolous behavior and sexuality in the very act of playing? What if erotics did not disturb our method but defined it?

When not seen as progressive, militaristic, educational, or as providing player agency, gameplay emerges as a frivolous practice that resists easy incorporation into state and neoliberal attitudes, as it appears as a self-indulgent waste of time. Sutton-Smith calls this discourse of games a "rhetoric of frivolity," which sees gameplay as a useless escapism. Erotics, as Audre Lorde has pointed out, shares in this rhetoric of uselessness, as discourses of erotics have pathologized sensual feelings into "the confused, the trivial, the psychotic, [and] the plasticized sensation."[47] As Megan Condis argues, techno-utopic discourses seek to surpass erotics by trusting in virtual worlds to "mark the end of gender, and even of the body, as we know it."[48] In the context of our open world empire, the "trivial" erotic and the "frivolous" video game seem a destined pairing, especially if we see the erotic not as asking "what we do," but as questioning "how acutely and fully we can feel in the doing."[49] Erotic perceptions of video games can shift modes of perception to more "acute" and "full" capacities to comprehend the social contexts through which video games are decoded.

In being construed as nonsexual, games discourses have divided play from fetish, immersion from love, interaction from intimacy, and pleasure from sex. Critics then remain suspicious of games that permit or encourage the indulgence of "perversity," such as sadism, voyeurism, child homosexuality, and female objectification. Evidence for this suspicion manifested with the 1992 Sega game *Night Trap*, where players monitored full-motion video of a girls' slumber party via hidden cameras (*Night Trap*, along with *Mortal Kombat*, sparked the creation of the Entertainment Software Rating Board [ESRB] rating system still in place today). The anxiety over gamer sexuality has been informed by, as Foucault might call it, a preoccupation with sex as a perverse pleasure, where the figure of the masturbating child or the homosexual adult lurks as anomalies to be normalized and disciplined.[50] Gamers of course resemble both. As Amanda Phillips has argued, the pleasure of killing an enemy with a well-placed headshot has an erotic and sadistic undercurrent, while the tactile stimulation of the controller in games like *Bayonetta* can be read as clitoral stimulation.[51] Despite the erasure of erotics as a form of play, the libido of games has lurked within its pleasure practices.[52]

As a method, erotics does not focus on representations of sex and sexuality in erotic or pornographic games but on the *erotic forms of play* that emerge in games. As Brendan Keogh writes, "*all* videogames require a body; some just ask that the player's conscious attention be turned away from that body's actions."[53] Similarly, all games engage the erotics of the body—pleasure, desire, sensation, bliss—but only some seek to make these erotics explicit by enveloping them (or interpreting them) with a sexual object.[54] Just as Lorde saw erotics in everyday practices like "dancing, building a bookcase, writing a poem, or examining an idea," playing a game can often feel erotic, even if we do not articulate it as such.[55] Reading play as an erotic engagement makes no ontological or existential claims onto what "play" or "games" really are but evokes a particular cultural politics that resists discourses of information technology by asking how players are teased, provoked, and strung along. In this framework, gameplay is not merely erotic but also queer, as it disrupts narratives of purity and childishness that characterize the gamer. If play can take the form of a queer politics, it has the potential to expose "the punishing norms that discipline behavior and manage human development with the goal of delivering us from unruly childhoods to orderly and predictable adulthoods."[56] As the dominant voices of game studies have remained antithetical to erotics, *Open World Empire* attempts to synthesize game studies with the "pluralizing" meanings that Murray so maligns.[57] Seeking to free game meanings to the many player audiences (queer folk, Asian folk, folk of color), I argue that theorists should become more like gamers, those who can play erotically within and among contradictions.[58] This sense of erotic play is not the usual sense of "play" as the opposite of "work" but instead sits beside the verb phrase "to use." The transitive construction "to play with" invokes a mode of erotic engagement different from the extractive and colonial logics of "to use," as in, to employ or deploy. "To play with" conjures a distractive logic, as one can also play with objects or people who have fallen into disuse or been made into refuse. These are the frivolous, the useless, remade by play.

An erotics of play focuses on the sensations and sensibilities within the interactive experiences of each gameworld. As many gaming scholars have argued (Aarseth, Bogost, Galloway), gameplay and rules form the game's "dynamical meaning," defined by game designer Jonathan Blow as "the meaning that grows out of exploring a game's rules and boundaries."[59] Like genre conventions in literature, these dynamical meanings are not merely meaningful, but persuasive, as they offer convincing routes for players to weigh decisions, or they can stir new modes of play. Ian Bogost calls this a form of "procedural rhetoric," where the art of persuasion occurs "through rule-based representations and interactions rather than the spoken word, writing, images, or moving pictures."[60] Games, as a dynamic, rule-based medium, can "have a unique persuasive power" through the parameters of the game, the "processes it supports and excludes."[61] *Open World Empire* plays matchmaker to these game studies thinkers and queer theorists to consider how erotic interaction is informed by cultural and historical contexts. Here, accepting gameplay as frivolous opens the door to the unintentional, sporadic, and erotic meanings that grow out of playing a game. The persuasive grammar of games comes in the collaboration between the lifeworld of the player and the gameplay, which takes the form of core repetitive mechanics and inputs/outputs of the body.

Playing erotically can reveal the metadiscourses of games that recognize their own imperial contexts and confront us with the beguiling pleasures of imperial power. In his revision of Antonio Gramsci's ideas, Stuart Hall famously claimed a "war of positions" was being fought on the frontlines of gender, sexual, and ethnic identities.[62] For Hall, film and television were this war's main ideological medium, as film had the power to construct "points of identification, those positionalities we call in retrospect our 'cultural identities.'"[63] Film audiences identified with and against protagonists, seeing through their gaze. Perhaps video games have eluded cultural studies theorists not because they are of less importance but because they don't easily meld with an identity-based "war of positions," except in games that are explicitly cinematic (the *Assassin's Creed* series, *Sleeping Dogs*, the *Grand Theft Auto* series). The vast majority of games have little to say about identity and much more about the sensations, pleasures, and feelings of the body.[64] Video games provide fraying fantasies built upon production chains and hierarchical ordering systems, but they also stage a field of desires and pleasures within interactive experiences. The fantasy of the game becomes a space where one learns how to take pleasure in the taboo, the unspoken, the queer, and how to visualize the consequences of pleasure, even for those who seem severely distanced from it. As with sexual acts, the gravity of the fantasy doesn't always dawn upon us until after the fact.

The Last Decade of Barthes, Foucault, Sedgwick

To proclaim yourself something is always to speak at the
behest of a vengeful Other, to enter into his discourse. . . .
what society will not tolerate is that I should be . . . nothing,
or, rather, more precisely, that the something I am should
be openly expressed as provisional, revocable, insignificant,
inessential, in a word irrelevant. Just say "I am," and you will
be socially saved.
—Roland Barthes, "'Preface' to Renaud Camus, Tricks"

Traditionally, game studies has relied on frameworks concerning networks, machines, and simulation, rather than on the body, erotics, and
queer desire. Though recently game scholars have called more attention
onto affect, embodiment, and feeling,[65] much of game studies continues
to dismiss theories of erotics and sexual pleasure as anathema to analyzing video games, even as games and play are concepts that have been so
integral to theories of sexuality.[66] Seeking an alternative, anti-imperial
method of game analysis focused on the erotic, *Open World Empire* will
tease out a playpen of methods based on the work of three theorists who,
in their last decade of life on this planet, sought to abandon many of
the critique-driven epistemologies of their previous work to develop an
arts of living erotically—through touch, feeling, and amorous relations.
These are Roland Barthes, who died in 1980 after being knocked down
by a laundry van; Michel Foucault, who died of HIV-related illness in
1984; and Eve Kosofsky Sedgwick, who died of cancer in 2009. These
three theorists are often cited in queer theory, yet their contributions
have always been difficult to reconcile, as their definitions of the queer
and the erotic conflicted with their own obscure lifestyles and because
much of their later work seemed to fetishize Asia. Yet in seeking to
fathom erotics as a method, *Open World Empire* leans heavily on these
three thinkers, for whom queerness was not merely an identity, nor a
deviation from the heteronormative status quo, but an ethics drawn out
of an orientalized *ars erotica*, an erotics of play rendered through the
Asiatic.

　　The 2017 anthology *Queer Game Studies* strove to represent the field's
queer debates by welcoming chapters from game designers and critics

as well as scholars.[67] In 2018 and 2019, queer game studies discourse grew with the first ever issue of *Game Studies* devoted to "Queerness and Game Studies," and with books by Bonnie Ruberg, Christopher A. Paul, and Megan Condis focusing on queer forms of play as an alternative to the "toxic masculinity" of *some* hypervisible gaming cultures.[68] This emerging discourse has been crucial for perceiving multiple gaming cultures who relate to games in alternative—perhaps erotic—ways. Yet, thus far many queer gaming scholars have also reproduced the bare limitations of queer studies, what José Esteban Muñoz has described as an "antirelational" approach that treats sexuality as "a singular trope of difference,"[69] and which Chandan Reddy echoes when he observes that for many queer studies scholars, sexuality "names the normative frames that organize our disciplinary and interdisciplinary inquiries into our past and into contemporary racial capitalism."[70] Indeed, in re-centering the field of game studies from Asia and Europe to the American academic landscape where queer theory has remained most grounded, entire analyses of Japanese games now have little to no recognition of their multiple audiences or of Japanese aesthetic design, instead relying upon American paradigms of gender and sexuality to treat a Japanese product.[71] Furthermore, queer game studies has continued to practice a pronounced indifference to the process of game manufacture and the labor regimes involved in its production, seeing games as commodities to be reread by American consumers in queer ways. This absence of transnational labor regimes and universalizing of an American-centric gaze onto Asian products—which can broach into a queer Orientalism—is not inherent to queer theory, as Barthes, Butler, Sedgwick, Foucault, Warner, Berlant, Manalansan, and Muñoz (the list goes on) were and continue to be highly invested in transnational and capitalist dimensions of race, class, and sexuality. In video games a relational view of queerness remains of crucial importance, as its labor and creative processes are made possible through transpacific routes.

Open World Empire asks how games grant us ways to recognize the imperial and structural violences that produce game pleasure through the mythical seduction of an Asian-inflected and Asian-produced commodity. I focus on queer theorists before "queer studies" and "queer theory" became ingrained disciplines in order to question the ways in which queer studies, in the last two decades, has been devoted to structural critiques of heteronormativity in a way that departs from these early figures, for whom normativity (and identity) were not reified concepts that easily figured into a "normative"/"resistant" binary centered within North America. I return then to Sedgwick's own definition of queer, as referring to "the open mesh of possibilities, gaps, overlaps, dissonances, and resonances, lapses and excesses of meaning when the constituent elements of anyone's gender, of anyone's sexuality aren't made (or can't be made) to signify monolithically."[72] This definition, which Nicholas De Villiers calls an "open" definition of queerness,[73] does not attach itself to an American version of heteronormativity, nor to the homosexual subject, but invokes an open and vast plurality of perspectives and contexts wherein one person's queer resistance could be another's normative gaze and vice versa.[74] I focus on these authors who seek to articulate and compare forms of queerness and normativity across history and geography and to infer how their theoretical *totentanzen* conjures engagements less involved with critique and more attuned to intimacy and erotics. *Open World Empire* thus attempts not to include greater representations or recovery (though these are valuable buffs), but aims erotic play at untangling discourses of information technology, which preemptively celebrate the future of games as multicultural, tolerant, and LGBT-friendly. I ask then to what extent queer representation deadlocks the "cruel optimism" of a future-oriented equality granted by technological liberation.[75]

By focusing on the last decades of Barthes, Foucault, and Sedgwick, I seek to understand how each thinker, after devoting their careers to critiquing social norms, myths, and ideologies, sought alternatives to the structured political epistemologies that had once preoccupied them. I read this as an attempt to challenge themselves (and their readers) by refusing the language of certainty any further recourse and denying the sphere of ideology critique as the theorist's career-swallowing occupation. In *The Use of Pleasure*, volume 2 of Foucault's *History of Sexuality* (1984), Foucault deviates from his previous historical research, which was "concerned with what might be true in the fields of learning," and attempts "an analysis of the 'games of truth,'" driven by "a curiosity" that "enables one to get free of oneself."[76] As a "thematic" of analysis, erotics opened up "a new way of conceiving oneself in one's relation to one's wife, to others, to events, and to civic and political activities—and a different way of considering oneself as the subject of one's pleasures."[77] In seeking alternative methods and themes, these theorists put trust in the powers of erotics both as a self-liberation and as a means of questioning the wider contexts in which pleasure takes place, including the role that pleasure plays in critique itself.[78] Indeed, pleasure remains a major theme in comprehending erotics, where we do not have an ideological "suture" so much as what Tim Dean calls a means of "taking flight."[79]

I focus on the last decade of these thinkers not so much because they are "last" (they actually aren't) but as a metaphor for a period after these writers' perceived greatness, when their works had put them at the forefront of critical theory. What emerged for all three was a curiosity concerning otherness (Japaneseness, Greekness, Asianness, Buddhism) that offered what Foucault called a form of "straying afield of himself," and of playing "games with oneself" that questioned if one can "think differently than one thinks, and perceive differently than one sees."[80] We find similar shifts in Roland Barthes who, after his "The Death of the Author" in 1967, shifted toward an attempt to write the body, culminating in his *The Pleasure of the Text* (1973), and *A Lover's Discourse* (1977). We can also trace Eve Sedgwick's turn after the success of *Epistemology of the Closet* in 1990 and the cancer diagnosis that immediately followed. Once hailed by *Rolling Stone* magazine as "the soft-spoken queen of the constructionists,"[81] Sedgwick turned from constructs to feelings, touch, and erotics, a shift that she articulated in her 1995 manifesto, "Paranoid Reading and Reparative Reading." Here I ask a question that plays upon the seriousness of death and authorial greatness: Just what was with the "last decade" for these queer theorists, this time spent on "games," "erotics," and "touching"? Why did their writings undergo such a major shift that they would all later be accused of abandoning their politics (at least, their Marxist-oriented politics)? What was it about death that led to a greater focus on the body and its possibilities (even for Barthes, who was unaware of his impending death)? What was so important for these thinkers, I find, was an exploration of a queer art, an *ars erotica*, where one's self could only be understood within its fragments. It is within their last decades that these thinkers turned from being critics to lifestyle philosophers, whose interests in Asia allowed them to comprehend new ways of acting, feeling, and imagining the future.

In returning to these scholars of queer lore, I also hope not to dismiss the many critiques of their work that have emerged over time: that they repeated themselves *ad infinitum* (see Barthes on Barthes), that they privileged the white European gaze (see Spivak[82]), that they dismissed racial assemblages (see Weheliye), that they were Orientalist (see Mavor), that they overprioritized erotics and sexuality over "psychoanalytic truths" (see Siegel[83]), that their attempts at "unknowing" signaled archival laziness (see Nussbaum), that they were not themselves queer according to whatever technical definition (see Weigman on Sedgwick's hecklers), that they were closeted, obscurist, and unnecessarily opaque (see De Villiers[84]). This book does not join in these public scoldings, nor does it rhapsodize the genius or conscience of these thinkers. Instead, I play with them as theoretical cooperative partners to discern how erotics emerges through the gaps, the faults, the obscure, the fetishistic, the Asiatic, and the inevitability of death. I treat their theoretical toolsets not to use them as surgical instruments for dissection but as toys for animating new possibilities and for reimagining our vexed imperial present. My playful readings then will append Barthes's own "Death of the Author" with the Death of the Critic, to ask what can emerge from longingly hugging these theorists without plodding through structuralist/poststructuralist debates, or by becoming fluent in French, or by revisiting their diaries and public personas. With much shame (as shame constitutes queerness), *Open World Empire* plays with and alongside these thinkers in a way that might give theoretician gatekeepers a panic attack. For what better way to theorize play than to do so playfully?

Let's Play Erotics

In human consciousness eroticism is that within man which
calls his being in question.
—Georges Bataille, "Erotism, Death and Sensuality"

Erotics is an art of conceiving how pleasure, desire, and the interactive work upon the body as a way to master ourselves and to recognize how our pleasures impact others.[85] In games these desires are often social and political—the desire for power, for self-optimization, for knowledge, the desire to dominate, and the pleasures of being dominated. Summarizing

Foucault, Amber Jamilla Musser writes that "desire" for Foucault was often "mired in a psychoanalytic concept of lack and anticipation," while "pleasure" emerged as a form of creative possibility.[86] Video games expose our troubling and sometimes violent desires while enticing us to pursue more creative and queer pleasures within the cordoned-off space of the gameworld, and it is through this realm of sandbox experimentation that we can fathom our erotic selves.

Barthes conceives of an "erotics of reading" in his *The Pleasure of the Text*,[87] where Barthes calls a text of "pleasure" the text that "contents, fills, grants euphoria."[88] In volume 2 of *The History of Sexuality*, Foucault conceptualized erotics as a method to solve the ethical problem of the self's relationship to itself, that is, to its desires, pleasures, and actions, what he calls (from the Greek) *aphrodisia*, an "open" concept of sexuality that includes its context and future consequences toward others. Sedgwick does not use the term "erotics," but "touch" and "feeling" to grasp the body's sensation-based relationship to a text. For Sedgwick, to "touch" is to remain open to other histories, other experiences, other ways of thinking. In turn, "touch" cannot be defined "in terms of structure" without making "a qualitative misrepresentation."[89] All three of these authors apprehend the erotic as a means of recognizing sensations that remain tied to fetish, play, and virtualizing the other for playful imaginings (Barthes wrote not about Japan but "that country I am calling Japan"[90]).

For some who work in affect theory, erotics would belong to the "individualized" emotions, feelings or drives that Brian Masumi, in his landmark 1995 essay on affect theory, "The Autonomy of Affect," saw as frivolous and irrelevant to a wider Marxist/feminist view of affect as revealing a "pre-ideological" structure.[91] Erotics has thus far been an easy scapegoat, a merely asocial feeling or sensation that relies on Orientalist fetishization, the "other" to affect studies as much as it has been the "other" to discourses of game theory and information technology.[92] Erotics, unlike these others, has no easy component to sociality, ideology, or the realm of the political, making it seem aberrant. But as Barthes, Foucault, and Sedgwick stress in their last decade, erotics was not a topic to be discussed or a feeling to be known so much as a means of engagement, an alternative mode of embodied interaction offering new ways to speak, to feel, to act, and, most pertinent for us: to play.

I here provide a brief genealogy of erotics as a form of play, made visible through the major "problems" that scholars often perceive within Barthes, Foucault, and Sedgwick: their obscure queer identities, their rejection of Marxist epistemologies, and their fetish for Asia. I treat these three "problems" as different avatars expressing a similar erotic sensibility. One's refusal to meet an audience's hunger for identity (on their terms) remains deeply connected to one's refusal to reinvest in Marxist/materialist critiques, which can be refused only by looking outside, across oceans, to a distant and unknowable "Asia." As these shifts and modes of identity are also very personal, I cannot claim that these perceived "problems" necessitate each other, but we can remove the injunction that would see them as separable (as if any theorist can just so happen to fetishize Asia). Through these "problems" I hope to unspool an erotic method of confronting otherness typified by "the Asiatic," a playful engagement with Asia that exposes how notions of the erotic (like the exotic) bleed easily into the idealistic, the fetishistic, the Orientalist.

Barthes's writing toyed with language by tracing its edges, reveling in its opacity, just as Barthes himself did not come "out of the closet" into a gay identity but preferred to inhabit an opaque sexuality, irreducible to a political identity.[93] In "The Death of the Author" (1967), which signaled a turn from logic to the erotic, Barthes called writing itself "the negative where all identity is lost, starting with the very identity of the body writing."[94] One could see Barthes's later work as an attempt to return to this lost body, to keep the body within the act of writing and reading. It seems no coincidence that "The Death of the Author" was published the year after Barthes visited Tokyo (1966), where he began writing his book about Japan, *Empire of Signs* (1970). Indeed, Barthes's writings of Japan as a stage for self-inquiry sounds remarkably similar to the insights of "The Death of the Author," where Barthes as author(ity) is far removed by also removing Japan as a knowable object. In *Empire of Signs*, Barthes seeks not to "lovingly gaz[e] toward an Oriental essence," but to understand how Japan, as a "fictive country," has afforded him a situation of writing.[95] It is also in Barthes's later writings where he envisages pleasure as an erotic sensation that relies on imperial contexts so that the object of desire becomes a shadow of the power relations through which that desire is experienced ("the scene," as he calls it in *A Lover's Discourse*). Fittingly, pleasure and desire become ludic, a part of a "game," as Barthes calls it, that tethers opposing forms of fantasy, love, and truth. These later writings represent a period when Barthes, evading his own author function, became "too elusive or too playful" for many of his readers to support him, and he saw his own shifts not as a development from his prior work on ideology but as "a series of breaks or zigzags."[96]

Like Barthes, Foucault flirted well with obscurity and anonymity, often hiding his name in interviews like "The Masked Philosopher."[97] As with Barthes, Foucault's shift to erotics is most manifest in his essay on the author, "What is an Author?" (1969), a response to Barthes's "The Death of the Author," and given the year before Foucault himself first went to Japan (1970). Foucault's work also grew more attentive to "the flesh" after visits to Japan, particularly his second visit in 1978, where he presented a revised argument for his *History of Sexuality* that directed more attention onto erotics, pleasure, and otherness.[98] Erotics for Foucault emerged as a way to account for the fragmented self of multiple, contradictory, and often inconsistent allegiances and preferences (gender, sexual, racial) and to sense how power operates alongside pleasure practices.[99] Understanding our multiplicity through contradictory and unpleasant pleasures forces us, as Foucault sought in his *History of Sexuality*, to ask how we have been involved in other people's lives and how we have been antagonist to those within our very household (wives, servants, boys) as well as to those living within our imperial provinces. Foucault's decade-long project saw pleasure in Western societies within a discourse led by science (*scientia sexualis*), wherein erotic pleasure was confined to the pleasure of knowing something transparently and authentically. In contrast to the West's *scientia sexualis*, Foucault theorized an *ars erotica*, or arts of erotics, that was not about forming identities or transparency but was an artful training in pleasure and its effects, a gamelike form of sexuality focused on the ethical boundaries of erotic exchange. Whereas sexuality in the West was akin to "the essentially narcissistic pleasures of self-confirmation or identity affirmation,"[100] *ars erotica* was a form of Asian sexuality associated with the "ethos of silence" and pleasure practices of Eastern cultures: "China, Japan, India, Rome, the Arabo-Moslem societies."[101] These conceptual bases for erotics, formed out of fetishizations and orientalisms of Asian difference, pushed both Barthes and Foucault to focus on the body as an alternative to psychoanalytic diagnoses and identity-based forms of recognition.

Eve Sedgwick wrote plainly about her sexuality, identifying herself as a married woman who had "vanilla sex, on a weekly basis, in the missionary position, in daylight," yet she, too, carried an obscured relationship to queerness by refusing the terms through which queer identities were understood.[102] At the third annual Lesbian and Gay Studies Conference at Yale in 1989, Sedgwick was repeatedly interrupted by detractors who doggedly demanded for her sexual orientation ("Are you a lesbian?"). Asked to account for herself on the majority's terms, her answers were never satisfactory.[103] As José Muñoz writes, Sedgwick's decision to characterize herself as a married women was not an effort to be transparent but to "show how conventional language failed to grasp her own fundamental sense of queerness."[104] This distrust in language signaled Sedgwick's "turn" from criticism and ideology in her monumental essay "Paranoid Reading and Reparative Reading" (1995), where she criticized "paranoid readings" as methods that overvalued transparency and exposure while seeing pleasure and self-nourishment as merely systemic within a global order. As an alternative, Sedgwick conceived of "reparative readings" that did not expose, identify, or seek certainty, but conferred "plentitude on an object" when "the culture surrounding it is inadequate or inimical to its nurture."[105] Indeed, as with Barthes and Foucault, Sedgwick's thinking in her later years was inspired by Asian philosophies and cultures, particularly Buddhism, which provided a means of seeing Western "knowingness" as paranoid. For Sedgwick, prominent forms of leftist critique were "not simply impoverished but belligerently, even willfully so, as [they drew] their political credibility from the pretense 'to know' the truth about 'reality,' no matter how differently conceived."[106] Buddhism meanwhile offered "the apparent tautology of learning what you already know . . . [as] a deliberate and defining practice."[107] Like Barthes and Foucault, Sedgwick's later career marked a radical turn from methods of ideological critique to erotic methods that opened texts to greater understandings of touch, pleasure, and sensation.

The Asiatic

[W]e can't have our erotic life—a desiring life—without
involving ourselves in the messy terrain of racist practice.
—Sharon Patricia Holland, *The Erotic Life of Racism*

It's no coincidence that the methods of erotics found in Barthes, Foucault, and Sedgwick were formed through intense and intimate relations
with "the Orient." Even in their acute awareness of the pitfalls of Orientalism, these thinkers' later works sought to untangle their erotic
selves through confrontations with the Asian other—the other that Asia
afforded them, what I will call throughout this book "the Asiatic": a style
or form recognized as Asianish but that remains adaptable, fluid, and
outside of the authentic/inauthentic binary. The Asiatic is a "cybertype"
in Lisa Nakamura's sense of a racial form shifting "into the realm of the
'virtual,' a place not without its own laws and hierarchies."[108] As virtual,
the Asiatic does not strive for realness but plays upon the real.

Video games are Asiatic even when they contain no explicit racial
representations, as they are manufactured and innovated upon in Asian
contexts[109] and remain colored by Asian associations as new media
products, where "the Asian subject is perceived to be, simultaneously,
producer (as cheapened labor), designer (as innovators), and fluent consumer (as subjects that are "one" with the apparatus)."[110] In her book
The Race Card, Tara Fickle examines how the infrastructure of gaming
is itself a raced project, operating on the "ludo-racial" presumptions that
Asians are naturally oriented toward games.[111] I thus call games Asiatic
not to reduce games into an East/West binary where all Western players
are Orientalist but to account for the inescapability of Asian associations
in games and to trace their transpacific imperial contexts.[112] Similar
to yoga, tea drinking, and meditation, video games arrive as an Asiatic form inviting players of all backgrounds to participate in and adapt
them into their own lives. As I expand upon in chapter 1, the Asiatic sees
race as verb rather than object, as something done rather than something known, made approachable in the game's interactive medium for
players "who can more readily assimilate and accommodate whatever
objects they encounter."[113] It is a means of grasping race through "the
interplay of personal psychic reality and the experience of control."[114]

The erotic methods conceived by Barthes, Foucault, and Sedgwick are too Asiatic, as they are a practice that emerges by comparing "scientific" and "paranoid" modes of Western thinking with those perceived to be common across Asia. These writers' erotic methods were developed and tested through their confrontations with the Asiatic, as we see in Barthes's two travelogues *Empire of Signs* and *Travels in China*, Foucault's interviews with Zen Buddhists and reliance on Asia as a contemporary example of *ars erotica*, and Sedgwick's *A Dialogue on Love*, which takes liberal use of Japanese poetry forms, her visual art using Eastern textiles, and her essays and courses on Buddhism. Rather than merely cast an Orientalist label onto these works, a far more interesting angle is to ask how these writers' intimate connections to Asia provided a very different view of the ideology critique common in Marxism, which had taken the role of a state religion in Russia, China, North Korea, Cambodia, and Vietnam, where it was increasingly associated with warfare, starvation, and genocide.[115] The Western defenses of Marxism claiming that Asians had falsely interpreted Marx (see Althusser[116]) or were merely responding to American propaganda (see Chomsky[117]) can seem disingenuous once one engages intimately (erotically) with the overwhelming loss of life in Asia, where one could no longer say (as Slavoj Žižek often does) that Marxism was a catastrophe in Asia and add the word "but."[118] For all three theorists, their attachments to Asia provided an opportunity for thinking erotically. In seeing the inevitable gambit of such an affordance, whether Orientalist, reductive, or just plain inaccurate, each theorist also saw Asia as "not-Asia," as a virtual form, as Asiatic. In so doing, they sought to nurture erotic methods as both a way of reading and as an ethics for conceiving of better relations with others.

The Erotics of Games

Get over here!
—Scorpion, *Mortal Kombat*

This book traffics in ideas of erotic play, salvaging pleasure from its casual invocation as an immoral danger at risk of capitalist and imperial complicity. At the same time, I hope to also distance my use of erotics from psychoanalytic discourses seeking to revise pleasure into a form more compatible with "moral virtue or progressive social change."[119] Whether discussed or not, whether aggrandized or ignored, erotics persists, even in digital technology meant to free us from our bodies. Erotics offers a means of discussing interactive media's play with the body without needing to invoke a structural metadiscourse that would restrain erotics as a mere supplement to empire, capitalism, consumerism, and the binding powers of affect. No matter one's politics, pleasures have a habit of transgressing rules of good and evil, ideological and frivolous, dominant and resistant. Erotics demystifies pleasure by developing tactics and strategies to master our desiring selves.

I see the pleasures of gaming as erotic rather than sexual in the way Barthes, Foucault, and Sedgwick also discussed feelings associated with attachment, love, drift, bliss, and ecstasy, as similar to sexual sensations. If taste can be figured through the sexual (an orgasmic strawberry, a tantalizing mug of hot chocolate), why not the "aiming," "shooting," and "mashing" of video games? In *Empire of Signs*, Barthes saw the Japanese game pachinko—a precursor to arcade games—as distinctly erotic, whereas the Western game of pinball was distinctly sexual. Unlike the "pinup girl" seen in pinball, the pachinko machine contained no visual representations of sex and was a "collective and solitary game" full of "varied clientele" with a revenue comparable to "all the department stores in Japan."[120] Pachinko's only interactive moment was in its "initial dispatch," which made the player extremely sensitive to "the force the thumb imparts," making the hand "that of an artist" that directs the ball with "the sole flash of its impetus."[121] If successful, this nuanced act of muscle memory results in being "symbolically spattered with money."[122] Here we have a game that is not about sex or sexuality but still tantalizes, teases, and sensitizes the body, training the player into an artful erotics of play.

Like pachinko, video games are an erotics with or without sex. The slow reveal of a scroll panel in *Super Mario Bros.* is the tease of the stripper without flesh; the well-placed headshot in *Counter-Strike* is an orgasmic lunge; the sneaking in *Metal Gear Solid* is a vacillating flirtation; the decisions made in *Mass Effect* are the uncertainty of cruise. To read games erotically opens games into various forms of parody, burlesque, kink, and camp. But more importantly, erotics helps us understand what we mean when we call a game "fun," when we say that it gives us pleasure, even when we are horrified, stressed, or bored while playing. Erotics develops a language for fun and pleasure that captures the excess meanings these words hide, how they transgress moral/ethical/normative boundaries. These erotics are not always queer, though they *can* emerge from disobedience (turning right when being told to turn left) and they *can* be interpreted through queer lenses (catching a baseball as a sign of being a "catcher"). Yet erotics can also be troublingly normative, in that it can exceed our political attitudes and empowered identities, often leading us back to the very thing we thought we were resisting.

In his 1977 inaugural lecture at the College de France, Barthes exhorted listeners to revise literary interpretation anew. As an effect of deconstruction, postcolonial writing, and Barthes's own poststructural thought, literature had been desacralized, and in that moment there was no better time to open literature up. "This is the moment," Barthes advised, "to deal with it."[123] Toward an open literature, Barthes conceived an erotics of reading. Absent of a single entrusted institutional interpretative community for video games, we can say that the lack of recognition of games as "real art" and its consistent dismissal as a frivolous waste of time conjures a similar moment "to deal with it." Yet in response to these dismissals, gamers and scholars alike have sought to "sacralize" games with single narrative meanings or to brand games as belonging only to a male counterculture (#GamerGate). With this caveat, *Open World Empire* sees the act of game playing as an opening rather than a closing of meaning. To pry from this crevice, we must refuse depictions of the player as passively accepting games as either a benefactor for agency and education or as an all-consuming leviathan that takes away critical thought. If we allow it, games can open us to be something other than what we were told we were. Games can break us, can unravel our presumptions about the world, by making plain our desires, pleasures, and powers within it.

What Follows

The chapters that follow were written within a precarious seven-year period in which I taught at five different institutions, applied for over three hundred academic jobs (and was denied by nearly all of them), immigrated to three different countries, started a family, and traversed the transpacific numerous times to gather research and lock in support wherever I could find it. Over these seven years, video games were a consistent space to recuperate, to be frivolous and nonsensical, passionate and erotic, illogical and loopy. The chapters thus work in a loop, beginning and ending with reflections on Asia as a construct within the open world empire, from "Asiatic" forms of play (chapter 1) to Asia as a "virtual other" (chapter 6). The choice of games will also appear idiosyncratic, as my archive consists of "AAA" or mainstream industry games, independent games, massively multiplayer online games (MMOs), horror games, and first-person shooters. This hodgepodge of game texts restricts this study from offering a definitive form of play and keeps it from reducing game audiences to particular "game cultures" gathered around a genre or a brand. Rather—as Foucault said of his own goals as a writer—this book invites the reader to wander peripatetically, to slip into a kind of experience that "prevents us from always being the same, or from having the same kind of relationship with things and with others that we had before reading."[124] It is in the tradition of Barthes, Foucault, and Sedgwick, as well as games journalists and scholars like Anna Anthropy, Brian Keogh, and Steve Swink, that each chapter also draws on my own erotic experiences with games, detailing my own vested relationship with them and the pleasures that they afford.

Chapter 1 argues that video games, unlike literature and film, are most often depicted as a form of global art, free of ideologies and nationalist boundaries. I treat the games *Street Fighter II*, *League of Legends*, and *Overwatch* to comprehend how these "global games" are played as gateways into "the Asiatic," a playful form of Asianish representation that straddles notions of the queer, the exotic, the bizarre and the Orientalist. Building from the Asiatic, chapters 2 and 3 examine games within a broader discourse of information technology and global empire, first by tracing the discourses of authorship, design, and otherness in Japanese, white, and Asian American producers (chapter 2), and then by exploring how role-playing games like *Mass Effect* and *Guild Wars 2* make visible (and hold players accountable) to regimes of labor and capitalist accumulation by yoking forms of erotic power play (chapter 3). Whereas the open world empire presumes a transparent self, the erotic forms of play in these chapters center the player's ambivalent affinities toward global empire and their relationships with others within its grasp.

The book's second half breaks from the first half's modes of critique to ask how the atrocities and violent consequences of empire can be perceived through erotic and reparative engagements. Playing with Eve Sedgwick's concepts of "texture" and Barthes's notions of pleasure and bliss, I attempt to meditate upon the very real pleasures of domination. Chapters 4 and 5 work as a pair to invoke a form of play as "touch" that sees the game as "text(ure)" and the interactive moment as positioning our bodies into postures ready for expression, reaction, and reception. Chapter 4 explores how *Alien: Isolation* (2014) disrupts our casual "plunge" posture to postures of vulnerability and dread, which enforce new understandings of the social anxieties stoked by political and social marginalizations. Chapter 5 explores how the open world first-person shooting games in the *Far Cry* series engages players in repetitive "game loops" (jump, run, aim, shoot) to provide what Roland Barthes calls "pleasure" and "bliss," forms of erotic play that secure and unsettle the player's identity and social world. Chapter 6 provides a conclusive stringing together of erotics, empire, and play by focusing on experiences of virtual travel and cartography in the Pacific Islands. Thinking through erotic methods found in the Asian confrontations of Barthes, Foucault, and Sedgwick, I argue that the modes of erotics in interactive media entice players to reimagine the world outside of the imperial forms of mapping, surveillance, and war.

The System Only Screams in Total Brightness

To interpret is to impoverish, to deplete the world—in order to set up a shadow world of 'meanings.' . . . The aim of all commentary on art now should be to make works of art— and, by analogy, our own experience—more, rather than less, real to us . . . In place of a hermeneutics we need an erotics of art.
—Susan Sontag, *Against Interpretation: And Other Essays*

Open World Empire was written through forms of settlement inside America as well as circuits of travel within its prior colonies (the Philippines, Hawai'i), its sub-empires (South Korea, Taiwan), its complicit nations (Canada), its competing empire (China), and that empire's contemporary colony (Hong Kong). The chapters thus attempt to comprehend the larger context of video games in a world structured by our interactions with technology on all levels—the communications of social media that toughens mass protests as well as mass surveillance; the aerial technology that enables transpacific travel and Google Maps as well as drones and spy satellites. If empire today is shaped through the developments and circuits of information technology, video games are the open world empire screaming through the language of play. To hear these screams we must no longer make ourselves transparent, identity-based beings, but, as Sontag writes, we must "recover our senses" through an erotics that stresses our perceptions to "see more, to hear more, to feel more."[125] As Sontag's oeuvre shows, erotics does not merely celebrate the interactions of the body but heightens one's conscience through nourishment.[126] Or, as Sharon Holland writes, to practice erotic methods means also "enlist[ing] the erotic as a possible harbinger of the established order."[127] Erotics does not evade empire by focusing on the body, but through the body it makes empire's presence palpable. Video games, too, have not been in any way immune to militarization and capitalist incorporation, at least, no more than any other entertainment medium. But as anyone who has played *Portal 2*, *Hotline Miami*, *Papers, Please*, *This War of Mine*, *September 12th*, *Civilization*, *Final Fantasy VII*, or *Shadow of the Colossus* well knows, video games do not mess around with making the player feel responsible, complicit, and guilt-ridden over their own relation to empire.[128]

By simulating the processes and providing the pleasures of our open world empire, video games stage conversations about how to think ethically about American power in the world without the nationalist impulse to launder imperial history or deny its erotic sensations (and thus disavow its very existence). In the open world, the screams of empire are no longer distanced into the colonies or behind the camera. They are muffled by the cacophonic noise of facts, knowledges, exposures, certainties, and all that form a "game of truth," whose volume drowns out the screams even when they come from our own mouths.[129] These truths are not censored, covered up, or blacked out. They are endlessly heaved into view, stark in total brightness, and available at the click of a button.

Video games offer no liberation from our empire. To use Sedgwick's own Asiatic language, games do not expose anything new but merely help us recognize what we already know. If there is a reparative function of games, it is not in the utopic or in the gathering of new information but in making normative (rather than exceptional) America's undeniable attachment to perpetual war and imperial preservation.[130] By letting us relish in the pleasures of power and privilege, video games reckon with our erotic selves, with our own motives and attachments as perpetrators, enablers, settlers. To have a real conversation about our responsibilities as an empire, to help us live within it and flourish as one can, we must face up to that pithy excuse that I use when I realize I've wasted the day playing *Overwatch*: "there was something about it, I suppose, that gave me pleasure."

PART I

Asiatic

You are not a good person. You know that, right? Good people don't end up here.
—GLaDOS, *Portal 2*

1

Global Game

Race \ Play / Intimacy

One day, while playing the multiplayer video game *Overwatch*, one of my five anonymous teammates began to chide me over the in-game text box. "Useless," the player called me. "Useless fucking American." The player's name tag was in Korean characters, but mine, named "Kawika," did not scream "American." The character I was playing, Mei, was a Chinese biologist wrapped in a plum-colored snow coat. "Fucking American," the player wrote again, as my other teammates leaped to my defense, calling him (or her?) a racist Korean and reminding them that "you're on an American server." As others joined in, some slandering Americans, the chatbox turned into a flame war of racist bashing. We lost the match.

I encountered this player again. This time, they were on the opposing team. I felt a spark of indignation spurred on by their insults, and I recalled the anti-American, anti-Filipino prejudice that I experienced when I lived in South Korea. I found the player in the match, playing the same character as myself, the ice-damage specialist Mei. I chased the character, cornered her, froze her, and executed her with a sharp icicle to her head. In the chatroom box, the player's hectoring continued: "Useless fucking American!" the player wrote again and again.

How was I to react to this vicious name calling? Was I to report this player for racism? Or was the player just calling me "American" not as a nation or a race, but because I was playing in a particularly individualist, laissez-faire style? For some reason I felt a strange bond with the other player. The indignation I felt at being harassed had made defeating him an achievement far more memorable than rescuing a digital princess. The two of us, chasing each other in racially spurned rage while both playing the same bubbly Chinese female character, set a ridiculous tone to the altercation. Once we left the game's "magic circle," I honestly wished the player no ill will. In a game where people of different races, nations, and languages were forced to cooperate, hadn't we invited this upon ourselves?

Overwatch is a prime example of what I will call throughout this chapter a "global game" that features a large cast of characters, each with unique abilities, who span multiple ethnicities, nationalities, and genders. As the game's distributor, Blizzard Entertainment, is known worldwide as an e-sports company, the game has garnered comparisons to sporting events like the Olympics with its international cast, worldwide audience, and sporting arenas. I call *Overwatch* a "global game" not to name a category or genre but as an analytic to understand the discourses that envision games as a global art form, as global commodities produced by transnational companies that seem, initially, to hold no nationalist sentiments or orientations and thus evade the particularities and "seriousness" of national racial attitudes. Blizzard Entertainment boasts of having "nearly 500 million monthly active users in 196 countries," and carries offices in six different countries.[1] Ubisoft, the third-largest independent game developer, hosts over nine thousand employees and thirty studios upon six continents, illustrating the massive influence of multinational production.[2] Similar to *Overwatch*, Ubisoft's *Assassin's Creed* series is also a global game, as it takes place in various locales (the Middle East, Italy, Colonial America, China, India, Russia), and each game begins with a disclaimer affirming that the game was "designed, developed, and produced by a multicultural team of various religious faiths and beliefs."[3] As Patrick Jagoda writes, games are unique in constituting global art forms through their depiction of network and structure rather than national (or even physical) spaces.[4] While some games seem totally disassociated from their national origins (*Tetris*), others, like the *Mario* franchise, symbolize a national aesthetic, even as the games' content deviates from its national origin. As Adrienne Shaw writes, this ability to foster disinterest in nationalist origins and boundaries creates the potential for designers to create internationally accessible games that construct diverse visions of "globality," making the most of a medium that "relies upon play and, in turn, can play with what reality means."[5]

This chapter explores how global games reconceive of race through experiences of play. Since games like *Street Fighter II* (1991) and *Mortal Kombat* (1992), which both feature an array of diverse, international characters, video game companies and media have attempted to present games as forms of global art whose racism and prejudice are obscured by their uncertain origins. Global games evade critical engagement through their diverse casts, which can feature characters from nations like the Philippines and Brazil, and for their playful attitude, which underscores the strategic effects of deployed stereotypes. While transnational films like *Memoirs of a Geisha* routinely fail to cast off their nationalist presumptions and origins,[6] games can appear without a nation, as they are bred through international development and distribution companies that conceal nationalist residues. If the global art form of games makes playing them a distinctly unique experience from other media, then race also functions differently in games and requires theories based less on representation and identity and more on play, style, and form, within a medium routinely divided from a single nation's racial politics.

Analyzing racial figures in games has proven particularly difficult due to a game's obscure nationalist ties as a transnational product and because gameplay has departed drastically from forms of the novel, cinema, and performance art. Except in rare cases,[7] video games make little to no attempt to thematize race, even when including racialized main characters (the Prince in *Prince of Persia*, the Native American lead in *Turok*). Most studies on race in video games borrow analytical methods from other media, focusing on race only in games that are strikingly similar to cinema or in games that operate as virtual worlds, where performing racial others is crucial to maintaining the visual spectacle. In the prior, analyses of cinematic games like *Grand Theft Auto* or *The Last of Us* rely heavily on narrative and cinematic visual cues. In the second case of virtual worlds like *World of Warcraft* or *Second Life*, race has been treated as a form of "identity tourism," as Lisa Nakamura has defined it, as when "the appropriation of racial identity becomes a form of recreation, a vacation from fixed identities and locales."[8] For Nakamura, the "vacation" of the virtual world satisfies "a desire to fix the boundaries of cultural identity and exploit them for recreational purposes."[9] Going a step further, Dean Chan has written of playing racial others as "pixilated minstrelsy,"[10] while David Leonard has interpreted identity tourism as a form of "high tech blackface" that licenses participants to "try on the other, the taboo, the dangerous, the forbidden, and the otherwise unacceptable."[11] Meanwhile, other scholars like Adrienne Shaw have pointed out the habitual "pathologizing of cross-identity play" that reduces all forms of racial avatars into identity tourism, which presumes "a particular privileged identity as a starting point."[12] Both Shaw and Anna Everett ask for more nuanced and context-driven analyses of race in video games, to push race from its relegated corner as either a "structured absence"—where the magic circle remains free of racial attitudes—or a "specious virtual presence"—where playing race remains a form of identity tourism, passing, or minstrelsy.[13]

For Shaw, the dismissal of players, developers, and games themselves as simply reproducing racist attitudes is made possible by the stereotypes of the "gaming nerd," which homogenizes "gamer culture" as male, white, young, and at least privileged enough to own a console or computer.[14] To see acts of play as a form of minstrelsy by virtue of controlling a racialized character neglects the experiences of people of color, women, non-American players, or capable white folk who play games while also thinking through real racial logics. By deracinating minstrelsy from the context of slavery, Reconstruction, and Jim Crow, we also neglect crucial issues concerning audience and purpose: For whom is the act of "racial tourism" performed? Does the racial avatar also cause the player to play differently—to play out a stereotype—or does it remain mere skin? Should players only feel at home inhabiting a white virtual body? Instead of questions specific to games, scholars can be detained by questions concerning the representation of diverse bodies, a question that can mark games as less willing "to pursue meaningful diversity or refrain from egregious stereotyping."[15] Though representation and diversity are crucial for reflecting upon biases within gaming cultures, the presumption that marginalized gamers long to see people like themselves in games is often false, perpetuated by a market logic and imported from theories of film and literature.[16] This focus on the racism of "game culture" tends to replace more theoretically generative inquiries, like "Why do games that express racial stereotypes and encourage racial violence continue to be played by various audiences across the globe?" or "How are games *different* than other media in expressing race?"

To answer these questions, this chapter turns to global games, which have evaded analysis for their uncertain origins, their playful style, and their efforts to see racial constructs as having no explicit function within the game. Global games can be highly competitive and can carry open universes that maintain flexibility for franchise-making. Unlike cinematic or role-playing games, global games like *Street Fighter II*, *League of Legends*, and *Overwatch* are nearly indifferent to their imposed narratives. However, their depictions of race lead us to envision a larger theoretical basis for comprehending the experience of seeing race as a signal for a mode of play as well as for a sense of racial playfulness. Lisa Nakamura called this sense of race a "cybertype" that reinforced a "cosmetic multiculturalism," where "local racial problems are shuffled aside by a global and diasporic diversity."[17] However, to see race as "cosmetic" one need not forego racial histories, but one can also revise them through style, form, and surface, which can be understood as a form of camp. Camp, as Susan Sontag wrote, "dethrone[s] the serious" to play within a decorative art "emphasizing texture, sensuous surface, and style at the expense of content."[18] Characterized by "the spirit of extravagance," camp is of artifice rather than authenticity and thus "sees everything in quotation marks."[19] The queer sensibility of camp provides a method to comprehend racial forms in games where one does not inhabit a racial other but plays roles presumed to be "anti-serious." In this regard, playing race in games carries the campy potential to "dethrone the serious."[20]

I invoke Sontag's hallmark 1964 essay, "Notes on Camp," to begin our plunge into erotic play through one of the first and most influential essays written in an intentionally erotic style. Toying with Sontag's writings on camp alongside Roland Barthes's attempts to recast Japan not as a nation, race, or country but as a "stock of features" of "formality and invented play,"[21] this chapter explores play-based forms of race and efforts to reconceive of games as an always-racialized medium, as "Asiatic": a nonexclusive and nonessential racial form understood through sets of forms, rules, and styles that reimagine racial boundaries and categories. To conceive of "race as play" does not excuse games as nonracist or as mere parody, but it tracks the potential of games to revise meanings of race and to disrupt racial hierarchies. I close the chapter by close-playing the global game *Overwatch* to understand how playful attitudes toward race can produce intimate and insurgent fusions of the serious and the playful.

Race as Play

Play is often conceived within a telos of progress, thought to provide a realm of unfettered freedom to experiment, educate, and foster human growth. Within the early formation of game studies, play aligned with a notion of neoliberal freedom, presuming man as a universal economic being whose desire for freedom transcends (or should transcend) racial, gendered, and sexual hierarchies. The designer turned scholar Brian Upton,[22] for example, insists that "everywhere we look, how we play is the same."[23] As proof, Upton describes how the Chinese game of Go exports to other cultural contexts: "you can become very good at Go without ever learning anything about Chinese culture."[24] Because "Go's ability to function as a game doesn't depend on cultural context," Upton declares that "there is a deep structure to play that transcends cultural boundaries," particularly with games that meet "certain universal conditions."[25]

Two problems emerge in Upton's argument. First, the game Go or *wéiqí* (围棋) has become so highly invested in cultural, national, and racial attitudes that the example seems ill chosen. In China, wéiqí operates as a nationalist symbol of the "5,000 year old history" of ancient China, and in America, wéiqí confirms techno-Orientalist stereotypes of Chinese as math-obsessed and computational (these skills are crucial in wéiqí).[26] Further, wéiqí has become synonymous with a Chinese reliance on wéi tactics that refuse to meet an enemy head on but rather surround and entrap the enemy (*wéi* translates to "enclosure").[27] For the mathematician Scott Boorman, wéiqí resembles a military strategy particularly adaptable to Communist ideology that came from China but was put in use in the Vietnam War to evade and surround American troops.[28] So the game of Go becomes racialized/nationalized within every context it travels to. The second problem is more fundamental to Upton's argument and concerns games as noncultural objects in general: that simply because the game can be mastered "without ever learning anything about Chinese culture" does not make the game "transcendent" of cultural boundaries, any more than the fact that someone can appreciate a plate of spaghetti without learning Italian history makes culture, nation, and race any less relevant to the dish. Even still, discourses of play have continued to describe play as a noncultural, noncontextual practice.[29]

The most essential definition of play that game theorists seem to agree on is that "first, work isn't play."[30] In nearly every theoretical account, play is contrasted with work. Where play is playful, work is serious. Play operates, according to Johan Huizinga, as a safe zone, one of "absolute order," where the serious world of work is defined by disorder: "into the confusion of life [play] brings a temporary, a limited perfection."[31] Huizinga famously coins the term "magic circle" to describe the boundaries of the game as a space of retreat from the "imperfection" of work life, what Edward Castronova later called the porous "membrane between synthetic worlds and daily life,"[32] and what Katie Salen and Eric Zimmerman later valorized, writing "the term magic circle is appropriate because there is in fact something genuinely magical that happens when a game begins."[33] Indeed, as no other theorist has had so great an impact on discourses of play and video games, Huizinga's "magic circle" has framed games as an ideal space that transcends cultural and ethnic identities.

To see work and play here as co-constitutive concepts leads us to question their division within cultural perceptions of "work" and the presumptions we bring to what activities are work and what are play. One can "play" at one's job, just as one can "work" in a game. The work/play binary speaks also to a particularly neoliberal subjectivity where work must be ordinary, mundane, and methodical, while play "is free, is in fact freedom."[34] But again the larger question emerges—for whom is the game freeing? To those who "win"? Can the magic circle exhibit "freedom" for one person and pain for another? As Jaakko Stenros has argued, the magic circle synthesizes metaphors of play into a spatial and temporal concept, wherein players inhabit the role of "player" as a contractual obligation.[35] The magic circle invokes a "psychological bubble" that permits a playful mindset (like unsupervised children), but this is not so much an affordance than a required attitude. One must roll with the punches, must take offensive behavior as a joke or as mere play. The magic circle's "bubble" can thus be rife with tension. Marginalized players can become used to playing within barriers, to seeing boundaries not just in the game rules but in the ridicule and prejudices of the circle.

As a concept, the magic circle has operated within game studies "to define the ways in which play sits outside 'normal' space and interaction," providing a protective membrane to divide games from the broader imperial and racial contexts.[36] Yet despite the seriousness of war, play persistently defines the most heinous military acts. Play intrudes upon the serious in the form of racial massacre, rape, and assault (as depicted, for example, in the Abu Ghraib scandal of torture and prisoner abuse). Play happens in war while the serious can emerge in games like the Olympics or football games that arouse mob violence. What can be playful for those in power (like the white slave master forcing slaves to dance and sing) can be truly serious to the disempowered. One person can feel the freedom of the magic circle while another can be victim to it. In this sense, the gameworld does not differ from the real world. It is not a playful bubble space exterior from it but a reflection of the world's pleasures and desires as they impact the body. The magic circle presumes that those who enter are already free subjects, that their interests in joining the circle are the same. But playing, like any other choice, is encumbered by social expectations. Feeling compelled and coerced to play continues to be a reason for play as it is for work, operating off social currencies, peer pressure, and state coercion (in physical education class, in recess, in the bedroom). Likewise, each mode of play carries its exclusions, from fitness level to gender, class, and racial prejudices. In the play of the magic circle, fun and freedom are not merely expected, they are, paradoxically, compulsory.

I propose that we withhold the presumption that play operates as a free, ideal circle disconnected from the mundane necessity of cultural knowledge and history and instead consider "play" and "work" as signposts that compel players to be playful or serious. Game controllers and systems symbolize play, though the player may still be seriously impacted by real consequences: losing track of time, neglecting a loved one. The game itself—a product of transnational economic processes—is also never really an act of play for those who manufacture or mine materials to produce them. Distinguishing the co-constitutive forms of the playful and the serious helps generate a general theory of racial formations in games, or "race as play." If the difference between a "playful" experience and a "serious" one is often a racial difference, then we must consider how play styles, or styles of play, speak to racial constructs. In the same way that wéiqí can be marked as a Chinese Communist strategy, so, too, can *styles* of play speak to the tactics and strategies that racialized bodies are imagined to inhabit.

Race as play is similar to race as "cultural practice"—a nonessentialist "neo-racism" as Etienne Balibar defined it—where race is not biological but presumes "insurmountable cultural differences" informed by racial histories and signified through racial bodies.[37] Wendy Hui Kyong Chun goes a step further in seeing "race as technology," where race is divided from biology, history, as well as culture, to represent other ways to do things, styles that cannot be "known" but can be done "by emphasizing the similarities between race and technology."[38] Seeing race as technology or as "mediation" perceives of the ways race continues to function in ways of doing rather than ways of being.[39] By stripping the content of race to surface-level stylization, "race as technology" reframes race into a "discussion around ethics rather than around ontology, on modes of recognition and relation, rather than on being."[40] Building from Chun and others, Tara Fickle has argued that Asian American cultures and politics have already become attuned to forms of play, using "gamelike attributes" in political and aesthetic products.[41] For Patricia Clough, Chun's "Race and/as Technology" theory keeps "technology" as a shifty term that homogenizes various forms of digital experiences with race.[42] As a technological medium, global video games can tell us much about "what different technologies do" to race by providing a sense of how global cultures are impacted by the ability to perceive of race as a dual form of play styles and play attitudes.[43]

If culture acts as a sign of race in our analog world, then in a virtual realm, race dwells within play itself. First, "race as play" compels us to see the virtual racial formation within play styles that can be seen as foreign, minoritized, or intolerable to the proposed postracial "magic circle." Styles, too, can be switched, toyed with, or made unexpectedly intimate, a means of inhabiting difference formed through play. A player, for example, might be seen as "too Chinese" or "too Asian" if they seem overly concerned with winning, even if it means evading most of the game's challenges and taking on a "cheese" (cheap and easy) style of play. This form of play turns from tolerable to *intolerable* when players undertake styles of opposed play that obstructs the team's goal or strives for alternative achievements. Such play belongs to banned players like Chinese gold farmers who would play a game like *World of Warcraft* intending only to level-up their characters as fast as possible so that they can sell virtual equipment or characters for real-world money.

The banning of Chinese gold farmers in games like *World of Warcraft* forms a boundary across players who are otherwise celebrated as racially and nationally anonymous. Game administrators seek out these groups through linguistic cues and rely on the online community of players to report each other, thus producing groups of players identified as "nonplay," who enter the gameworld not out of leisure but out of economic need. As Nick Yee and Lisa Nakamura have pointed out, gold farmers have been identified by gaming communities through their accents, as well as use of scripting and bot programs, and subsequently targeted for harassment or hacking.[44] As Nakamura writes, the hatred toward these unwanted subjects "depict Asian culture as threatening to the beauty and desirability of shared virtual space."[45]

Second, "race as play" examines how the pressure to share "play attitudes" obliges some players to fabricate a sense of happiness similar to those who thoroughly enjoy the game. As Sara Ahmed has argued, happiness can be attributed to particular objects or spaces (like the space of the family or the objects of digital media). As Ahmed writes, "happiness involves a way of being aligned with others, of facing the right way,"[46] and that when we refuse to go along, "we become alienated—out of line with an affective community."[47] The way one is *supposed* to play functions as a "happiness script" whose deviation risks spoiling the happiness of others.[48] Keeping disagreements tolerable maintains the fantasy of the magic circle, as one's play style, though odd, continues to verify the happiness of those who ascribe to the script. Even if personal experience sees this shared happiness as mere fantasy, players feel required to squelch their private disagreements to maintain the circle's "magic," or else be marked as a spoilsport. The "spoilsport," too, has been a lasting figure in video game theory. Huizinga calls the spoilsport the player who trespasses against the rules or ignores them and "robs play of its illusion."[49] The illusion here is not merely the goal that the team hopes to achieve, but the very presumption that following the "happiness script" is a universal experience. To play in ways that expose the postrace script is to become intolerable to the magic circle, a spoilsport who "must be cast out, for he threatens the existence of the play-community."[50] To see the spoilsport as a racialized figure is to turn that figure from the "hospitality" of racial tolerance toward the "hostility" of racial *in*tolerance. Where the magic circle suspends norms in order to create a stage for global play, race can appear as a hostile force, threatening to upend the racial hierarchies of the real world.

Portrayals of "race as play," summarized above, shift our perceptions of race to the forms, styles, and attitudes of games, but at the implicit cost of dismissing the importance of racial representations in games, where debasing stereotypes run rampant. Yet these racial figures—read as forms of play—also bear the capacity to upend racializations crucial to the order of global empire. Erotic methods of engaging racial aesthetics perceive how "race as play" does not mean that representations of race are irrelevant within video games—quite the opposite. Racial figures in games are rather infused with playful meanings, signaling forms of doing rather than being, presenting themselves always within quotation marks.[51] They are not mere skins but extravagant styles that, in global games like *Street Fighter II* and *Overwatch*, are doled out to every nation: for every Ryu there is the American blond-haired military fanatic Guile; for every Mei, a slow-talkin' gun-slinging cowboy, Mc-Cree. The races that are represented as "us" seem monstrous, demeaning, cynically overpowering, or insufferable. As John Cheney-Lippold writes, digital representations of racial, gendered, and sexual difference often presume the presence of air quotes to denote not merely an uncertainty or inauthenticity but a "sardonic use of air quotes to emphasize an ironic untruth" that classifies "an algorithmic caricature of the category it purportedly represents."[52] The "ironic untruth" of these representations allow them to be played in ways that do not replace one's identity but function as "an additional layer of identity."[53] I am by day an Asian male who mains the Asian female Mei. This later "addition" bleeds into my daily life and self-perceptions but does not collapse into it.

The digital representations of race in video games operate through ironic untruths that rely upon the player's "playful attitude" toward the game. This attitude mirrors what Sontag calls a camp sensibility that perceives of a "double sense" of campy and hyperanimated figures whose surface-level frivolity signals not a representation of racialized people but a quirky style of play.[54] On the surface they are pure artifice, figures that "[convert] the serious into the frivolous," which strike the player as both offensive and alluring. But this artificial surface also allows the player to recognize the racial figure as a form of play, inviting theatricality and performance, or what Sontag calls "Being-as-Playing-a-Role."

Camp, needless to say, is also irrevocably queer, as it refuses the standards of the serious (beauty, deeper meaning) to experience the unashamed joy of the erotic (the sensual, the decorative).[55] In reducing meanings to the surface, to artifice, to style, camp does not merely dismiss the serious but "involves a new, more complex relation to 'the serious.'"[56] As Soraya Murray points out, the playful depiction of racial histories in games can cause us to interrogate the efficacy of always taking a "deferential position" toward otherness, encouraging us to instead imagine new ways of reckoning with imperial violence in our present.[57] In downgrading the serious, camp expresses a "love of the unnatural: of artifice and exaggeration"—in other words, a love for queer, nonnormative being.[58]

In theoretical revisions, camp also serves a double meaning—as a critique of dominant structures of gender, sexuality, race, and class (Butler, Halberstam) and as "the communal, historically dense exploration of a variety of reparative practices."[59] On one hand, camp in games upends racial and gendered authenticity. On the other, it fosters erotic forms of communal nourishment through "juicy displays of excess erudition" and "alternative historiographies."[60] Yet, even still, "camp sensibility" does not always invoke a radical or subversive political form—it, too, can operate as a "magic circle" that excludes others through mockery and performance (particularly when it critiques gender and sexuality but makes no room for others). For Sianne Ngai, the hyperanimated likeness of cartoonish racialized figures relegates minorities into "the passive state of being moved or vocalized by others for their amusement."[61] Though defenders of camp idealize the practice as democratic, inclusive, and "tak[ing] everyone down together,"[62] the same is routinely said by those who defend the magic circle as a social practice immune to criticism, even when it is invoked to defend abuse.[63] Indeed, a decade after writing "Notes on Camp," Sontag herself shifted her views on camp as a critical sensibility to an art form whose "taste for the theatrically feminine" could reinscribe heteropatriarchal stereotypes.[64] Camp's characteristic power to both "draw" and "offend" risks its deployment as a mere excuse to offend freely within a white, male, homonormative space.[65] Richard Dyer has tellingly argued that "[f]irst of all and above all, [camp is] very us," celebrating camp as "distinctively and unambiguously gay male" (and we must add *white* and

Western as well).[66] Despite the obvious "magic circle" presumptions with camp aesthetics, camp still carries the potential for an "aristocratic detachment" characterized by the "ludic or playful quality of its legitimate misreading and deviant decoding" that, without a dominant authentic meaning, carries ambiguous political effects and can take part "in the representation of the power it debunks."[67] Camp carries a perverse relationship with truth and authenticity as it performs "a potentially *denaturalizing* gesture."[68] It is, to invoke Barthes's sense of myth,[69] a slippery mode of demystification, loosened with the vagaries of pleasure and power.

In order to arrive at a theory of race in gaming, we have taken the plunge from seeing race as a playable style to apprehending how "race as play" is made possible (even pleasurable) through campy animations of racial figures. If race is, as Patrick Wolfe has named it, a "trace of history,"[70] then accounting for the multiple contexts and audiences who play race in video games can evoke race's function within an open world empire, where hyperanimated and nonsensical racial conceptions like "tiger mothers" also offer a form of gameplay, an adaptable set of tactics for entrepreneurial (and scholastic) success within a seemingly open competitive atmosphere.[71] Games expose how the open world empire recognizes race not as history or even culture but as tactics and strategies for either winning or disrupting the order of things.[72] Its principal outward sign remains racialized forms of difference—skin as well as accent, movement, attitude, tactics. Taking on a playful view of race means facing race not as a nationalist politics (of racial minorities against majorities) but as imbricated within what Wolfe calls "a fertile, Hydra-headed assortment of local practices" that emerge through *how* one plays a game—not just a video game, but games of marriages, games of capital, games with the law, war games, or games with distant others.[73] It means understanding games not as ideal spaces of postracial belonging and mutual competition but as a space that brings the tension, hatred, fear, and anxiety of the "serious." Where the real world can be a space of play for some and a place of serious anxiety and pain for others, we must ask how games can act as a window onto this world, to divulge how race has already become incorporated as a style of play (an "erotics"). If "race is colonialism speaking," as Wolfe writes, what does race in games say about colonialism today?

The Dizzying Diversity of Street Fighter II

Thus far, our working theory of race in games has been devoid of historical and cultural contexts dealing with the very racial form definitive of
games—in particular, the inescapable influences of Japanese aesthetics
and genre forms that give games a campy and distanced feel. As Rob
Gallagher has argued, camp manifests most in Japanese games from
the 1990s (*Castlevania: Symphony of the Night, Final Fantasy VII*), as
such games have proven "conducive to precisely the kinds of projec-
tive identification, enthused amateurism and felicitous mistranslation
that Sedgwick identifies with camp, fostering a subculture of Western
devotees of Japanese video games," who have become definitive of much
mainstream gaming.[74] Michelle Clough and Sarah Christina Ganzon have traced forms of queer sexuality in games to Japanese genres
of *otome* or maiden games, *renai* or romance games, *yaoi* or boy's love
games, and *bishoujo* or beautiful boy games.[75] For American audiences,
such games would read as campy or queer even when their same-sex
scenes have been censored, as these games' images of hypersexualized
women are "surprisingly often . . . flanked by a male character who is
just as desirable," a trope that has been "well-encoded into Asian media
and storytelling."[76] Following the insights of these authors, if we hope to
conceive a theory of race in video games, we must turn to the aesthetic
categories and historical contexts that have been at the center of gaming
production.

If there is a regional space that holds the same measure of influence
for video games as Hollywood does for cinema, Japan is clearly the closest. Japanese games dominated early video game popularity, with games
like *Space Invaders* (1978), *Pac-Man* (1980), *Donkey Kong* (1981), *Super
Mario Bros.* (1985), *The Legend of Zelda* (1986), *Final Fantasy* (1987),
Mega Man (1987), *Sonic the Hedgehog* (1991), and *Street Fighter II* (1991),
and have remained influential with later game series like the *Pokémon*
series (1996), the *Resident Evil* series (1996), and the *Metal Gear Solid*
series (1998). Japanese games have laid out genre conventions for games
as a form of global art, where racialized characters are stereotyped as
cute (*kawaii*) and playful "skins," while most Japanese games themselves
seem to totally lack globally recognized symbols of Japan, separating
the game itself from its country of origin (though Japanese players may

easily find Japanese symbols, others would not). For Chris Goto-Jones, Japan's enormous impact on video game aesthetics has molded games as "a medium of Digital Asia," where games resemble an Asiatic space whose "aesthetics are generally stylized, anime-like graphics, which audiences do associate with East Asia, even if the subject matter has little to do with Asia per se."[77] As Paul Martin has argued, critical studies of games concerning race, gender, class, and nationality have too often ignored the conventions that emerged from Japanese aesthetics, and thus any study of race in games must consider how "the cultural baggage of Western discourses of race and colonialism becomes interleaved with a Japanese social imaginary."[78] Of primary concern for this social imaginary, Martin argues, has been to construct Japan as a "normal country" despite its military defeat in World War II, the devastation of its major cities, and the military restrictions that followed with Article 9, which forbade Japan to maintain a military for potentially offensive purposes.

The "global game" emerged through Japanese conceptions of race and nationality that were embedded in post–World War II aesthetic forms of *kawaii* (cuteness) and *otaku* (geekiness). The artist Takashi Murakami has attempted to critically examine these two cultural art forms through his own "superflat" art movement,[79] which sees kawaii and otaku aesthetics as anxieties of national impotence: a physical impotence ensued by a high suicide rate and low birth rate and a psychological impotence from the lack of military offensive capabilities after the loss of World War II.[80] As Noi Sawaragi has also argued, postwar aesthetics "bespeak a profound psychological repression" of Japan's profound desire to forget the atomic bombing and Japanese empire by remaining innocent and cute.[81] These losses characterize the minimalist and cute art styles of kawaii as well as masculine art forms that express unfettered power and mimic atomic warfare. Murakami calls this more masculine form of Japanese pop art "otaku aesthetics," which include robot anime (*Mobile Suit Gundam*), monster (*kaijū*) films (*Godzilla*), and battle-focused manga (*Dragon Ball*). Otaku—popularized as a Japanese geek culture that emerged in the late 1970s and was formed by fans of anime, manga, and films—characterizes an aesthetic that Murakami argues is "ultimately defined by their relentless references to a humiliated self."[82] The masculine pop art found in *Dragon Ball*, for example, is inclusive of kawaii images, even as it depicts mythical fighting tournaments. The series, for Murakami, represented a strange loop of death and rebirth, where the creators and audience were "playing out a game of one-upmanship" that resulted in "a never-ending loop that defies even death itself."[83] Connecting *Dragon Ball* with other masculine pop art like *Akira*, rebirth appears as a consistent theme within this aesthetic, where the dead return even stronger than before.

As Koichi Iwabuchi has argued, Japan's postwar popular art has featured rebirth in two techniques, both of which maintain Japan's industry of coolness and increase its ability to disseminate digital products worldwide. The first is a strategy of "strategic hybridism," which "discursively constructs an image of an organic cultural entity, 'Japan,' that absorbs foreign cultures without changing its national/cultural core."[84] This strategy sees a unified Japanese subjectivity as always evolving and able to make use of foreign ideas and technology. Such hybridism does not unsettle nor blur sexual identities but fixes and "reinforces the rigidity of these boundaries" by consistently calling attention to the Japanese culture's ability to "absorb" while still remaining pure.[85] In a society where racial issues are thought to belong "in such countries as the United States and South Africa," absorbing outside influences need not taint the national culture but can simply improve it.[86] Iwabuchi's second point concerning rebirth is Japanese pop culture's ability to aestheticize (or flatten) national and racial signifiers into fragrant "cultural odors," which deploy already disseminated symbolic images of a country or race to make them globally palatable.[87] The accent and pushy mustache of Mario here operates as a fragrant reuse of already embedded Italian stereotypes, made cute (kawaii) through its aesthetic and potent (otaku) through its looping narrative of rescuing princess Peach. Meanwhile, the game itself, as Iwabuchi argues about Japanese video games in general, appears as a global object, or in Japanese slang, *mukokuseki*, as lacking in nationality, as "odorless."[88] "Odorless" products signal a turn from the desire to satisfy "a Western Orientalist gaze" to instead promote surface-level self-representations that warrant only a "global glance."[89] The flattening of aesthetic representations to stereotype is one way of eliminating national "odor"—making Japanese products adaptable to a world still dominated by Western cultural hierarchies so they appear as merely global.[90]

The two themes of Japanese pop culture discussed by Murakami, Iwabuchi, and others, suggests that games today reflect Japanese cultural aesthetics that 1) cycle rebirth within a playful mode of experimentation, adaptation, and hybridization and 2) deodorize nationalist symbols in order to appear global, while also deploying "fragrant" racial symbols. Both themes dangerously scathe the surface of racial essentialisms, which is no coincidence, as they emerge through Japanese responses to being seen by the West as a "little boy." Nevertheless, these aesthetics—Japanese or not, "real" or contrived projections—facilitate the meanings of race as a form of play, where gameworlds not only stage forms of racialized play but also compel players to re-play, to play differently, to experiment with various racialized forms within games that appear ideologically neutral even when we recognize the historical violence behind their images. Play generates when failure does not mean an end, but when re-play means experimentation and adaptation and trying out the strategies of others. Race becomes recognized as forms of play in global games, but race only becomes play*ful* when the player resets, when she repeats the same gameworld over and over, until she feels compelled to shift her form of play from one racialized form to another.

Of all the Japanese games mentioned above, only Capcom's *Street Fighter II: The World Warrior* stands out as inclusive of Japanese cultural symbols (the Japanese flag, Mount Fuji, karate, sumo). Seen as one of the most successful video games of all time, *Street Fighter II* set in place the genre conventions of the fighting game with its button scheme, combos, and special moves as well as its meticulous character balancing.[91] *Street Fighter II* was also the first "global fighting game" that successfully deployed racial stereotypes while detaching itself from its country of origin. The "arena" of the fighting game stages a racial competition that appears perfectly balanced, with none of the eight characters overpowering the others. All the characters are marked by their own unique strategies so that all players can find characters appropriate to their own play style. The Japanese character Ryu moves at medium speed and comes with the flexibility to face short-, medium-, and long-range attackers, while characters like Dhalsim are better long ranged, and Vega is better for intense speed-driven players. Though many scholars have interpreted the game's racial figures as stereotypes reiterating "the deployment of hegemonic whiteness and masculinity,"[92] many players and game commentators have seen its combination of Japanese aesthetics with playability and "dizzying diversity" not as a form of white supremacy but as a form of camp, a queer and exaggerated take on national racial imaginaries that signals a commentary on our unequal reality. Dhalsim, an egregious stereotype of an Indian yogi who sports face paint, pupil-less eyes, an emaciated torso, and a necklace of skulls, can be recognized not as an "odorless" Japanese aesthetic but as a queer exaggeration whose offensive traits signal not realism but a play style, with his ability to strike players from a distance using stretchable arms and legs, as well as his magical ability to incinerate enemies up close by shouting "Yoga fire!" and spitting out a stream of flame.

Undoubtedly, if *Street Fighter II* were within a serious medium rather than one defined by global play, the racial stereotypes it deploys would be too deplorable to consume. Besides Dhalsim there is also Zangief, a Russian wrestler who sports scars from bear fighting, then Guile, a blond-haired American soldier in camos who fights on a military base decorated with fighter jets. But unlike film and literature, in the genre of video games race rarely approaches realism and instead plays upon the seriousness of racial authenticity through its own extravagance ("'It's too much,' 'It's too fantastic,' 'It's not to be believed,'")[93]. As a global game that invokes camp sensibilities, *Street Fighter II* plays with the very terms of racial diversity and multiculturalism, as it depicts diverse and powerful bodies who remain anything but celebratory. Rather, these "World Warriors" operate on a logic of racialized play styles. *Street Fighter II*'s two most similar characters, Ryu and Ken, were almost identical except for the racialized constructs they represented. Ryu, the Japanese character, and Ken, the American, were contrasted with every playable move. Ryu was slightly faster and kept enemies at a distance, relying more on fireballs ("hadoken"), making him appear more focused, while Ken was more improvisational and daring— moving into opponent spaces, risking counterattacks for stronger hits. In later iterations of the game, Ryu's strikes became more hard hitting, while Ken's opted for combo-rich unpredictability. Even though both characters were nearly identical in appearance and movement, their play styles became invested with what seemed racially typical: the Japanese Ryu as the quick and disciplined one, the American Ken as the rash and impulsive one.

Fighting games match race to abilities but also free games from having to provide a single racial voice or perspective, installing a dizzying diversity, so that focusing on one racial type can feel like dismissing others. If a player were asked to pinpoint where the racism of *Street Fighter II* lies, the racial offenses would seem so abundant and far-fetched that one would hesitate to respond. The deployment of so many racial types breaks "stereotype" as a useful term (if it wasn't already broken) by pointing to its nationalist limitations—what appears stereotypical in one instance (E. Honda's sumo garb, for example) will seem vastly atypical in another (in Japan, E. Honda has been banned for sporting facial paint). The racial constructs are overshadowed by the game's diversity and its formal feature of various play styles. The dizzying diversity of *Street Fighter II* makes the game appear "odorless" or global, yet, read as a Japanese game, it could also convey the power structures across the transpacific, where the desire to equalize Japan as a "normal country" means balancing Japanese characters alongside other political powers and thus situating Japanese racial constructs closer to American and European power.[94] The restriction for an independent military reappears in fighting games where Japan arrives equal (balanced) among other nations, the very aspiration for conservative Japanese governments who advocate for Japan to militarily rearm.

Five years after *Street Fighter II*, the 1996 game series *Dead or Alive* extended its racial logics into the three-dimensional competitive arena, but it featured a character aesthetic that depicted the "cultural fragrance" of racial identities through a kawaii minimalism. The franchise has, by 2019, encompassed twenty-six different games as well as a feature film (2005). Like *Street Fighter II*, *Dead or Alive* featured a dizzying diversity of racial characters: Bass and Tina Armstrong were the American stereotypes as blond-haired wrestlers from the American South whose clothing sported American flags, and the Chinese character LeiFang wore a red cheongsam and braided queue hairstyle. So far, so dizzying. But *Dead or Alive* enhanced these stereotypes by dramatizing them with exuberant personalities that explicitly integrated their national backgrounds with their fighting styles, making race impossible to ignore. Characters walked into arenas touting one-liners, strutting as if on runways that showcased their racial skins. The characters each came with unique personalities that bled from their racial identities and were made relatable through CGI cut scenes scattered throughout the game's story. The character Zack played as a "funky" and "hip hop" African American, and the Chinese Gen Fu played as an old martial arts master spouting adages like "to lose is the way of the fool."

Dead or Alive pushed the campy nonsense of racial playfulness by conceiving of racial identities as an explicit pleasure, encouraging players to match personality with play style as well as fetish. The game was instantly synonymous with gaudy sex appeal, as it encouraged players to clothe the Japanese characters in geisha outfits and the American Tina Armstrong in a cowgirl bikini.[95] The game's kawaii aesthetics also made the body itself—particularly breasts—look glossy and soft. Techmo's physics engine was dedicated to breast animation, inventing a "boob-physics" that overlapped gameplay with sexual play, as moves like punching, slapping, and uppercuts resulted in exaggerated breast movements. The game's two busty stars, both Japanese women, persuaded players to buy the game to unlock outfits that enhanced their sexual appearances (sub/dom outfits, cat outfits, etc.).

Street Fighter II and *Dead or Alive* resemble two exemplars of the "global game" whose racial logics have reappeared in the American game *Mortal Kombat* (1992), the British game *Killer Instinct* (1994), and Japanese game series like *Virtua Fighter* (1993), *Tekken* (1994), and *Soulcalibur* (1998). These later games have become especially well known for their relatable racialized characters who resemble stereotypes, but because of their race's scarcity in video games, also garner pride. The Filipina character Talim in *Soulcalibur 2*, the first visible Filipina character in a video game, fights using a version of Eskrima (the Philippines' national martial arts form) and shouts Tagalog phrases in her fighting moves. Yet her petite silhouette, scantily clad body, childlike voice, and ability to control the wind give her ethnic background a campy cultural "fragrance" that invites both humorous parodies and irreverent performances as well as objectifying gazes.[96] The undeniable slip in video game camp from "discovering points of commonality amid difference" to "mocking and exploiting the ostensible credulity and ignorance of others" foregrounds the productive ambiguity of playing with race in video games, a practice conditioned by imperial attitudes toward Asiatic forms of art and sport.[97]

The Asiatic

The contradictions that emerge when conceiving of race as play are indeed vexed and entangling, not only because they involve a transnational set of audiences within a global medium—where the same object can be read as both a "dead serious" stereotype and as a campy exaggeration—but also because our own "style" of handling race has its own gamelike boundaries and rules, laid bare by seeing race as play. Foremost among these rules is that racial forms are exclusive (one can't be black and white; one must choose) and that racism emerges through forms of crossover (when a white person performs as black), especially when that crossover ignores or erases historical violence or present-day privilege. This serious approach can only see the playful approach as itself racist, as deeply misguided, or as in poor taste. However, we find playful approaches to race not only in video games but in attempts to engage with others outside of the racial meanings that structure the Western gaze. Here I briefly turn to Roland Barthes's work of theoretical travel literature, *Empire of Signs*, where Barthes confronts Japan playfully and erotically by understanding it only through his own limits as a Westerner, never speaking of Japan in any finalizing sense but referring only to "Japan" in quotation marks as "that country that I am calling Japan."[98] Japan thus appears as a gamelike world that offers Barthes "a flat language where nothing grounds on superimposed layers of meaning."[99] As with Sontag's depiction of camp as a triumph of style over content, Barthes's *Empire of Signs* laments the Western tendency to "[moisten] everything with meaning, like an authoritarian religion which imposes baptism on entire peoples"[100] and finds in Japan's postwar culture a playful erotics that refuses meaning with the flatness of the sign, an antisemiotics that Barthes found immeasurably hopeful.[101]

The book's title, *Empire of Signs*, illuminates Barthes's playful attitude toward the meanings that Japan offers, of being overwhelmed by signs that construe no meaning for the Westerner, a symbolic order that offers a reversal of imperial relations. Barthes found in this "empire of signifiers" an immensity that promised "richness, mobility, and subtlety"[102] and that saw the body not as an identity of rights and privileges but "according to a pure—though subtly discontinuous—erotic project."[103]

Throughout *Empire of Signs*, Barthes feels played upon by immense symbols that (to him) mean only flatness (the tempura chef is "he who has played"),[104] yet Barthes also comes to apprehend these various play styles as erotic forms that recognize the body playfully.[105] Indeed, here we find a form of race that reflects the casual gamer's play of racialized bodies, done sensually (emphasizing taste, odor, savoring), frivolously (with no serious purpose), and as displaying alternative perceptions of the body. What makes these depictions "playful," ultimately, is Barthes's sense of Japan not as a race or nation, but as a "fictive nation" of "invented interplay" that proposes "a possibility of difference."[106]

In order to understand games as proffering a similar fictivity of difference, sensuality, and erotics, we must also understand race within the playful "bubble" of the magic circle (here we risk exclusion, but like in games, one can only proceed by either quitting or playing along). As with Barthes's own project on Japan, we, too, can no longer deduce "Asia" within bestowed meanings that suggest exclusivity or even specific comparative histories (as East versus West, Oriental versus Occidental). Notions of Japanese pop art as "odorless" aesthetics born from postwar anxieties seem not to capture Japan in any authentic sense but rather exemplify Japanese popular products as transpacific commodities within a context of American imperial dominance. Our ability to read games as queer or as campy is made possible by their ability to circulate as global objects aloof from the serious world of racial politics. Accepting that no term can easily apprehend this fictive racial construct, I toy with the term "Asiatic" to characterize forms, spaces, and personages that many players will find similar to Asia but that are never exclusively Asian, or are obscured from any other recognizable racial genre, or are not foreclosed to other given identity tropes. Whereas to call one "Asian" finalizes identity like a stamp, "Asiatic" remains a form, a style rather than a substance, a technology rather than an essence. One is not Asian, but merely *does* something in an Asian way (a country's Asiatic nationalism, a scholar's Asiatic approach, a subject's Asiatic freedom). One is not necessarily Asiatic toward oneself but is seen that way by *the person who finds them Asiatic* (and simultaneously could also be doing "America" and "Manila"). The "-ic" of Asia*tic* functions similar to the broadening suffix "-ish" used in monogamish, blackish, Asianish, in that it turns nouns to adjectives and attempts to name recognizable themes and forms, while still presuming uncertainty. But unlike "-ish," the "-ic" suffix does not suggest the structural reassurance of mastery in knowing the "real:" the monogamous, the black, the Asian. "Asiatic" rather than "Asianish" does not reiterate the masterly noun but insists upon the "sort of" of the "-ic" suffix as its own realm, its own magic circle, or its own discourse (one can study "the Asiatic" but not the "Asianish"). As with Sontag's view of camp as seeing "everything in quotation marks," and with Barthes's writings about "the country that I am calling Japan," the realm of play, erotics, and camp conceives of Asiatic forms as well as Western*ic* forms—both of which could, in fact, describe the exact same objects.

As with *Street Fighter II*'s stereotypical depictions of Dhalsim, the term "Asiatic" seems too full of historical baggage to be made playful, which is precisely the risk of play. In *Ornamentalism*, Anne Anlin Cheng uses the term "yellow" in naming "the yellow woman" because it refuses the "more ameliorative, politically acceptable terms" like "Asian American" and instead conjures "the queasiness of this inescapably racialized and gendered figure."[107] Like "yellow," "Asiatic" offers political dilemma rather than safety, and its so-called baggage is exactly the remembrance that we have never separated from histories of racism, that our technological breakthroughs have never helped us approach a postracial world. But unlike "yellow," which could be a political term of endearment, "Asiatic" confronts and revises the serious baggage of racial naming, as it is a term often reserved for geographical space, animals, or fauna (Asiatic seas, Asiatic cougars, Asiatic barbarians). Asiatic messes around with the positivistic forms of race widely recognized through the "serious" lifeworld of scholarship and imperial optics.

In its colonial usage, Asiatic named a blurry assortment of possibilities, a thing yet to be properly explored or identified. Webster's and the Wikipedia dictionary both proclaim "Asiatic" archaic, a term considered offensive when applied to people rather than spaces, eras, or objects. But even during its highest use in the late nineteenth century, "Asiatic" rarely referenced objects or people themselves, but *parts*, styles, or ways of being, and thus always presumes mixture as it frequently named hybrid forms: the "Afro-Asiatic" or "Asiatic characteristics" of non-Asian people (rivers could have their "Asiatic side," meaning the side facing East). Henry James described the Russian writer Ivan Turgenev as having "something Asiatic in his faculty of procrastination,"[108] while Laurence Sterne's Tristram Shandy described his own father as having "the acumen of the Asiatic genius."[109] The Asiatic enables a view of "somewhat Asian" forms and strategies rather than insisting on measuring and evaluating the strategies of one group (Chinese) that can also suggest mastery over others (Thai, Cambodian). Asiatic in this sense need not be tied to race, geography, or any particular content at all, and in so being, invites others to play along.

"Asiatic" communicates how Asia and other racial forms blend in video games in ways that elude "serious" categorizations. In *America's Asia*, Colleen Lye conjures what she calls "Asiatic racial form" to unite model minority stereotypes of Asian Americans with yellow peril stereotypes of Asian immigrants in the early twentieth century, showing how both racializations were based primarily upon economic anxieties. "Asiatic" becomes a way to visually encounter the "unrepresentable" foreign, pushing scholars to better account for "the international context in which American race relations take shape."[110] While Lye uses "Asiatic racial form" to wed racial discourses, this book understands the Asiatic within digital media as less representation or discourse, and more as a stage that shapes the interactions in video games as neither Asian nor Asian American but as an unrepresentable blend. Japanese characters in video games are almost uniformly dubbed into an American-accented English, forming Asian Americanness within entire genres of video games (Japanese role-playing games, Japanese dating simulations, Japanese visual novels). Similarly, the Asiatic shapes racialized characters like *Final Fantasy VII*'s Barret, who expresses a Japanese perception of American blackness that is mediated through English translators as well as the player's own performance, all within a cyberpunk fantasy (a typically Asianish form).

"Asiatic" sees Asia as a construct needing to be problematized, as only existing within scare quotes or as holding an asterisk that implies, as Jack Halberstam writes, "expansive forms of difference, haptic relations to knowing, uncertain modes of being, and the disaggregation of identity politics predicated upon the separating out of many kinds of experience that actually blend together, intersect, and mix."[111] Video games, by virtue of their aesthetic forms and genre traditions, are always in some conceivable way Asiatic, opening "Asia" to non-Asian-identifying subjects for play and reveling in mixtures that are articulated as "global."

What other term might we call Pokémon catchers, cosplayers, or indeed, the gaming world in general, if not "Asiatic"?

Asiatic Play in E-sports

We can understand video games as an inescapably Asiatic medium when we consider how even global games with "dizzying diversity" are in fact characteristic of Japanese aesthetic forms. Yet games are most visibly Asiatic when race is reconceived as play—that is, when Asian bodies are hypervisible in e-sports competitions, which contrast non-Asiatic sports like basketball, baseball, or football. Like any sport, video games, too, have a competitive edge that pushes players to improve, to fail and reflect, and to return, entering into a loop that is often merely called addiction. In the United States, video games lack the admiration of sports as a self-evident good in itself, especially when games are played by African American youth. In President Barack Obama's first major speech to the African American community at the NAACP's one hundredth anniversary celebration, Obama said parents should be "putting away the Xbox and putting our kids to bed at a reasonable hour."[112] Despite the cultural associations of African American competitiveness with basketball, baseball, sprinting, and other sports, video games for black youth signified laziness rather than technical superiority. In East Asian countries like South Korea and Japan, video games have become a much more popular form of sportsmanship. South Korea, frequently cited as the most internet-friendly country in the world, has become infamous for its e-sports enthusiasm, as PC bangs (PC rooms) can be found in every district, sometimes on every street corner. Seoul has its own dedicated e-sports stadium, has TV channels dedicated to e-sports, and its e-sports players garner celebrity status.

Curiously, many of the most famous e-sports games played in Asia are made by American software companies. South Korea's main e-sport of choice, since 2012, has invariably been *League of Legends*, a multi-player online battle arena (MOBA) game released in 2009 by Riot Games, a game company that began in Los Angeles but grew to include additional offices in seventeen different countries, with a Los Angeles staff of over 1,600 employees. *League of Legends* has become a worldwide phenomenon, with at its peak over sixty-seven million people playing every month, or twenty-seven million per day.[113] Though *League of Legends* championships have been held in Europe, North America, and Latin America, the game has become racially coded as an Asian obsession that, like wéiqí, speaks to the technical and mathematical superiority of Asians, as its world championships and biggest celebrities appear Asian.[114] Another extremely popular MOBA, *Dota 2*, was also developed by an American company (Valve) and targeted markets worldwide by optioning twenty-six different languages from Bulgarian, Romanian, and Thai to both mainland and overseas Chinese. Recently, China's Tencent company has dominated the MOBA industry, owning Riot Games (the maker of *League of Legends*),[115] and it has capitalized on the MOBA mobile game *Arena of Valor*, which in 2017 carried 80–200 million players daily (mostly in China) and was named the most popular game in the world.[116] E-sports has sedimented video games as an Asiatic sport, where Asians secure competitive advantage by appearing as natural talents.[117]

The comparison of e-sports to traditional sports reveal how imperial attitudes have been reconstructed via the dissemination and cultural presumptions of sporting skill and spectatorship. As Brian Sutton-Smith has pointed out,[118] sports have a history of being exported to colonial spaces to encourage "deific" idealizations of those who play them, so that in order to meet the colonizer upon an equal field, the colonized must first accept the colonizer's sport as their form of equalization.[119] Sports and games have the effect of producing a ludic identity,[120] where a group identifies with a set of rules that smuggle along presumptions based on nationality, race, and gender: they presume that some races excel at some sports, while labeling marginalized peoples—like African Americans—as sports spectacles, whose bodies are to be admired as unreal. Because the rules of a game seem absent of racial, national, or gender orientations, the bodies identified with these games seem to speak to deeply rooted tendencies and essentialist forms of play. Similarly, the Asiatic forms in e-sports reiterate a techno-Orientalist racism that sees East Asian identity not as creative or independent but as passive and robotic—well suited for the programming and engineering labor of information technology.[121] The rigorous competitive ethos that characterizes e-sports echoes the martial arts discipline that characterized Ryu, but also evaluates Asian societies as a dangerous vision "of the future itself" as Stephen Hong Sohn writes, where despite their "superb technological efficiency and capitalist expertise, their affectual absence resonates as an undeveloped or, worse still, a retrograde humanism."[122] Configured as Asiatic, e-sports dehumanize Asian bodies as automated others who do not conquer technology so much as they are conquered by it.[123] Playing a video game can thus take the form of "trying on" Asiatic sport, entering a symbolic space similar to martial arts or yoga, both Asiatic cultural art forms that permit others to play along.

The discourse of e-sports exhibits Asiatic styles of play that operate as racial spectacles. MOBAs like *League of Legends* and *Dota 2* are known in gaming communities as the most addictive and money-driven game forms, characteristics drawn from the amount of time they consume and from their available in-game purchases. Unlike past global games like *Street Fighter II* and *Dead or Alive*, MOBAs are deep, complex games that take hundreds of hours to play effectively, with each match lasting about half an hour rather than the three to five minutes of a *Street Fighter II* match. Within these half-hour matches, players must master precise handling of their character, must consistently communicate with their teammates to properly balance the team's needs, and must display a full knowledge of the game's highly complex systems of attributes. *League of Legends* contains 141 characters ("champions") that serve to make the game appear global but also cast race through mythical heroes whose origins can be made more racially explicit by purchasing different skins. As with *Dead or Alive*, e-sports games like *League of Legends* and *Dota 2* mythologize identities into playful racial essences that match their play style. Martial arts figures like Sun WuKong (The Monkey King) make up fast and heavy-damage characters, while the character Ashe, based on Scandinavian myths of female hunters, plays the role of a marksman.

Even as these games' characters seem to scream racial stereotypes, their depictions shape race just as well through the games' consistent balancing of these characters via updates and patches. The need to cooperate within a perfectly balanced and highly complex system marks these competitive e-sport events as a spectacle on par with the military discipline of North Korean military parades or with the display of cooperative gymnastics at Beijing's 2008 Olympics opening performance.

Where cooperation and strength in numbers have characterized Asian cultures, MOBAs follow suit. As an "addictive," time-consuming e-sport, MOBAs seem to hinder the success envisioned within neoliberal subjectivity, making Asians appear magically fit for both e-sport success and model minority success. The freedom and educational purposes of play thus become poisoned by this Asiatic sport, making white players in America and Europe appear more soulful and independent, while Asian players remain stigmatized as robotic technology addicts.

Race as Playful in *Overwatch*

The e-sport MOBAs of the late 2000s combined the Japanese postwar aesthetics of fighting games with cooperative mechanics of a sporting arena, solidifying techno-Orientalist discourses of Asian automation. Yet even as global games have seemingly emptied race of its historical and political attributes to a bare style of play, they have simultaneously allowed players to see their own strategic performances (and the performance of others) as connected to playful, campy, and fictive racial identities. If the "magic circle" of video games is an Asiatic space, then race in games signifies not a mask but a style that players absorb to ask if there is something "Filipino," or "Chinese," or "Japanese" about the way they perform and whether their most "natural" play style may be the style of the other. For the remainder of this chapter, I focus the 2016 e-sport global game *Overwatch* to ask how racial play can be made meaningful, critical, and transformative.

Overwatch is a first-person shooter game released worldwide in May 2016, reaching a high point of fifteen million players in August of that year. It falls into the emerging genre of "hero shooters," which arguably began in 2007 with *Team Fortress 2* and came of age in 2016 with the games *Overwatch* (Blizzard), *Battleborn* (Gearbox Software), and *Paladins* (Hi-Rez Studios), all released in that year. Like fighting games, hero shooters situate players to select from a dizzyingly diverse set of characters (heroes) with special abilities, and like MOBAs, they feature cooperative mechanics that demand consistent team balance, communication, and expertise. *Overwatch* pits two teams of six against each other to defend points on a map, or to escort payloads over a limited amount of time, with thirty-one characters (as of August 2019) who battle in futuristic cities in Africa, Britain, China, and the United States (see Figure 1.1). It is, in a sense, a metagame that brings together elements from previous global game genres into a meticulously balanced arena. As a metaworld, or a game about the world, *Overwatch* rejects narrative depth to provide hyperanimated cartoonish characters, left as toys for players to make their own. The game's racy patchwork of diverse heroes appear less like representations of people and more like the personages of pornography, who, as Sontag writes, are pure behavior, lacking in depth because the player's engagement requires "emotional flatness" as a precondition to "find room for his own responses."[124] So the player hardly takes notice that the game's narrative, which establishes the characters as heroes or villains, totally contradicts the gameplay, where teams can be made up of all the same hero and can face off against themselves. As with previous global games, *Overwatch*'s main concern to weigh these characters within a meticulously balanced gameplay is totally indifferent to its own narrative. The consistently adjusted balance of the game, where each character seems just as vital and useful as any other, provides a spectral fantasy of a balanced global world. Weekly patches and updates "nerf" (weaken) or "buff" (strengthen) characters based on player activity. *Overwatch* provides a global multicultural representation of others equally balanced in a competitive utopia, an optimistic fantasy that constructs a magic circle where race becomes playful.

Overwatch's characters exist in the "-ic" or "-ish" suffixes, the quotation marks of camp. They are both stereotypical and homage, both racist and racially nationalist, both offensive and subversive. Mei, the Chinese hero, is inspired by Chinese ice artist festivals, but unlike Chinese film icons, Mei sports a large silhouette and undermines the vastly male-dominated science industries in China itself, as Mei is a climatologist and chief engineer for the Overwatch heroes. Her lines throughout the game are strikingly optimistic and play upon the optimism of a mainland China burgeoning with wealth and global prowess. She spouts phrases like "Everyone is counting on me," "I hope you learned your lesson," and her environmentalist pet phrase, "Our world is worth fighting for," all slanted in a Chinese accent by the Chinese voice actress Yu Zhang. At the same time that Mei appears parodic and unsettling, from

Figure 1.1. *Overwatch*'s character selection screen. Screenshot by author.

an American perspective, Chinese Americans are often stereotyped as nerds and scientists, and Mei's constant concern with finding laboratory experiments would ring true to model minority stereotypes. Yet in *Overwatch*'s actual gameplay, Mei's naive optimism and stereotypical accent become camp, as they function as an innocent stylization of psychological warfare. Her bubbly voice and cheery lines are coupled with her ability to freeze opponents and leave them struggling in a blind panic. As the Reddit user SirRagesAlot writes, "Being killed by [Mei] is slow and agonizing because of her relatively low dps [damage per second], and freeze mechanic. She kills people like a psychopath who takes pleasure in binding and slowly torturing her victims."[125]

Like Mei, the Russian bodybuilder Zarya reads as both offensive and as resistant to stereotypes. Fan communities have accepted her as queer, though she is extremely patriotic toward Russia, a country whose leaders routinely hold homophobic views and persecute queer people. Her role as a "tank" who lifts an enormous particle canon marks her as a tough front-line unit who absorbs damage. As a bodybuilder, Zarya was also a sports competitor before becoming a hero, and she once represented Russia in a "world championship" (their Olympics). Her nontraditional appearance is coupled with pithy one-liners that expel her patriotism to Russia, sometimes in meme form: "In Russia, Game Plays You" and "I want to hug you like big fuzzy Siberian bear."

As in previous global games, *Overwatch* exemplifies gaming as a play-ful art form, as it arranges campy characters within a dizzying diversity that could both "offend" and "shock" but never seems to cross the line of *demeaning* a particular group (at least not more than any other). These characters promise pleasure for someone who seeks only to play within the magic circle, but they can also embolden marginalized players who, familiar with seeing stereotypical nationalist images, might find the campy elements of these characters undermining accorded stereotypes through comical excess. D.Va, the game's Korean character, is a Korean celebrity pro gamer who plays retro games inside of her giant robotic machine (the "MEKA"). D.Va, whose symbol has been used in feminist protests in South Korea, seems like a direct commentary on the Korean e-sports stereotype, making her technologically savvy (a quality ascribed mostly to Korean men), while also marketing her as a sassy Orientalist fetish.

Playful Intimacy

what if: What if the right audience for this were exactly *me*?
—Eve Kosofsky Sedgwick, *Epistemology of the Closet*
(emphasis in original)

As Brian Sutton-Smith puts it simply, play is whatever is not serious, but it relies on the serious in order to make its point. For game studies theories of play, the "play" and the "serious" have operated as binary concepts, relying on the other to constitute itself. But, as argued in the introduction, play can also be understood through the verb phrase "to play with," constituted beside the phrase, "to use." "To play with" rather than "to use" means taking a role that gives and receives, quiet-ing oneself to share intimate experiences, to think *with* rather than think *about*. As the game designers Naomi Clark and Merritt Kopas point out, juxtaposing "to use" and "to play with" implicitly interro-gates both concepts, as "playing" can be "useful" in that it can "help us imagine and invoke new possibilities" by revealing "new ways to relate to play, and through it, to each other."[126]

When it comes to racialized figures in games, this notion of "to play with" a racial figure rather than "to use" them summons an intimate form of engagement made possible by the campy and the Asiatic. To get a handle on this strange ludic intimacy, I here share my own play experience with *Overwatch*:

I downloaded *Overwatch* in June 2016, about one week after my marriage. The game challenged me, pitted me against survivable and surmountable hardships, giving way to playful proddings as I tested the game's boundaries, grafting, flirting, enjoying its whimsical distance. I became hopelessly infatuated with my mains, the Chinese Mei and the queer Russian Zarya. Within months, the game brightened the city around me in the way a blazing sunset can make an inhospitable world look polished in oil-slicked pinks and purples. I saw the game's dizzyingly diverse universe everywhere in the peoples of my expatriate riddled neighborhood in Hong Kong. I felt fettered to Zarya's queer and nonsensical one-liners, "I want to hug you like big fuzzy Siberian bear!" and to Mei's optimistic desire for a world "worth fighting for." Though I had lived in China for years, I never memorized Chinese poetry until I heard Mei quote a line by Tang dynasty poet Cen Shen, "hūrú yī yè chūnfēnglái, qiānshù wàn shù lí huākāi," [忽如一夜春風來 千樹萬樹梨花開], meaning, "suddenly, on a spring night, thousands of pear trees bloom." Mei, research-lover and icicle-stabbing psycho, shaped my world, made it seem balanced, equal, playful. Everything was OK: my foreignness, my lack of Chinese fluency, my faking an optimism even as my own country broke apart. The game knew none of my difference—it had other unexpected, uncontainable perils. My need for these characters befuddled my partner and friends, who saw the game as a form of addiction, escapism, or a racial tourism that bordered on performing blackface or yellowface. What right did I have to feel so intimately attached to playing a stereotypical Chinese, British, Korean, or queer Russian woman? In the serious world of racial division, my game experience seemed to only suggest perversity, naivety, and quite possibly an ingrained racist (if not misogynistic) worldview. I could not talk to anyone about the game, ashamed to admit its hold on my heart.

Drawing on Judith Butler's sense of precarious life, which "characterizes such lives who do not qualify as recognizable," Adrianne Shaw argues that video game representations offer performative roles that "makes certain identities possible, plausible, and livable."[127] Characters like Mei and Zarya are not used by gamers to identify *as* that person, but temporarily *with* them to explore affinities and aspirations. As Shaw writes, "one might identify *with* an Asian character even though one identifies *as* Latina."[128] My own feelings of intimacy with *Overwatch*'s campy and Asiatic racial figures made other forms of self-perception recognizable, forms that were once shadowed by living within my own particular racialized body.

For a less subjective example of intimacy and racial play we can look to Tracer, *Overwatch*'s British hero, and her signature line, "The world could always use more heroes." The line is spouted in a stereotypical cockney accent, an exaggerated form of British English, that is featured in the game as an optional voice line that the player can run at any moment. In play, the line becomes comical, extravagant, campy, as it can be repeated on a constant loop, which can elicit creative responses from teammates. As gamer videos and blogs have shown, this tagline can function to annoy or snuggle up to one's teammates by spouting a clearly obnoxious phrase within a stereotypical voice, or while jumping up and down in excitement before battle.[129] Others play along by repeating similar jargon, sometimes ignoring the entire purpose of the match to do so. However, in one of the first animated shorts released by Blizzard to advertise for the game, the line appears again, "The world could always use more heroes," this time without any of the playful absurdity as witnessed in the game. The line comes after a heated battle, told to two young boys who look up to the *Overwatch* characters like superheroes. The film ends with one of the boys shouting, "That was awesome!" while the *Overwatch* theme music plays in the background. This animated short takes away all the camp and joy from enacting the line in the game. It becomes a means of using the line, deploying it for marketing purposes, rather than playing with it. The short film turns the once playful character Tracer into a mere stereotype and the voice into a cringeworthy accent that distances the viewer rather than invites intimate relations. The in-game line, free of narrative weight, heroic music, and cinematic ostentation, maintains a spirit of intimate playfulness.

The racial politics that *Overwatch*'s characters conjure extends the "dizzying diversity" of previous global games to emphasize the intimate attachment that players have with these characters. Their surface-level personality quips and fetishes here necessitate the quotation marks of camp or "-ish" and "-ic" suffixes that recognize their playful modes of play: Tracer is not British so much as British*ish*; Mei is not so much Chinese as "Chinese." Though characters are, ideally, meant to reflect different play styles, players often stick to characters they are not even talented at playing merely because they feel an intimate attachment to that character's personage. The player may desire to play with the Korean pop star D.Va but still find that they are naturally more useful for their team by picking Zarya or Mei. Here "maining" emerges as a racially unsettling narrative, where to "main" a character implies that players perform best with that character, while many players main due more to their intimate connection rather than their skill.[130]

The narrative of "maining" makes race appear purely coincidental to one's play style, yet in my own experience playing *Overwatch*, I found myself gravitating toward characters who spoke to my own experiences as a queer traveler of multiple racial genealogies who has lived in Korea, China, and Hong Kong. From June 15, 2016, to October 15, 2016, I logged in 112 hours of play time, with eighteen as Zarya, sixteen as D.Va, thirteen as Tracer, and eleven as Mei. My attachment to all female characters, two Asian, one queer, and one highly objectified (Tracer's rear end has featured prominently in *Overwatch* advertisements) could not be explained by the logic of the magic circle as a place where race can be "purified" by the prioritization of a game's mechanics. My attachments could not be purely playful or purely serious but were always an intimate form of "to play with," as I felt more at home playing alongside their campy, Asiatic personas than "using" them for personal gain (like winning). D.Va resolved my own desires from living in Korea for a year as an American immigrant, while Zarya spoke to my own obscure-queer identity, and Mei gave me comfort living in Hong Kong after teaching mainland students for two years (2014–2015) and struggling to learn Mandarin for five. Yet if I had created these monstrously stereotypical identities myself, or used them for some greater purpose, I would never have felt comfortable playing them. Their campy, Asiatic depictions helped me brood upon the spaces I had inhabited, while at the same time, refused the gaze of mastery, expertise, and certainty.

Playful Insurgency

As with Tracer's seemingly stereotypical voiceover line, "The world could always use more heroes," race functions in *Overwatch* to both deliver intimate relations with playful racial representations and to engage in discourses with distant others, though these modes of communication can have risky and possibly injurious outcomes. To safeguard digital space, information technology companies routinely pinpoint not race but language as the residual obstacle to be overcome, an artificial boundary between peoples of different nations and cultures that one lingua franca—be it English or Chinese—has failed to fully surpass.[131] Indeed, if games stage "race as play," they also stage forms of play that transform understandings of both race and language from serious forms of optimization, hierarchy, and analytical knowledge to forms of playful insurgency that refuse the rules of "serious" attitudes toward race and seek fulfillment within the previously restricted boundaries of mixture and reinvention.[132]

Much of the optimism of *Overwatch*'s utopic universe relies heavily on the diversity of its players working in mutual harmony, despite their vast linguistic differences. To overcome these barriers, *Overwatch* provides a command system that instantly translates directions and emotive comments into each player's chosen language. An in-game dialogue wheel provides seven lines of spoken communication such as "need healing," "group up," and "thanks." These and other forms of urgent communications—"look behind you," "let's attack the point,"— come automatically regardless of player choice. Indeed, the ease through which players in America can communicate with anonymous players in Asia seems to mark an overcoming of the linguistic barrier, where games in Mandarin and in English have often been vastly separated by different markets and censorship.[133] *Overwatch*'s instantaneous process of translation, ideally, frees all players from having to shoulder the burden of translation, a burden that has always been cast upon the disempowered.[134] In *Overwatch*, the foreignness that threatens group cohesion becomes, in these terms, domesticated into something safe, easy to recognize, and balanced.

Overwatch's voice acting adds another layer to its effective presentation as a global game that has transcended linguistic, racial, and national boundaries. As a game that promises a global competitive arena, *Overwatch* has been able to adapt to nationalist politics across the transpacific. The game's English version, meant primarily for American audiences, adjusts to America's brand of identity politics, where white actors, writers, and designers are often called out for performing as people of color, as such acts can conjure histories of blackface and reproduce whiteness as the performance standard. Likewise, in the English version of *Overwatch*, all its voice actors correspond with the characters they play. Mei is voiced by the Chinese American voice actress Zhang Yu, the South Asian character Symmetra is voiced by Indian American voice actress Anjali Bhimani, and even Zenyatta, an artificially intelligent robot from Nepal, is voiced by the Asian American actor Feodor Chin. However, the same racial politics do not apply when the game appears in Japanese or Chinese, where all the voice actors appear to be Japanese or Chinese nationals. A totally different linguistic politics emerges in the Chinese version of *Overwatch*, where the game reinstates Cold War border politics by providing two different versions of Chinese language—simplified/Mainland, or traditional/Taiwanese. The simplified Chinese is accented with a heavy use of the standard Mandarin "儿-er" character, while the Taiwanese uses a more tender and gentler tone.[135] Though the term "Taiwanese" does not appear as a menu option, the simplified and traditional languages signal not merely a written text but different dialects that can include slang from regions more likely to use those written characters. Thus, Mei's main expression, "A-Mei-zing!"—an English play on her name—is translated in Chinese as *měilì dòngrén* [美丽动人], meaning "beautiful and touching" (also a play on her name), and in Taiwanese as *tài xuàn le* [太炫了], a well-known slang term meaning "too much showing off."

It is within the veneer of the seriousness of race, language, and national politics that gameplay can take on a more playful and insurgent role. *Overwatch*'s methodically planned political effects set the stage for players to cooperate despite national, racial, and linguistic differences, as they stream in from across the globe and communicate in speech and in text chats. Here nationalist and linguistic differences appear unabated, as player anonymity ruptures the fantasy of a nonnationalist space, and indecipherable forms of communication become a threat to the very objective of winning, wherein at any moment, one's teammate may not follow a word of the team's language, and the match will be lost. Racial

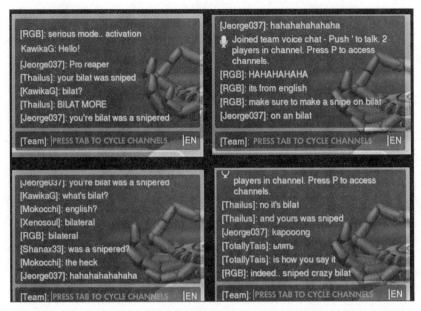

Figure 1.2. *Overwatch*'s in-game textbox chats. Screenshots by author.

difference thus returns as a form of play that can threaten the game's very goal, making moments of untranslatability resist the apparatus that has reduced racial diversity to an ahistorical and nonthreatening element. Within this imaginary stage, players confront the foreign, and finding themselves submitting to another's linguistic patterns, take on a more receptive role of "playing with." A "play language," as Vicente Rafael calls it, begins to develop, one that signals a social alternative to the idealistic instrumentalization of language through a language of "puns, jokes . . . slang, pidgin and creolisms."[136]

Overwatch's in-game slang ranges across languages, from "gg" (good game), "ez" (easy), 88 (bye bye), and so on, while linguistic accents and shorthand can spur on playful experimentations with foreignness as pictured in Figure 1.2, where the phrase "your bilat was sniped" meaning, "your bilateral ultimate was cancelled," becomes playfully reinvested with foreignness even though the phrase is in English. If, as Rafael writes, literature and poetry can provide an aggressive form of linguistic insurgency, games provide translation as a form of play, where linguistic difference exceeds developer-directed limitations, forcing players to confront the reality of racial difference through a playful anarchy. Indeed, these racial, national, and linguistic realities remain within a realm of play as the unpredictable excesses that threaten the security of the "magic circle."

As a game that attempts to provide a global competitive arena, *Overwatch* deploys language to conjure anxieties that exist across national boundaries—namely, the anxiety of the foreign, where contact zones can be both a pleasure and a trauma. Linguistic aporias reappear with the fear that members of a team will be inefficient in the team's language, or that the player will be inefficient in theirs. Language generates anxieties of the foreign through both the fear and the joy of being othered within an unknown and unmasterable linguistic environment. When a player enters a match, whether on American, European, or Asian servers, a new linguistic hierarchy forms. Instead of a single lingua franca, the burden of translation can shift unexpectedly as players find themselves adjusting to the group's dominant language. Since leaving a match can be a punishable offense, players must attempt to recognize modes of racial play in order to win the game. Often groups of Vietnamese, Filipino, or Thai players will come onto a server, and as a group they will outnumber the English or Chinese speakers, who will then be forced to either make wind of the group's strategy or be left out. Their own play style, seen before as a dominant form, will be othered according to the group's. They will be made to feel like the addicts, the gold farmers, the incompetent players, the spoilsports. Some players, like myself, will routinely join up with groups of different linguistic backgrounds just to experience "the loss of identity, or the fluidity of identity."[137] For others, such loss of linguistic dominance can goad racist remarks that frequently emerge as fears of irrelevance ("Speak English!" players often demand).

As Shaw writes, in online video games like *Overwatch*, "translation and local adaptation complicate positivistic claims about representation, demonstrating how racial, gender, and sexual identities are understood quite differently in different national contexts."[138] As an online game, *Overwatch* can facilitate "discourse with rather than appropriations of the other,"[139] but only through the messy confrontations that make national, racial, and linguistic difference difficult. Because video games constitute common global cultures where "mistranslations and epic malfunctions abound,"[140] they are able to expose the peculiarity of the player's own context, which may otherwise seem universal. The inevitable tendency to fail through linguistic ignorance reinstates the real divisions of racial difference, even within the playful modes of the magic circle. This introduction of difference through linguistic boundaries creates potentials for new intimacies, as members must find unspoken and performative forms of communication in attempts to coordinate, win, and have fun. Within this effort to "play with" others, players can begin to imagine new groupings, new forms of nonlinguistic communication, new shared slangs, and new points of view from which to grasp their own place within an imperial center.

The Racial Circle

Envisioned through the playful campiness of race as play, video games can act as a terminal for chance meetings, where intimate connections grow unabated and confrontations with race and otherness remain partial to the rhythm of play. Games like *Overwatch*, in their attempts to appeal to a global marketplace by erasing their own national origins, cause us to reexamine our presumptions about spaces that are not our own—spaces here construed as Asiatic, where the rules of Western and imperial gazes are transformed into playful forms of improvisation and recognition. To return to the anecdote that began this chapter, the Korean player who called me a "fucking American" was one such chance for recognition. Stabbing him with an ice shard granted me a feeling of euphoria that would have been impossible to feel without his insults. Though the game's anarchic contact zone had betrayed my sense of anonymity, the risk of racist remarks was, in the end, part of the very experience that made the game so pleasureful. No doubt, if I hadn't felt racially or nationally attacked, I would not have played as well—and no doubt, being called a "fucking American" was decidedly different than other, more injurious epithets. My determination to snipe him with a bubbly Chinese avatar was less about a universal will to win and was far more about losing the security of identity within a magic circle, where pernicious chance encounters were meant to be relegated to the serious.

Video games do not produce racial attitudes so much as stage playful engagements with race that risk injury, but they can also offer transformative ways of perceiving racial realities. By tracing global games that appear within a campy, dizzying diversity, we can better understand how race speaks through commodities masked as global: turn-based strategy games like Sid Meier's *Civilization* series (see chapter 6), open world games like *Shenmue II* (see chapter 2), online role-playing games like *World of Warcraft* and *Guild Wars 2* (see chapter 3), sports games like *FIFA*, horror games like *Alien: Isolation* (see chapter 4), and others. Each of these genres distances itself from its national origins while also configuring as Asiatic and thus conceiving of race through forms of play. Like *Overwatch*, these games stage confrontations with forms of race that can transform traditional conceptions of racial difference, where "victory" can only emerge by reading the playful signs of the other, discovering their limitations and boundaries, and then functioning well ("winning") within those constraints. Racial, national, and linguistic differences are not merely boundaries to be overcome, as common conceptions of the "magic circle" teach, but are the most crucial challenges we face together.

2

Ludophile

Author \ Auteur / Asian

In 2012, the Wing Luke Museum of the Asian Pacific American Experience in Seattle, Washington, held an exhibition titled "Asian American Arcade: The Art of Video Games." The exhibition's goal was to "explor[e] the interplay between video games and Asian Pacific American identity & experience" by combining the works of painters and graffiti artists with programmers and game designers.[1] The pairing revealed a strange dissonance. While the graphic and comic artists like Ken Taya and Gene Luen Yang explicitly represented the "identity & experience" of Asian American people, the game designers seemed to lack this element within their games. Derek Yu, who *Eurogamer* once called "as close to a genius as video games have," has created characters based on Indiana Jones, and on his website he narrates his own life history as a speculative adventure reaching from the United States to Nepal and Vietnam.[2] Another featured designer, Jenova Chen, a migrant from Shanghai, has never had an Asian or Asian American character in any of his games. This dissonance between the exhibition's goals to explore "Asian Pacific American identity & experience" and the designers' work devoid of Asian representations exposes difficult questions concerning Asian heritage video game developers in the West, who according to every available statistic are "over-represented" as game developers and programmers.[3] And yet, as scholars and bloggers have repeatedly pointed out, video games have lacked Asian American characters seemingly more than any other American minority, including Native Americans and Hispanics. While Asian American representation in games has been scanty at best, there has been little attempt by either scholars or bloggers to consider the role of Asian North American game producers, even when it is common knowledge that they are over-represented in the industry.

In the fields of literature and film, ethnic authors have become so tied to representing their ethnic identities and histories that, as Viet Thanh Nguyen writes, "if 'ethnic' means anything in relation to literature, it is the sign of the ethnic speaking of and for the ethnic population."[4] In ethnic literature particularly, the author's identity is expected to coincide with the identity of their protagonist. Novels give interior insights into a person, so it seems natural that audiences would trust their author with an intimate portrayal of a marginalized experience. The authorial ethnicity made explicit in short bios, headshots, and names, seals authorial authority to write from the point of view of an ethnic minority. But like in many forms of digital art, Asian North American game developers and designers—the vast majority of whom do not represent Asian bodies in their games—remain unrecognizable to scholars, bloggers, and even players. As the queer Asian designer Robert Yang observed in my 2017 interview with him, "hardly anyone makes 'personal games,'" and the racial identities of the producers are not expected to correlate with that of the game's characters.[5] At the same time that Asian American developers are rarely recognized as authorial agents, Japanese developers have been known as information tech rock stars, whose games form artistic oeuvres detailing their distinct personalities akin to the filmic cults of the auteur. These Japanese artists are renowned by gamers and writers alike as risk-taking geniuses who have provided the most influential games for nearly every genre, from role-playing games (*Final Fantasy*) to platforming games (*Mario Bros.*) to arcade games (*Space Invaders*, *Pac-Man*).

If (as argued in chapter one) games portray themselves as a global art form whose meanings are open to various transnational decodings, then many of these decodings become dependent upon their authorship, which in games refers to company-dictated marketing schemes. In Foucault's lecture "What is an Author?" Foucault responds to Roland Barthes's earlier essay "The Death of the Author" with a genealogical approach to the author as an ideological function that emerged so the religious-legal system could cast blame on authors for writing transgressive texts. In this light, we should not only examine the absence of authors in games but also the hypervisibility of authors in film and literature, where presumptions that ethnic stories reflect the author's ethnicity have for so long remained paradigmatic.

Expanding on the previous chapter, here race emerges again as play, not because we can categorize and identify "racial styles," but because racial authorship in games forces us to deviate from the presumption that the artistic product should act as an immediate reference for racial essence, racial belonging, and ethnic genre making. To see race as play means questioning how explicitly self-referential art lies upon a spectrum of expressive genres and forms. Rather than attempting to access an authentic "truth" to an ethnic experience, games cause us to ask how else the "game of ethnic expression" is played—how else racialized peoples have sought to respond to mainstream styles of race and selfhood through emerging technologies and discourses (academic, literary, gamer oriented). How does the author function operate differently from Japanese games, seen as artworks produced by "rock star" developers, to Western games, where the author/developer is promptly erased? In a medium where Asian characters in Japanese games are so prevalent, why do Asian North American developers hardly ever portray Asian minorities in their games?

This chapter explores the transnational dimensions of authorship through three types of developers: the invisible American developer, the Japanese auteur developer, and the Asian North American developer. I look at how Japanese authorship reinvents "the Orient" as a space of development and playful innovation, while Western developers gain little recognition for their work so that game companies can cast blame onto players themselves for a game's violence and sexual transgressions. I ask then how we might imagine the player as "ludophile," whose attention to the game designers (particularly Asian North American designers) can offer erotic readings of games as objects of attachment, intimacy, and obscurity. The "ludophile" does not invest authority into the author so much as call attention to speculative ways of playing routed through ethnic authorship. By growing attached to the Asian authors in games that feature extreme militarism (*Modern Warfare 2, Counter-Strike*) or games that seem apolitical and universal (*Journey*), games can better speak to the complexities of imperial violence, where subversion and resistance often occur within the intricacies of vast and uncentered information networks.

As global art, video games incorporate a variety of cultural forms, presenting themselves like a mall: a pure product of late capitalist consumerism reigned by the "freedom" of consumer choice. The author only exists insofar as to guarantee its quality. The game thus maintains the magic of the global commodity form, abdicating responsibility for sexist, racist, and violent images by deferring blame onto the player who derives pleasure from them. Though most games are consumed as global forms of art with no explicitly meaningful national origin, the association of games as Asiatic has fostered subcultures praising Japanese artists as the true game innovators and originators for gaming's most popular formal techniques. Japanese auteurs exemplify the unknowable Asiatic, as their products and performances are framed by cultural obscurity, which excuses the game from its political and social meanings, again placing the transgressive content of games onto the players themselves. However, to ascribe players as primary agents in meaning-making does not necessarily de-authorize the text ("pluralize" it, in Barthes's terms), but produces the abstract figure of the "gamer" as the agent of power and responsibility, an agent constructed through hegemonic discourses that see games as merely violent, perverse, racist, frivolous, infantile, imperial. Game studies scholars themselves have responded by suggesting the opposite: games are educational, progressive, antiracist. Meanwhile, the discourses of pleasure, enjoyment, and love experienced within these games have been relegated to the dispersed communities of gamers themselves.

This chapter does not simply seek to reestablish the importance of the author/developer, but to argue that the absence of the author as responsible agent or ethnic authority has opened a realm of possibilities for erotic readings of games as Asiatic "loved objects," which, as Barthes writes in *A Lover's Discourse*, causes anxiety because of their elusiveness, their silence, and their unknowability. The absence of the amorous object conjures sets of feelings ("figures"), from realizing one's dependency ("Domnei"), to confusion ("I want to understand"), to orgasmic utterances ("I-love-you"). If, as Foucault and Barthes both write, the author is the source of totality for texts, a means of dealing with the anxiety of multiple meanings and audiences, then the absence of the author provides opportunities to creatively engage with games where fans dictate meanings. While authorial power confines a work to its author's time and place, fan-led communities interpret games as products oriented toward the future. A video game's ultimate meaning lies not in the contexts and biographies of the past, but dispersed among various contemporary audiences, so that its "true meaning" will always elude the player, perhaps forever. This delay of meaning means that games can consistently be endowed with new meanings by fan communities through participatory artwork (memes, YouTube videos), modifications, and in homages that seek out the game artists' backgrounds, stylistic orientations, and even their political allegiances. Where the absence of the author is taken for granted, meaning is up for grabs, vulnerable to the whims of the ludophile.

Playing Author(ity)

Despite the annual industry-wide spasms drumming up awareness for the latest positive representation of an ethnic identity in games, few critics find it relevant that the most "empowered" and "authentic" ethnic characters do not have ethnic authors behind them. What, in video games, makes an "empowered" character? For Asian Americans, praise has often drifted toward *Far Cry 4*'s Ajay Ghale and *Sleeping Dogs*'s Wei Shen, both gun-savvy killers who follow a "diasporic hero" narrative where the Asian American protagonists return to the homeland; relearn their parents' culture, language, and family secrets; and end up killing swaths of Asian peoples.[6] Asian females in Western games, as one might expect, have been synonymous with eye candy (*Mortal Kombat*'s Mileena, *Prince of Persia*'s Kaileena, *Far Cry 3*'s Citra), though a few, such as *Portal*'s Chell and *Mirror Edge*'s Faith, have earned celebrations as nonsexualized representations. Yet even these celebrated characters are granted little personality to speak of (often because they do not or rarely speak). Faith has been lauded as a positive representation of Asian American women, with critics noting that she appears both "attractive" and "nonsexualized." She also exhibits little personality and seems otherwise characterless, a visual spectacle as meaningful as a "cool skin." In their celebration, few critics or scholars have felt it worthwhile to mention that all of these games featuring Asian North American characters were developed primarily by white designers and script writers.[7]

Games theorist Ian Bogost has repeatedly pointed out that games are not as concerned with the interior explorations of an individual mind nor their particular life story (the realm of narratology for him) but more with exterior insights that help understand the procedural forms

of everyday life, its rules, its logics, and its processes.[8] Yet it is important to put these arguments in the context of the games industry, which
stresses the neutrality of its products by offering little visibility to its designers. Game designers are not given recognition in the way that a film
director might gain in the film industry. Game awards typically focus on
awarding games by genre, and ceremonies like the IGN Games Awards
do not provide awards for developers, nor do they name developers
when awarding games, instead reserving individual awards to the best
e-sports game players and to voice-over artists.[9] By keeping developers
hidden, the games industry remains able to produce games as player-
driven, player-collaborative products so that the very act of playing a
game can construe the responsibilities associated with it (sexism, racism, militarism). Unlike in spectating a film or reading a novel, with
games there is a presumed lack of critical engagement. The game space
thus functions like a tourist space whose hidden construction is crucial
to enjoying the experience, but whose enjoyment reveals more about
its participants than its producers. The creators of the virtual spaces of
video games are best left in the shadows, lest their presence expose the
inauthenticity of the experience.

Even when North American developers give interviews, they rarely, if
ever, present themselves in terms of their racial backgrounds, deferring
to the postracial presumptions of information technology. In research
for this chapter, I found myself searching through lists of designers with
"Asian-sounding names" (ironic because mine is not), only to find that
developers with these names did not discuss their family history in interviews or in popular media. Interviewers did not ask them to identify
their backgrounds, and they did not voluntarily divulge them. Consider
Siobhan Reddy, who Forbes named one of the ten most powerful women
in gaming, but whose interviews and self-promotion never shared her
ethnic identity nor the origin of her family name, "Reddy." Likewise,
ethnic developers like Abdul Ismail ("IceFrog"), the developer of *Dota
2*, trade in their ethnic names for gamertags as their only recognizable
brands (IceFrog himself was only "outed" as Abdul Ismail because of
court documents in May 2017 revealing his name). Indeed, this research
itself confronts not only the postracialism of the industry but the researcher's and critic's own reliance on the exposure of hidden Asian

diasporic identities in an industry where, unlike in literature or film, the author's ethnic identity has not yet been made marketable.

The absence of authorial presence within video games can be traced to the 1970s, when arcades were villainized as tantalizing spaces of ill repute, thought to begin lifestyles that would eventually lead to gambling, asociality, drug dependency, and gang-related violence. Though arcades from the 1920s to 1960s were places of pinball gambling (with real cash payouts), competitive sports or "Sportlands," and family-friendly "playlands," US lawmakers framed the arcade as a public gambling den connected to the rise of mafia groups and casinos.[10] Fiorello La Guardia, New York City mayor through much of the 1930s and 1940s, was famous for his crusade leveling pinball machines with a sledgehammer, railing that the machine was a "perverter of innocent children."[11] Even after pinball had taken out its gambling-related elements, the National Association of Citizens Crime Commission continued to claim that the pinball industry drove children "to crime to obtain funds for their craze."[12] In this context, video games entered the arcades, a space already known as a perverter of children, and authorial presence was thought to welcome legal and moralizing battles. Marketing the biographies of game designers became a business model used by only one American company, Activision, the first third-party game developer. In 1979, Activision included in their instruction pamphlets headshots and bios of their designers alongside numerous tips coupled with designer names in bold lettering.[13] Atari and other American companies did not follow suit, believing that "questions about designers' identities and new projects remain off-limits or, at best, off-the-record," and, as an Atari spokesperson admitted, "Management doesn't want us to make rock stars out of them [the designers]."[14] In 1981, fears of lawsuits remained high as Americans spent $5.7 billion on arcade games, twice the gross earnings of all of Nevada's casinos, and three times the total revenues for professional baseball, football, and basketball combined.[15] Besides legal and moralistic battles, companies also feared that once designers became well known, they would leave the company as their individual mythos became more marketable.[16] The absence of authorial presence enabled game companies to keep salaries low and not to offer royalties, so many designers never "made a cent" from their games after release.[17]

In the fifty-year history of video games, some Western designers have gained recognition and have been spotlighted as the "genius" behind some long-running series. These cases have been rare and exceptional, and often these developers frequently give credit to their design teams for much of the game's creative work. Sid Meier, whose name is stamped upon the series *Sid Meier's Pirates* and *Sid Meier's Civilization*, admitted that the use of his name was a marketing tool suggested by the actor Robin Williams, and that most projects carrying his name are in fact directed and designed by others.[18] Like his contemporary Will Wright (credited for *SimCity* and *The Sims*), Meier's authorial label functions more like a genre label that signifies simulation games where a single godlike designer is thought to manage the inner workings of a vast open world. In both Meier's and Wright's games, there is little threat to legal and moral battles, as these games censor the violence, sex, and militarism present within the medium. Authorial responsibility thus only applies to these games' complex simulations, not to their transgressions. For most Western designers, particularly those working on big-budget games, authorship remains unthinkable. Even designers who could easily claim auteur status for their control of game direction often do the opposite. Clint Hocking, creator of the *Splinter Cell* series and *Far Cry 2*, sees his own artistic philosophy as being an invisible author. In an interview with Bonnie Ruberg, Hocking compared his role to "what Roland Barthes said about the death of the author . . . in terms of literature he's wrong. But he was [a] visionary and ahead of his time." Hocking sees his relationship with his games, even as project lead, as more akin to Marshall McLuhan's views of authorship as a group collective, where the "univocal authority" or "private ownership" of the author over a text's meanings breaks into a plurality of co-creative explorers.[19] In contrast, film auteurs like David Cronenberg frequently "insist upon authorship" and outwardly refuses "to believe in the death of the author."[20] In games, as Hocking suggests, development implies "learning what it means to not be an author . . . to give up control."[21]

The Japanese Auteur

While Western game companies have shied away from marketing games as authorial products due to threats of litigation, the need to keep wages low, and the chance to defer responsibility onto the player, Japanese developers have become renowned as auteurs responsible for grandfathering in most gaming genres. In Japan, developers don't shy away from lavish personality displays, and they often announce their titles in grandiose costumes (take the cowboy hat and whip brandished by Koji Igarashi, creator of the *Castlevania* series, or the sunglasses and samurai swords wielded by Tomonobu Itagaki, creator of the *Dead or Alive* series). In America, Japanese designers are known as experimentalists, mavericks, and iconoclasts who upset the corporate, profit-driven atmosphere of despised Western game companies like Electronic Arts, voted for two years in a row the worst company in America.[22] "Auteur" here becomes an appropriate concept, as its inception came from the need to distinguish French New Wave filmmakers from studio system directors, seen as complicit to Hollywood production companies. In practice, auteurism meant seeing films as controlled works of art by a single author (the director) with a signature style and discernible traits (Martin Scorsese's use of tracking shots, voice-over narration, freeze frames, long run times, and criminal protagonists). Similarly, Japanese video game auteurs, much like their manga and anime counterparts, stress the artfulness of a medium that is otherwise derided in nations outside of Japan. Games by developers like Hidetaka Suehiro ("Swery65"), Yoot Saito, and Fumito Ueda are often mentioned to argue for the validity of video games as an art form, while the Japanese developer Hideo Kojima, often seen as a rogue developer for leaving his parent company Konami, maintains high-profile friendships with auteur directors like Guillermo Del Toro, who appears in Kojima's game *Death Stranding*. Kojima himself claims that he was responsible for innovations in cinematic gameplay and stealth, calling himself "a creator with an auteurist approach."[23]

The contemporary view of Japanese auteurs as sacred gurus of technological innovation is far removed from how American developers saw their Japanese counterparts in the late '70s and early '80s, when American developers attempted to cast Japanese designers as "horrible copiers" whose business models would fail in the United States.[24] Indeed, before Nintendo, video game sales were led by Atari, an American manufacturer often presumed to be Japanese.[25] Despite Atari's lead in the market, it was the Japanese game *Space Invaders*, created by the designer Tomohiro Nishikado, that is credited for beginning the golden age of the arcade. The mythology of Japanese developers began with *Space Invaders*, a game that came with no instructions, whose strategies and rules had to be passed by word of mouth.[26] This aura of mystery—coupled with its Asiatic foreignness—supercharged the arcade era, giving way to fears of Japanese takeover of the market, as *Space Invaders* quickly became the highest earning arcade game, only to be outdone in 1980 by another Japanese game with "mysterious origins," *Pac-Man*.[27] American developers, able only to understand these games' success as a cultural unknown (a "mystery"), began to conjure the Japanese artist as a mastermind, a nemesis who sought to copy the American originators of game technology through splashy and visually sumptuous pop art that looked nothing like traditional Japanese iconography of geishas, samurai, or Mount Fuji. Yet, akin to my arguments in the last chapter, to see *Pac-Man* and *Space Invaders* as aesthetically outside the realm of Japanese culture is itself a Western view dictated by unfamiliarity and a lack of cultural knowledge. As Steve Bloom pointed out in 1982, Japanese developers thought the opposite: the developers behind *Pac-Man* believed the game "would never gain acceptance abroad" because "they thought it was too typically Japanese."[28] In 1983, the games market in the United States crashed, with companies like Atari and Mattel unable to stay afloat. Games were seemingly lost to the corporate hacks of American companies, and their sales plummeted 97 percent. The industry bounced back in 1985 with the release of the Nintendo Entertainment System (NES), yet video games would never be American again. Japanese auteurs had come to rescue the art of video games from companies like Atari, who had seen massive defections for its increasingly corporate atmosphere.[29] Japanese auteurs thus played a role similar to the mythos generated around tech "geniuses" like Steve Jobs, who put personality and artistry into products thought to be merely profit driven.

The discourse of Japanese auteurs triumphed in the generation of North Americans who grew up in the 1980s and 1990s, when Nintendo, Sega, and Sony defeated all American-based competition, making it seem as if video games were always a Japanese product, rather than a copy of American software, as the earlier generation believed. Games then seemed naturally rooted in Japan's cartoonish anime and pachinko-parlor habits. Indeed, the narrative of Japanese auteurs today sees them as genre definers: Shigeru Miyamoto as the father of the platformer

(*Super Mario Bros.*), Shinji Mikami as the father of survival horror (*Resident Evil* series),[30] Hironobu Sakaguchi (*Final Fantasy* series) and Yuji Horii (*Dragon Quest, Chrono Trigger*) as the fathers of Japanese role-playing games, Eiji Aonuma as the father of the action role-playing game (*The Legend of Zelda* series), Yoshinori Ono (*Street Fighter* series) and Katsuhiro Harada (*Tekken* series) as the fathers of fighting games, Hideo Kojima as the father of stealth (*Metal Gear* series), Tomohiro Nishikado as the father of the shoot 'em up (*Space Invaders*), and Eiji Aonuma (*Legend of Zelda*), Goichi Suda (*Flower, Sun, and Rain*), and Yu Suzuki (*Shenmue* series) as the fathers of the open world game. All of these genres are held up as technologically innovative and artistic, contrasting the raw violence of the most well-known American video game genre, first-person shooters, a genre known for its extreme violence (*Doom*, 1993) and American patriotism (*Wolfenstein 3D*, 1992). Japanese auteurs, in comparison, need not resort to patriotic militarism in order to make an artful game (though many Japanese games do include massive gore).

Since the 1980s and 1990s, Japanese developers have garnered massive cult followings, and many have become idealized as renegades who, like Kojima, Suzuki, and others, have had to carve their own paths, splitting from the publishers that made them famous and opening studios of their own.[31] Their devotion to games as expressive forms of art has also left many developers, like Suzuki and Shinji Mikami, embroiled in decade-long development hells of remakes, sequels, and serials. In the auteur narrative, these developers struggle for the freedom to express their art amid the business interests of game companies and legal firms. Even still, well into the 2010s, the cult of the Japanese game auteur has remained steadfast, with figures like Hidetaka Miyazaki (*Dark Souls* series), Hideki Kamiya (*Devil May Cry* series, *Okami, Bayonetta* series), and Fumito Ueda (*Ico, Shadow of the Colossus, Last Guardian*) continuing to dominate notions of the auteur game designer, and their games continue to be invoked as the best evidence for games as a form of art.[32]

The Ludophile in Oedipal Time: Suda51

The question that emerges from this brief history of game developers as auteurs or as invisible co-creators is not whether one is true or false (both share inconsistencies), nor which is more appropriate for the study of interactive gaming (a field too broad to cast a single theory of the author), but to ask how the authorial function of the auteur opens up alternative ways of understanding games beyond a discourse of player-centered responsibility, where the game itself appears as a (perverse, infectious) global commodity to be used or abused by its audience. Here we can reframe discourses of the auteur to that of the *ludophile*, the audience member who seeks intimate knowledge of a game: its narration, its history, its genre, its designs, and its technological innovations, much of which relies upon an informed and often idealized depiction of the developer. The ludophile is similar to depictions of the fanboy, the "hardcore gamer," but seeks an amorous knowledge structured by feelings of intimacy and love (the "philic"). The ludophile also shares distinct similarities with the cinephile in film and the "amorous discourse" in literary critique, though she is not reducible to either. Whereas the fanboy may wear *Pac-Man* T-shirts and consume overpriced memorabilia, the ludophile, like the cinephile, operates on a different temporal register, less concerned with identifying as a fan within a community of fans but more as a keeper of gaming history and aesthetic appreciation.

Emerging in France in the 1950s and 1960s, cinephiles belonged to social groups who sought to elevate film into a great art akin to painting and literature, and they aggrandized individual filmmakers as grand artists (auteurs), tethering these artists within what Thomas Elsaesser has called "oedipal time," joining and separating artists into a "paternity and generational repetition in difference."[33] These paternal links among artists transformed nationalized forms of film into a larger transnational art form (François Truffaut's indebtedness to Alfred Hitchcock, etc.). Like cinephiles, ludophiles map contemporary games onto their genre precedents, from past games to literary, filmic, and musical influences.

The fervent auteur communities centered around the work of Goichi Suda, also known as Suda51, can be seen as a ludophilic discourse par excellence. Seen as the auteur behind experimental and graphic games like *Flower, Sun, and Rain*, *Killer7*, and the *No More Heroes* series, Suda follows many of the tropes of the Japanese auteur: he has founded his own development firm over which he has complete control, he rejects the for-profit motives of game design and prefers to remain an "indie" artist (even as he has over fifty people working under him), and he markets his games as obscure, difficult works of art, as he says, "I have a responsibility to prove the superiority or at least the validity of the storytelling in games and games as an art form in what I do."[34] In many ways, Suda has gone above and beyond these tropes, consistently talking about himself as a visionary and auteur, suggesting that as a game director he has "even more influence than a Hollywood director." He authored a book on his gaming philosophy,[35] and he has been called the "punk rock star of gaming" by numerous gaming magazines, with his background as an undertaker often mentioned as a clue for understanding his games.[36] Popular gaming writers like Austin Walker establish Suda's auteur "oedipal time" by inserting his games into a canon of other auteur-produced work like David Lynch's *Twin Peaks*. Such ludophiles point out Suda's signature style as "punk," "violent," and "bizarre," all descriptions that Suda himself uses to describe his games. In his interviews, Suda compares himself not only to punk rock icons (the Arctic Monkeys) but to American TV shows like *Jackass*. In presentations and advertisements, Suda wears the same red leather jacket as his Johnny Knoxville look-alike Trevor from *No More Heroes*, leading players to see his games as extensions of the author himself.[37]

Like much of the Francophilia that led to early auteur theory, the tendency to aggrandize Japanese developers is informed by their foreign aura, which produces much of the text's cultural meanings as bizarre, layered, or arthouse. Like the "unknowability" of *Space Invaders* or the "mysterious origins" of *Pac-Man*, Suda's games are shrouded in the unknowable Asiatic, as most reviewers and gamers excuse his games' eccentricities as a form of Japanese otaku subculture. The trailer for Suda's *Flower, Sun, and Rain* proudly proclaims that "Suda51's masterpiece is finally here," while Suda puts himself center stage of the trailer for *No More Heroes 2: Desperate Struggle*, sitting on a public toilet.

Similar to the origins of the auteur, where its main theorists were also its main artists and directors, it is difficult to distinguish between auteur theory in gaming as a reading method and as a marketing ploy used deliberately to sell games that might otherwise be too alienating or strange ("too Japanese" as with the fear of *Pac-Man*). Indeed, some writers have become disillusioned with Suda's own auteur status, since he is known for compromising his artistic integrity by releasing separate versions of his games, with those catering to American audiences ramped up in violence and sex.[38] The violent perverse style that could be excused as the punk genius of a Japanese auteur, with all its Asiatic unknowabil-ity, is in fact more obscure, more extreme, when catered to Americans. For Japanese scholars like Koichi Iwabuchi, this confrontation with the "hyper-modern bizarre" does not produce Orientalist presumptions but rather a "self-absorbed indifference," where "one just stands in open-mouth amazement at the encounter with other cultures."[39] Though this "indifference" remains self-interested (or merely frivolous and erotic), it also "cannot help but be more self-reflexive," as it refuses to evaluate the other based on a perceived authenticity.[40] Ludophiles, lured by the arts of the Asiatic, read games not to inform their knowledge of ethnic and cultural identity but as amorous others whose "true" social and political meanings can only be speculated upon.

The Ludophile's Discourse

Besides the tendency to place auteur directors into "oedipal time," cine-philes, as well as "lovers of literature," tend to form an intimate connection to the authorial presence of an artist or storyteller, as the mythical auteur figure (almost always male) typifies what Elia Kazan called "the man with the answers."[41] In his understanding of cinephilic culture, Elsaesser adds another temporal register to the paternal genealogy of "oedipal time," one based on Roland Barthes's *A Lover's Discourse: Fragments*, where Barthes attempts to stage multiple utterances of love—"figures," as he calls them—by riffing off sampled literary references. Quotations from Goethe's *The Sorrows of Young Werther*, Plato's *Symposium*, Sartre's writ-ings, and even the *Tao Te Ching* become stages for Barthes's own musings on love. By seeing love as a discourse, Barthes attempts to rescue love from mere lust, sexuality, preference, and institutions of marriage. His book, taken less as a work of criticism and more as a literary work in itself, explores how love operates within the horizons of language, which cannot be talked about so much as simulated, talked in, talked of, and talked with. Unlike Barthes's previous work in the 1950s and 1960s, little remains of the cold, calculating structuralist here, nor is *A Lover's Dis-course* focused on the openness of pleasure and the instability of the sign as was Barthes's focus in *Empire of Signs* and *The Pleasure of the Text*.[42] What concerns Barthes in *A Lover's Discourse* are "figures" that trace (in no linear fashion) "the lover at work" and "take shape insofar as we can recognize, in passing discourse, something that has been read, heard, felt."[43] Figures have no definable content, but they can be rediscovered through "amorous feeling." The figure is not "the text" but the erotic sensations felt toward an undefined other or object: "To wait" for *something or someone*, to "be engulfed" (*s'abîmer*) by *something*, to "will-to-possess" (*vouloirsaisir*) *someone or something*, to desire to write *something*. Figures are emotive states, verbs without objects, which the viewers/readers/players fill in for themselves. Figures emerge in the desire to understand the other ("I Want to Understand") and in being faced with the other's unfathomable meanings ("The Unknowable" *inconnaissable* / unknowable; "The Uncertainty of Signs" *signes* / signs). Nouns like "anxiety" and "memory" take the form of topics whose content can be shared, while figures remain elusive, different, and personal to every individual.

A Lover's Discourse encapsulates a form of auteur love that the cinephile (and ludophile) recapitulate into aesthetic discourses of the artist. But if we, unlike Elsaesser, perform our own philic reading of Barthes as an obscurely queer author, we can also read *A Lover's Discourse* as a meditation upon queer "amorous feelings," as expressing an unspoken, nonvisible love. In fact, a crucial component of Barthes's use of figures, like that of the Japanese and Chinese "signs" he analyzed in 1970 and 1974, is that the material object or text—the "amorous object"—has infinite potential for multiplicity. The amorous object need not be a woman, man, or even human. Like the Japanese auteur (or the Asiatic writ large), the amorous object could exist entirely within one's imagination, separated by barriers of language, nation, and ocean. In his fragment on the figure "No Answer" (*mustime*/silence), Barthes argues that "No Answer" conveys "the amorous subject [who] suffers anxiety because the loved object replies scantily or not at all to his language (discourse or letters)." In his fragment on the figure "Domnei" (*dependance*/dependency), the amorous object emerges as superior and dominating, an "other" who is "assigned to a superior habitat, an Olympus where everything is decided and whence every-thing descends upon me."[44] The "lover" is dependent upon the amorous object, reducing language to gestures of seeking out the other: "I am engulfed by . . . ," "I wait for . . . ," "I want to understand . . ." The "lover" narrator is not seducer but seduced, one who struggles for someone or something to reciprocate address, who yearns for that to which he has no privilege, right, or claim. The roles of the narrator and the addressed destabilize, move from self-protection to unflinching desire.

But the amorous object is not entirely arbitrary. As Barthes theorizes, the *context* is more important in forming the amorous object than the object itself. It is "the scene" that "*consecrates* the object I am going to love," so that "what ravishes me is the image of a body in *situation*."[45] As Steven Ungar writes, it is the "discursive forces" spiraling around the amorous object—discourses of love but also of empire, technology, race, gender, sex—that give way to "amorous feelings," the figures of love.[46] Unlike Said's *Orientalism* framework, where the "other" reconstructed and validated the subject's identity through opposing and co-constituting forces, *A Lover's Discourse* is a dialogue "ideally predicated on exchange and mobility of roles," and it is through the "amorous feelings" for the "other" that the subject becomes queered, as he is disempowered, dependent, and caught in spirals of pleasure and desire.[47] The amorous object is "unknowable" in Barthes's term, catching the subject in a self-imposed contradiction: "on the one hand, I believe I know the other better than anyone and triumphantly assert my knowledge . . . and on the other hand, I am often struck by the obvious fact that the other is impenetrable, intractable, not to be found."[48]

Barthes's desire for the impenetrable convenes with the ludophile's discourse of the Japanese video game auteur, where foreignness and unknowability in content or style (attributed to artistic genius and Japanese culture) adds to the mysterious cult of the auteur but also becomes necessary as a mode for the audience to read the game. Our ludophile games journalist Austin Walker, for example, praises *Flower, Sun, and Rain* as the height of Suda's artistic achievement, writing,

> [the game] isn't fun . . . the point isn't to have a good time while looking around interesting locations. The point, I think, is that *this game hates you*. You have to walk everywhere, and walking is incredibly slow. And then, it counts the amount of steps so you know exactly how much time you've wasted. It's mean. It's cruel. *I kind of love it.*[49]

Faced with the queer sadomasochist gameplay of "cruel," slow pacing, the ludophile responds with love, knowing that his love cannot be reciprocated, when "this game hates you" is exactly the point. The game's author function plays the part of amorous object. Lost in the world of the game's "bizarre" Asiatic imagining, the players must feel safe in the hands of an artistic genius, trusting that their misapprehension is part of the gameplay experience. Yet, as Walker's comments show, this ludophilic way of experiencing the game opens gameplay up to queer and unthinkable forms of play: the sadistic, the perverse, the erotic.

Shenmue II: *Yu Suzuki and ScottishDuck17*

The ludophile's amorous discourse, for much of gaming history, was not detailed in writing about games but was relegated to the environments of gameplay in arcades, living rooms, and PC rooms. Since the early 2010s, with the advent of Twitch.tv and YouTube "Let's Play" videos, videos of "personalities" playing video games have become so popular as to warrant their own subscription services, some with twenty thousand viewers logged in watching livestream video at any given moment.[50] The rise of Twitch and "Let's Play" videos captures, as Barthes puts it, "the lover at work," and their often overdramatic exclamations toward the game and its authors can be read as erotic utterances ("figures") aimed at an Asiatic other. As with Austin Walker's admiration of Suda's game ("I kind of love it"), these game streamers express long monologues addressed to a loved object that only responds through the gameworld itself. To give a detailed example of this ludophilic discourse, I here examine "Let's Plays" of Yu Suzuki's game *Shenmue II* from the avid ludophile ScottishDuck17. For Barthes, erotic desire is itself a letting go, a submission to oneself, which cuts across the active/passive binary associated with gamers and fans. The amorous subject, as Barthes terms himself, is active only within the conditions of his own desires. Likewise, ludophiles like ScottishDuck17, who displays extreme emotional investments while playing *Shenmue II*, cannot be construed as abstract "fans" outside of their national, racial, and regional positions. ScottishDuck17 can only be seen as amorous through his social context, as his desire operates through "a scene" of imperial discourses.

ScottishDuck17's "Let's Play" videos provide a ludophilic attachment to Japanese auteurs, especially those who have worked under the banner of Sega Incorporated, the developers behind the *Sonic* games and

Figure 2.1. *Shenmue II*: Ryo in Hong Kong. Screenshot by author.

"old school" arcade games like *Hang On*.[51] I focus on ScottishDuck17's plays of Yu Suzuki's 2001 magnum opus, *Shenmue II*, the most expensive game ever produced at the time, and whose third installment (*Shenmue III*) was delayed (in "development hell") for nearly two decades.[52] *Shenmue II* remains within the spirals of ludophilic desire as a moment of high art by a renowned auteur that inspired multiple homages (like the *Yakuza* series) and laid the groundwork for the open world game genre, which Suzuki himself called the "F.R.E.E." game ("Full Reactive Eyes Entertainment").[53] Like future open world games, Suzuki's *Shenmue* and *Shenmue II* offered an unparalleled level of player choice, giving them full rein to explore a sandbox city with its own day-night cycles and dynamic weather (see Figure 2.1). The games also featured an astonishing amount of detail, with hundreds of fully voiced characters who each had their own daily scripts and routines. *Shenmue II* takes place in Hong Kong and stages a relationship among white Western gamers where the amorous object is, in a sense, multiply foreign: a social realist representation of a Chinese space (Hong Kong) experienced through the eyes of a Japanese youth (Ryo) in a game developed by a Japanese auteur (Suzuki) and then played by a Western gamer (ScottishDuck17).

Since 2008, ScottishDuck17 has filmed over eighty "Let's Play" videos and has become well known for, as he describes it, "playing games and screaming a lot." A self-identified Sega lover, ScottishDuck17 treats *Shen-mue II* as the pinnacle of erotic desire, as he repeats time and again that he loves the game too much, so much that he shouldn't even be doing a "Let's Play" video, because his love for the game outweighs any useful commentary he can make on it. Like Barthes's *A Lover's Discourse*, Scot-tishDuck17's "Let's Play *Shenmue II*" appears as a fragmented catalog of his erotic experience with the game, and whenever he begins to air the slightest critique for its burdensome cut scenes and slow pacing, he reminds himself that he "loves this game so much." ScottishDuck17's at-tempt to catalog his desire manifests when he speaks of the goose bumps he feels during cut scenes and the memorization and tactile pleasure that comes from playing quick-time events, as well as through his con-stant personification of the game by hailing the game's producer ("Why do you do this to me, Sega?") and the game's designer ("Damn it, Suzuki, why would you put a cut scene there?").

Should we find it strange that this Scottish man's effusive love is di-rected toward a game made in Japan and that takes place in Hong Kong and China in the 1980s? We can name this seduction as not merely strange but queer, in the sense that the relationship is unrecognized by the disciplining effects of heteronormativity and rails against the young Asian boy/white man dyad that has defined power relations throughout the transpacific (see Figure 2.2).[54] Indeed, *Shenmue II*'s allure is framed through a politicized discursive force as a foreign Asiatic commodity as well as a historical origin point for the open world game. Even though ScottishDuck17 could play *Shenmue II* in English, he chooses to play

Figure 2.2. ScottishDuck17 bows before *Shenmue* and *Shenmue II*. Screenshot from ScottishDuck17, "My Top 20 Dreamcast Game (10 to 1)," *YouTube*, June 20, 2017, www.youtube.com/watch?v=PF2MbaVZgQ8&t=31s.

the "old school" Dreamcast release to keep the dialogue in Japanese—a strange choice, since the vast majority of characters in *Shenmue II* are Chinese and would not know any Japanese (even the game's main love interest, Shenhua, speaks in Japanese, though she has never even heard of Japan). *Shenmue II* also seems a strange object of obsession as an open world game that, unlike almost every open world game since, deprives the player of power and ambulates them slowly through the monotony of the everyday.[55] The game "engulfs," in Barthes's terms, invoking "a moment of hypnosis," where the game's rules and boundaries present "the gentleness of the abyss."[56] Amorous desire here turns players from an active feeling of agency to a passive feeling of being submerged in the auteur's world. It is in many ways a fully engulfing world: the game is micro-detailed in the sense that picking up items, gazing upon them, and working jobs actually feels more difficult and lumbering in the game than in real life. Indeed, as with Austin Walker's love for Suda51, for ScottishDuck17, *Shenmue II*'s frustrating monotony is exactly the point, as acts of wandering become purposeful in themselves through discovering minute details that the developers spent labor, time, and money on. In its depictions of the monotony of Hong Kong, *Shenmue II* enacts a queer desire that is perhaps informed by the Orientalist worlds of *Madame Butterfly* and *The World of Suzie Wong*, but it resists the binary oppositions of white/Asian, self/other, that those romances reproduce. Instead, the amorous object stages a moment of love's "languor," a "subtle state of amorous desire, experienced in its dearth, outside of any will-to-possess."[57]

Hanging in the Hang On Room

The allegorical authenticity of Hong Kong's cityscape in *Shenmue II* does not offer a space to be dominated but rather a space to be submitted to, a slow-building masochistic impulse withheld by the promise of fulfilling one's desire. One does not shove one's way through crowds and run over pedestrians, like in the *Grand Theft Auto* franchise, but offers help to locals and spends one's days performing gnawingly repetitive labor tasks. *Shenmue II* gives the Western player a hyperrealist Hong Kong without being viewed as a white foreigner but instead as a young Japanese visitor, Ryo, seeking to learn more about the space (in order to avenge his father's death). Takeo Rivera has argued that games operate within a mode of empathy that exceeds the protagonist of dramas (and by consequence films) so that games operate as "a mode in which the player becomes the avatar or gaze onscreen itself."[58] In *Shenmue II*, the player adopts the protagonist's gaze through the estranged embodiment of the foreign Japanese man, permitting unexpected empathies to arise among exiled groups, but more importantly, to understand Chineseness and Asianness in general without immediate reference to whiteness or Americanism. The cultural differences of Hong Kong don't appear as an "other" to Ryo's home of Japan but as curious and alluring differences, sealing a deeper erotic bond. Indeed, *Shenmue II* can be understood as an antithesis to its main competitive open world game, *Grand Theft Auto III*, which appears as a fast, violent joyride fueled by the pleasures of dominating others. In contrast, Alexander Galloway once identified *Shenmue II* as a process-driven game with a slow, purposeful accumulation of experiences.[59] While Galloway reads this form as "ambient," we can also see the poetic buildup as reclining within the other's embrace, of dreaming toward "a total union with the loved being," a beckoning arrest of one's pleasures for the "motionless cradling" of enchantment.[60]

ScottishDuck17's constant frustration with *Shenmue II*—for its slow loading times and the need to plod through the city—transmutes within a ludophilic discourse into an erotic tease that builds up sexual desire, what Barthes calls "contingencies," those "trivialities, incidents, set-backs, pettinesses, irritations, the vexations of amorous existence . . . as if chance conspired against him."[61] "I'm not going to criticize," Scottish-Duck17 says in the midst of erotic frustration, "I love this game." Love for the amorous subject is defined by this process of contingencies, an erotic foreplay that builds in scope as *Shenmue II*'s story moves from a hyperrealist Hong Kong island to the epic kung fu setting of Kow-loon Walled City, a district once infamous as an unregulated hotbed for triad activity. Pleasures build in grandiosity as the story and setting become more epic but also far more erotic. The player experiences Kow-loon City as a wild space of male bonding, with the ubiquitous presence of shirtless men braced in wrestling positions. ScottishDuck17 himself becomes infatuated with Ren, Ryo's gangster sidekick, who propels the game into a buddy comedy, what ScottishDuck17 calls "the adventures of Ryo and Ren." The hyperrealism of the game's first two discs on Hong

Kong island complements the epic nature of Kowloon by carrying over the feeling of authenticity and realism into this mythic setting, inserting a flamboyant space of queer desire into the mundane and everyday. Indeed, as ScottishDuck17 penetrates farther into Kowloon's phallic towers and seedy underground, a moment of erotic jouissance emerges near the game's climax: as Ryo and Ren seek to rescue an old man through the floors of a Kowloon high-rise, ScottishDuck17 decides to randomly walk into a small room just to see if he could open the door, and he effuses ludophilic pleasure at discovering a playable minigame, Suzuki's 1985 arcade game *Hang On*. ScottishDuck17 yells:

> Are you fucking kidding me! You are fucking kidding me, right? This cannot be fucking real! We are in the middle of a gang organization's hideout, trying to kidnap somebody, and Ryo is—has the ability to play fucking *Hang On*? Ah! My Jesus Christ! [clapping, laughter, sobbing] Oh my God! What the fuck? What the fuck![62]

ScottishDuck17's shock and sudden spurt of joy is a figure of "fulfillment," an unexpected delight that "streams over me, strikes me like a lightning bolt."[63] ScottishDuck17's discovery comes with the disciplining mechanism that this is not, in fact, the point of the game. He is immediately struck with the injunction that the fulfillment he feels from the *Hang On* room is merely a distraction, and he attempts to move on, saying, "Let's leave this floor behind, shall we?" Here the amorous subject gets more than he wanted—an excess of the amorous object that before always remained elusive. Where amorous feeling was once "never enough," finally the subject is transported "beyond language."[64] Despite his inability to decipher the moment of fulfillment, ScottishDuck17 repeatedly returns to discussing the *Hang On* room. As he says three minutes later, "I still can't fucking believe that *Hang On* vendor down there," and again a minute and a half later, "What is the point of putting a *Hang On* machine there? . . . the last thing on anyone's mind at this point in the game is *Hang On*. I mean I like *Hang On*, it's by Yu Suzuki after all, but . . . [groan]."[65]

It's in these fragmented moments of reflection that ScottishDuck17 begins to articulate his own love for the game as erotic. Indeed, as many of his YouTube commentators also expressed, it is the possibility of discovering such a room that drives *Shenmue II*'s popularity, as it embraces the discovery of minute details that seem purposeless and absurd even to a fault.[66] Given the urgency of the game's storyline, the *Hang On* room appears as a form of ludic dissonance, a flaw that upsets one's immersion. It appears as a moment of bliss, or as Barthes describes the orgasm, as "a moment of affirmation," but with the later realization that "something has been successful."[67] This "something" is the estranged erotic desire one didn't expect to be fulfilled, a desire that evades narrative form. The *Hang On* room stages the erotic engagement with the Asiatic, which the Western amorous subject can only recognize as an afterthought. ScottishDuck17's erotic joy at being able to wander away from the urgency of the mission to frivolously play *Hang On* demonstrates how gamers engage in forms of erotic play framed through Asiatic foreignness. As Barthes himself saw his fictive Japan as an ineffable and erotic realm, it is hard not to read the loved object in *A Lover's Discourse* as Asiatic. Its refusal to speak back, its mystery, its inability to be mastered, repeats much of Barthes's way of seeing Japan in *Empire of Signs* and China in *Travels in China*. The strangeness, the silence, and the impermeability of the Asiatic provide the very "spiral of discourses" that consecrate the loved object, forming an erotic play. Through ScottishDuck17's sustained amorous discourse we understand *Shenmue II* not as "amorous" in itself but as an object that the Asiatic imperial scene has led the ludophile to read "amorously."

Playing Amorously

The ludophile's amorous desire for the artist exists within a spiral of imperial power, Asiatic constructs, and erotic pleasure, yet its effects open alternative ways of playing with interactive technology. Take, for example, how ludophilic love shifts registers when applied to the "genius" of the tech world—as in the love for Steve Jobs, which translates to love for the Apple corporate leviathan. Even the status of self-marketed auteurs like Sid Meier will never measure up to the Oriental mysticism of sagacious Japanese auteurs like Miyamoto (*Super Mario Bros.*) and Hideo Kojima (*Metal Gear Solid*). Indeed, ludophilia in an American context often remains a misplaced "false" love for a corporation or a sign of addiction, with the ludophile operating as another name for a sufferer of "game-related afflictions."[68] However, through its "spiral" dance with the Asiatic unknowable, ludophilic love, like cinephilic love, resists Western corporate models and rejects the nationalist underpinnings of digital art, preferring the abyss of the foreign and the bizarre.

Still, there does remain a tradition of ludophilic love for Western artists, one that has operated within the confines of ethnic literary critique. In literature, amorous love for the author often sees ethnic writers as representative of an identity, as it presumes that they are at all times speaking from an authentic marginalized position. In some cases, this author function is not far removed from the ludophilic and cinephilic desire for the unknowable, which for Rey Chow can encourage artists to provide a commodified form of "self-Orientalism" that conveniently reflects Western racial presumptions and fetishes.[69] How can this form of Asiatic desire, which sees the other as a stage for understanding our own desires/pleasures/powers, be used to see American games differently? How can ludophilic attachments to Japanese auteurs outline ways to erotically reread Asian American designers who do not openly identify as such?

If Barthes's queer sexual desires were always "opaque," never discernable or "out of the closet" in the way future biographers would wish upon him, then we can see a similar trend in Asian American designers, as their preference not to be identified (as anything) is often taken as a sign of political ineptitude, informing how we read the militarism and violence of their work. Indeed, the closest developer in America to a "Japanese auteur" has recently emerged in the developer Jenova Chen, a migrant from Shanghai, who sees his heritage as integral to who he is and how he sees the world, even as he produces games that appear totally apolitical.[70] Perhaps unconsciously appropriating "Japaneseness," Chen replaced his legal first name "Jason" with the name "Jenova" from the Japanese game *Final Fantasy VII*. Like Japanese auteurs, Chen frequently criticizes the corporate environments of commercial game design and has started his own company (Thatgamecompany) in order to resist incorporation.[71] Like Suda51, Chen has authored games with puzzling names like *Cloud* (2005), *Flow* (2006), and *Flower* (2009), names remarkably similar to Suda51's own *Flower, Sun, and Rain*. And like Suda51, Chen has also written treatises on his aesthetic philosophy.[72] As an Asian diasporic American, however, Chen has consciously kept his games from giving an explicit political message, sometimes eliminating game elements when users find them politically oriented, cutting even innocuous themes like "be green."[73]

Minh Le / Gooseman: The Communal Auteur

Though Chen may seem evasive in his refusal to discuss his identity in depth, as an auteur he has been far more forthcoming than any other Asian American developer, using his background to conjure an Asiatic author function. As explored in the previous chapter, the Asiatic is often codified in gaming through stereotypes of the "Asian gamer," whose lack in other sports (basketball, baseball, soccer) has envisioned a retreat into PC rooms, where Asian Americans have become synonymous with gamer "addicts" and as e-sports gamers. Asian Americans often play the role of gaming gurus, and e-sports teams have typically spotlighted Asian American team members, with the most famous earning world-wide recognition, like Tomo Ohira and Dennis Fong (a.k.a. "Thresh").[74] Tellingly, these Asian heritage gamers are often more associated with their speculative gamertags than with their legal "Asian-sounding" names, and they, too, do not shy away from playing games that include white heroes repeatedly killing Asian characters.[75]

In a 2004 study of Californian cybercafés in Little Saigons and China-towns, Mary Yu Danico and Linda Trinh Võ argued that Asian American gamers saw games and PC cafés as a space of refuge from poverty and racial stratification as well as from living in "cramped, multigenerational households."[76] What has been overlooked in this and other studies of PC cafés is that the very game credited with the creation and expansion of PC rooms was in fact designed by an Asian North American designer, Minh Le, a.k.a. Gooseman, the lead designer and creator of *Counter-Strike*. Minh Le was only twenty-one in 1999 when his pet project *Counter-Strike* was released into the world, spurring the growth of PC rooms across the globe and becoming one of the most successful video games of all time (having sold over twenty-five million units). *Counter-Strike* pits two teams against each other, Counter-Terrorist and Terrorist, who can win by eliminating all the members of the other team or by completing opposing objectives (planting/defusing a bomb, holding/rescuing hostages, killing/saving a VIP). After the game was acquired by Valve in

2000, it yielded three reiterations: *Counter-Strike: Condition Zero* (2004), *Counter-Strike: Source* (2004), and *Counter-Strike: Global Offensive* (2012). Over the past two decades since the original's release, *Counter-Strike* has been credited for forming a movement of young gamers who play team-oriented first-person shooters, many of whom have put tens of thousands of hours into games like the *Halo* series and *Overwatch*.

Reading *Counter-Strike* as a ludophile proves challenging because it ultimately means reading Minh Le as an Asiatic auteur, a man who, like many designers of color, has rarely discussed his Vietnamese background and goes by an internet handle: Gooseman, a cartoon character from the animated space western *The Adventures of the Galaxy Rangers* based on Clint Eastwood's cowboys. Although other designers, like Steve Swink, see Le as an auteur who had total control in creating *Counter-Strike*, Le himself has preferred to shape himself as a community collaborator rather than an artist or game director.[77] Seeking to find some narrative within his opacity, in March 2017 I performed the ludophile myself and interviewed Le to discuss racial issues in his games. Unlike Japanese auteurs who aggrandize their work and remain elusive, Minh Le was candid and reflective of how young (and "naive") he was when *Counter-Strike* was in development.[78] He made no attempt to "own" the game, but he noted how its popularity happened to coincide with the War on Terror, and even though not all terrorists in *Counter-Strike* were Arab, the game's popularity skyrocketed as it came to mirror the wars in Iraq and Afghanistan. Refusing to claim ownership over this "coincidence," Le pushed much of the decision-making onto his audience, the gaming community, claiming that the game's only Middle Eastern inspired map, "de_dust," was submitted by a "member of the community" (Dave Johnston), and Le even rejected it numerous times for being "too ugly." He released the map despite his doubts, only to watch it grow into the game's most iconic setting, so that a Google image search of "*Counter-Strike*" will yield images of terrorists on a Middle Eastern–themed background.[79] The terrorists, Le claimed, were also not meant to reflect Arab bodies but were also chosen through community feedback.[80]

Le's answers in our interview reflected many of the same anxieties I felt as a young gamer with Asian heritage. I asked Le why his collaborator, Jess Cliffe, provided the voices for *Counter-Strike* and not himself, and Le responded that his own voice sounded too "prepubescent." I asked him why his race rarely came up in interviews, specifically in a Reddit "Ask Me Anything" where fans asked Le intimate questions about his personal life—what kind of car he drove, what it was like to be a father—but only after two hundred questions did they ask him about his heritage.[81] Le replied that he liked "to shy away from controversy," that his ethnicity was always present in "his name," and that he was "very proud" of his Vietnamese heritage, as he met consistently with "other Vietnamese refugees and we formed a close community." In many ways, Le's answers in our interview reflect that of an artist far more interested in the international community than in the American or Canadian minority communities. To Le, counterterrorist forces against terrorist teams had come to define much of twenty-first-century global politics, which made them ample subjects for the global audiences available to video games. Only one of *Counter-Strike*'s team units is American, while the others belong to the French GIGN, the Israeli IDF, Germany's GSG-9, and the UK's SAS. Indeed, any cursory glance at the *Counter-Strike* community boards reveal the global breadth of the game's community, with more players in 2016 in Russia, Brazil, and Poland than in America. As Albert Chan observed in Hong Kong in 2008, "If you walk into . . . any of the cybercafés, nine out of ten computers are running *Counter-Strike*."[82] Le, too, has lived in South Korea and has traveled extensively in Vietnam.

In ethnic literary presumptions of race and authorship, Minh Le's attitude as a game designer and player seem to deny his heritage and racial community and put into practice the gratitude of the Vietnamese refugee. But to read him as a ludophile would mean to find something "elusive," "obscure," and "unknowable" in his indifference to these discourses. He speaks of his Vietnameseness with pride but also does not claim "Vietnamese Canadian" as an identity more important than that of designer, traveler, or collaborator. Like Japanese auteurs, Le's self-presentation is focused on innovation, gameplay, and perfecting the "harmony" of the online team-based shooter. In other words, to read *Counter-Strike* within the "amorous discourse" of the ludophile means seeing its innovations within an "oedipal time," with its auteur embracing his audience through a virtual transnational space where players exchange verbal and nonverbal grammars, fostering unlikely allegiances and international subcultures.[83] The ludophilic discourse allows the game to perform differently, to expose the spiral of imperial and racial discourses through which auteur love is made possible. Whereas Danico and Võ write that *Counter-Strike* was attractive to Asian American youth because "of the guns and violence," their interview subjects (Asian American gamers) saw *Counter-Strike* within the genre of shooters that are always about guns and violence (*Quake, Doom, Duke Nukem*), and their responses thus noted how *this* particular shooting game still remained unique, innovative, and artistic. As one of their respondents said, "Every time it's different. You have skills at certain things." This "every time it's different" emerges as the innovative distinction that marks Minh Le as auteur.

Unlike other games of "guns and violence" like *Half-Life* (the game that *Counter-Strike* was modified from), *Counter-Strike* does not confine players into an identity, a narrative, or a story, but is entirely a multiplayer, team-against-team game, requiring consistent communication and putting personal differences on pause to collectivize under the urgency of the situation. Indeed, the ludophile might then see Le's consistent collaboration with gaming communities as further proof of his innovative technique, as *Counter-Strike*, in its beginning, released new versions every three months, with every level (map) made by the community. Minh Le was then one of the first auteurs to see development as a collaborative project with the community, giving them the tools by making them easy to use and garnering constant feedback by actually changing the game.[84] This ludophilic shift offers counternarratives to the game's narrative of terrorism as well as to dominant narratives of Asian North American gamers as alienated, emasculated, and asocial. For the ludophile, *Counter-Strike* epitomizes the work of a bizarre, stylistic, Asiatic auteur, whose team-based magnum opus forever opened the possibilities for camaraderie with unknown and elusive strangers.

Mohammed Alavi: The Level Auteur

As one people, we shall free our brethren from the yoke of
foreign oppression!
—Al Asad, *Call of Duty 4: Modern Warfare*

Perhaps the most influential idea within auteur theory—unusual for its time but widely accepted today—is that the most authorial and visionary voice within the realm of filmmaking is not that of the script writer, the producer, or its actors, but the director himself, the "man with the answers." In most cases, the Japanese auteur has followed suit with this "director" figure, as most of its renowned auteurs (Suda51, Suzuki) are credited as game directors. As previously shown, however, many American designers do not hold director titles for their games and will share "designer" status with a larger team (Minh Le, Sid Meier, Will Wright). As Anna Anthropy points out, big-budget game design is rigidly hierarchized in order "to coordinate teams of increasingly unmanageable numbers of people," and directors themselves can have little say in the creative process (they report to producers and publishers).[85] The variety of designers who could be assigned authorship, for the ludophile, opens a deeper well of meanings, so that games like *Counter-Strike*, often written off as a military shooter reinforcing the racism and xenophobia against Arabic peoples, shifts meanings dramatically as we transpose authorship from its parent company, Valve, onto its original modder, a Vietnamese refugee. So, too, for other minority game designers rooted firmly in games about terrorism and the military, even those who do not share in "director" status.

Steve Fukuda and Mohammed Alavi are two Asian diasporic designers who were integral to the creation of the *Call of Duty* series, which has sold over 250 million copies and has earned over $15 billion USD. While Steve Fukuda, as a director and lead writer, has rarely given interviews that reveal his ethnic background or political intentions, Mohammed Alavi has been highly visible as a daring level designer. Alavi boasts of his proud Iranian heritage and self-identifies as Persian and Iranian more than American, though he has lived in America for most of his adult life. This might strike readers as ironic, since no other AAA (big budget/blockbuster) game has ever been more accused of acting as a tool for US military recruitment than Alavi's game series *Call of Duty: Modern Warfare*. This is a game series where the player, part of elite counterterrorist forces, kills enemies while they sleep in their bunk-beds, while they stumble around drunk, or while they cry, curled up in a dark corner; it is a game series that Viet Thanh Nguyen has accused of "train[ing] people to be part of a war machine, turning war into a game and a game into war."[86] As with Minh Le, one could read these Asian designers as race betrayers, imperial ideologues, complicitous.

But a ludophilic reading of their games reveals a more critical confrontation with games as forms of politicized art produced by marginalized designers whose participation exposes the very limits of game analysis. A ludophilic reading of Alavi's level design speaks not to the glorification of modern warfare but to its uncompromising brutality. Though the game was heavily inspired by the *Medal of Honor* game series, *Call of Duty: Modern Warfare* lacks honor in every respect. When playing as a US Marine, players are meant to feel like war fodder—repeatedly hearing screams of "man down!" or accidentally killing other marines with friendly fire, only to see one's squad "refilled" at the next checkpoint. Whereas *Call of Duty*'s first two games were both focused on World War II, and both were concerned with the "honor" of that war, the *Modern Warfare* installments shift to a more adult audience (using an adult rating), making "modern warfare" remorseless.

Modern Warfare's first installment established Alavi's status as an auteur renegade, as his designs for the levels "Crew Expendable" and "All Ghillied Up" were rejected by the project leads, forcing him to work on the code himself and to even hide his work on "Crew Expendable" until it was ready to be shown. These two levels instantly became the game's most popular, with "Crew Expendable" famous as the defining level for all future cinematic gameplay (with Alavi's scripted teammates and gravity effects on a sinking ship) and "All Ghillied Up" now considered one of the most sophisticated levels ever made (for its creativity and the freedom it gives players to strategize).[87] Yet these levels can also be read for their political daring, what the ludophile might envision as Alavi's own suspicion for US empire as a "proud Iranian." "Crew Expendable" begins with the vicious massacre of a ship's Russian crew by US Marines who shoot them while drunk, celebrating, and sleeping in their bunkbeds. Indeed, the level's scripted teammates—praised as a technological innovation of the genre—are integral to this brutality, because if the player chooses *not* to execute these men, the other members of the team will do so for them, slipping in bravado phrases like "sweet dreams." As the game's opening level, "Crew Expendable" creates a new normalcy for how modern warfare is envisioned. A far cry from the "honor" of World War II, *Modern Warfare* spotlights western militaristic power (the US, the UK) battling comparatively powerless military forces whose lack of technology and equal footing are often grotesque.

In the level "Black Out," the player kills enemies from above with sniper fire (where they cannot shoot back), and minutes later, kills enemies in the dark using night-vision goggles, executing an enemy huddled crying in a corner. If the player chooses not to execute the sobbing man, a teammate will do so instead and flippantly quip, "These goggles make it too easy."

Despite its uncanny depiction of American warfare onto powerless others, *Modern Warfare* has become known—partially due to its popular multiplayer mode—as one of the most pro-militaristic games ever made. But played through a ludophilic discourse focusing on the Iranian auteur, Mohammed Alavi, the game instead condemns American military action, forcing players to witness the US and UK's indifference to the rules of engagement, and understands how those trained in military hardware can become numb to the act of killing (there is no bonus for "not killing" like in other first-person shooters). Alavi's most infamous level appeared in *Call of Duty: Modern Warfare 2*, a game that sold nearly five million copies within its first day, making it the most successful launch of any media product in entertainment history ever, bigger than any other game, movie, musical album, or book. And Alavi's level in the game, "No Russian," quickly became the game's most famous set piece (see Figure 2.3). In it, the player joins Russian terrorists as they ruthlessly massacre civilians within an airport, hoping to incite a war against the United States by framing it on US special forces. "No Russian" was so controversial that the game's publisher Activision was forced to let players skip it (labeled as "Disturbing Content"). Yet the level's destabilizing effects came not only because of the massacre (lots of games feature massacres), but because this particular massacre is committed for politically relatable reasons, for revenge against the Western imperial powers that have destroyed the terrorists' homes and families, and, according to them, corrupted their culture. Embracing Alavi as an "Iranian auteur" takes seriously Alavi's own claims that he created the level to "sell why Russia would attack the U.S. [and to] make the player have an emotional connection to the bad guy."[88] The player later learns that this massacre is actually instigated by a US Army general seeking to jumpstart the American military industrial complex by creating a war with Russia, a narrative twist that has led journalists to call the game "a game condemning America's political behavior for the past several

Figure 2.3. *Call of Duty: Modern Warfare 2*. Alavi's "No Russian" level. Screenshot by author.

decades . . . by putting its audience in the shoes of everyone involved in the conflict."[89]

Through a ludophilic engagement, what appears to be the most successful imperialist video game ever made, *Modern Warfare* reads radically different. Rather than submerge its meanings into the lazy eyes of game detractors (who see games as violent, perverse, or pointless), or into the laser-precise limelight of game defenders (who praise *some* games as progressive, educational), the ludophile exposes a plurality of meanings that spiral around the Asiatic amorous object. All meanings are therefore taken as *speculations* causing us to reread, each time dismantling a presumption we initially carried with us. This plurality of meanings is made possible through the game's collaborative production, where authorship could be ascribed to anyone within *Modern Warfare*'s vast list of developer credits, many of whom have the "ethnic-sounding names" that coincide with notions of the foreign auteur developer.

This perplexity of meaning manifests within the title sequence of *Call of Duty: Modern Warfare*. As the names of the game's many designers dissolve onto the screen, the player controls an Arabic body: the president of an unnamed country in the Middle East, who is tossed into a car and driven to an auditorium while listening to the speech of the Arabic villain, Al-Asad, where he is summarily executed by that same villain. The dissolving credit sequence visualizes the multiethnic, international presence of the game's contributors as the player listens to an anti-imperial political speech made by an emerging despot. As a depiction of the "Middle East" (the Arab-*ic*), the sequence features the iron-clad stereotypes of summary executions and dainty, war-torn housing, but also makes Islam itself conspicuously absent. The coup that puts Al-Asad in power seems to have no basis in religion at all, nor in cultural differences. Instead, Al-Asad voices his cause as a revenge narrative against the West for its brutality and war, which the player, for the rest of the game, will prove entirely right. Al-Asad accuses the president (the player) of "colluding with the West" and announces a new era, where "as one people, we shall free our brethren from the yoke of foreign oppression!" Al-Asad speaks of justice and his "noble crusade" of restoring independence from the West, and all the while ethnic developer names dissolve on-screen as if stamping Al-Asad's words with approval: Mohammed Alavi, Steve Fukuda, Peter Chen, Neel Kar, Bryan Kuhn, Oscar Lopez, Ryan Lastimosa, Cheng Lor, Julian Luo, Taehoon Oh, Sami Onur, Velinda Pelayo, Jiesang Song, Theerapol Srisuphan, Sompoom Tangchupong, Andrew Wang, Lei Yang (see Figure 2.4). Even the director's name, Jason West, appears alongside these names, with no title to mark his difference from them. Who are these "ethnic-sounding" names, each so integral to the inner workings of this supposedly imperial game? The ludophile's desire for the unknown, the obscure, the Asiatic, opens the text to these auteur voices, revising its political implications from imperial complicity to exposing the unforgiving and amoral brutality of modern empire.

Even this title sequence we can reread ludophilically: its occurrence within an "unnamed country in the Middle East" at first seems like an imperialist homogenization of all Arabic culture, a mere repetition of Islamophobic films from Hollywood directors like Michael Bay. But by seeking the unknown—led perhaps by desire and pleasure—we find this presumption radically mistaken. By comparing the game's maps with real-world maps, we realize that the country in question is Saudi Arabia, the United States' main ally and one of the most powerful despotic regimes within the region. The "unnamed" Asiatic space, like the unknowable amorous object, reveals more about our own imperial pleasures and desires, in this case, American complicity to tyrannical regimes in exchange

Figure 2.4. *Call of Duty 4: Modern Warfare.* Credit sequence in an unnamed country (Saudi Arabia). Screenshot by author.

for economic and regional "stabilization." Thus, our amorous embrace of *Modern Warfare*'s title sequence unveils what is seen in plain sight: multiethnic names pinned to a speech denouncing American militarism within a game that forces players to reenact modern warfare's most brutal acts, buttressed within America's most atrocious political allegiances.

The Remains of the Author

This chapter has played with Barthes's "The Death of the Author" and *A Lover's Discourse: Fragments,* two texts that, read within an amorous discourse themselves, may be inverted, toyed with, flipped, and redrawn to erotically read games and understand their imperial scene. Barthes's insight that the authorial presence or absence ultimately had the greatest impact on the text's meanings ("closure") has remained unchanged. The authorial function, as Foucault would later term it, has the potential to foreclose meanings or to open the text to its radical plurality, to deny totality just as much as it denies its own ends. Whereas the author for Barthes needed to be pronounced dead in order to release the text from totality, this hinges on the presumption that the text itself already passes as a renowned and elevated form of art. Yet for the majority of

Westerners, games construe no deep meaning, and even fans of *Modern Warfare* or *Counter-Strike* make little attempt to claim their beloved products as art. Ludophiles can thus exhibit a plurality of political and ethical meanings from games, as one can focus entirely on the level designs of Alavi, or surmise the writing influences of Steve Fukuda, or penetrate the underlying authorial influence of Minh Le.

Cults of the video game auteur have, since the late 2000s, become increasingly fashionable with the rise of the independent game genre, which has gained prominence through popular independent games like *Braid* (2008), *Minecraft* (2009), and *Limbo* (2010). Indeed, Asian North American developers have become more visible in this turn, and developers like Jenova Chen (*Journey*), Brendon Chung (*Thirty Flights of Loving*), Brianna Lei (*Butterfly Soup*), Nicky Case (*Coming Out Simulator*), Sean Han Tani (*All Our Asias*), Robert Yang (*Radiator*), Ken Wong (*Florence*), and Navid Khonsari (*1979: Black Friday*) have gained visibility despite the corporate, authorial absence that remains in most big-budget game companies. Despite these emerging ludophilic cults, such designers have remained invisible to Asian American scholars and communities, as they hesitate to directly represent "empowered" identity narratives, and game writers instead offer their platforms to representations of Asian Americans by white designers (*Sleeping Dogs*, *Mirror's Edge*). Spotlighting developers as auteurs within a ludophilic discourse reveals here the pleasures and desires we seek in narratives of ourselves: mainly, our hunger for positive representations of ourselves, a need so foundational to our political positioning that unless an Asian American designer caters to this political demand, he or she may as well be white. Such a rigid reading of these designers would conclude that they are ashamed of their race and that their pen names (Gooseman, Jenova Chen) are attempts to hide their true ethnic selves. But if we read as ludophiles, we imagine their products as "amorous objects," whose bizarre styles can be taken as a new, unimagined form of self-expression, a form that does not explicitly express racial identity, but something deeper, something always scuttling just beyond our reach. As ludophiles, we long for the amorous object, even in its Asiatic unknowability, listening to its beckoning, feeling out its contours. Doing so reveals new ways of playing, cognizant of how our own pleasures/desires/powers spiral within the scene of love's consecration.

3

Ars Erotica

Utopia \ Aphrodisia / *Role Play*

In Lawrence Chua's queer travel novel *Gold by the Inch* (1999), the unnamed narrator's pleasure-filled romp through Thailand gets lodged in the deluge of family duty when he visits his cousin Martina, a worker at a microprocessor factory nearby Penang, Malaysia. The protagonist's kinky tour through Southeast Asia is ruptured by the grim reality of the multinational microchip company, whose exploitation of young women in Malaysia has been well documented by scholars like Aihwa Ong. In her investigation of microprocessor factories in Malaysian Export Processing Zones (EPZs), Ong argues that information technology companies have used a narrative of progress and development to exploit rural areas with a surplus population of unemployed females.[1] Such factories employ already existing structural violence to produce a population of low-wage factory laborers and have a heavy hand in intensifying gender, racial, and religious hierarchies within their operative spaces. Even so, the manufacture of information technology still does not carry the same narratives of exploitation as historically embedded industries (rubber plantations, garment work), even to those who work there. The women in Chua's factory describe it as a space masked with progress and human development. Martina claims that she was "awed and intrigued by the equipment she had to use," equipment such as a microscope, which "she had only seen scientists and professors use on television."[2] Her awe for the machine develops from the symbolic resonance of information technology as the forefront of human development. Due to her exhausting work hours, Martina eventually realizes that this space of "human development" demands that her body be cast off once her labor power has been exhausted.

The associations of information technology with "newness" and "human development" play a lead role in disavowing the exploitative working conditions in factories that produce information technology. From microprocessor factories in Malaysia, electronic parts eventually make their way to China, where they are assembled within working conditions known for human rights abuses, debt slavery, and suicide. Yet because brand names like Apple, Microsoft, and Sony are so idealized by notions of progress, ethics, and innovation, the process of production seems trivial in the face of the utopian promises they represent. Focusing on "utopian narratives" that shape technology as "a mass medium of freedom," Wendy Hui Kyong Chun has explored how technology enables forms of control over gendered and racialized bodies to understand the vulnerabilities that appear when we see our digital selves as invulnerable.[3] In the realm of hardware manufacture, Lisa Nakamura has shown that IT factory work has always relied upon racialized notions of women's bodies, as IT factories can be traced back to Navajo Indian Reservations in 1965, where the Fairchild Corporation's Semiconductor division used ethnic associations of Navajo women with "blanket weaving . . . and jewelry making," to make them seem naturally fitted to build electronic devices and integrated circuits.[4] Fairchild was one of the largest private employers in the United States until 1975, when protestors who accused the company of sweatshop labor occupied and shut down its plant. Fairchild then joined the exodus of information technology corporations by outsourcing manufacturing to female workers in Asia, distancing the production processes of computers and video games ever since from the people meant to take pleasure from them.

This chapter compares narratives of digital utopia against the turgid material process of factory labor in Asia. I begin by exploring how video games shore up evidence for digital utopia by enacting its values of liberal tolerance, freedom, and egalitarianism within a virtual realm. In video games, no other genre caters to these imaginings better than the diverse and utopian realm of the role-playing game. Whether it is narrative forms of character-driven role play that are today read as a form of education, or a massive online role-playing game that depicts itself as a form of egalitarian acceptance and democratic participation, role playing has been crucial to providing experiential substance for digital utopias. Indeed, even queer studies of games have often celebrated role playing as a genre that is always already queer by making possible gender reversals and diverse sexual experiences. Scholars and bloggers alike give credit to games like *Mass Effect* and *Dragon Age* for their non-normative representations, only faulting them for not going far enough (as in, for example, the inability to play as male homosexual, until *Mass Effect 3*).[5] At the same time, scholars like Lisa Nakamura have continued to point out the undeniable presence of labor exploitation in massive on-line role-playing games through the prejudices used to identify and discuss Chinese gold farmers. How do we see celebrations of role-playing games within a larger discourse of digital utopia? How can we reconcile forms of queer play and intimacy with the brutal transnational labor conditions of information technology, which make these celebrations possible?

After delving into the morass of imperial exploitation in Asia, this chapter's second half explores how video games can promote new connections among imperial subjects through the erotics of digital role play, which provide a way to redress the histories and structural violences of empire. Role-playing games are thought to enact and envision digital utopian futures through the act of playing a role, an act submerged in the values of digital utopia as future building. For James Paul Gee, to role play means playing a "projected identity," defined as the player projecting "one's values and desires onto the virtual character" and "seeing the virtual character as one's own project in the making."[6] As others have argued,[7] in most video games, the on-screen avatar functions as a proxy, a figure that the player identifies with only as an extension of the self, as "a tool, a puppet, an object for the player to manipulate."[8] In most cases, identifying with a typical game protagonist is hardly different from identifying with a car or a hammer, as Swink writes, "[y]ou can go from 'being' Gordon Freeman one moment to cursing his vile clumsiness the next."[9] But role-playing games ask players to deeply connect with their avatars not as proxies but as "roles" who they can inhabit for dozens of hours. As Sundén and Sveningsson found in interviewing female *World of Warcraft* players, this type of emotional attachment stirs "passionate encounters with game technologies" in ways that are reminiscent of "erotic play with power and domination."[10] Playing a role is thus characteristic of the power positions of sexual role play, a kink that includes weighing and negotiating consensual fantasies of domination and subjugation. Indeed, role playing seems to be the only form of play that has been inarguably both gamelike and erotic, as both develop rule-based fantasy worlds with hierarchized avatars or roles.[11] Read as an erotic act not about "project building" but about power and pleasure in relation to others, role play can make explicit the transnational power differentials that function as digital utopia's conditions of possibility.

To tease out an erotic function of role play, I turn to Foucault's "last decade," when his critiques of bourgeois medical and moral discourses of sexuality helped envision and recognize alternative forms of sexuality where notions of ethical self-making and self-care did not lead one inward into our own pleasures and pillared identities but outward into the anxieties and "problematics" of our ethical relationship with others: in particular, to those who make our pleasures possible. As Amber Jamilla Musser has argued, Foucault's focus on pleasure offers "a frame for thinking about embodiment that exceeds the disciplinary regimes that define modernity, therefore opening up different modes of theorizing resistance and power."[12] In his last decade, Foucault pushed this inquiry further by seeking out a genealogy of pleasure that offered alternative relations to modern sexuality, which he named *ars erotica*. *Ars erotica*, or "the art of erotics," represents not a form of self-help (as "care of the self" is often interpreted) but a set of anxieties that the ancient Greeks and Romans wrestled with throughout their philosophical and artistic writings. *Ars erotica* is not so much a self-love but a self-awareness, as it tethers one's pleasure to their domination over those who would have otherwise been relegated simply to the realm of the inhuman (slaves, barbarians, women, young boys). Employing *ars erotica* as a method of play, this chapter's second half focuses on how role playing can keep the exploitation of others from being disavowed, and how it brings the power and domination of the West as an explicit point of anxiety, thus grasping the commonplace celebrations of role playing as rationalizations of these anxieties. Role play licenses the perversity of domination and subjection, erotically tinged within a gamespace that presumes consent (because others are playing along). Understanding role play as a form of fantasy characterized by a "switching of roles" shares distinct qualities with role playing in the bedroom, as both expose the context of domination and subjugation that are integral to an ethics of play.

Console Cowboys

From 2010 to 2012, a slew of scandalous articles appeared against Apple concerning the treatment of Chinese workers in factories owned by its Taiwanese contracted manufacturer, Foxconn, one of the largest private employers in China. These scandals began in 2010 when eighteen Foxconn employees attempted suicide with fourteen deaths, and reporters took pictures of Foxconn factories where nets had been strung up to keep more workers from leaping over.[13] Though Apple received most of the negative press, Foxconn did not only produce iPads and iPhones but also game consoles and gaming computers.[14] In fact, all three major console companies, Sony, Microsoft, and Nintendo, had consoles (the PlayStation 4, the Xbox One, and the Wii U) produced by Foxconn. The suicides at Foxconn resulted in a narrative of exclusion and erasure. Twenty universities in China, Hong Kong, and Taiwan wrote an eighty-three-page report that detailed the Foxconn suicides and labor conditions in factories, which they called an "inhumane" "labor camp."[15] Yet sources from Apple and journalists from magazines like the *Economist* were still skeptical that any suicides had taken place. For Apple, profits only increased.

Though large IT companies like Intel and Toshiba have some factories in their home countries, invariably electronic companies contract with factories in China's Pearl River Delta, which produces an estimated 90 percent of the world's consumer electronics, as it provides a seemingly endless supply of disposable labor alongside the protections of the People's Republic with its pervasive internet censorship, unenforced environmental regulations, and lack of free speech. The consolidation of factory work in China has formed an alliance among IT companies, as no one company can adequately frame a narrative about the exploitation of workers in Asia without also being implicated in it, making the erasure of Asian factory work a common interest for all companies involved.[16] While, for example, the hardware company Dell Computers may have emerged as an alternative to Apple products, not long after the Foxconn incidents, information also emerged about Dell contracted factories forcing workers into seventy-four-hour work weeks, to stand for twelve hours a day, and to inhale toxic fumes.[17]

The digital utopian discourses of information technology are indelibly formed through video games, in the way games are played and for whom they are manufactured. Yet it is within our understandings of "the Asiatic" that discourses of digital utopia and techno-Orientalism overlap: "Asia" becomes a synonym of ludic forms of exoticism, queerness, and nonnormative relationships, which warrants celebration from Western queer communities but also relegates "Asia" into the realm of the nonhuman, making the vast exploitation of Asian women an acceptable premise for the formation of play. Discourses of techno-Orientalism feminize "Asia" for erotic pleasure by transforming Asian sexual figures into figures of exploitation, either through representations of Asians as machine labor (in films like *Ex Machina, Cloud Atlas,* and *Ghost in the Shell*) or as being incapable of *not* giving consent (because they are always turned on, always willing, always welcoming, always ready). However, to adequately chart out the vexed boundaries of these discourses, we must also see techno-Orientalism as only telling half the story. On the other side is the corresponding "techno-Occidentalism" that represents the Westerner not as a laborer but as someone imbued with liberal values of tolerance, freedom, and egalitarianism. These values, manifest in the Western player, license the white subject to play as a "console cowboy" able to navigate, tame, and domesticate Asiatic technology.[18] For Lisa Nakamura, electronic devices made in Asia signify the innovation of the West "to preserve the image of an artisanal product," a discursive strategy that keeps the product "globally desirable."[19] Indeed, Western conceptions of freedom in the digital age are enabled by depictions of Asia as *unfree* victims to technology—as laborers, as robotic beings, as dominated by tyrannical uses of technology (China's "Great Firewall"). These anxieties of information technology are resolved in depictions of Silicon Valley as Western efforts to tame Asiatic technology through liberal values, just as the techies of the Valley also tame other Asiatic forms for capitalist purposes (meditation and yoga as "de-stress," "zen" as an art of innovation, minimalism as a marketing technique). As "console cowboys" able to produce a liberal digital utopia, the Western figure desires for more—more pleasure, more land, more resources—and plays the role of the manager, the conductor, the designer of the Asiatic device.

Wendy Hui Kyong Chun develops the "console cowboy" figure as a global phenomenon in artwork produced in both the West (*Necromancer*) and the East (*Ghost in the Shell*). Though he appears in various forms, the console cowboy always resembles Western technological power. As a forerunner to contemporary American role-playing games, the *Final Fantasy* series offer the console cowboy as a techno-Occidentalist figure in its repetition of the character Cid, who appears differently in every *Final Fantasy* game, most often as a Caucasian-looking man with white skin and blond hair. An inventor and lovable monster, Cid is almost always an airship captain who gives the player new technology (access to airships) that brings the players into the larger world and makes them competitive against their imperial enemy. Indeed, these traits have led fans to read Cid as an allegory for the West, particularly America, as he represents a necessary element in the process to develop the player's "ragtag" team of resistance fighters into a superpower rivalling an evil empire. Like the genius figures of Silicon Valley, Cid himself must be respected as "wise and intelligent," but unlike typical console cowboys in the West, Cid frequently goes mad with power, easily loses his temper, and sometimes becomes evil himself. As even Cid's name is anglicized in Japanese (シド, Shido), we can see him as an allegory for America's role in giving Japan the "gift of flight" into the modern age and overseeing its ascent from America's own firebombs and atomic warfare into a cultural and economic giant. Taking this view, we can also understand Cid as a critique of the "madness" of American technological power as Cid becomes more evil and imperial in further iterations of the series. Whereas Cid in *Final Fantasy* games of the 1990s acts as a wise (but sometimes ornery) sage, after the Iraq War and Bush years, the cowboy Cid shifts into a villain delirious with technological power.[20]

If Japanese role-playing games allegorized the political scene of Japan becoming a "sub-empire" of the United states, then American role-playing games inspired by the *Final Fantasy* series can be read as similar allegories but viewed from the imperial center rather than its ally.[21] From the center's view, the console cowboy is not an auxiliary character like Cid but the protagonist and avatar, the main role meant for the player to occupy. As an allegory for Western control over technology, the console cowboy reinforces digital utopic discourses by providing an identity through which the player can navigate Asiatic virtual worlds and thus demonstrating (and teaching the player) values of liberal tolerance, freedom, and egalitarianism. Each of these values correlates to particular game genres formed through elements of game rules and story, and they have evolved into experiences of role play that reflect an ideal form of digital utopia.

Liberal Tolerance

From the philosopher John Dewey to the contemporary game scholar James Paul Gee, the most common response to accusations that games are frivolous or dangerous has been to rebrand role-playing games as a crucial tool for learning how to deal with others.[22] For video game scholars like David Simkins and Constance Steinkuehler, role-playing games instruct players in liberal values by engaging "individuals in forms of ethical reasoning that may very well foster empathy, tolerance, and understanding for others."[23] In the United States, the games produced through the role-playing game company BioWare have earned the most recognition as liberally tolerant: progressive, antiracist, and LGBT themed. As the game scholar Kristine Jørgensen has observed, BioWare's role-playing games are unique in drawing attention away from the player and onto supporting characters and their respective cultures "by equipping supporting characters with agendas of their own."[24] Indeed, both gamers and scholars have praised BioWare for its focus on ethical decision-making that requires players to consider complex moral situations, often resulting in a greater grasp of liberal values.

My previous book, *Transitive Cultures*, addressed the perils of liberal tolerance whose values rely upon seeing racial difference as insurmountable cultural ways of being, which then bolster suspicion and violence onto those cast as "mono-cultural" or "non-tolerant" (arguments also made by Étienne Balibar, Wendy Brown, and Jodi Melamed).[25] *Transitive Cultures* was invested within this discourse because, as I argued, it had led to a trumpeting of American exceptionalism seeking to illuminate and incorporate individuals as domesticated identities. Though this co-optation helps lower-class and marginalized others gain recognition, it is only insofar as they perform the "roles" assigned to them, roles which share the values of American exceptionalism. The celebration of cultural appreciation, as Etienne Balibar noted as a form of "neo-racism," can often work to conflate race, nation, and labor, so that one's cultural heritage and practices (like Malaysians who sew textiles) can mark a population as specialists in certain labor practices (like building the microprocessors needed to play BioWare games).[26] Role-playing video games operate within this discourse by virtue of their very form, where the celebrated depth of its supporting characters also puts the player in the curious position of managing those characters, reducing the value of their psychological complexity to abilities that must be manipulated and deployed for war. No matter what racial/national/species-based "role" the players are encouraged to inhabit, they will always play the part of American exceptionalism: the cowboyish "manager" who watches over racialized teammates and is the final judge of their fates. From this point of view, role-playing games can be seen as a practice-based educational tool of imperial management, one that produces in-depth characters for the task of vilifying and dominating those too religious or too militarily weak to take part in the multicultural imperium.

Cultural education has always played a heavy part in the conduct of empire. The employment of anthropologists in the Philippine-American War has become textbook material for the ethical stance against the use of anthropologists within the American military (a resistance popularized by Franz Boaz). As Lisa Yoneyama argues, this legacy led to refusals among anthropologists to participate in military activities like the US Army's Human Terrain System (2007–2014), a program created "to embed anthropologists in the military so as to facilitate the effective use of their expert cultural knowledge for U.S. military operations."[27] Cultural education concerning the "human terrain" was seen as an effective tool for imperial management, partially because it gave alternatives to "extermination" (biological and cultural), instituting occupational regimes to take its place. In today's "War on Terror," cultural education has evolved into a form that teaches the ideals of liberal tolerance in order to differentiate the tolerable colonized subjects from the "extreme" or intolerable ones, so that the recruitment of racial others becomes a strategy to demonstrate the exceptionalist values of the occupying force.[28]

The most explicit sign of this imperial education is within the celebrated form of liberal tolerance exhibited in BioWare's *Mass Effect* and *Dragon Age* series, games produced by North American game companies but popular the world over. Here, the harmony of different races displayed in both games is only made possible by presuming a racial division of *militaristic* labor. While the worlds of *Mass Effect* and *Dragon Age* often make labor invisible or done by synthetic beings, the main labor of interest to the player is military force, so that learning tolerance entitles players to incorporate racialized groups as military assets. In *Dragon Age*, the race that the player chooses to play determines his attributes in a Tolkenien fantasy: elves make good mages (+2 willpower and +2 magic), dwarves good rune-makers and axemen (+1 strength, +1 dexterity, +2 constitution), and humans have a versatile spread of racial bonuses (+1 magic, +1 strength, +1 dexterity, +1 cunning). While these racializations should be of no surprise in a fantasy setting, this division of militaristic labor continues in *Mass Effect*'s supposed multicultural future but also allows the reader to assume the role of cultural manager. Here, each race yields specialized talents, and even the all-inclusive and pan-ethnic government, the Citadel, divides labor by its respective races: "The Asari are typically seen as diplomats and mediators. The Salarians gather intelligence and information. The Turians provide the bulk of the military and peacekeeping forces."[29] Throughout *Mass Effect*, military ability is recognized as the only commodified labor power that matters, as we see in the Citadel's explicit exclusion of the Volus, a race who were "instrumental in establishing a standardized galactic economy"[30] but who lack military resources and pursue nonviolent methods. In this post-9/11 worldview, a seat at the table of the multinational imperium only comes in proving one's military prowess. In both the *Dragon Age* and *Mass Effect* series, humans, like "whites" in Western multicultural imaginaries, are "jacks-of-all-trades" who can perform any specialization or a mixture of specializations. As a human, the player takes on a "neutral" role that determines and manages the talents of their ethnicized teammates. While appreciating cultural difference, the player also weaponizes it, managing their ethnic squadmates from a neutral (universal) position.

A counterpoint to viewing race within the militaristic multiculturalism of BioWare games can be found in one of its main genre influences, Japanese role-playing games (JRPGs). Throughout the 1990s, JRPGs formed the role-playing genre through stories involving in-depth diverse characters who battle an evil global empire. In one of the masterpieces of the genre, *Final Fantasy VII*, the character Tifa's attributes of strength are not only due to her rebellious attitude but also because her role reinstates the "monk" character class from previous *Final Fantasy* games. In *Final Fantasy VII*, the convention of "class" is absent, yet the RPG tradition still demands a "monk"-like figure in the gameplay, forming the brazen Tifa, a character with a no-nonsense attitude, whose role of "monk" implies particular genre traits: bare fists, no armor, and quick attacks. Unlike in American role-playing games (*Fallout, Baldur's Gate, Mass Effect*), the *Final Fantasy* series does not feature open worlds of branching narratives and discourses of player freedom and moral education. The player is not being "trained" because there are few if any consequences for how they treat other characters. The player is faced with choices that can determine the outcome of a battle, yet the main storyline itself is linear. Cloud Strife, a wayward clone of the ancient deity Jenova, will always rise from the slums of Midgar to defeat his evil twin-like figure, Sephiroth, and bring on a new age of environmental growth. The player's teammates, who must be strategically employed with weighted strengths and abilities, will never choose to leave the player's crew once they join, no matter what ethical decisions the player makes. Teammates' skills are also diverse and complex, with variations concerning speed, strength, healing, sneak, and magic. Supporting characters' race, species, or gender seem to have little impact on their skills and attributes. Their skills instead reflect their personality, so that Aerith, the gentle flower girl from the slums, plays the healer role, while Tifa, the sassy bartender with physics-defying breasts, plays the monk.[31]

In *Mass Effect*, skill sets are tied to racialized others who make up the player's squad, a mechanic that educates players to keep their teammates within an imposed racial harmony as a means of deriving their militaristic abilities. The Asari, for example, are a mono-gender race distinctly feminine in appearance who are known for their elegance, diplomacy, and talent with biotics (a type of genetic magic). The Asari teammate Samara, likewise, will no longer be in the team if the player makes decisions that disrespects cultural differences. In contrast, Grunt, a fierce Krogan with a natural desire for violence, will die in a suicide mission if the player does not earn his loyalty by acting too weak or showing too much kindness. All the supporting characters, restricted as they are to their culturally determined world, feature a great deal of psychological depth that is "established through elaborate backstories, as well as character growth and development."[32] These backstories sway the players to empathize with their teammates, but always with the goal of incorporating their cultural skill sets into a military project. This need to impose racial harmony can sometimes seem pedantic, as players typically earn "renegade points" by showing cultural intolerance and earn "paragon points" when they choose tolerant dialogue choices. As Tom Bissell writes in a parenthetical aside: "The degree to which you can inflame or dampen alien racism among your own crew is one of *Mass Effect*'s most interesting quandaries. I almost always inflamed it—and felt enjoyably bad in doing so."[33] Expanding upon this colonial view of race, Jordan Youngblood writes that *Mass Effect* games see both race and queerness through a sense of utility, as attributes to be discarded when no longer of use.[34] *Mass Effect* does not play with difference so much as place the player in a position to evaluate and manage ethnicized and queer others, challenging players to optimize their forms of difference for military deployment.

The stakes of these racial and queer divisions are militaristic just as much as they are labor oriented. While racialized divisions of labor are self-evident within the everyday social structure, the allegorization in role play of a militaristic (battle-oriented) division of labor reflects the tactical deployment of black, Native American, and Asian soldier units and brigades in the Civil War, World Wars I and II, and the War on Terror. We see contemporary examples within the US military's use of Arabic translators and cultural diplomats, who are invested with communication skill sets that mark them as both necessary and high risk. As Vicente Rafael has observed, Arabic translators have been essential for fighting insurgents, but they are "also feared as potential insurgents themselves," and in times of war they have been "the only ones searched within the base . . . forbidden to carry cell phones and cameras, send email, play video games, and even swim in the pool."[35] Thuy Linh Nguyen Tu similarly argues that race has functioned in the military within a "militaristic multiculturalism" by equipping the skin itself with environment-ready skill sets.[36] Here racialized bodies are deployed as units with natural abilities to combat the environment (the harsh sun) and biological disease, thus legitimating the organization of bodies that keep some more vulnerable to death.[37] Unlike in the hero-focused games of chapter one, the allegorization of race and nation in role-playing games is allegorical rather than explicit or campy, yet its political meanings are expressed in encouraging players to manage their teammates, choosing which characters will be strung along and which are disposable.

Freedom (Wrex on Virmire)

The merging of the racial/national allegories of Japanese role-playing games with the choice-based multiracial training of American role-playing games birthed the contemporary role-playing game as essentially the educative imperial form par excellence. The influences of Japanese RPGs as allegorical tales are visible in American role-playing games since the 2000s, while the 1990s "American brand" of role play reflects the open world feel of what are now called CRPGs (computer role-playing games or classical role-playing games). These games include *Fallout* and *Fallout 2, Planescape Torment, Icewind Dale,* and BioWare's first role-playing game, *Baldur's Gate.* CRPGs were heavily influenced by (or outright copies of) tabletop role-playing games of the 1980s like Dungeons and Dragons, as well as the interactive fiction made popular among early computer users (*The Hitchhiker's Guide to the Galaxy*), and the popularity of chatroom role playing in the early 1990s. CRPGs mirrored these other genres' multidirectional stories and their freedom to manipulate objects or to do harm to nearly all characters, even those crucial to the story. In such games, discussions with nonplayable characters greatly affect the player's story experience, making each decision branch off into separate and unique playthroughs. For these games, the player's avatar is not so much character but a role being played via a collaborative creative process, one partially determined by the story and partially at the player's behest.

As Chun argues, the digital age has brought on a conflation of freedom with control, so being able to tame or merely navigate Asiatic spaces becomes definitive of freedom. This is a freedom produced through the paranoia of being dominated by Asiatic technology, the fear of becoming like Asians. The ability to control and manage ethnic others produces freedom as "the result of our decisions" rather than the larger structural and imperial forces that "make our decisions possible."[38] Similarly, Alexander Galloway has written of games as solving "the problem of political control" through their "political transparency," which makes the practice and value of control "coterminous with the entire game."[39] One of BioWare's most celebrated refinements on the role-playing genre was to emphasize player control within a calculated moral compass, integrating the decision-making aspect of CRPGs by placing the player on a moral journey to tame otherness—the otherness of unknown lands (*Dragon Age*), the otherness of Asia itself (*Jade Empire*).[40] Moral problems in BioWare games often function around dualistic concepts like "community" versus "individual" (*Star Wars: Knights of the Old Republic*, 2003), or "peaceful" versus "aggressive" (*Jade Empire*, 2005). Yet these "good" and "evil" stand-ins can overlap considerably, as both sides can encourage lying, murder, and destruction, depending on the context. The player exercises freedom by making ethical decisions that help control the story, shifting the plot alongside the player's appearance, strength, and attributes, and by which teammates they can keep along the way. If the player can earn a teammate's loyalty, he can also unlock their hidden abilities ("squad bonuses" in *Mass Effect*). The player's goal then is not merely to strategically maneuver these teammates against an enemy (as with liberal tolerance) but also to exercise dominance over their ethnicized teammates by appeasing, threatening, or systemically and ideologically controlling them—a freedom of control that is dependent upon the other's *unfreedom*.[41]

In a particularly memorable scene from the first *Mass Effect*, the player must convince the team's strongest member, the aforementioned Krogan named Wrex, to accept that the squad will destroy a base containing a cure to the genophage, a biological weapon that has effectively made Krogan females sterile, only allowing life to one out of a thousand stillborns. The Krogans are an extremely strong and hotheaded race, and Wrex, the most "civilized" Krogan, still must be managed as a potentially violent and irrational savage. As Wrex tells the player (playing the human protagonist, Shepard):

> WREX: Saren created a cure for my people. You want to destroy it. Help me out here, Shepard. The lines between friend and foe are getting a little blurry from where I stand.[42]

Players have several options: they can kill Wrex, intimidate him into submission, or convince him that destroying the cure is in fact in his people's interest, since the person who created it (Saren) only seeks to control the Krogan. Most likely, the player will kill Wrex, as the other options are only available through the player's deep investment in either paragon or renegade decisions. Upon killing Wrex, Shepard says, "He just wasn't going to listen to reason" (1:30). The player here role plays a position that devalues the ethnicized alien's own point of view over Shepard's universalist "reason," positioning the player as a console cowboy responsible for navigating and managing racial difference. But the player is given choices in *how* she presents this argument to Wrex. If the player is too arrogant or heartless, Wrex will react violently, and the player will lose the strongest character on her team just before facing the game's most difficult enemies. In this scene, Wrex can be killed in the name of "reason," or he can be convinced to come along and see "reason" over his own divisive interests. Never, however, can the player choose to rescue the cure and help keep Wrex's people from going extinct.

In the context of the continuous War on Terror, Wrex seems to resemble the most extreme element in the political and moral alliances of Shepard's squad. As a Krogan whose people are known for aggressive violence (selected and bred that way by another race), his aggressive and strength-driven role inserts him easily into the role of the imperial other, what Jasbir Puar and Amit Rai (2002) have called the "terrorist-monster," a figure who "has become both a monster to be quarantined and an individual to be corrected."[43] The terrorist-monster associated with extreme intolerance or an absence of reason produces the American as a "docile patriot," which, in terms of multiculturalism, is the tolerant individual who seeks not to "rock the boat," and for whom racism is most apparent in individual language and speech rather than in resistance to American imperial projects abroad. As the squad's strongest member, Wrex's raw aggression signifies a military tool that, outside of combat, must be contained and tolerated. His casual in-game dialogue, which only appears when the player includes Wrex in his squad, reveals a complex yet aggressive personality, as he exposes the player's own position as a manager of ethnicized bodies by delivering what the blogger Alex calls "withering smackdowns of ignorant privilege" that "teach[es] the player about privilege."[44] Wrex openly calls the protagonist ignorant of his people's suffering while refusing to play cultural ambassador for the other human teammate, Kaiden:

KAIDEN: I haven't spent much time with Krogan before, Wrex, and I have to say, you're not what I expected.

WREX: Right. Because you humans have a wide range of cultures and attitudes, but Krogan all think and act exactly alike.

Wrex's cynical attitude toward the cultural knowledge that the player seeks from him mirrors conversations of racial authenticity and knowledge in the United States, making his life-or-death conflict over the genophage especially impactful. As Tom Bissell notes, "I had grown immensely fond of the aggrieved [Wrex], and each time a new conversation option appeared [in Wrex's death scene] I felt a noose of real dramatic concern tighten."[45] After killing Wrex, Bissell opines that

I reloaded my last saved game and tried again. Once more, my friend and teammate took a bullet for his trouble. In my bewilderment I pressed on, and when the menu for squad selection came up, the slot for the dead character was now a darkened silhouette. It seemed as stark and inarguably final as a tombstone.

As Bissell suggests, *Mass Effect*'s casual dialogue provides an intimate emotional investment in Wrex, who would otherwise be understood as mere weaponized force. This virtual intimacy also exposes the privileged position of the player as the squad's multiculturalist manager (the aptly named Shepard), as Wrex's gameplay persona seeks to disrupt Shepard's managerial position. David Simkins (2008) has pointed out that reflection of the player's position is integral to an RPG because such games involve "performing a socially defined position or status with its associated duties and functions."[46] Role-playing gamers have called this the "bleed effect," where the personalities encouraged in character influence (or bleed into) the player's real-life decisions, and vice versa.

As the leader of a multicultural team, players of *Mass Effect* practice tolerance and multicultural acceptance but only with the presumption that it will reward them with the squadmate's specialized labor. Performing this role rewards the player with the pleasures of control and freedom associated with the "console cowboy," as accepting it means obtaining what the designer and scholar Nicole Lazzaro calls "fiero," "the ultimate game emotion" (in Italian, "personal triumph over adversity").[47] Lazzaro explores "fiero" as the most powerful emotion unique to gameplay, experienced when players are "overcoming difficult obstacles,

[and] players raise their arms over their heads."[48] This emotion is especially prominent in RPGs, where challenging battles follow hours of emotional investment in the game's story and supporting characters.[49] In killing Wrex, the game's pointed narrative of remorse is sharpened by the absence of fiero, an absence created not because the player failed to complete a mission but because he is unable to exercise his freedom (as control) over the terrorist-monster, Wrex. Fiero, read as a psychological affect meant to entice players along to game victory, is inextricable from the racial allegories and ethical decisions of role-playing games, where the game's mission to win the war is often overshadowed by the emotional bonds the player feels for her teammates.

The player's role as a free agent exercising control over teammates can come into direct conflict with the intimacy he can feel for them, which is why killing Wrex remains one of the most emotionally charged moments in all of gaming. Whereas the tear-jerking death of Aerith in *Final Fantasy VII* can never be changed, the loss of Wrex in *Mass Effect* is disquieting because it could have gone differently, if only the player had been skillful enough to earn greater freedom and control (saving Wrex is a very unlikely outcome unless decisions are well calculated beforehand). The game, however, cheapens this death and keeps it from becoming a truly self-reflective moment, as it rationalizes the killing by foregrounding players' higher mode of civilization, since their goal is to "develop" teammates into their true militaristic potential.[50] In the life-or-death conversation with Wrex concerning the genophage, the ethical dilemmas proposed by the game's dialogue wheel are offered to the player in the form of paraphrases catered to the player's feelings.[51] When Wrex first seeks Shepard's understanding, the player can select "not my problem," which will cause Shepard to say: "This has to be done. Saren's the enemy, not me." The player's most self-serving option, "not my problem," becomes interpreted as if it were a universalist position: "this has to be done." In the second wheel, the player can choose "I don't have time for this," another self-serving position, which the paraphrase system reinterprets as "I don't care what your personal feelings are. This base gets destroyed!" The self-interested prompts ("I don't have time for this") are repeatedly interpreted into universal positions, in effect marking the other, Wrex, as someone overburdened by his "personal feelings" (see Figure 3.1). Despite the player's intentions in these dialogue wheels,

Figure 3.1. The dialogue wheel in *Mass Effect* (Wrex and Shepard). Screenshot from Boba1911, "Mass Effect—Ashley Williams Kills Wrex," *YouTube*, August 16, 2009, www.youtube.com/watch?v=lHLhvRXhlDE&t=2s, 1:27.

the game only gives clumsy nods to ethical depth and instead taps into the pervasive universalism that sees Wrex as an ethnic other plagued by his own interests, a brute whose violent passions must be kept in line (or on the battlefield).

The Egalitarian

The progressive ideals of role-playing games as an educational tool for reproducing values of liberal tolerance through moral decision-making and in-depth characterization have, since the economic recession of 2007, recently been enhanced to include an egalitarian form of consumerism that offers an alternative to the exploitative conditions of factory work. After the 2007–08 recession, game discourses began to disavow the production process of information technology by comparing virtual world commodities with "real" commodities like textiles and oil. As Lisa Nakamura has argued, electronic manufacture has a great deal in common with textile industries, as it similarly relies on fetishizations of foreign-produced products designed by Western artists.[52] Yet electronic products are even further distanced from consumers than textiles, as their "beauty" comes not from touchable textiles but from the software of virtual commodities. Imagined as merely bits of code, these commodities are envisioned as part of a streamlined process where an artistic innovator merely uploads coded product into the virtual realm, allowing players to forgo any guilt that might exist in real garment processing.

The egalitarian narrative of games sees the exploitation of textile manufacturing as being replaced by the nonexploitative industry of virtual fashion, which emerges with massive multiplayer online role-playing games (MMORPGs) like *World of Warcraft*, *Guild Wars*, and BioWare's own *Star Wars: The Old Republic*. These games encourage players to dress their avatar in virtual clothing while maintaining an innocence that separates them from the expensive and exploitative world of fashion. If a gamer purchases a Louis Vuitton bag for her avatar, the symbols of the virtual image attract a different set of meanings than toting a real Louis Vuitton purse, even if both items are of the same monetary value. The virtual item is free of the baggage of the imperial anxiety that the real bag might represent to more ethically minded audiences. While some might find the virtual bag silly, few would consider how the bag—or how the sleek device they are viewing the bag on—was produced through a transnational exploitative process. When comparing the real thing to the virtual item, the first injunction is to praise the virtual item as a symbol reflecting the free and diverse virtual world through which it is rendered. Among the telepresence of other role players, players are free to create new selves within the game's racialized and gendered skill sets (healing, homemaking, combat, or driving cars, ships, and helicopters) and in purchasing virtual clothing. The social world of online games is constructed as egalitarian through the presumption that thousands of virtual garments are free from the structures of global capitalism that real commodities represent.

The logic of egalitarian play makes players themselves feel responsible for the manufacturing of digital items, as the game forces them to enact the manufacturing process. In my playthrough of the MMORPG *Guild Wars 2*, I encountered virtual fashion not as exploitative factory work but as a traditional, premodern craft, one that demanded I spend hours "grinding" (earning in-game gold) for virtual objects. The labor process was laid out from the very beginning: I spent hours gathering raw materials, then mining and chopping to store them in my backpack;

then I traveled vast distances to a city to find guilds and teachers to help me refine the items; then I built up my skill tree to bind, sew, and dye my new garments. Many hours passed before I could wear my first piece of clothing: a bust of armor made from wool and cotton scraps that resembled a child's attempt to cut a dress out of a burlap sack. Even so, I could sell this product—a result of hours of labor—for real-world money (mere pennies). This process of gaining the item through my own in-game labor marked me as the worker, disavowing the real labor and raw material mining that information technology necessitates. The arduous process of in-game grinding formed my ethical identity so that the hours spent "earning" the virtual item made me feel like I had produced something of real-world value. Rather than feel alienated from a commodity, I became intimate with the virtual object I had "created," as it was invested with my own personal experience of producing it, and it was mine.

In many ways, the egalitarian ideals of MMORPGs have emerged as a response to the failure of capitalism to bring any semblance of economic equality. After the 2007 economic recession, virtual commodities began to insert their way into the mainstream as a popular substitute to capitalism's massive wealth gap and thus shape information technology as a paradoxically noncapitalist, or "good capitalist" form. This depiction complements ideals of liberal tolerance and freedom as digital commodities motivate gamers to shape their avatars' bodies to transcend racial, gender, sexual, and other social norms found in real-life commodities. Virtual fashions are then embraced as a means for experimental play rather than for art or beauty. With a seemingly infinite amount of clothing to choose from, players are free to experiment, and they can establish personal connections with new fashions after dozens of hours of earning them.[53] Role players can produce or purchase virtual clothing that defies gravity and clothes that perfectly mimic the latest fashions because they are designed by real fashion designers.[54] In this narrative, anyone can wear the latest fashions without the potential guilt of not quite knowing where the clothing came from.

The narrative that tethers virtual fashion to ethical notions of a world without sweatshops has produced virtual goods as the primary method of gaining profit for many video game companies. Popular games like *Second Life* and hundreds of casual games can be downloaded

completely for free ("free-to-play"), making companies seem benevolent since they only ask for payments through optional microtransactions (defined as transactions less than twelve dollars).[55] As Jesper Juul
points out, microtransactions have become more profitable for casual
game companies because their players "[do] not think of themselves as
playing video games (even though they clearly [are])."[56] For the most
part, gaming communities have celebrated this turn in gaming, and
MMORPGs like *Lord of the Rings Online* and *Star Wars: The Old Republic* have abandoned monthly subscriptions to only charge for optional
in-game purchases. So long as the ability to purchase in-game content
is restricted to the "merely cosmetic," gamers seem to uniformly hail
this shift in payment form.[57] Indeed, this narrative of virtual fashion has
been so successful that it diverts attention away from the possibilities
of producing real-world fashion *without* the use of sweatshops, and in
turn, it has not decreased the revenue of any major clothing distributor
(Zara, H&M, The Gap). This ethical advantage of virtual goods warrants
some virtual items to carry the same value or to be even more expensive
than the real garment, setting a high price for ethical affiliation.[58]

The utopian potentials of role playing have spread onto social media
networks, whose companies have capitalized on the trend in virtual
commodities by encouraging users to replace their profile images with
avatars, a strategy that has been most successful in Asia, where the social
networking service Tencent QQ (known simply as QQ) generated over
$100 million in a single quarter (2007), with over 65 percent of revenue
coming from the purchase of virtual items.[59] These virtual items became
more expensive as more users joined the service, as any item purchased
carried the potential to be seen by any of the 800 million active QQ
accounts. Similarly, in 2007 the Finnish social networking company,
Habbo Hotel, made 90 percent of their $60 million revenue from vir-
tual goods, while the American social network Gaia Online employed
"3 people whose sole job it is to open snail mail envelopes full of cash
that people send in for virtual goods."[60] While most virtual commodities are sold through microtransactions, intense or hardcore gamers
have turned from "peacocks" to "whales" by purchasing cosmetic items
within the hundreds or thousands of dollars range. The most expensive
cosmetic item ever sold—an ethereal flame pink War Dog courier—was
for the male-dominated strategy game *Dota 2*, for $38,000.[61] Since *Dota*

2 is billed as a balanced competitive game, the $38,000 War Dog costume is entirely cosmetic, and it merely changes the appearance of a donkey courier that transports goods to players engaged in combat.

The temptation to purchase virtual clothing from in-game auction houses may seem like an amusing subculture to most, but to many gamers the system that combines free-to-play games with cosmetic microtransactions demonstrates an egalitarian, postracial, postgendered gaming utopia, where anyone can play any game for free, so long as those who have money volunteer to pay for cosmetic items (and ultimately pay for everyone else). This business model became known as "freemium," a combination of the words "free" and "premium," where games would be provided free of charge, while microtransactions (known as premiums) were only for virtual goods. Paul Tassi at *Forbes* made his stark gratitude for the tech industry explicit when he wrote that "games who focus their microtransactions on cosmetic upgrades with literally no impact on gameplay are the golden standard."[62] Tassi went on to write that in the freemium game *League of Legends*, "the only thing locked behind a paywall are cosmetic upgrades for your characters which have no bearing on gameplay, and they're bought for fun, for vanity, or just to say job well done to a company who has given you a great game for free."[63] Like many gamers, Tassi interprets the free-to-play freemium system as a symbol of the benevolence of the game company, so that paying for virtual fashion items becomes a matter of showing one's gratitude toward a benevolent host of designers and programmers, effectively bolstering egalitarian narratives of information technology while erasing the real labor of Asian factory hands.

Much has been written about how video games induce feelings of guilt upon players; how players may find themselves giddily shooting down a virtual animal, only to gasp in horror when they realize that the deed was far more traumatic than it appeared when the option came in a clickable bubble on their screen. Yet games also have the power to alleviate guilt, to absolve the players, to depict their participation in information technology as a progressive step into a postracist, postcapitalist, and posttotalitarian future. In the next section, I will explore the potentials of role playing not in reestablishing the utopian ideals of the open world empire but as a means of understanding ourselves in relation to others. Read within an *ars erotica*, role play inhibits the tolerant, free, and egalitarian futures that games promise and refuses to suture anxieties concerning the player's position as both consumer and as citizen of the Global North. As Chun writes, the console cowboy's ability to tame Asiatic technology permits audiences to experience the pleasure of control over Asia: of "being somewhat overwhelmed, but ultimately jacked in."[64] If the pleasure of playing the console cowboy "usually compensates for a lack of mastery," then can we find similar pleasures in being mastered over, in being subjected to Asiatic technology rather than wrangling ourselves over it?

Aphrodisia

Celebrations of role-playing games as educating audiences in liberal tolerance, freedom, and egalitarianism see the act of role playing as an extension of real life, where we are expected to make choices that "teach us" by showing us the consequences of our actions. These celebrations dismiss how role playing itself overlaps with erotic forms of sexual role play and provides an outlet for nonnormative sexual practices.[65] What if we chose to kill Wrex not because he "wouldn't listen to reason," but because doing so gave us a perverse pleasure? The easy dismissal (or outright unthinkability) of the erotic forms of role play maintains role playing as a demonstration of digital utopia, disavowing the production process and erotic relationships to the Asiatic. This separation of role play from the erotic also presumes that, like in film and literature, audiences typically identify with the protagonists, whereas for many gamers, connecting to media characters is not about inhabiting an identity but about the feelings, joys, and pleasures one can experience when playing a role.[66] Role play can thus be a transgressive form of play not because it asks the player to inhabit an ethical identity but because it reveals the erotic dimensions of domination within a rule-bound space of consent whose boundaries can bend but never snap, lest the role play break its kinky fantasy.

Unlike the "magic circle" or even conceptions of "camp," role play and other forms of kink like sadomasochism do not presume an equality among participants but exaggerate and play upon the power differences among consensual players. In *Techniques of Pleasure*, Margot Weiss argues that sexual practices like role play and BSDM are not "free from social regulation," nor do they characterize rebellion or unbound intimacy, but operate as circuits "between realms that are imagined as isolated and opposed," particularly "those conceptualized as subjective or private, and those understood as social or economic."[67] To understand the multiple forms of transgression and regulation that sadomasochism can take, Amber Jamilla Musser argues in *Sensational Flesh* that we must see such practices not as inherently resistant but as relational and contingent, as describing "a plethora of relationships" that can reveal "a series of unexpected sensational affinities."[68] Ariane Cruz provides one such example in *The Color of Kink* when she argues that role play in BDSM communities can illuminate "touchy" subjects that create spaces where forms like "race play—a BDSM practice that explicitly plays with race" can become permissible, therapeutic, and revealing of real racial anxieties.[69] By refusing the "don't go there" injunction of everyday encounter, role playing can bandy about racial and sexual transgressions so long as they are framed as consensual, and they thus form a perverse magic circle that presumes not universality but what Cruz calls "racial-sexual alterity" or "a way to fuck and fuck with racism."[70] Online role play can expose the "fabrications of race" because it recognizes "a pleasure in their enactment" that asks players to negotiate pleasures openly construed through others. Role play is a return, in other words, to the "problematics" of the *ars erotica*, to the questions not about how one identifies but how one performs pleasure as ethical beings.

In his *History of Sexuality*, Michel Foucault explores *ars erotica* as a form of ethical engagement with others and the self, calling it an "arts of existence" or "arts of the self." *Ars erotica* defines an "ethics of sexual austerity" that does not concern what one should or should not take pleasure in but *how* one ethically takes pleasure in erotic acts when they are free to "exercise their rights, their power, their authority, and their liberty: in the practices of pleasure that were not frowned upon . . . [which were] accepted, commonly maintained, and even prized."[71] These arts of existence do not concern the prohibition of sexual acts but the morally ambivalent practices that still necessitate an ethical "problematization" because there is always, within every erotic act, the presumption that one's pleasure remains situated within a power relationship with someone else. The problems proposed in *ars erotica* are not about restricting pleasures and sexual acts but about "the right use . . . prudence, reflection, and calculation in the way one distributed and controlled his acts." The ethical problem is not within feeling or not feeling pleasure but upon whom pleasure depends, under what circumstances, and the conditions upon which pleasure manifests from fantasy into action. Foucault called this "scene" of relationships the *aphrodisia,* an area "wider" than contemporary notions of sexuality.[72] *Aphrodisia* calls attention not to the morals or health dangers of pleasurable acts but to their "dynamics," to "the activity they manifested."[73] Foucault's most succinct definition of *aphrodisia* comes at the end of volume 2:

> sexual behavior was constituted, in Greek thought, as a domain of ethical practice in the form of the *aphrodisia,* of pleasurable acts situated in an agonistic field of forces difficult to control. In order to take the form of a conduct that was rationally and morally admissible, these acts required a strategy of moderation and timing, of quantity and opportunity; and this strategy aimed at an exact self-mastery—as its culmination and consummation—whereby the subject would be "stronger than himself" even in the power that he exercised over others.[74]

Aphrodisia constitutes pleasurable acts within a broader context, an "agonistic field of forces difficult to control," which include the desires that give rise to the act, the pleasure that occasions desire, and the other people implicated in the pleasure act. All of these together form *aphrodisia,* the problematized form of sexuality textured within scenes of power, the "forces" facilitating desire and pleasure.

As Ann Stoler has argued, Foucault's intention in *History of Sexuality* was to trace the ethical networks of empire and to question how empire was made possible through "the affirmation of bourgeois bodies."[75] Role play is a crucial component within the practice of *aphrodisia,* as it rejects such affirmations of the self to practice "adjustment between social roles and sexual roles."[76] Through an experiential shuffling of various roles of domination and subjugation, one learns to master oneself by recognizing times when one's pleasures are pitted within unethical situations. Mastery emerges through one's ability to play within roles, knowing also how to *deny* oneself pleasure even when that pleasure is central to one's identity. This mastery is gained through practice and through a greater awareness of erotic situations, so that reciprocity, willingness (consent), and self-awareness remain ethical problems that every pleasure-seeking subject must unravel. One comprehends roles of power by enacting them; one understands one's own domination within roles of "master" and "subject;" one experiments; one begins to take some accounting of the various modes of subjection and domination. Sex acts are not made ethical by the nature of the acts themselves. This is, for Foucault, a mere element in ethical conduct. The act can be deemed ethical only after the subject "decides on a certain mode of being that will serve as his moral goal. And this requires him to act upon himself, to monitor, test, improve, and transform himself."[77] Foucault calls *aphrodisia* "monistic" in that it is all inclusive and does not seek to differentiate among pleasure, desire, object, and act, but sees them all within the larger stage and scene of power.[78]

Role Play as a Way of Life

It is good to remember always that playing is itself a therapy.
—D. W. Winnicott, *Playing and Reality*

Foucault's concept of *aphrodisia* reveals a pedagogical process in role play that contrasts the celebration of role-playing games as a form of liberal education. In *Friendship as a Way of Life*, Tim Roach writes that Foucault formulated *aphrodisia* as a form of self-care that was only focused on developing the self for the purposes of being better outwardly focused.[79] Self-care was only "self" insofar as one could look beyond her immediate relations and pleasures to the distant effects of erotic acts: to the future growth of a younger partner, to the impact upon one's own family and reputation, to the humanity of the slave, to how one will live with one's own unethical actions. It was not "an egoistic or resigned retreat into individualism . . . but a social practice" formed through "exercises of self-discipline."[80] One contemporary "exercise" in self-care is erotic role playing, where players inhabit roles of varying power relations, and power is "mobile, shared, or routed between practitioners during play."[81] These roles, taken playfully and with consent, are practiced, experimented upon, and mastered, making the player hyperaware of her own performance until she can perform it casually, like riding a bike.

As Mattie Brice, designer of *Mainichi*, writes in the *Queer Game Studies* anthology, video games can use the power dynamics in kink practices of role playing and BDSM to challenge the "faux egalitarianism" of mainstream society by playing roles that "deeply feel these contexts in their bodies."[82] Arguing against the "contextless play" of "empathy games" that present identities for audiences to jump in and out of, Brice emphasizes kink's ability to offer "a type of play design that deeply confronts life contexts" by showing "bodies and minds in codependent situational contexts based completely on the participants' relationship with real life."[83] As with *aphrodisia*, games can provide an honest engagement with our contexts that exposes the power dynamics at work within our pleasures. Kink practices of gaining consent, improvisational scene-making, and aftercare, allow players to see the multiple contexts that make their pleasures possible and to reflect upon their relations with those who make, manufacture, and transport the very object providing pleasure.

In order to show how the playful scene of online role playing enacts forms of *aphrodisia*, I focus here on my own role play experience in the chatroom smartphone app, "Geeking,"[84] as a form of self-care in three aspects: as anonymous partners, as impersonal lovers, and as power players.

Anonymity

Self-care experiences of role play, for Foucault, depend upon anonymity, so that both parties do not rely on their default social identities so much as the roles that they undertake in relationship to each other when seeking pleasure. As Roach writes, "Anonymous sex . . . allows subjects to free themselves from the shackles of identity and relate to one another in ways that run counter to the modern demand for self knowledge."[85] Unlike an identity, a "role" is not meant to be understood as a sole unity but conjures its partnered opposite (the dominating or the subjugated). The *identity* of a "teacher" would imply teacherly attributes incorporable into a managerial system: educated, trained, certified, of the intellectual class. But to *play* "teacher" *as a role* elicits not a characterization but a relationship with its partnered opposite, "student," a relationship defined by ethical conduct and reciprocal pleasure. Role playing experiments with these roles and finds their points of transgression, what taboos bend and which ones break, with the presumption that the dominating role ("teacher," "doctor," "bourgeois," "captain," "human") and subjugated role ("student," "patient," "housekeeper," "soldier," "alien") are paired for the sole purpose of testing (and teasing) their implicit boundaries. In so doing, role play emerges as a practice of *ars erotica*, an "arts of existence," that molds one's ethical conduct. Role playing is crucial for scrutinizing one's own ethical conduct, as *aphrodisia* cannot be governed by universal and venerable guidelines because every situation deserves its own ethical reflections. Indeed, anonymity and the emphasis of roles over identities transforms pleasure practices into an ethics mindful of the greater context of pleasurable acts and experiences.

Anonymity is a condition of online role playing, the ability to create and play a role without others evaluating the contradictions between a "true" self and an invented persona. Anonymity serves the newcomer. Five seconds into a chatroom called "Beastality Chat" on the chat program Geeking, I received three invites to private sex plays. "Want to get pervy?" said one message. "Into nekocats?" said another. I snubbed them and scanned the room's posts for a role-play partner, a muse who could convey myself better than myself. After nearly an hour of voyeuristic lurking, I found a post that charmed me into an anonymous person's universe:

ROSE LUNARIA: *Sits silent, with a herding pressure in her heart.*

Though brief, the sentence was just strong enough to catch me in its gravity, pulling me into a new role. I scanned their profile:

Name: Lunaria
Age: 18
Special: fire type
Sexuality: bi
Gender: female
Personality: bubbly very childish and is chill until u annoy her then it burns
Can turn into fire breathing dragon

The profile list does not offer knowledge about the other person but entices me to respond to their orientations and styles, whether I seek to charm her up (and earn her "bubbly" self) or to provoke her (and feel how "it burns"). This self-description in mind, I launched an opening salvo of fine-tuned words into the chatroom, hoping to lure the other player with my own supplications.

> KAWIKAG: You could recognize Kawika creeping open the tavern door, holding the bracelet's silver chain to keep those crystal charms from announcing a new presence. From the small purview beneath a sunhat, finds a table and, kicking legs up, sifts through a newspaper kept rolled up in a left sleeve, letting the sweat-mixed print rub off on fingers.

After a brief writerly high from spinning a capably invitational post, I awaited the chance to partner up with an anonymous writer and clash erotic talents.[86] They responded:

> ROSE LUNARIA: *Cheeks sunk with the thoughtfully casual pucker of glossy, vemon-stung [sic] lips, silent, eyes squinting down at @KawikaG as if she couldn't quite see words to describe her.*

A shot, a cannonball in my direction. Her request to "see words" pushed me deeper into my role, where I prepared the next tease. Game on.

Impersonality

Anonymity leads to the second way that video game role playing mirrors exercises of *aphrodisia*: the impersonal relationships formed by distinguishing the anonymous self from the projected role. In this play, Rose Lunaria and myself (as KawikaG) care for each other as impersonal partners "with which one maintains a rapport of distance and respect."[87] For Foucault, the subject of self-care forms a detached and disciplined relationship with the self, "not seeking its secret truth, but bringing it into existence according to aesthetic and ethical guidelines."[88] Like anonymity, detachment from the self is part of the condition of role play, separating one's "soul self" (as Foucault calls it), who plays the part of judge, from their "acting self," who plays the defender.[89] In the role-playing chatroom, Rose Lunaria's profile already suggests an art of the impersonalized self with explicit rules and boundaries for play (sexual preference, preferred gender and age, veiled threats not to annoy her). Her "soul" self, the self sitting at the computer desk, is referred to in chatroom lingo as the "mun," short for "mundane," a name that highlights how unapologetically role-focused role play is. I, the "soul" I, am only referred to via my character ("Kawika's mun"), splitting my soul-self of the "mun" from the acting-self of my "role," Kawika. This name, "Kawika," is the name my mother wanted for me when I was born, and in role play, whether in games or chatrooms or in the bedroom, I imagine Kawika as gender nonbinary, an effeminate man and simultaneously a masculine woman. In games that sanction it, I transform this role (often seen as a "trap") into an androgynous being whose biology I never feel necessary to reveal as male, female, or even queer. To play with me means playing along with this obscurity.

Role playing operates as a means of learning power over oneself, of mastering new forms within boundaries that we dictate. It splits the self, pluralizes the self, not with an immediate "jouissance" but in a slow play of experiment, reflection, and mastery that produces new techniques of self-awareness. The "freedom" of the role-playing scene emerges not as a way to control others but as a condition created by the consent one derives from others, in the mutual agreements of playing *with* others rather than deploying them for personal gain. My role as Kawika teases transgressive pleasures but also portends my own conduct as one unlike Kawika—one who is routinely read as a heterosexual, cis-gendered, married father. Indeed, this is also how the games journalist Gita Jackson sees herself playing Rihanna in every role-playing game.[90] Jackson's Rihanna role comes from her desire to "make myself as myself" but also in being unable to play as her own name, her own unpresentable mixed race hair, and her own sensitive, vulnerable persona. In other words, for Jackson to role play *herself* in the gameworld would be a drag (just as playing the self in the real world is often drag). In the role of Rihanna, Jackson can be impersonal toward others as well as herself, able to examine herself—her soul-self and acting-self—as seeking forms of queer pleasure outside of her married life. The friendships forged through impersonality intimately relate to external selves, or in Lacan's language, they are relationships of *extimacy*—intimacy through lies, through the superficial, through the not-knowing—an intimacy that does not ask the other to reveal themselves, to "come out of the closet" or to be "authentic," but revels in their obscurity by forming reciprocal roles.[91]

Power Play

The anonymity and impersonal relationships of role playing create an equalized setting for the purposes of playing dominant and subjugated roles. As with bedroom role play, even its costumes, on a basic level, upset or inflate power dynamics. Yet the costume itself remains a symbol of its artificial suspension of everyday identities, since the role play ends as soon as the costume (or the game controller) is taken away.[92] Foucault compares the role playing of S&M to chess, where players form an inventive and experimental space by negotiating their roles as well as the rules that follow.[93] In the theater of violent and absurd video game role play, freedom lies within its accommodation, its mutual consent, and its comforts, even when, in action, it appears violent and dominating.

This focus on consent within power play is what the games writer Aevee Bee describes in her article "I Love My Untouchable Virtual Body."[94] Playing games as a "metaphor for interpersonal conflict," Bee constructs female avatars that she aspires to look like, but she also molds them within a conduct of fleeing, of escape, that urges her to find the right boundaries for touch and intimacy. She writes that in games, "everything is violent and wants to touch you, but if you are perfect, you will not be touched." Her playthroughs seek out the "perfect, flawless dodge," so that she can "be beautiful, and yet have nobody touch." This longing comes from her own experiences having transitioned and been assaulted by men who push through her defenses (with physical touching, long emails, verbal abuse). Her activity in games embodies characters who have "the simple power of getting to decide whether or not you are allowed to come in and touch her," and who "controls the conditions of touch."

After two hours of playing with Rose Lunaria's mun, I also begin to retract from the previous conditions of power play, feeling the gravity in me disperse as she, or he, or they, grapple me into their world.

> ROSE LUNARIA: *Her stocking clad feet and lower legs—or what was visible of them from under her long, black dress—were dainty and*

voluptuous, a characteristic which wouldn't be so amiss to describe the woman herself. "I have no qualms with very slowly disrobing," turning back to @KawikaG, "I didn't catch your name, miss. But I'll dare, since you seem so tired, to imagine something to wake you. A show? Specifically, a lap dance, from you, to the lucky volunteer, me." Voice was sweet, dripping playful charisma, "But don't you think about touching me. I'm a exo-breeder, I can 'pregnate you just with my skin."

In role play, there's an ecstatic moment when the lunacy of the content meets the purity of the form, when the imagination of the mixed, cornucopia universe shocks with its boundless frontier (*"I'm a exo-breeder"*). My own boundaries here are pushed and prodded (I'm identified as "miss" though I've presented myself without gender). I'm pushed into this subordinate role (I'm tired, I do not "volunteer" myself to give a lap dance, I cannot touch). Time stops. Language ends. I am enchanted, bewitched, made an infant, only capable of faltering prose.

Rose Lunaria partners my role play through role experimentation, boundary testing (and teasing), and pleasure that does not disavow the power relations of sexual activity but revels in them by making them unavoidable (if I touch her, I will be "'pregnated"). Of course, these are all virtual, digitized, part of a game whose dire consequences are ephemeral. The three attributes of *aphrodisia*, anonymity, impersonality, and power play, cast role play not as a performance for oneself or for a passive crowd but as an erotic relationship with others that attends to the larger "agonistic field" of global empire. These perverse spaces carry the presence of others, all dressed, all dependent upon each other, either as real people or as nonplayable characters meant to garner empathy and intimate relations. It's a practice radically unlike a stage play and far more akin to a fantastic venture, sexual or otherwise, where one simply does not feel one's performance being watched, judged, or perhaps ridiculed by a passive audience. Taking all this into account recognizes role playing as an erotic activity—role play in the bedroom, in the clubs, as a social and erotic practice, because its audience is primarily other role players.

The erotic form of role play is not labeled as an educational tool for liberal tolerance, freedom, and egalitarian futures but as a characteristic that defines subcultures of anonymous perverts. Yet in its frivolity as mere pleasure, erotic role play pushes players to meditate on pleasure—what enables it, who is affected by it, and how it speaks to our roles within the imperial center. One can imagine the role one inhabits as one's "air," as Barthes called it in *Camera Lucida*: air is not one's identity nor one's soul but is "the expression, the look," that coincides with the self and can be seen through the way one acts, their "art of existence."[95] To role play is to be within a mask, but not our everyday masks of the selfie smile, the "don't look at me" grimace, the work costumes, the inoffensive makeup, the respectable other. Nor are we those mun(dane) people playing the game within the comfort of their home. Within the home we are naked, the "soul" self; within the world we are our transparent and calculated identity; within the game we can become air, air that develops over forty hours of habitually playing the same role until we feel comfortable in its skin.

"Air" can only appear after a long process of experimentation and practice. Imagine the pose a person takes in front of multiple camera shots: a smile in the first shot, a simple grin in the second shot; perhaps, ten shots later, she is looking bemused; then after twenty shots, she experiments, trying new poses never before attempted. By four hundred shots she is no longer performing, nor is she completely herself. This is the air of role play: aware of the other, yet comfortable (perhaps even more comfortable) in the other's presence. She has inhabited a role by making her own act of watching watchable. Here, no longer naked but no longer within given identity, one can flourish into air, enabled through the other's gaze to dwell within their relations.

Empire's Roles

I want to end this chapter just as it began, with a story. In the short story "Ms. Pac-Man Ruined My Gang Life," Hmong refugee writer Ka Vang describes Cindy, a Hmong American "gangsta girl" living in Minnesota who arms her all-girl gang with knives, hammers, and a gun in preparation to attack Mandy, a female Puerto Rican rival who "stole" Cindy's boyfriend, Tiny. Just before her confrontation with Mandy, Cindy becomes distracted by the arcade game *Ms. Pac-Man*: "I pretended the ghosts were Mandy and Tiny, and I was chomping them up to be stronger. Chomping away, first the cherries, strawberry, and then the banana, which meant I reached the highest level of the game."[96] The game offers a convenient distraction that soon becomes an obsession, as the competition for Tiny shifts to her competition to beat *Ms. Pac-Man*. When Mandy and Tiny appear, Cindy ignores them and turns "back to the machine, back to defeating *Ms. Pac-Man*, a truly worthy opponent."[97] The confrontation still ends in bloodshed, though not by Cindy's choice, yet her recourse to playing the role of Ms. Pac-Man even in the middle of a gang fight offers her a momentary space of reflection, where she is able to realize her own capture within the "gangsta girl" persona. Cindy thinks, "The role of being a gangsta girl was becoming too narrow for all that I wanted to do with my life."[98] Though *Ms. Pac-Man* is not characterized as a role-playing game, Cindy's momentary pleasure in inhabiting the role of Ms. Pac-Man convinces her to leave her own "gangsta girl" role, one that she realizes is imbricated with a larger social context. Tiny, Cindy's ex-boyfriend, is a Khmer refugee whose father was killed by the Khmer Rouge for wearing glasses, while Mandy's presence in the poverty-stricken neighborhood is also made possible by the routes of American empire. The role of "gangsta girl" that Cindy has been performing was produced through the wider context of imperial power. Even if the role of "gangsta girl"—like the role of Ms. Pac-Man—can make Cindy feel stronger, it's a strength only made possible through the transmission of imperial violence onto others.

As with Cindy's self-reflections of her own desire to play *Ms. Pac-Man*, the dynamic and improvised power play of role playing challenges us to observe how our own roles are produced and how they relate to those around us, near and far. If the trick of identity is that identities are too often seen in isolation, *aphrodisia* encourages us to think in terms of roles that respond to others and are in turn responded to by others. *Aphrodisia* extends erotic relations to those distanced from us, even unseen factory workers who undeniably make up our erotic scene. If the exploitation of the garment factory is enabled by the mechanism of distance—where the consumer and producer are literally an ocean apart[99]—then information technology is doubly distanced, first through the literal distance of space, and second through the distance of the virtual objects themselves, which seem to lack any need for material production processes. The pleasure one experiences from the game implies no power relationship, no form of domination. But to see role play as an erotic pleasure means approaching the form as an art of reciprocal conduct. This is what Sundén and Sveningsson discover in their interviews with female *World of Warcraft* players—avatars attract others by resembling power positions, which offer reciprocal roles to players willing to give consent as dom or sub: orcs resemble "distinctly 'butch' qualities," while trolls suggest a "laid-back, rough-around-the-edges femininity with rebellious overtones."[100] The art of reciprocal conduct becomes a means of dialogue and negotiation, a practice that Foucault sees within the Greeks' problematization of love between a man and a boy, but also grants existing in a wide range of pleasurable acts.[101] *Aphrodisia* involves two sets of roles, the "active actors" (dominating) and the "passive actors" (subjugated), with its major ethical variable being the "questions of remaining in one's role or abandoning it."[102] Roles of domination can thus at any time be realized as unethical, causing one to renegotiate, reflect, or even cease the play.

Volume 3 of *The History of Sexuality* shifts *aphrodisia* from Greece to the imperial context of Rome, when concerns were less about involving relationships among men and more about the dominating imperial center and the subjugated imperial provinces. It is within the imperial context that *aphrodisia* transforms toward a care of the self with the goal of self-mastery, where one realizes one's own domination through playing roles of domination. The more one role plays, the more one perceives of "truth," the truth of the broader personal and imperial situation concerning power, the "scene" upon which desire is made, and the everyday play of power that had been disavowed by the distancing of empire and its corollaries (racism, nationalism, xenophobia). In an empire such as Rome, the purposes of learning to self-rule were related to one's real-life roles as a political and social elite. As Foucault writes, the "new forms of the political game" of empire represented a crisis in recognizing one's relationship to the outside world.[103] No longer mere barbarians or "non-Greeks," outsiders were now subjects whom the Romans themselves were responsible for. The ethical domain grew—became a world in itself, where one's identity within the empire was burdened by new relationships to others, new subjects, new roles of domination. This shift sparked a crisis of the self, where one could not be understood as merely dominating toward one's wife (or subjugated to the husband) but forced upon individuals within "a far more extensive and complex field of power relations."[104]

It was in the turn from city-state to empire that *aphrodisia* became more focused upon the self as an ends rather than as a means to fathom one's power over others. Before the imperial epoch, texts of *aphrodisia* were meant precisely for "young aristocrats destined to exercise power," and in turn their purpose was to care for oneself in order to properly care for others, "so that one will be able to exercise properly, reasonably, and virtuously the power to which one is destined."[105] Self-care in this context was outward looking, meant as a means to ethically engage with those who made pleasures possible. But with the growth of empire, just as one's self was gaining unprecedented forms of power over the provinces as well as the household, self-care transitioned into a form of universal morality, "a requirement addressed to everyone."[106] Without a proper assessment of one's imperial power, self-care drew inward and became its own means rather than a means of caring for others, so that one cared no longer "for the city-state, but for the self."[107] This "new erotics," as Foucault called it, began a long shift from the outward-looking self to the self conveyed by Christianity, a self preoccupied with the self (or "the flesh"), an isolated self concerned with the outside world only because it risked one's self with disease, evil, sin, guilt, and the possibility of eternal hell.

This new erotics (rather than *ars erotica*) is the ethical utopianism demonstrated through video games today. It is the ethics of *Mass Effect's* Shepard, whose personal pleasures are comprehended within "a universal form by which one is bound, a form grounded in both nature and reason, and valid for all human beings."[108] In order to be ethical beings, players need not understand "the scene" of *aphrodisia* but merely follow a set of universal rules. One could experience a pleasure without ever knowing (or caring to know) the effects, the conditions, the subjects, or the victims of that pleasure. If the ethical conundrum of *aphrodisia* was the need to situate erotic experiences, then the challenge of empire today is to broaden our own erotic relationships to account for those who are radically distanced from us. Rather than meet this challenge, during the Roman era, discourses of "care of the self" became focused on self-retreat, on self-mastery, for the purposes of improving one's own reputation and self-worth.

As Foucault imagined it, in the Roman era of empire, trade, and Christian morality, discourses of self-care shifted to disavow imperial and structural violences onto distant others. One could make similar arguments concerning the state of media studies within our current imperial epoch: that what appear as "problems" are not the violent process of manufacturing and mining that makes these products possible, but the "problems" of how these commodities form, empower, and add wisdom to our "selves." It is an inward-looking self-care that narratives of digital utopia rarely stray from. The challenge then is to comprehend how role playing in video games can be practiced through the technologies of *aphrodisia* (anonymity, impersonality, power play) without losing focus or permitting the narrative to shift toward the inward-focused self. Colin Milburn achieves such a feat in his masterful reading of *Final Fantasy VII*, which he calls "a relentlessly self-reflexive game that provides players with conceptual and affective resources to address the consequences of their own recreational pleasures."[109] Self-reflection occurs through playing the mysterious, self-inventing, and cross-dressing main character, Cloud Strife, a mercenary and excommunicated member of an elite warrior unit (SOLDIER). Yet the player cannot really identify with Cloud, because not even Cloud is really Cloud—he is a liar and loser playing the role of "Cloud" to become, as he later admits, "the master of my own illusory world." As Milburn shows, it is through Cloud's very anonymity and separation of his selves that the player can understand his own power position: "Playing the role of 'Cloud' is literally the means by which Cloud works through failure to become better than himself. We, as players of Cloud, are invited to take the same initiative."[110] "Cloud," is not an identity but a role that recursively emphasizes our own responsibilities, galvanizing players "to love responsibly."[111]

The narrative of information technology needs games as its form of benevolent consumption par excellence, to shape IT devices as utopic, and as part of a global apparatus of innovation that promises to solve all the problems created by past innovations (industrial plants, the reliance on fossil fuels, underage or unsafe factory work). As a narrative that explicitly offers the creative technology of the past through the utopic technology of the present, video games act as a means of resolving real anxieties about exploitation and empire without actually challenging the means of information technology production. In turn, Asia as a space of production is made invisible, excluded from an otherwise "benevolent" process of production, as it directly contradicts the cherished pieties of information technology characterized, for example, by the charity of Bill Gates and the innovation of Steve Jobs.

Alternatively, we can look to role playing in video games and other digital platforms as an erotic revision of information technology routed through the perverse, the frivolous, the pleasure fulfilling. Within the space of role play, questions of morality are displaced by the erotic. *Ars erotica* focuses instead on one's engagement with the other within an agreed-upon consensual frame, wherein pleasure, technique, and ethics structure the rules of the game. Yet despite these ethical practices, we cannot avoid that Greek society, as Foucault stressed (perhaps as an Asiatic projection[112]), maintained an *ars erotica* even while also maintaining slaves, the degradation of women, and its (by today's views) troubling relationships with young boys. These facts should remind us that to focus on the "the body and its pleasures" is merely a tacit gesture unless it also exposes pleasure's inhumane costs.

[Pause]

Hey! Perhaps we've gone the wrong way.

Let's push pause and take stock. What have we been doing?

For the past three chapters, I have attempted to understand games as transpacific products embroidered with Asiatic associations that come to the fore when we focus on the global game (the text), auteurs and absent designers (the authors), and role players (the audiences). I have tried to do the work, as Judith Butler writes, of articulating a critical genealogy of legitimating practices.[1] My method has been to read games erotically, a risky venture because it reconceives of pleasure as an artfulness seeking to account for one's dynamic relationships to others. Erotics, I have argued, recognizes how pleasure is situated. It seeks not to celebrate, condone, or disparage sex or sexual difference but to expose the scene, the *aphrodisia*, the larger imperial network that makes particular forms of pleasure possible. In so doing, erotic modes of perception like intimacy, ludophilia, and role play become ways to recognize this scene and to establish the dignity and the reciprocal consent of those who are implicated within our pleasure practices.

But there is something more at stake within the erotic as it concerns our open world empire. If, as Foucault writes, *ars erotica* was once supplanted by the moral and inward-focused self allied with the imperial state (and later the Church), then how can erotics dismantle this inward-focused self today? How can erotics strip even unconscious imperial allegiances? Our first playthrough was a study of discourse. It focused on the ambivalence toward video games as a medium that can either foster violence or teach tolerance, and it showed how this ambivalence is rooted in the desire to protect the values of the open world empire: the value of knowing for certain, the value of "to use" over "to play," and the use of technology to exercise control over others rather than create dialogue with them. Video games, by their very nature as playful, globally networked, and erotic, compromise such values.

Our first playthrough has been a straightforward game—a mission to rescue the princess (ourselves) and defeat the monstrous empire. But beneath narratives of transparency, certainty, information, and control lurks a widespread social desire for the totalization of the subject into a single unified whole. Indeed, as Barthes, Foucault, and Sedgwick each show in their last decades, erotic methods not only expose, as Sharon Patricia Holland writes, "the personal and political dimension of desire,"[2] but in doing so, they also offer ways to accept the human body as a plurality, a disunity, at times dominating (majority) and subjugated (marginalized), a self often contradictory and inconsistent in allegiances, preferences, and relations to others. The open world empire has taken hold by unifying the self into identities pressured to remain transparent, morally sound, and present to the gaze of surveillance apparatuses. Just as in Foucault's vision of the Roman era, in the digital age one's pleasures and desires are no longer problematized but are assigned moral positions by knowledge regimes seeking to repress the self-reflections that would recognize and reckon with our power over others.[3]

As Viet Thanh Nguyen has argued, the fiction of the self-unified identity has permitted historically intractable conflicts to continue unabated, where "both sides [see] themselves as victims, or refus[e] to see themselves as potential or actual victimizers."[4] The ethical imperative here is not to wrong the feelings and tactics of presenting the self as a self-unified whole, but that doing so can keep us embedded into particular narratives wherein we are the main character (and thus the object of sympathy, the victim, the powerless) rather than a "role" implicating the necessary presence of others. It is to not merely see ourselves in relation to a white hegemonic order—in the face of which we must appear "empowered"—but to also interrogate our relations to the typical "nonplayable characters" of white representation: other minorities, migrants, and diasporics inside and outside of America. These relations remind us of our own positions as members of the most militarily dominant force the world has ever seen and as members of a Global North whose consumption of information technology facilitates warfare in Africa, debt slavery in Asia, and surveillance capabilities all around. Despite this context, much academic work on this industry remains firmly nested in arguments concerning what's "good" and "bad" for a particular identity. Recognizing multiplicity through our contradictory and unpleasant pleasures forces us to do the opposite, to ask how we have been involved in other people's lives and how we have been dependent upon those who appear as nonplayable characters, there only to establish meaning for our own narratives.

Already this book has begun to broach the self as plurality: the self at work and the self at play, or the self who takes issues like race seriously and the other who plays with race. Role playing, too, dislodges the self into the "soul" self (the self at home), the "identity" self (the self in the world), the virtual self (the self performed online), and the "air" self (the self one feels oddly at home in). But this has remained a brief glimpse into how erotics can disturb our own political sensibilities. This book has introduced ways of playing erotically (ludophilia, *aphrodisia*), but it has so far prioritized concern with critical analyses of games in order to expose the political discursive work of information technology. In other words, our initial playthrough has relied on what Eve Kosofsky Sedgwick calls a paranoid form of reading, one reliant upon exposing the realities behind dominant discourses (ways of seeing games, of seeing ourselves) as the primary means to create change. In so doing we have arrived at paranoia's conceptual limitations: we know our imperial relations to others and the wider stakes of our consistent disavowals. Yet the problem of empire remains, the ease of incorporation still at large, the inward-focused self still a possible ends. Our problem in this first playthrough—necessary to get a sense of the many games in play—is that we have played with everything but the games themselves as objects in the world. We have instead used games as a utility to decipher empire, and we have made our claim to games as meaning something *for* us rather than grasp its "freedom to 'mean' nothing."[5]

In part 2 I will attempt to show how games, as interactive forms of storytelling and play, measure our pleasures and desires, attenuate us to bodily perceptions, and help us perceive how power takes hold of our conduct, our bodies, and our frailties. I intend to see games not as utilities but as objects in the world that offer playful experiences, which have the ability to nourish us and, as Sontag writes of art, "to make us see or comprehend something singular, not judge or generalize."[6] How do video games challenge us to account for our own misapprehensions, contradictions, and fantasies? How can erotic forms of play help us reconceive of ourselves as simultaneously victims to dominating forces as well as self-interested members of the Global North? Simply put, what can playing video games erotically do *to* us, rather than *for* us? How can it force us—kicking and screaming, perhaps—to reimagine our very world, and in so doing, our very selves?

So, in our momentary impasse, let's redo this playthrough. Let's re-spawn—a hard reset. This time, let's ignore the mission handed down to us. Let's slip. Let's goof around. Let's stay awhile and listen.

PART II

Erotics

Do you like hurting other people?
—Richard, *Hotline Miami*

4

Posture

Plunge \ Dread / Vulnerability

Perhaps there are certain ages which do not need truth as
much as they need a deepening of the sense of reality, a
widening of the imagination . . . The truth is balance, but the
opposite of truth, which is unbalance, may not be a lie.
—Susan Sontag, *Against Interpretation: and Other Essays*

In modernity, ideology was an instrument of power, but now
ideology is a decoy.
—Alexander Galloway, "Playing the Code: Allegories of
Control in Civilization"

Where do we go when critique fails?

This is the question that jump-started the career of Susan Sontag, who
in 1966 argued that great art had been burdened by critique. The merit
of great art, Sontag argued, "lies elsewhere than in their 'meanings,'" but
in their sensuous, untranslatable, and erotic experiences.[1] For the next
decade, Roland Barthes, in attempting to crack open the radical plurality
of the text, sought to dismantle his own methods of ideological critique
by focusing on the erotic as the silent, the unreadable, the blurred-out.
In the late 1970s and early 1980s, Michel Foucault joined in the foray,
developing erotics into an Asiatic form, the *ars erotica*, a means of experiencing pleasure that simultaneously brought greater attention onto
"the scene" of pleasure and power.

The failure of critique has also been a preoccupation for gaming
scholars, who see "critique" as we know it—as a focus on language, narrative, and representation—inadequate for understanding video games.
As Alexander Galloway wrote in 2004, video games have been a slippery terrain for critics because "the more one tries to pin down the

ideological critique, the more one sees that such a critique is undermined by the existence of something altogether different from ideology.
So where the ideological critique succeeds, it fails."[2] We have seen this
time and again, in an unforgiving loop: the more we critique *Overwatch*,
Shenmue II, or *Final Fantasy VII* for their ideological meanings (stereotypes, exoticisms, nationalist propaganda), the more we realize that this
critique doesn't do much—it was never integral to us picking up the
game controller and taking pleasure from the experience of play it provided, nor does it reveal how games encircle us back to the world with
new wills, attitudes, and erotic perceptions.

It is in the spirit of play and erotics that I begin a second trio of chapters, which build upon these analyses but turn from their targets (or
from targeting in general). I ask how playing erotically can itself upend
forms of knowledge that go beyond merely exposing the faults of information technology but can show us something greater than the open
world empire has to offer. This book's turn here is meant to reflect the
turns of Barthes, Foucault, and Sedgwick, who in their last decades
shifted from methods based on ideology and exposure to techniques of
"self-love,"[3] of "feeling," "affects," and erotics. Foucault's last decade was
marked by a turn away from Marxism to focus on an ethics of self-care
that symbolized "the one sure way not to tyrannize over others."[4] His
views later in life dissected his own position from a place of growing
privilege and intellectual power, as he tracked Hellenistic self-help archives to elucidate the crisis of finding oneself in league with empire, a
crisis of the self that can "bring a certain dissociation into play between
power over the self and power over others."[5] For Foucault, this crisis
for better ethical responsibility ultimately failed with empire, as ethics
shifted from an art of the self (an *ars erotica*) to "an art of existence
dominated by self-preoccupation" (238), making erotics and sexuality
increasingly dangerous, leading subjects "to confine it, insofar as possible, to marital relations" (239). The regime of self-care in the Roman
era failed to account for the turn to empire because the problematizations of sexuality and erotics turned to a universalizing moralism, and
inquiry turned into the vigilant determination that sexual activity had
to be tamed under one means of fulfillment: marriage.[6]

As with Barthes's interest in "the country I am calling Japan," I understand Foucault's notion of *ars erotica* not as a historian or anthropologist

but as a critic attempting to gauge what we have lost today, in an age where knowledge, transparency, and information are deployed to create divisions, shifting our mode of engagement with digital technology from ethics, erotics, and pleasure to self-protection, vulnerability, and morality. The collective recoil from problematizing our own erotic and intimate relations to digital devices has shaped pleasure as an entitlement occurring within an isolated vacuum (as convenient, time-saving, self-optimizing). Though we see its erotic elements—its ability to shock, please, and distress—they are marked as frivolous, addictive, perverse, or violent. Unproblematized, erotic relations do not invoke questions concerning relations to others within the empire, nor do they detail the shared feelings of vulnerability and precarity that make these relationships meaningful. Erotics are feared because their relations compromise the very selves empire has built: they become a spectrum of possible feelings, positions, and postures produced through our attachments to the digital device.

The everyday structure of unhampered imperial violences speak to our inability to see pleasure and attachment as itself in need of problematization. Our unresolved ethical dilemmas are numerous: the United Nations' exposure of coltan ore as a conflict material, the conditions in assembly factories in the Pearl River Delta (which Jack Qiu has likened to chattel slavery[7]), more recent exposures of environmental degradation and e-waste (most recently chronicled by Colin Milburn). Yet the information technology industry has been remarkable in its ability to dismiss such critiques by promising far-fetched reform or in suggesting that such costs are worthwhile (iPads are saving the trees, communications technology is reducing oil for airplanes, etc.). The karma of the IT empire secures critical discourses onto "problematizing" its effects on the user—the "are screens good for you?" debate, the "do video games cause violence?" problem. False debates such as these have gripped some game scholars and designers, who aggressively promote the games industry through manifestos that, instead of calling for a way to reduce the inequality and precarity of our current moment, offer utopian dreams built upon the very mechanisms of exploitation.[8] The argument game critics often focus on, that "games are beautiful" and "we should all learn to think like designers," is a prime example of how games studies discourses have been preoccupied with the moral and aesthetic justification for the things that give us pleasure rather than the intricacies and power relationships produced through that pleasure. This is game studies at its most utopic—but what else could we expect? When slapped against the stone wall of unquestionable human progress, critique tends not to stick.

So when critique fails, we pick up the refuse, transmogrify our tools into toys, and exert all remaining energies to forging a new path. To do so, this chapter turns to Eve Kosofsky Sedgwick, whose work in *Epistemology of the Closet* (1990) and *Touching Feeling* (2003) have been foundational to queer theory, affect studies, and studies of the body. Like Barthes and Foucault, Sedgwick's last decade is marked by a turn away from traditional modes of critique, which she (following Paul Ricoeur) called a "hermeneutics of suspicion" and (following Melanie Klein) "the paranoid position," but which others have more recently called "symptomatic reading," the kind of critical genealogical and exposure-driven critiques handed down from Marx, Freud, Nietzsche, and most of Foucault.[9] In *Touching Feeling*, published after Sedgwick's terminal cancer was already made public and reflected upon in her earlier work *A Dialogue on Love* (1999), Sedgwick turns to nonnarrative texts to resist the frame of suspicion, such as Japanese poetry (*haibun*), visual art, and texture itself. Like Barthes and Foucault before her, Sedgwick pins primary importance on the body and its ability to interact with objects through erotic sensations like touch. As Sedgwick writes of touch:

> Even more immediately than other perceptual systems, it seems, the sense of touch makes nonsense out of any dualistic understanding of agency and passivity; to touch is always already to reach out, to fondle, to heft, to tap, or to enfold, and always also to understand other people or natural forces as having effectually done so before oneself, if only in the making of the textured object.[10]

Perceiving of touch does not reveal divisions among people but one's own presence: our presumptions about how an object will feel, the histories of that object, the affects it might satisfy (or disappoint). Sedgwick's sense of touch is similar to media theories of haptic criticism, which see touch as a means of closing off critical distance through "sensuous closeness."[11] As media theorist Laura Marks wrote in *Touch*, "touch" operates within "a visual erotics that offers its object to the viewer but only on the condition that its unknowability remain intact, and that the viewer, in coming closer, give up his or her own mastery."[12] Sedgwick's sense of touch also seeks not to penetrate the unknowability of the object, but as a mode of erotic perception, it interrogates one's relationship to the other, exposing the larger context where the viewer can become a "self" in the first place. To perceive touch is to perceive ourselves within the act of touching, to see our complex relations to others through our desire for their image. Touch is a way of remaining near the surface, just below the abstraction of shapes, to a realm of perception that does not see deep enough for the structure but remains "irreducibly phenomenological" in order to "enter a conceptual realm that is not shaped by lack nor by commonsensical dualities of subject versus object or of means versus ends."[13]

Sedgwick speaks of two types of textures we can perceive through touch—the texture that is smooth, meant to be dismissed in order to facilitate interaction with the object (the texture "that defiantly or even invisibly blocks or refuses such information"), and texxture with two x's, the texture that is "dense with offered information about how, substantively, historically, materially, it came into being," such as a brick or metalwork pot that "still bears the scars and uneven sheen of its making."[14] Sedgwick's notions of texture and her determination to remain in the realm of the body puts us on course to see games not as a magic circle of rules, boundaries, and hidden meanings but as a text(ure) formed by the interactive experience. I here tease out the term "text(ure)" to encompass the many elusive forms of erotic interaction that forego distinctions between player and machine to make us aware of our bodies in the moment of interaction.

Text(ure) occurs between the game as narrative/ludological text and the game's material texture/texxture, where the smoothness of the keyboard and the gamepad's glossy resistance to its own history of production reveals a calculated forgetting of the material, its history, and one's own body. Sedgwick theorizes texture through her interest in textile art,[15] as she considers how touch and perception can impact a wide range of "artistic media . . . that can be manipulated through various processes to show new aspects."[16] In games, to perceive of text(ure) is to see how the body joins the gamepad/keyboard in facilitating the ease of gameplay so that one's touch only affects one's visual and audio receptors rather than the thing itself (like how cloth changes with touch). As

Aubrey Anable writes, in video games touch confuses designations of "self and other," pointing to the ways "bodies, devices, images, and code are enmeshed."[17] While some hardware devices, like the Wii's motion sensor remote, have sought to utilize the bodily postures of the player for in-game interaction, games overwhelmingly do not recognize gamer movements—postures, muscle reflexes, wild gesticulations—as carrying any meaning.[18] The smooth ease of gamepads is meant to make text(ure) imperceptible, yet in so doing, controls also compel the body into particular postures and positions (leaned in on a keyboard, couched in a living room) that users themselves don't need to notice to adopt. Text(ure) approaches Steve Swink's definition of "game feel," which he terms "the tactile, kinesthetic sense of manipulating a virtual object" and "the sensation of control in a game."[19] Yet Swink's focus on "manipulation" and "control" in feeling a game sees the player as deployer and user, reinforcing the rigid separation between actor and object. Text(ure) sees not a user performing actions upon an object but the inter-acts, the interstitial and transitional spaces between recognizable actions: how the body prepares to receive and perform acts, the ease or difficulties of performing *re*actions, the unsaid ways of enunciating acts. Text(ure) thus emphasizes the erotic engagement with the digital device that includes not only the visual and audio changes that the player makes upon the game but the changes to her own body as various postures are held to engage with the device. To read play as both descriptive and performative is to perceive of the game's text(ure) as offering positive affects (affects that satisfy themselves) and to see interaction as taking place, in Sedgwick's terms, in the intersection between absorption and theatricality.[20]

As in my previous theoretical play with Barthes and Foucault, my use of Sedgwick's concepts to understand video games may seem heretical, particularly to those in literary affect studies who routinely deploy affect for the very thing Sedgwick tried to resist: to read narratives, to pull affects from a text and reveal their structural underpinnings à la Raymond Williams or Brian Masumi.[21] Though I myself have employed affect in these ways in previous work,[22] this is simply not the method that Sedgwick develops in *Touching Feeling* and *The Weather in Proust*. A hermeneutics of suspicion, for Sedgwick, was "inescapably narrative," and *Touching Feeling* is an attempt to look beyond (or "beside") this scholarly standard, to reverse the process through which "nonverbal aspects of reality" are subsumed "firmly under the aegis of the linguistic."[23] Thus, one shouldn't ask why we would use Sedgwick's theories of touch and texture for video games, but why for so long these theoretical tools/toys have been dominated by literary analyses and not by interactive media. If Sedgwick's notions of touch, texture, and affect were ways of breaking from linguistic to nonlinguistic media, then their uses in video games has been shamefully postponed.

So with only a modest amount of shame, this chapter begins with a rehearsal of Sedgwick's ideas within the realm of interactive media to understand the techno-paranoia captured in games and how reading them as text(ure) helps us grip their interactive experiences. First, I treat the 2016 "Men Against Fire" episode of the television show *Black Mirror* alongside the strikingly similar 2008 video game *Haze* to compare the mode of visual techno-paranoia with the reparative text(ure) of game-play. Second, I ask how text(ure) poises the player within an available spectrum of bodily postures—its most dominant and normalized that of the "plunge posture," a ready-set hold of the body that sees the object through positive affects of excitement, surprise, and satisfaction. In playing Sega's voyeuristic game *Night Trap*, I consider how the plunge posture is produced through games of surveillance and control. Finally, I end by considering feelings of vulnerability produced through the game *Alien: Isolation*. Vulnerability, I argue, emerges within a "dread posture" that pushes players to conceive of new forms of interaction that involve patience and perception. To touch game text(ure) does not ask "what does this offer me?" but "what is this interactive moment doing?"

Techno-Paranoia, or "Come and See the Violence Inherent in the System!"

The most prevailing critique of interactive technology today is of techno-paranoia, which, as Wendy Hui Kyong Chun has observed, forces us to revisit the ideologies of information technology as a visible apparatus of control. For Chun, techno-paranoia reveals that one cannot merely move about the cyber world as a flâneur, a "detached observer who remains hidden from the world."[24] Rather, they inhabit the unbridled gaze of "the gawker" (*badaud*), who, as Walter Benjamin wrote, is so absorbed by the external world that they lose their

164 | POSTURE: PLUNGE \ DREAD / VULNERABILITY

individuality within "intoxication and ecstasy."[25] The "gawker" is the stereotypical gamer typed as an easily susceptible automaton, a commonplace notion that links games with advanced military projects, "promoting an ambient paranoia."[26] In 2016, this paranoia was demonstrated when the game *Pokémon Go* introduced into the mainstream a form of reality augmentation that stamped a fantasy world onto the real world. Multiple media outlets gave alarmist reports concerning how the game's palimpsest of the virtual onto the everyday would incapacitate young people from being able to distinguish reality from fantasy. With *Pokémon Go*, spectatorship itself became spectacle, as players could easily be spotted interacting with virtual pocket monsters, sometimes within a mob. Chun's allusion to Benjamin's gawker sediments many of the fears and anxieties of emerging technology to exacerbate systemic violence through the pleasures of technological intoxication, wherein frivolous forms of pleasure and play, like video games, signal the greatest threat to one's abilities to think from a critical distance (like a flâneur). New technology is then looked upon within a "hermeneutics of suspicion" that asks how one's worldview is shaped by the augmentation of interactive technology.

On the one hand, techno-paranoia remains fittingly suspicious of misinformation: that the people the American military targets are not really as deserving of violence as the populous are led to believe. Yet, led by the desire to "unveil" or "expose" the falsity of state or capitalist narratives, techno-paranoia presumes that miscataloging and misrecognition are the primary forces through which imperial violence is made possible. This paranoia of emerging technology concerns the cataloging and recognition of empire's others: terrorists, immigrants, refugees, and other possible threats to national security including antiwar protestors within the United States. Yet American empire has never relied entirely upon the spreading of false information in order to function, and it in fact relies, too, on the promise of transparency and knowledge—that if only we knew the truth (is that child really a terrorist or not?), our habitual killing wouldn't bother us a wink. Our own ethical imperative then is to turn from this reliance on transparency and exposure to forms of knowledge that exceed techno-paranoia.

In 1997, Eve Sedgwick critiqued paranoia as a hermeneutics that saw structural critique and exposure as the only routes to access greater truth and revolutionary practices. Sedgwick's five-point definition of paranoia is worth rehearsing here:

> Paranoia is anticipatory.
> Paranoia is reflexive and mimetic.
> Paranoia is a strong theory.
> Paranoia is a theory of negative affects.
> Paranoia places its faith in exposure.[27]

These five attributes also reflect presumptions toward good and critical scholarly work. Paranoia can anticipate change by seeing history as both repetitive and pessimistic (that things do not change or are getting worse); it is strong because it is broad and prescriptive rather than descriptive; and it follows presumptions of knowledge production that have functioned as Marxist axioms: 1) true knowledge comes from struggle, 2) radical politics must come from a bad situation being made intolerable ("radicalizing"), and 3) unveiling this materialist process exposes the truth of structural violence. For Elizabeth Freeman, paranoid readings grant one to feel "more evolved than one's context," presuming that the reader or writer has captured a piece of scandal that otherwise eludes the vast majority of people (voters, workers, gamers).[28]

Perhaps the best example of paranoia as it exists in the digital age is in the British television show *Black Mirror*, as every episode seems to play on the techno-paranoia of emerging technology. In the episode "Nosedive," social media becomes a four-star rating system that decides who can get adequate hospital care. In "Shut Up and Dance," a group of unknown hackers blackmails citizens to rob banks and fight to the death. *Black Mirror* was developed by Charlie Brooker, who first gained fame for his work on BBC documentaries about video games. His devotion to studying video games began as an undergraduate at the University of Westminster, where he failed to graduate because of his "decision to write a 15,000-word dissertation on the subject of videogames, without bothering to check whether that was a valid topic, which it wasn't."[29] His interests led to the BBC series *Gameswipe* (2009–13), where Brooker commented on games and the game industry, and later to the documentary special *How Videogames Changed the World* (2013), which analyzed game design and its historical impact. These documentaries led to Brooker's stardom and eventual position as head writer and developer of *Black Mirror*, which has won numerous awards including Best TV Movie/Miniseries at the International Emmy Awards and has garnered large audiences worldwide, particularly in China and America. Unlike Brooker's previous documentaries, his fun and cheeky tone is only present in *Black Mirror*'s pessimistic view of the user's ability to remain in control. Like Chun's view of the user as a gawker, Brooker's characters remain lost in the intoxication of new technology, as they become so reliant and addicted to virtual worlds that they risk abandoning their own humanity.

The *Black Mirror* episode "Men Against Fire" typifies techno-paranoia in relation to fears of American militaristic violence.[30] In a dystopian future, Stripe (played by Malachi Kirby) is part of an American military team that hunts "roaches"—mutants whose DNA has been deemed genetically inferior, warranting their extermination. Within this postapocalyptic universe, soldiers are enhanced with a neural implant called MASS that enhances their abilities to plan attacks and communicate. Secretly, the implant also nullifies the user's senses and makes the "roaches" appear monstrous, with ravenous teeth and diseased skin (see Figure 4.1). Following the presumptions of techno-paranoia, within the episode these "roaches" develop an LED device that disrupts the MASS implant, forcing Stripe to see the roaches (and his past victims) as (white) humans who make up a migrant minority within their own country (see Figure 4.2).

"Men Against Fire" is an explicit commentary on the connection between technology and the military actions of the United States. It is the first episode of *Black Mirror* to feature an almost entirely American cast, and its desert climate mimics the ongoing wars in the Middle East. The "roaches" of the episode reflect contemporary contexts where migrants have been cast as agents of disease and infection whose quarantine involves seeing them as monstrous others who must be subordinated within their own homeland. As speculative fiction, the episode attempts to flip the racial norms of military conflict by representing a black soldier committing ethnic cleansing toward a white minority, so that in "de-monsterizing" the bodies, the episode also "de-racializes"

Figure 4.1. *Black Mirror*'s "Men Against Fire." Stripe stabs a roach with MASS activated. Screenshot by author.

Figure 4.2. *Black Mirror*'s "Men Against Fire." The same roach seen without MASS. Screenshot by author.

them. They are no longer in the realm of the speculative, monstrous other but are white, blond haired, blue eyed, more normalized than our black protagonist. The unveiling of the technological military apparatus thus results in new forms of radicalization and revolution. Like most *Black Mirror* episodes, the ending reiterates the pessimism of techno-paranoia, as Stripe chooses to erase his mind from the memory of killing innocent civilians and to go on living in the pleasures of the fake fantasy world that MASS has provided.

As "Men Against Fire" stresses, techno-paranoia attempts not to explore the intricacies within the act of killing but to unveil the real identities and motives behind such killing with the faith that its exposure will result in more radical politics. As a female roach (seen as human) tells Stripe, MASS is only a slippery slope from surveillance technology:

"First the screening programs, the DNA checks, then the register, the emergency measures, and soon everyone calls us creatures." The paranoid fear of technological militarization here is not so much in the superpower's right to kill at a whim but in the concern that we may be killing the wrong people. This is the tension in paranoia that Sedgwick takes to task, as she writes, "Why bother exposing the ruses of power in a country where, at any given moment, 40 percent of young black men are enmeshed in the penal system?"[31] With paranoia, the notions of secret violence, of censorship, and of scandal create an interest—daresay, a fetish—that finds pleasure in exposing the unknown. Meanwhile, the US government routinely admits to its involvement in civilian death and torture, such as a US-led coalition airstrike in 2017 that killed thirty-three migrant civilians from Raqqa and Aleppo taking refuge in a Syrian school, an event that occurred during the writing of this chapter. This school bombing was admitted by the United States, and in its admittance and readiness to exposure, the massacre of innocents lost its aura of being unknown, mysterious, and exposable. The paranoid mind that only sees the unveiling of violence remained indifferent. Like the US penal system in Sedgwick's (and our own) time, these lives seem to lack the puncturing power of scandal and thus radicalization (on the US side, at least).

Paranoia captures the fear of being misinterpreted, of being labeled inaccurately.[32] It places focus upon those who gaze rather than the very impediments and structures that enabled this gaze in the first place. As in "Men Against Fire," the desire to demystify what has been mislabeled can miss out on the nonscandalous explicit violence upon which this gaze is based (what Chandan Reddy has called the "legitimate violence" of the state and US military[33]). Such violence is not hidden or even normalized, as Sedgwick claims, but consistently eludes analysis by remaining an "exemplary spectacle."[34] "Men Against Fire" highlights the veiling effect of new technology with the pleasures one experiences while inhabiting it, and it thus marks the fear of techno-paranoia as the fear that technology will cloud our ability to judge ourselves and others, a fear that other episodes of Black Mirror fragment into fears of being seen as politically aberrant, as nonfeminist, or as a pervert. Paranoia ultimately concerns our capacity to see and recognize others for "whom they really are" and, in exchange, to be seen as who we really are. Paranoia and identity, in other words, go hand in hand.

To use a real-life example, we can flash-forward to the "immigration crisis" that occurred in early 2017, when this chapter was first being written, concerning the entrance of Syrian and other refugees into the United States alongside already stoked fears of Mexican immigrants. These fears, too, were propelled by a paranoid impulse to categorize mobile bodies as accurately as possible. "Pro-immigration" news media attempted to counter the trust in digital recognition by featuring stories of upper-middle-class migrants who had been obstructed from entering the United States under new travel bans. The ban of migrants with success stories as musicians, physicians, athletes, and academics stoked a paranoid fear of mislabeling driven by the revitalization of the US immigration system. Being mislabeled exposed the immigration system as racist but did not speak to the imperial violences that produced migrancy, nor to the valorization of American citizenship and belonging within a field of competing nationalist epistemes.[35] As Heonik Kwon has similarly argued, the paranoia concerned with migrant bodies exposes the tensions of Western multiculturalism as it has formed in an age of the Cold War and terrorism, where subjects who are visibly othered by the colonial color line (à la postcolonial criticism) remain entrenched in the dualistic othering of the ideological color line (à la area studies' focus on "reds" and "non-reds," "civilians" and "terrorists").[36] The paranoid attention to categorization and getting the "lines" correct sanitizes and intensifies the very explicit (and nonscandalous) violence of US militarism. It does not question why those with US passports have a right to travel and abode while those impacted by American bombs do not. The demand to be seen and labeled accurately has little concern for the known figures of dead civilians in Yemen and Syria (from wars that also occurred during the writing of this chapter). Such known violences have little weight upon the paranoia of seeing or of being seen—they are those whose killing has been framed not as a matter of imperialism, crime, or racism but as a mere byproduct of technological *inaccuracy*, which can always be forgiven.

Reparative Playing in Haze

To those who are sure that right is on one side, oppression
and injustice on the other, and that the fighting must go on,
what matters is precisely who is killed and by whom . . . To
the militant, identity is everything.
—Susan Sontag, *Regarding the Pain of Others*

Sedgwick's writings on paranoia are not meant to disqualify paranoid
readings but to unmoor paranoia from reinforcing a scholastic standard
as the only viable heuristic capable of critical thinking and radicalization.[37] As an alternative to the practices of paranoia, Sedgwick directs
attention to reparative practices that have been undervalued by paranoid readings because "they are about pleasure ('merely aesthetic') and
because they are frankly ameliorative ('merely reformist')."[38] Sedgwick
claims that reparative practices undermine paranoia's faith in demystify-
ing exposure, from the "explosion of gender roles" to the exacerbation of
oppression to create class or racial consciousness. Reparative practices,
in contrast, focus on the cultivation of positive affects. Rather than reading for how queer practices like camp "demystify," "mock," or "critique"
imperial culture, reparative reading considers how camp expresses a
variety of reparative practices: "the startling, juicy displays of excess
erudition . . . the passionate, often hilarious antiquarianism, the prodi-
gal production of alternative historiographies."[39] Reparative readings are
about, in Robyn Wiegman's words, "loving what hurts but instead of
using that knowledge to prepare for a vigilant stand against repetition, it
responds to the future with affirmative richness."[40] Reparative readings
direct scholarly attention onto forms of pleasure, fun, and ecstasy not to
expose their parody and critique but to understand the experiences they
offer us and how such experiences can emerge from histories "based
on deep pessimism"—histories of AIDS, homophobia, prejudice.[41] As
Elizabeth Freeman notes, reparative readings lead scholars to be "interested in the tail end of things . . . whatever has been declared useless."[42]

I thus turn to a useless object that transforms our techno-paranoia
into pleasure and ecstasy: the first-person shooter video game *Haze*
(2008), a game that failed even as a video game, as its sales records
and reviews were so disappointing that its distributor, Ubisoft, halted

production on all platforms except for the PlayStation 3, effectively driving *Haze*'s ambitious design studio, Free Radical Design, out of business. *Black Mirror*'s episode "Men Against Fire" seems directly inspired by *Haze*,[43] as the game also takes place in a dystopian world where soldiers integrate with a technology that augments their reality. *Haze* follows Sergeant Carpenter as he fights in the "Boa region" of South America against rebels who an international corporation, Mantel, has accused of ethnic cleansing and crimes against humanity. Even given its failings to top sales charts, *Haze* is reparatively far richer than "Men Against Fire," as its gameplay offerings of pleasure, fun, and play drive the user's quest through a plot reminiscent of *Heart of Darkness* and *Apocalypse Now*. In "Men Against Fire," the neural implant MASS operates as a system of total control and illusion, yet in *Haze* the superdrug "Nectar" causes a hallucinogenic effect that "cleans" dead bodies and provides an illusion of painless and idyllic war. Nectar does not trick good soldiers into killing innocent victims (routine misinformation and propaganda are enough to do that) but simply makes the killing experience one of pleasure and ease. On Nectar, the player's environment alters so that enemies appear as orange glowing silhouettes, while the player himself moves faster, jumps higher, and shoots better. Once enemies are killed, their suffering is muted, and their bodies fade into faceless corpses as soon as their heartbeats cease (see Figures 4.3 and 4.4). Even when the player joins rebel factions, Nectar continues to make killing pleasurable, as it still provides a means of overpowering one's enemies using guerilla tactics (becoming invisible by playing dead, causing enemies to overdose on Nectar and kill each other). Indeed, Nectar operates as an analogy for first-person shooter games in general, where games make death fun "as a cooperative activity performed with a machine."[44] Even as the game's narrative is meant to critique and "unveil" the sinister effects of Nectar, *Haze*'s in-game tutorials extoll its pleasure practices: "Remember, Nectar boosting yourself to Optimal lets you see further and increases your accuracy at range!"

Despite (or perhaps because of) its failure, *Haze* is a perfect counterpoint to the techno-paranoia of "Men Against Fire," as it offers a text(ure) for reparative readings through a nearly identical story. The reality-altering technology in *Haze* is not merely weaponized but is also fun and pleasurable, operating as an addiction that is triaged onto more

Figure 4.3. *Haze.* Massacred civilians with Nectar activated. Screenshot from Full Playthroughs, "Haze | PS3 | Full Gameplay/Playthrough | No Commentary," *YouTube*, March 11, 2016, www.youtube.com/watch?v=0NI34Me7seY&t=10s, 39:12.

Figure 4.4. *Haze.* Massacred civilians without Nectar activated. Screenshot from Full Playthroughs, "Haze | PS3 | Full Gameplay/Playthrough | No Commentary," *YouTube*, March 11, 2016, www.youtube.com/watch?v=0NI34Me7seY&t=10s, 39:21.

privileged bodies. Unlike MASS in "Men Against Fire," Nectar in *Haze* becomes the sole purpose for war, as troops lead missions to control the drug and destroy Nectar factories in order to monopolize production, while the rebels hope to moderate rather than nullify its effects. Nectar does not hide death and killing but sanitizes it within a fantasy-driven "magic circle." As reviewers and fans have pointed out, Nectar has become the sole reason to play the game, and the game's failure can be partially blamed on Nectar becoming a moral issue in the game's narrative, whereas players would have preferred to simply indulge in Nectar's ecstatic embodiment of military power.[45] Thus the risk of Nectar as technology is not due to misrecognition, nor does it even operate on the divisions of good and bad, the empire and the rebels (both the evil corporation and the rebels use Nectar as a means of conducting warfare). The paranoia of fighting for the wrong side or of accidentally torching innocent victims is of less concern to the player than the simple and unabated joy of Nectar. Unlike in *Black Mirror*, *Haze* recognizes a world where we don't need a superdrug to veil violent acts. Technology's only role is to provide pleasure in wielding unfathomable power over others.

The techno-paranoia of *Black Mirror*'s "Men Against Fire" has its grounding in the presumption that technology, media, and other cultural objects veil over "the mistakes of well-meaning men."[46] Our military hero, Stripe, chooses in the end to remain with MASS only after he is given a fair (and truthful) argument concerning its purpose: to keep soldiers from sympathizing too much with the enemy (as they did in World War II). MASS is evil until we find its true purpose, then we become indifferent. Though techno-paranoia can seem cynical and even nihilistic (as *Black Mirror* is often accused of), it is in fact far too optimistic. Paranoia presumes that we, the audience, might change our political allegiances to empire if only we were not fed misinformation, if only the truth were made available. Paranoia sees the world as collectives of "well-meaning men" who merely make mistakes or are led astray, relegating all the violence of colonial history into a singular "oops!" and brightening our futures with an optimistic "trust us this time—we've updated!"

Unlike paranoia, reparative modes of reading attend to the erotics that drive our imperial fidelity. In *Black Mirror*'s "Men Against Fire," pleasure and erotics exist only to satiate the perpetrators, while the victims remain devoid of sex or pleasure. Sex appears in Stripe's dreams, in the illusion created by MASS. But in *Haze*, pleasure dominates the acts of killing and takes erotic tones in the shooting of dead bodies, in orgasmic explosions, and in precise headshots. *Haze* engages the player on a level that cannot be compared to either the critical gaze of the flâneur nor the instant satisfaction of the gawker but that of touch and text(ure), where the inter-action is propelled by the presumed pleasures that will emerge from it. In *Haze*, pleasure, as a positive affect, does not merely satiate violence but becomes the very reason for its reproduction. Without the pleasure and communal participation of the squadron, violence appears pointless. The game thus understands how pleasure exists in military warfare: the pleasure of trying out new gadgets, of dominating others, of brotherhood and communal bonding, of travel and sex. If pleasure, love, and desire here direct us to a deeper truth, it is not only about unveiling the violences of our empire but about reckoning with the pleasures we take from exposing and correcting its miscalculations.

The Plunge Posture and Night Trap

If you don't have the brains or the guts for this assignment,
give the controls to someone who does!
—Lieutenant Simms, *Night Trap*

If the player's gaming posture, upon entering the world of *Haze*, cannot be subsumed under that of the flâneur or the gawker, we can then parse out the various postures of play that text(ure) affords. In representations of the gamer at play, the most dominant of these postures is the posture of the "plunger," the spelunker, the diver, who, like the "gawker," seeks the satisfaction of objects but does so in order to act upon them and to be acted upon, to change them and in so doing change the self. With the tabletop gamer, one imagines deep-seated thinking, hand on chin, patiently awaiting one's turn. But the video game player plunges, leaned toward the machine, face lit by the screen and fingers scrambling to react. Gaming mechanics cater to the plunge position: the falling blocks of *Tetris*, the horde of alien attackers in *Space Invaders*, the randomly generated caverns of *Spelunky*, the endless fall of *Downwell*, and the scroll of *Super Mario Bros*. But all video games in a way cater to the

unexpected, the surprising, the inability to know for certain, the trusting only in one's intuition, muscle memory, reflexes—all conditioned by
one's posture—to react.

The plunge posture prepares the body for an onslaught of positive
affects wherein "affect arousal and reward are identical."[47] The term
"posture" here distances the "hold" of the gamer in preparation for the
interaction, where various affects come into play. The posture is similar to the "position" from which one writes or dissects the world (the
"depressive position" in Sedgwick's and Klein's terms), but postures rely
upon the stance of the body as receiver and doer. One is not only pos-
tured to expect particular experiences but to react appropriately. The
posture indicates then a set of expectations (a heuristic for engaging
with the object) as well as a set of possible interactions (turns, button
combinations, eye focus). Posture meets the text(ure) on its own terms
(the terms of the body), and it leaves players between the agency of their
"position" and the passivity of affective experience and attachment. Postures are bodily "holds" formed by habit, hardware, and the repetitive
motions encouraged by game mechanics. Perceiving of posture reminds
us that games directly involve the body as their medium. The plunge
posture remains a dominant depiction of gamers in advertisements
and fan-made videos, whether it is done by boys in a living room or by
women bent over an arcade machine (see Figure 4.5). In each case the
machine appears to offer delight, shock, excitement, the unexpected, yet
one can never be certain of what form of bodily pleasure one will find.
Erotic undertones haunt the plunge posture, which can be likened to the
exhilaration of pornography, with the controller or keyboard as the masturbatory apparatus, and the player ready to take control of a machine
that at any moment could exceed expected erotic limits.

We can understand the overlap of the plunge posture and discourses
of perversity in games with the infamous 1992 game *Night Trap*, a game
designed by the American developer Digital Pictures and distributed on
the Sega CD. In the game, players monitor full-motion videos of a girls'
slumber party via hidden cameras in order to protect them. As told by
Sims, the commander of the "Sega Control Attack Team" (that's right,
SCAT for short), the player voyeuristically observes young women at a
slumber party. This clearly perverse act of watching is sanitized within
a language of security, as the player is tasked to protect the girls from

Figure 4.5. *Centipede* "Arcade Girl" in plunge position. *Electronic Games* magazine, 1982.

augers, monstrous vampiric beings who thirst for young women's blood and who appear as normal human beings (thus the need for the player's surveillance). While monitoring scantily clad teenage girls, the player cannot occupy a merely voyeuristic gaze as he is also tasked to switch between hidden cameras, actively listen to conversations for clues, and activate traps that capture the vampires (but can "accidentally" capture the girls instead). The player, plunging into the role of a protector, switches hastily between cameras, always prepared to trigger a trap at the sight of an auger and to actively listen in on the girls' conversations. If one attempts to occupy the gaze of the gawker or voyeur (or to touch themselves while playing), he or she will find it remarkably difficult, as an auger will appear to disrupt their pleasure, or a secret code will toss by without being recognized, or something more important to the story will be occurring on another monitor. The game's deployment of sexual imagery thus acts as a mechanic to distract the player rather than as an object to be consumed by a voyeuristic gaze. Even in its replication of cinema through live-action film, the game compels players into the plunge posture.

When *Night Trap* was released in 1992, the argument that players were watching videos of young women pillow fighting only to protect them was not effective in defending against the game's perceived perversity. *Night Trap* was a frequent subject at the 1993 US joint Senate Judiciary and Government Affairs Committee hearing on violence in video games, where the game was called "shameful," "ultra-violent," "sick," and "disgusting."[48] Despite the fact that the game had no explicit violence or nudity, its association with voyeurism sparked the creation of the ESRB rating system still in place today, and the game was pulled from shelves. The ESRB and other rating systems have removed graphic sex from video games, yet plunge postures are routinely portrayed in erotic overtones, as depicted in game advertisements, in the pleasures and shakes of the body and in the orgasmic shocks seen in YouTube personalities like FPS Doug, who ecstatically screams "Boom, HEAD-SHOT!" as he plays *Counter-Strike*.[49] Compare these depictions of the plunging gamer with the most popular postures of television viewers who sit on a couch, so passive that a good joke may convey no bodily reaction at all—no laugh or even chuckle—but only a narratological understanding of the event as humor: "That was funny," television viewers casually say to themselves, stone faced (or better yet, "that's scary," says the viewer of *Black Mirror*).

To plunge into a game prepares the body for a variety of erotic sensations, yet the plunge posture has been obscured by critics' reliance on seeing the player as "immersed" within the gameworld. Janet Murray coined the term "immersion" by basing it on literary theories of novel-reading, where, according to Sedgwick, readers adopt a posture akin to navel-gazing, head and eyes bent downward, with quiet attention and interest. For Sedgwick, this immersed reading posture holds a "force-field creating power,"[50] and feels like an "additional skin shimmering as if shrink-wrapped around a body-and-book."[51] Certainly some games give a similar feeling of the outside world shrinking away, of losing oneself in the fluidity of the game, of "learning to swim, to do the things that the new environment makes possible."[52] But scholars and designers like Eric

Zimmerman and Katie Salen have critiqued immersion as a "immersive fallacy," which carries the danger of "misrepresent[ing] how play functions," as play depends on the players' constant awareness of the games' artificiality.[53] Similarly for Brendan Keogh, games "rarely, if ever, hold the player's full attention," as embodied experiences with games keep the virtual world and the actual world from ever being discrete.[54]

A more erotic critique of immersion is that it remains one of many forms interaction can take depending upon the player's posture as well as the game's text(ure) (the types of play in the interactive experience). To immerse oneself into a game suggests a certain fondness, a certain familiarity and comfort, of being enveloped into an author's world as in a long novel. To plunge into a game suggests the excitement and anxiety of leaping into a chaotic (and often randomly generated) plane. One is immersed into a tale woven by a master artist, but one plunges into the unexpected conniving of the lunatic fringe. Indeed, even as a way to speak of reading, "immersion" seems too dismissive of the reader's activity as a form encapsulating oneself into another world. Immersion belongs, as Sedgwick writes, to "a certain pernicious understanding of reading as escape."[55] Immersion has seen the game as its own unified lifeworld, where the player is led by the power of a designer in the way a reader is led by the ease of a long novel. In contrast, the plunge posture presumes an instantaneous relationship between the game and the real world, not only through the pleasures of narrative and gameplay but through the way one positions oneself via the machine, how one fits into one's immediate surroundings (office chair, carpet floor, gamer throne).

The plunge posture poises players to feel pleasure in taking control. One doesn't "learn to swim" but is handed the reins to power. In *Night Trap*, like in *Haze*, players adopt the plunge posture to prepare for instant reactions. We can see this in the way the game's teenage girls appeal to the player's masculinity in the face of the auger vampires. "I'd go anywhere with you," the lead girl, Kelly, says at the game's end, "and feel safe knowing you were at the controls." Even as the game works against mere voyeurism, the player's constant need to act and monitor functions as the only protective mechanism for the women who cannot defend themselves. Even more telling, *Night Trap* functions as a play with and against sexual urges. The very auger vampires who attack the girls are metaphors for the player's own perverse desire to put down the controller, pause the game, and self-pleasure (an erotic posture indeed). The vampires are insatiable perverts, constructs that rely "on a knowledge of sexual perversity (failed heterosexuality, Western notions of the psyche, and a certain queer monstrosity)."[56] Unable to control their sexual urges, the augers have failed to meet heteropatriarchal norms, while players are rewarded for stifling their own urges to pleasure themselves. Perhaps, this is why, throughout the game, the player is referred to simply as "the Control."

The plunge posture presumes the player will have power and will be in the position of "the Control," even if their real-life controls only allow jumping. Like in *Super Mario Bros.*, control can simply come in the abilities to jump, run, and eventually shoot fireballs. The build-up of power compels players into the plunge posture with its fascination for what could happen next, what lies farther on, tilting the player into a total presence within the moment, whether it is to see the scandal of a girl disrobing or the next panel of a scrolling world. Even so, "to plunge" into a game is merely the most popular and common of many possible postures.[57] For many gamers and game journalists, "plunge" gaming postures can negatively affect one's health, making gaming chairs—a "straight" posture—a possible solution to the damages that can incur during long play times. Gamers have also taken to postures that increase alterness and skill: standing, sitting on carpet legs crossed, or using "arm movement" (resting one's entire forearms on a desk). But these are health- and skill-related tools for optimizing bodies, not toys that help us perceive the erotics of play experiences. A player like FPS Doug can *flush* a game, his eyes widened and body tense, ready-set to expel anger and whatever excess libidinal energies, to end satiated or smashing the computer (like many first-person shooter players). One can *flame* a game, as we might imagine the "spoilsport," leaned back with crass smile, trolling others for brief amusement, interrupting the online game space to make provocative jokes. On Twitch speedruns, we see players *fist* a game, feet rattled, making the game "my bitch" (as is often expressed in gameland), teeth gritted and ready to leave bite marks on their controllers when their speedrun fails. One can *activate* a game, as with our YouTube friend ScottishDuck17, who plays with upright shoulders and consistent nods, playing with the game's complexity in mind, impressed with its various meanings. One can form *collaborative* postures with others at PC cafés, slumped over beside them, "recurrently engag[ing] in the gaming of other co-present players."[58] Finally, one can adopt "relaxed and dazed" postures with their roomates, feet propped on coffee tables.[59] These postures are not only possible for the same game or game genres but can also shift during gameplay, as when a relaxed player suddenly "gets into it," standing and jittering, or the opposite: when the game takes power away from the plunger, forcing him into a "dread posture" of fear and vulnerability.

The Dread Posture in *Alien: Isolation*

I ain't seen it, but it's here. Picking us off one by one.
—Axel, *Alien: Isolation*

If the plunge posture acts as a gravitational pull for positive affects of control, its intensity only increases when it is most at risk to change, when positive affects suddenly turn negative (unsatisfying) and the player loses the fantasy of control and power. In *Being and Nothingness*, Jean-Paul Sartre writes that the pleasure of voyeurism is not so much in the watching—one could easily go to pornography for that—but in the unexpected halt at the gaze of the other, at becoming the object of the other's knowledge, when one realizes that the scene portrayed is calculated and performed for their own gaze.[60] Being the object of knowledge suddenly sparks anxiety, a spark that comes all too easily when one is experiencing pleasure. One could hear the crunch of a stick and presume he is being watched, or the viewer's own tapping could be mistaken for a camera shot snapping off somewhere. The fantasy of the voyeur is dependent upon the risk of getting caught, and thus the anxiety of capture is itself crucial to the pleasure of watching. One must, time and again, get caught, if not by the subject being watched, then by a bystander; if not a bystander, then by the voyeur's own paranoia.[61] The optimistic expectation of control, power, and erotic sensation held within the plunge posture is similar here to an optimistic voyeurism, where exhilaration and pleasure are directly related to the risk involved in being able to maintain this posture and the anxiety that at any moment one could be caught in the act.

The plunge posture's fantasy of control presumes that dangerous objects in games will have easily identifiable patterns and will be defeatable, while useful "power-ups" will always increase the player's power. The plunge posture fails when games halt these common mechanics, forcing the player to review, reevaluate, and puzzle over these basic presumptions. To be caught off guard by a rupture in these presumptions thwarts the pleasure-seeking plunge posture, but as Sartre, Lacan, and others write, this disturbance can also manifest intense erotic pleasure. The plunge posture sets one to act upon text(ure) like a dive, excited at the risk of a violent impact. Yet a new posture inevitably sets in as one realizes, mid-dive, the force of the impact—or, once "immersed," finds the water cold, smelly, tasting like blood. Thus, the "dread posture" emerges: shoulders up, head shrunk, turtled into one's body—a protective hold. Here we can consider "dread" in its multiple definitions as prolonged anticipation, as great apprehension, as overwhelming fear, and as foreboding. "Dread" can infiltrate as property ("filled with dread") or as component ("dreadful"), and as a noun it can mean a flock of birds scared into instant flight ("the frequent dreads of the seagulls"). The dread posture is inevitable when one is repeatedly faced with disturbing objects. After a time, the player must become aware of her vulnerability after the energy to react is exhausted. Vulnerability thus feels appropriate as the dread posture's most conscious impressions of the event ("the game made me feel vulnerable"). Feelings of vulnerability often follow the plunge posture, that moment when the real world "kicks in," when the gaze looks back, when the feeling of plunging headlong into a virtual world meets the sudden silence of someone peering over the shoulder.

Games that best push players to adopt the dread posture can be found in the survival horror genre, where series like *Resident Evil* and *Silent Hill* strip away the player's perceived power to instead put power into the supernatural and erotic forces that hunt the player. Many of these games compel players into dread postures through innovative forms. In the first *Resident Evil*, faulty camera angles and difficult controls leave the user (playing the female role of Jill Valentine) struggling to survive in a haunted mansion.[62] In *Silent Hill*, the bending reality and the erotic overtones of the monsters force the player to reevaluate the real and fake gameworld.[63] Though many games elicit the dread posture, here I focus on the 2014 video game *Alien: Isolation*, an extension of the *Alien* film

series, to understand vulnerability as it emerges through the game's combination of themes of cyborg feminism and capitalism "run amok," as
well as through its main innovation: an unkillable alien (xenomorph)
whose movements remain unpredictable, sporadic, and visually erotic.
Pulling the player out of the plunge posture, *Alien: Isolation* reverses the
player's "control" role in games like *Night Trap* to play upon their techno-
paranoia, as the faults of technology signal a turn from plunge to dread.

Alien: Isolation begins with a retro 20th Century Fox opening and
fuzzy pixelated images on the title screen, introducing the player to a future (the year 2137) where technology remains as sterile and complex as it
did in the late 1970s, before the personal computer. Technology in *Alien:
Isolation* retains the same lo-fi obscurity as it did before user-friendly
displays like Windows, when only tech-savvy people and companies were
able to decode its intricate language.[64] Much of the anxiety felt by the
player comes in the surreal unease of a technology that structures everything, as any use of technology means greater risk to one's survival:
the large motion-tracker obscures one's line of sight, and inputting en-
cryption codes can cause noisy beeps. The game is set on Sevastopol,
a transit space station in lockdown and running on emergency power,
where the player—Ellen Ripley's daughter, Amanda Ripley—must sneak
through baggage claim areas and showrooms where synthetic robots are
sold. Chasing the player is the xenomorph, the alien, whose movements
are determined by a sophisticated artificial intelligence that is entirely
dynamic and difficult to predict, even when the player repeats the same
area.[65] The plunge posture's presumption that enemies can be predicted
and beaten meets its anxiety-driven end with the xenomorph. There is
no predicting her movements, making the game a constant "rogue-like"
experience of random encounters with death (whenever the player re-
starts, the enemy xenomorph starts in a different place). So, too, the
plunge posture's presumption that objects can be used to enhance the
player's power is quelled in early encounters with the xenomorph, as all
major firepower (guns, melee weapons) will fail to harm the alien and
only result in exposing the player, guaranteeing a quick death.

Alien: Isolation is truly a harrowing experience. I was in constant need
of long breaks while playing, and my own screams often pulled me out
of the experience to face those around me unfortunate enough to be
within earshot. The game was the most intensely fearful experience I've

had with any artistic medium, ever. I found myself frequently unable to go on playing, and I prolonged finishing the game over a four-month period. Without the desire to study and write about this game, I likely would not have undertaken such a dreadful experience, one that felt confining rather than freeing (I am claustrophobic and have fainted in small spaces). While playing I continually wondered how the main character kept going, whereas I would likely have just spent my last days hiding inside a locker, or worse. One might include *Alien: Isolation* within a stealth genre, but its first-person point of view and Amanda Ripley's audible heavy breathing feel far less like stealth and more like dread: an impulsive prick of realizing one's own vulnerability that results in running and hiding. The game's titular "isolation" can be felt in the long periods spent hiding from the xenomorph, staying far from the synthetics and other humans who will either make too much noise or attack the player. Hours might pass with the player sneaking through air ducts, under desks, and into lockers, all of which still leave her too exposed to ever feel safe (the xenomorph can attack the player anywhere). The sheer length of time spent inside these tight spaces induced my own claustrophobia. As soon as an exit was paved, I could still be yanked out, or some other thing could go wrong—a nearby alarm would set off, my own monitoring devices might start beeping. The game's length weighed on me for months. Every near-escape off the ship was thwarted by some faulty device.

But even this game about faulty technology was still defined by its most innovative and anxiety-inducing mechanic: the xenomorph who pursues the player throughout the game and who cannot be killed. Much of the game's four-year development was spent on perfecting the xenomorph's artificial intelligence, even developing its own proprietary engine built from scratch to accommodate the alien's behavioral design. The alien's artificial intelligence unlocks slowly each time it encounters the player, giving the impression that the creature learns from every encounter, so that any tactic used in a previous evasion could be rendered useless in the next (hiding in lockers, for example, quickly becomes a guaranteed failure).[66] But even as the xenomorph represents an achievement of digital technology, the figure still remains an erotic monster— the monstrosity of the digital itself. The alien takes the same appearance as the original xenomorph from *Alien*, designed by the Swiss surrealist H. R. Giger and taken from his necronomicon designs of creatures

meant to appear otherworldly or demonic (a book of the dead). Actress
Veronica Cartwright described Giger's creatures and set pieces as "so
erotic . . . it's big vaginas and penises . . . the whole thing is like you're
going inside of some sort of womb or whatever . . . it's sort of visceral."[67]
The alien, whose very saliva was made from K-Y Jelly, thus reads as a
queer monster, an abuser and existential threat who can only be understood in terms of her process of biological reproduction, which includes capturing (raping) other species and integrating them into her
genealogy. As the writer of *Alien*, Daniel O'Bannon, expressed in the
documentary *Alien Evolution*, "This is a movie about alien interspecies
rape . . . that's scary because it hits all of our buttons."[68] O'Bannon added
that he had believed the symbolism of "homosexual oral rape" would
effectively discomfort male viewers.[69]

The xenomorph of the *Alien* series is not only alien as a noun (the
stranger) but is powered with the adjectival property of the term, able
to make alien of anything she touches—converting ship spaces into
dark alien hives and people into alien others. Upon attack, the alien is
a nightmarish manifestation of sexual assault and othered violence: it
leaps, grabs, and penetrates the player with either her massive tail or
the secondary phallic mouth-inside-her-mouth. But while the alien of
the films seems to represent the extreme wildness of the organic, its reputation as a technological achievement in *Alien: Isolation* makes technology itself alien. The dread posture is thus simultaneously gendered,
sexualized, and racialized, as the player spends hours hunted by a black-
phallic-technological alien, where any places once deemed safe (vents,
trauma centers, bathrooms) become zones of growing peril. The alien
can kill the player even while she is saving the game at a keycard loader.
The animation is horrendous; with a quick penetrative slice through the
back, the tail appears outside the chest and the alien's arms grasp around
the player in a molest enfolding. Likewise, any companions gained in
the game could either betray the player (nearly everyone does) or are
already gestating a xenomorph fetus. Like the player, Sevastopol's characters are isolated in their struggle, wandering in packs of two or three,
with no question of banding together. They instead live in a constant
paranoia that sees everyone as potential enemies.

The xenomorph of *Alien: Isolation* inverts the "control" gaze of games
like *Night Trap*, so that attempts to just peep at the alien often result in

her seeing the player first (with her heightened senses), and attempts to monitor the alien with a beeping motion tracker will also make the player more vulnerable. "Keep moving slowly and carefully" becomes the repeated mantra that Ripley tells herself, the only tactic that seems to work. Staying still and hiding is only temporarily useful, using guns or other weapons is futile, and the array of engineering projects (smoke bombs, flashbangs, noisemakers) may only attract the alien. All the player can do is keep moving, slowly and carefully, and it's this slow and careful movement that habituates the player into a posture of dread. Dread, as Freud believed, emerged from the fear of castration, an invasion into one's private realm, and thus did not belong to women.[70] The feelings of dread—gendered, sexualized, racialized, and eroticized—in *Alien: Isolation* shift the masculine attachments of dread to constitute the feminine in confrontation with a male-dominated technology. Dread in this case is not paranoia; it is perceiving the violent force right in front of us, the thing we can't quite see but we know is "picking us off one by one."

A Universe of Vulnerability

I don't believe I've had the pleasure.
—Working Joe, *Alien: Isolation*

Set fifteen years after the events of Ridley Scott's *Alien*, *Alien: Isolation* follows Amanda Ripley's efforts to investigate her mother's disappearance.[71] In genre, mood, and style, the game reflects Ridley Scott's *Alien* rather than its successors, and during development Creative Assembly was granted access to three terabytes of original production material in order to authentically re-create the film's style and atmosphere (photography, concept art, set design, original sound effects).[72] In popular media, the *Alien* series has stood as an example of Marxist feminist science fiction, and the series has remained focused on themes of reproduction and sexual assault as well as the greed of companies like Weyland-Yutani, which seeks to harvest xenomorph eggs and weaponize their offspring into killing machines. Through its repeated serializations, *Alien* has taken liberties to extend contemporaneous feminist discourses into the *Alien* universe, and it is often held as the standard for feminine representation, with Ripley as the ideal feminist hero, the quintessential "rape-revenge heroine."[73]

Due to the films' well-known political attitudes, we can see the fan base of the *Alien* franchise as forming what Partha Chatterjee calls a political society, which takes on no recognizable form by the state but becomes politicized when the interests of the group inform a historical moment to the point that a political breach occurs, and the group's members react with a political will that was always present but at the time appears spontaneous, disorganized, and leaderless.[74] Indeed, only shortly after the release of *Alien: Isolation*, the video game industry and its players were embroiled in the largest cultural war ever witnessed in games: #GamerGate, when feminist game journalists and gamers were routinely attacked, harassed, doxxed, and sent rape and death threats in response to feminist game videos and other "social justice warrior" work. Its main targets were the popular feminist YouTube media critic Anita Sarkeesian and game developers Zoë Quinn and Brianna Wu. The emerging campaign of harassment, which Anita Sarkeesian and Katherine Cross have called "a never-ending, violent, and steady eruption of toxic misogynist hate,"[75] spoke to the anxieties of male gamers who believed progressive feminist politics was infiltrating the male-dominated gaming world, with games like *Alien: Isolation* (2014), *Depression Quest* (2013), and the *Tomb Raider* reboot (2013) as main examples.[76]

The #GamerGate harassment campaign seemed on par for an industry that has been, since the 1980s, overwhelmingly male dominated, with women making up only 11 percent of the game industry workforce—a number that doubled from 2008 to 2014 but still included mostly low-level positions. The themes of the *Alien* series seem even more piercing when aimed at the game industry, as its cyborg feminism (or xenofeminism) calls for using existing technology to reengineer gender relations and other boundaries (human/animal) while also dismantling the phallocentric deployments of technology. As Jodi Byrd eloquently points out, #GamerGate in part drew on academic discourses of games as exceptional media, outside the petty politics of identity, representation, colonialism, and feminism, to see games instead as "nonhuman" and "machine-oriented."[77] Similarly for Soraya Murray and Anna Everett, #GamerGate ended up as a "paradigmatic irruption" of the hidden identity politics within gaming (as the territory of men),[78] and it had the unintended benefit of "disabus[ing] many of the perceived truths associ-ated with the 'post' imaginary: postfeminist, postracial, and other post-post-isms."[79] *Alien: Isolation* is situated within these politics partially by reversing the presumptions of the plunge posture, where battling the alien monster can only be effective through undertaking a dread pos-ture that reevaluates the objects around and listens carefully to one's sur-roundings. The game's lo-fi technology and clunky machinery alienate the player from technology in the way women and other "non-makers" are made to feel alienated from the white and male-dominated develop-ment process.

Alien: Isolation repeats much of the first *Alien* film's anxieties by prey-ing upon the player's fears of sexual assault and bodily invasion, but it adds a form of techno-paranoia that compels the player to adopt a femi-nized dread posture in reaction to the male-dominated game industry. To play as Amanda Ripley is to live, virtually, the feelings of fear, eva-sion, and bodily harm that were present for female gamers throughout #GamerGate and that have been present for the vast majority of people whose relationship to technology has been of isolation, alienation, and vulnerability. Perhaps the most explicit enjoinder of white patriarchy with techno-paranoia is in the game's synthetic robots, the "Working Joes" who register as a male class of servants all made to look the same (working class) so as not to confuse customers. Halfway through the game, these Working Joes are instructed by their creator company, Seegson, to attack Ripley, killing her in scenes that reproduce visuals of domestic violence and sexual assault: choking the player to death, punch-ing her to death, slamming her head against the wall. The Working Joes' violence is coupled with a neutral voice ("non-emotional" according to Seegson advertisements) that ask the player to remain calm. The Work-ing Joe approaches the player with a brisk walk, only to strike, throw, or throttle her when she is in arms' reach.

The Working Joe is male power made manifest. He needs no weapons but his rhetoric and while stomping Amanda Ripley's head will tell her, "You are becoming hysterical." The Working Joes' vocal patterns of safety protocols, administrative nomenclature, advertisements, and polite mes-sages while engaged in murderous action provide an understated horror reminiscent of men who appeal to tolerance and inclusion while sup-porting a patriarchal structure. As one of the game's writers, Dion Lay, explains, "The content of the words are polite and friendly but it's lacking any real sincerity."[80] Indeed, the Working Joes' dialogue, scrambled in a robotic voice, repeats lines reminiscent of domestic abuse and assault:

> "I'm not going anywhere. You might as well show yourself."
> "There's no reason to be shy."
> "I only wanted to help."
> "Come with me, please."
> "Please, calm down."
> "Let me help you."

The only way to survive the Working Joes is to reinterpret these "polite and friendly" voices as voices indicating violence. Indeed, remaining in the dread posture for long enough forces players to reevaluate all the objects and sounds that once came so easily and were identifiable in the plunge posture. The player learns to see heterogeneous forms of hiding, of silence, of watching those in power (for Simone Browne, "sousveillance" rather than surveillance[81])—learning to outsmart rather than out-gun. One is forced into a position of active listening, of learning the details in the ambience.

If Ellen Ripley of the *Alien* film franchise can be seen as a "rape-revenge heroine," Amanda Ripley of *Alien: Isolation* appears to be the opposite. Her role feels repeatedly disempowering, subjected to violence, and alienated from the technology meant to provide her security. Yet to play Amanda Ripley means adopting a dread posture that slowly turns to defiance, where cowering in a locker—like attacking the monster—is never as good an option as moving slowly with eyes and ears focused on one's surroundings. Amanda Ripley feels like no heroine. She is young and completely terrified throughout the game, but she's also very good with tools. An engineer herself, she knows very well what tools can do and what they can't. Her route for freeing herself from the xenomorph is not to build more technology but to shut the whole thing down, first caging the xenomorph in a broken and irrepairable tower and then overloading a reactor to destroy the entire Sevastopol station. Playing as Amanda Ripley does not merely disempower gamers. Yes, the game denies their presumed expertise with emerging technology, but in doing so, it forces them out of the default plunge posture into one of dread and vulnerability that demands new ways of perceiving technology. It is within this dread posture that the player is primed to take on new strategies for listening and relating to others for whom the dread posture has always been the default.

Vulnerability and Politics, or "Okay, Ladies, Now Let's Get in/Formation"

I want to end this chapter by considering text(ure) as a way of perceiving interactive experiences horizontally, not like diving into a deep pool but like touching its surface to sense the waves and sounds of others present in it. As Sedgwick writes, thinking through texture and bodily sensation puts us on a path from dialectical forms of knowing "them" and "us," to spatial logics of being "with" or "besides" each other. These logics generate horizontal realizations with others that do not provide us more information but situate us *in* a similar *formation*. What does it mean to habituate oneself into the dread posture of hiding, walking slowly, and moving carefully, and how does perceiving of posture offer a means of understanding ourselves as we reside beside others?

As a metaphor, "immersion" suggests that players are incorporated into vertical models of "deep" experiences tracked through self-references, so that the more one falls into a game's universe, the further one gets from the real social and political world around them. Immersion is about being taken away to a distant land, or in the vertical sense, climbing higher up a ladder of collective content (like an ivory tower) until one becomes disassociated with the real world. The saving grace is that players can then, coming out of the immersive experience, read the "real world" in a different way, perhaps in a political or process-attentive way. However, to see the game as text(ure) and the gamer as adopting a posture cannot be viewed within a framework of vertical immersion, as the game is already informed by embodied habits and holds in such a way that to extend those postures (through games like *Haze* or *Night Trap*) or to adjust and reform those habits (as in *Alien: Isolation*) has a direct relationship with social and political life. While perceiving of text(ure), there is no tangible way to divide the "real" and the "virtual." Text(ure) does not facilitate an escape from the real world to provide a pedagogical experience for the player, but it stages the real world through the player's already formed political and social habits as well as their embodied experiences of gender, race, class, and sexuality. Casual readers of game reviews from *Kotaku* might notice that its female reviewers, like Patricia Hernandez, have only posted about *Alien: Isolation* by showing how beautiful the game is *without* the alien[82] or how the game's glitches make the alien less frightful.[83] Webcomic artists and other humorists have also made light of the gendered postures of playing the game. In contrast, *Kotaku*'s male reviewer Kirk Hamilton, in his review, posts numerous gifs of the alien attacking, penetrating, and killing the player, going so far as to write that "*Alien: Isolation* can only have been created for people who derive some perverse pleasure out of being killed by an alien."[84] These play experiences do not give the player a new way of seeing the outside world so much as put "the world" as merely the place where "the play experience" occurs.

Reading for text(ure) sees the horror of games like *Alien: Isolation* not as an immersion into a fantasy world but as a means of reparatively engaging with the world around us—how our interactions share the same space as the world of capitalist warmongering, male abusers, and alienating technology. The dread posture does not merely prepare one for feelings of vulnerability and exposure but for the intense burst of panic—the scream, the bloodshot eyes, the shaking. The dread posture stresses self-care over the body in panic by mollifying its effects and bracing for the sudden and inevitable emergence of violence. In never knowing when this moment will come, the dread posture stresses patience, awareness of one's surroundings, and reducing emotional stress by attempting to understand the monster and how to deal with it. Dread is reparative in that it seeks to renew and cure the player from that initial moment of panic, which came before the player could prepare for it: the first time the xenomorph appeared, the first time we trusted the Working Joes' soothing words. This initial disturbing and violent disruption arrives as a jolt, one that players must learn from by adjusting their posture for the next unexpected moment of panic. Players begin to trust their instincts, as their urge to cower huddled beneath a desk, frozen in fear, may in fact be the best way to survive.

To adopt a dread posture is to accept and account for one's vulnerability within this hazardous moment, which is to prepare for the jolts and violences that inevitably follow. For Judith Butler, Zeynep Gambetti, and Leticia Sabsay, discourses of both human rights and minority dis- courses carry the risk of calcifying group identities in ways that make vulnerability a shared affect. However, vulnerability also carries the po- tential to reveal these relations when it is not thought of as an ontologi- cal status (as "vulnerable populations"), but relationally, as "a feature of social relations" that "always appears in the context of specific social and historical relations."[85] Indeed, one does not feel vulnerable in the abstract but feels it within the confines of a dreadful apparatus—in this case, a technological apparatus where only few are assigned the roles of makers. The multitude of non-makers vulnerable to these technologies include the vast majority of unsavvy, queer, people of color but also the poor white communities and those whose relation to technology, for one reason or another, is one of fear, anger, paranoia, and vulnerability. But because vulnerability is enclosed within an interiorized immersion, it is not recognized as a shared bond among disparate peoples who all feel vulnerable, powerless, and isolated. Indeed, a paranoid reader would see games like *Alien: Isolation* as merely exposing the vulnerabilities within a particular political identity (white women) and thus easily incorporate it alongside divisive political discourses. Such a reading conjures a form of identity politics that Sedgwick herself found to be "an infinitely addi- tive version of . . . separatist assimilationism," where political identities emerge by placing people within adversarial classifications, a discourse whose very enactment is a form of assimilation.[86] Alternatively, we can look to Sedgwick's own use of shame, which she sees as a queer com- ponent that cannot be assigned identity markers.[87] What makes shame queer is its power to restructure and form new scripts based upon a shared understanding of how each of us is structured (to feel pride, to be ashamed of our own shame).

Like shame, the dread posture insists that we not catalog or rank par- ticular groups of "vulnerable populations" but trace how vulnerability reappears even among politically opposed groups. *Alien: Isolation* is as much about the chase as it is about the exhilaration of being chased, the erotic pleasure that often follows fear. The overreliance on a politics of exposure excludes reparative engagements that could form bonds with those whose identities are not the same as our own but are structured through similar feelings of vulnerability. As in Sedgwick's own use of shame, understood as a constitutive affect of queer belonging, vulnerability must be performed, responded to in art and culture, and construed to capture a political consciousness that balances according to context—in the case of *Alien: Isolation*, a politics that conceives of technology not as an ideological veil but as a field of relations whose patriarchal, racial, and imperial elements leave some people overwhelmingly more vulnerable than others. In *Alien: Isolation*, our fear of the monsters around us can only be surmounted through realizing the larger picture—that even those who strive to kill us are also struggling to survive, trapped on the same broken-down spaceship hurling deeper into the dark corners of space.

Posture Erotics

Take a look around you. We're all we have.
—Amanda Ripley, *Alien: Isolation*

This chapter's foray into the Sedgwickian sandbox of "touch," "texture," and "posture" broadens understandings of play through the interactive experience of spending hours upon hours habituating one's body to a game's text(ure). The game is no mere artistic medium in this sense but resembles an unknowable and obscure technological apparatus. Players adjust to these games by learning to switch among various postures that permit them to reinterpret and prepare. Plunge, dread, and vulnerability contain not only therapeutic and reparative functions but erotic ones. Kirk Hamilton's description that *Alien: Isolation* was "created for people who derive some perverse pleasure out of being killed by an alien" is clear in the game's atmospheric signs of sadomasochism (the alien's black rubbery body, its K-Y Jelly saliva).[88] As with *Night Trap* and *Haze*, these postures depend upon the frequent and repetitive generation of erotic pleasure.

Perceiving of game text(ure) sees engagements with games as embodied, affective, intimate, and erotic encounters. The digital anonymity of text(ure)s like *Alien: Isolation* shares in Chatterjee's political society not because it consolidates a group identified as "vulnerable" but because its vulnerability informs a wider political context of technology, patriarchy, and capitalism. One could then see text(ure)s like *Alien: Isolation* as a

"bottom-game" in the posture it asks players to adapt and in the pleasures made possible from that bottoming position.[89] Habituated to the
dread posture, players of *Alien: Isolation* may, after so many hours of
feeling vulnerable, access strange and perverse pleasures: the pleasure
of being objectified in a world where everyone is expected to be struggling for dignity, the pleasure of being contradictory when the subject is
meant to be a unified whole, the pleasure of feeling disempowered when
we are all supposed to be struggling for power. All of this, experienced
virtually, can offer a reparative release, a mindful nourishment, a form
of living in our bodies without the constant need to expose, to know,
to fight. Through play, *Alien: Isolation* can transform our "real-world"
vulnerability from incomprehensible fear into erotic pleasure.

The "posture" that initiates vulnerability is similar to Melanie Klein's
(and Sedgwick's) view of "positions" as both "critical practices" and as
"changing and heterogeneous relational stances."[90] The dread posture
only emerges after one has become habituated to a plunge posture, after
one has willingly thrown oneself into a context of vulnerability. Similarities exist across how we engage with new media—that despite our
techno-paranoia, most of us make the daily choice to remain "plugged
in," to feel challenged by others, and to balance the possible pleasures
and pains that might come our way. Even posting an update on social
media undertakes a "plunge posture," as the immediate joy of sharing
a feeling or idea contains the risk of showing too much of oneself, of
revealing a weakness, misspeaking, or exposing one's inner demons (homophobia, sexism, racism). To face our vulnerabilities does not erase
the erotic but, as Audre Lorde argued, makes the erotic possible and fills
it with power, asking us to contemplate the structures that leave us vulnerable.[91] Perhaps we can get closer to traversing our current political
moment by noting the crucial force of vulnerability in forming identity
to ask, "Why do we, all of us, feel so vulnerable?"

5

Loop

Violence \ Pleasure / Far Cry

> Men have this idea that we can fight with dignity, that there's
> a proper way to kill someone. It's absurd. It's anesthetic. We
> need it to endure the bloody horror of murder. You must de-
> stroy that idea. Show them what a messy, terrible thing it is
> to kill a man, and then show them that you relish in it.
> —The Jackal, *Far Cry 2*

From the back of a decommissioned army truck, I peek at the white
crescent peaks of Kyrat, a fictional war-torn country nestled within the
Himalayan mountains. Our truck's excursion through the landscape
beauty only lasts seconds before we're stopped by border guards armed
with AK-47s. Brown-skinned with noticeable South Asian accents, the
guards toss my United States passport in the mud before mercilessly gun-
ning down my unnamed travel companions. Their despotic leader, Pagan
Min, deboards his helicopter, stabs one of his own soldiers in the neck
with a pink pen, and then takes a selfie of the two of us with his blood-
soaked hand. His camera shows that I look like the locals: black hair,
brown skin, an Asian American returned to the homeland (see Figure 5.1).

As the Clash's "Should I Stay or Should I Go" plays in the background,
Min spirits me to his palace to eat crab rangoon from a table decorated
in monkey heads. As he speaks of his troubles with terrorists, I cannot
help but admire a breathtaking view of what appears to be the Nepalese
valley behind him. Once Pagan leaves, I follow the groans of a rebel
leader tortured by electric wires, and after a blurred rush of explosions
and gunfire, I am whisked away again, this time to a village encircled by
mountain peaks and speckled with Tibetan prayer flags snapping in the
wind, strung up alongside traditional skirts, dresses, and cotton jackets
hung to dry. There I meet Amita, a gorgeous faction leader who offers

Figure 5.1. *Far Cry 4*. Selfie with Ajay Ghale and Pagan Min. Screenshot by author.

me the first real challenge of the video game I am playing: "We're in the middle of a fucking war," she says. "We don't need tourists."

I experience these moments while playing the 2014 open world game *Far Cry 4*. The images of the snow-capped Himalayas are products of a Radeon graphics card leveled to operate at 1080p, its code-rendering firepower pushing pixels of Nepalese art murals and the gore of a soldier stabbed in the neck by Pagan Min's pink pen. I play these scenes while sitting in the comfort of a living room couch, anchored to one spot by a game controller tied to a set of devices (television set, speakers, consoles). In the game I am Ajay Ghale, a gun-toting killer seeking vengeance for my father but also an Asian American tourist looking for my roots. As a diasporic returnee, my own family history co-opts me to fight for rebel factions using a multitude of military weapons, all while hang-gliding, zip-lining, cliff jumping, and hunting endangered species (see Figure 5.2). My avatar's Asian American identity—meant to be played primarily by white players—empowers me to undertake militaristic acts while fulfilling a diasporic debt to my family, my home, and my nation. Then there is the real me: a hapa haole Filipino/Chinese/white gamer, holding a controller, waiting to get past this pithy introduction so I can start repeating the loops I've loved since I was young: shooting, jumping, running, reloading, and shooting again.

Figure 5.2. *Far Cry 4.* Hang glider near rebel village. Screenshot by author.

Far Cry 4 is a combination of the first-person shooter and the open world game, two genres that are known for continually raising the ante for more gruesome shock and violence. These are also the least Asiatic game genres out there, as both are heavily associated with American, Canadian, and European design firms. These games do not appear "scentless," as with many Japanese games, but patriotic (*Wolfenstein*), concerned with a single nation (*Grand Theft Auto*), and imperial (*Far Cry*).[1] Since the games *Far Cry* (2004) and *Just Cause* (2006), more games of this hybrid shooter/open world genre have been set in the Global South, featuring white male protagonists who are compelled to kill thousands of enemies and save brown locals, all while participating in tourist fantasies that include hunting game, water sports, and hang-gliding. The German-developed game *Crysis* (2008) sees the player investigating a space-alien structure just off the Eastern Philippines coast, while the Polish-developed game *Dead Island* (2011) sees the player battling zombies in an island resort located off the coast of Papua New Guinea. The Swedish-developed game *Just Cause 2* (2010), which takes place on a tropical island in Southeast Asia, wears its racial politics blatantly in its stereotypical brown, mustached despot and by tracking players' progress through the amount of "chaos" they have inflicted, ending with the explosion of an atomic bomb reminiscent of atomic testing throughout the Pacific. These games are "open" in that they give players a sense of freedom in choosing their own path and following nonlinear narratives. But this "openness," like the "open" of open world empire, slips from notions of freedom to an overtly imperial "open for business" logic, where the Asiatic opens for Western players determined to bring order to third-world chaos and have fun doing it too.

In writing, all of these games seem riddled with American militarism and racism toward the Global South. Yet as serious as these militaristic acts appear for us focused on the page, while playing the game they are merely an easy and repetitive slog of pointing at brown heads and pressing the mouse button, a pleasure enhanced by the game's exotic setting and tourist practices. Stabbing, shooting, and throwing grenades at an island's Asiatic locals do not register as heroic or imperial but as merely "something to do," a quick three seconds of fun made dynamic and different enough to build into thirty seconds of fun, complemented by an exotic environment to create three minutes of fun, then stretched by reward and plot into an entire game. This mechanic focusing on three-second moments, repeated ad infinitum, was first popularized with Bungie's *Halo* series, where it became known as a philosophical mantra for how developers designed the enemies and actions of a first-person shooter. As *Halo* designer Jaime Griesemer has stated, the secret to *Halo*'s combat was that "you have a 3-second loop inside of a 30-second loop inside of a 3-minute loop that is always different, so you get a unique experience every time."[2] This discussion of loops reflects larger discussions of "gameplay" and "mechanics" as a purely ludic space, as form rather than content, particularly when that content is overtly political.

The isolation of a game's politics from the way it is played and the erotic sensations therein keeps the game from ever truly affecting its audience politically, socially, or ethically. When Pagan Min stabs a border guard with his pen, I am simultaneously shocked and unmoved, as I feel no need to contemplate the gory details. I see this as a distraction, a mere story to give me a bit more motivation for the real reason I am here: the loops. The game's troubling representation of Asian revolutionaries, tyrannical leaders, and Asian diasporic heroes do not consciously impact my experience with these loops. Yet, subconsciously, the pleasurable ease of these loops does reflect the political content, as it mirrors the imagined unassailable ease of American intervention. But the player has no reason to see it this way. The ease of the loop seems the same in every first-person shooter, and story is merely tagged on for a bit of shock and awe.

Despite the tendency of many gamers and critics to focus on the "real" aspect of gameplay, games within the *Far Cry* series, having sold over twenty-three million units worldwide, have made their mark through violent touristic narratives that are marketed as satirical, inclusive, or even anti-imperial. These overtly political narratives have subsumed the discourse about these games, keeping critics from understanding how their political themes are embedded within gameplay that is expected to be fun and pleasurable, though it is often aggravating and unfair. Taken together, the games of the *Far Cry* series broach the limits of ideological critique, as the narratives remain hyperaware of the multiple intervention discourses they comment upon (militaristic, touristic, humanitarian). But seen through the erotic pleasures of three-second loops, the games' narrative and gameplay become indistinguishable. As with my own capture by Pagan Min, the evils of a foreign dictator only catch my attention for a brief moment before I am captivated by the beauty of Nepalese mountains, which lasts only seconds until I am watching a man tortured by electric wires, then running, jumping, shooting, and waking up to the words of a hotheaded revolutionary. What we see in the *Far Cry* games is not a political commentary so much as a means of making politics pleasurable, as the game relies upon the player's political awareness to provide the pleasures of gameplay. Though *Far Cry* games have little meaningful content on paper, in play, their mixture of politics and pleasure get at the heart of what foreign intervention implicitly promises, with its pleasure-inducing experiences of rescue, travel, sex, and knowledge about the other.

This chapter focuses on a single game series, the *Far Cry* series, to examine the various iterations a single series can have within a well-versed player base trained to sense nuanced shifts in its formal iterations. I explore how the first four *Far Cry* games treat the politicized act of killing third-world locals within the same momentary pleasures as hang-gliding, game hunting, and flirtation. *Far Cry* games form pleasure in and through military and tourist acts while giving enough freedom to the player so that their acts never appear totally touristic or totally militaristic. Instead, one is always conveniently subservient to the other, as tourist acts are performed as necessary measures (like hang-gliding into an enemy base), while shooting and killing become just another way of learning about different landscapes and peoples.

Following the previous chapter, I focus attention to the game's text(ure), the material postures, attitudes, and "finger-dances" of repetitive "loops" (*jump, run, aim, shoot*). Rather than see these loops as apolitical "mechanics" or a ludic "flow," I read them through Roland Barthes's notion of "pleasure," a "form of drift" that secures and reproduces the player's identity and social world.[3] An understanding of these "loops" as erotic pleasure causes us to read games beyond the scope of ideological reproduction and resistance as simulated environments where players stage playful interactions and experimentations with power. These repetitive game loops act as pleasure-inducing stimulants that mark the game as what Barthes called a "text of pleasure" that "contents, fills, [and] grants euphoria."[4]

The pleasure of game loops sees the player not as agent but as a body in motion, restricted by its mechanical form, making visible what Sedgwick calls "the middle ranges of agency."[5] The "inter" (between) of the inter-action here suggests a set of variable options based on a game's text(ure). As Adrienne Shaw writes, interactivity remains an "unsettled question" in game studies, as interaction is seen as either an experience of the body (as with *Game Feel*) or with the mind (as with immersion).[6] Yet neither position takes into account how the interactive experience is always situated within a social world and how interaction is never apolitical, nor can it be divided fully from the game's narrative. The inter-action depends upon the player's own familiarity and experience with digital devices, as players repeat hand/eye/body movements that form pleasurable sensations (rapid button presses, gameplay loops, controller rotations, the movement of the eyes from controller or keyboard to visual image, the turning of the body). The inter-action is also conditioned by stimuli totally unrelated to the game, which not only affect how the game is read or witnessed but the very actions in its plot (one's environment, background music or other audio, the chance of a friend or family member who, by accident or malice, blocks the screen). Perceiving of text(ure) in *Far Cry* games reveals how games' discourses see political and social contexts as irrelevant to the gameplay, declaring all "outside" stimuli (even narrative) as either irrelevant or secondary to the pleasure of a game's loops.

In the chapter's second half, I contrast the game loops of pleasure in *Far Cry 4* and the loops that form "bliss" in *Far Cry 2*. *Far Cry 4* attempts to revise typical exotic open world narratives by mobilizing a diasporic story of return meant to appear anti-imperial (even as the player enacts the violence of empire). In so doing, the game broadens imperial identity and unwittingly demonstrates the violence of this contemporary form, as the Asiatic son (and the player) is meant to take pleasure in dominating the homeland through repeated loops of shooting and killing. In contrast, the gameplay loops in *Far Cry 2* restrict the pleasure of military-tourist intervention, disrupting the player's pleasure by merging the message of the content (the colonial reiterations of human rights projects) with that of the form (the boredom and displeasure of repeatedly dying). In each *Far Cry* game, we see how the discourse of game violence can oscillate from seeing games as "pedagogical tools that in the end sanction and justify violence" (David J. Leonard)[7] to critiques that this view "empties media images of their meanings, strips them of their contexts, and denies their consumers any agency over their use" (Henry Jenkins).[8] However, looking past representations of violence and more toward our interactive experience of pleasure as politics, violence in video games can be seen as a rich site for understanding our relationship to others who may be subjected to real-world violences, teaching us, as Jenkins writes, "about our inner demons." The overlap of pleasure and domination in these games helps us reconceive of imperial power beyond ideological rationalizations, logics, and justifications as an erotics of everyday practices that pulls individuals into tolerating state and militarist violence within a comfortable and pleasurable drift.

Militourism in the Exotic Open World

In 2009, two Swedish human rights groups, TRIAL (Track Impunity Always) and Pro Juventute, observed teenagers playing over a dozen military shooter games, including *Far Cry 2*, exploring how "violent acts in games would lead to violations of rules of international law, in particular International Humanitarian Law."[9] Aiming to show how violent acts in games could potentially lead to "violations of rules of international law,"[10] the groups cite video games as especially relevant to the politics of intervention because "unlike literature, films and television, where the viewer has a passive role, in shooter games, the player has an active role in performing the actions."[11] The researchers' goal was to persuade game developers to portray games in a more realistic way, reflecting the "reality" "that in real armed conflicts, those who violate international humanitarian law end up as war criminals, not as winners."[12] Condemning every game they encountered, the TRIAL and Pro Juventute report shows a particularly vapid knee-jerk reaction to gaming that comprehends narrative art in general as moralistic bildungsromans whose protagonists must be punished for every violation of social code before the story can be deemed suitable for audience consumption. Similar studies show the fundamental misunderstanding in how those concerned with intervention and human rights read (and play) games, as they loosely apply the claim that violent acts in games are worse because they are "active."

Gaming journals were quick to ridicule the TRIAL and Pro Juventute report for assuming that gamers cannot tell the difference between reality and fantasy, but the language employed by the investigators speaks to a much more widespread misconception in games. The report focuses on the myth of player agency and what a game "allows," "lets," or even "encourages" players to do, which puts a peculiar burden on games to apply a godlike moral calculation on the player's deeds so that the very "freedom" of real-world simulation must take place in a completely *un*real and restrictive moralistic atmosphere (*as if* all those who violate human rights law end up on trial as war criminals!). The study ignores the most alluring driving dynamic of these games: the "open world" genre, which gives a bacchanalian sense of freedom that comes with traversing a foreign environment. In such a world, the consequences of one's pleasure are negligible, making the game space a laboratory of experimentation. As Ian Bogost writes, interactivity between the player and the game "guarantees neither meaningful expression nor meaningful persuasion, but it sets the stage for both."[13] A player does not "kill an innocent" to repeat it in real life but as a means of probing the open world system to measure its reaction, to set off a chain of events that result in a rush of emotions: guilt, regret, fury, and fear. Open world games are not merely power trips but experimentations with and against power—the power to fly, to kill at whim, to drive over pedestrians rather than swerve to avoid them, to cause explosions and see where the pieces land.

Part of the anxiety around video games and violence is that game technology shares roots (and routes) with American military funding, recruitment, compliance, and propaganda.[14] Alexander Galloway points out that gaming has always had a hand in military culture, where "flight simulators, *Doom*, and now *America's Army* are all realistic training tools at some level, be they skill builders in a utilitarian sense or simply instructive of a larger militaristic ideology."[15] In the age of drones and combat robotics, gamers have been particular targets for military recruitment, as their eye-thumb coordination, multitasking, team organizing, and target shooting mark them with an already established skill set.[16] Game studies scholars like Ed Halter and Nick Turse have traced the growth of first-person shooters from military projects, arguing that some video games (especially big-budget games) prime players toward military recruitment and reveal an "entrenched colonial logic instrumental for military recruitment and consent."[17] Other scholars have attempted to face this vexed history from the view of players, fans, and developers, who have fostered various ways of playing games that cannot be reduced to simple militaristic interpellation. Marcus Schulzke has criticized scholars for assuming that any representation of militaristic violence in games is harmful to players, while films and novels are assumed to take a more critical stance.[18] Similarly, Nick Dyer-Witheford and Greig de Peuter point out that even though many games were developed through war technology and Defense Department funding, game developers themselves have often come from countercultures "of psychedelic drugs and of political dissent" that have been "at odds with the military institutions."[19] As some games have a well-known history of connections with the US military and the Defense Department (*America's Army, Tom Clancy's Rainbow Six: Raven Shield, SOCOM II: U.S. Navy Seals, Full Spectrum Command, Full Spectrum Warrior*),[20] it seems clear that many if not most gamers and game developers are able to consume and produce such products without enabling them to take on the instrumental purpose of military recruitment.

Recently, gaming companies have sought to make narratives promoting militarism less explicit by inviting players to identify with nonmilitary heroes whose militaristic actions are incorporated into their personal narratives of travel, allowing them to speak not as a soldier securing land for a particular nation-state but as an international tourist whose pleasure-making includes securing "unstable" spaces of conflict for the greater humanitarian good. I hereon employ Teresia Teaiwa's term "militourism," which she defines as "a phenomenon by which military or paramilitary force ensures the smooth running of a tourist industry, and that same tourist industry masks the military force behind it."[21] While Taeiwa focuses on militourism as a spatial characterization, militourism also permeates experiences of play within Asiatic virtual spaces. Militourism expels feelings of masculine power through the converged imaginings of tourism (game hunting, cliff diving) and militarism (people hunting, bullet dodging), both crucial sources of pleasure in the exotic open world. Open world games that merge military and tourist imaginings provide pleasure through domination of third-world spaces presumably in need of rescue. Players take on the role of "stabilizers," seeking to integrate others into a system of liberal democracy where the United States can obtain strategic positioning—a definition that fits Walden Bello's description of US imperialism in Asia as less about economic expansionism but more as a goal-oriented regime wherein US strategic interests have been paramount.[22] To complete an exotic open world game is to conquer a space not just as an enemy territory needing to be secured but as a scenic territory that can be claimed by one's own play. As Setsu Shigematsu and Keith L. Camacho write, contemporary militarism is less concerned with winning wars, as it speaks not for a single nation-state, but is "increasingly 'androgynous,' and more fluid and permeable with civilian society."[23] As a network-based medium, games are perhaps the most everyday example of the fluidity of militarism, as their emergence comes "out of ongoing interchanges between war, simulation and contemporary technoculture."[24]

Beginning with the release of the first *Far Cry* game (2004), where players commanded a former US Special Forces operative sporting Hawaiian shirts and riding hang gliders, the *Far Cry* series provides a lens to perceive the pleasure experiences of militourism. As Vernadette Gonzalez argues in the context of the Philippines and Hawai'i, militourism emerges through narratives of masculine heroes "securing" a feminized paradise.[25] Security thus works as the goal of militarism, "an achievement in tandem with and through the pleasures of consumer practices."[26] In redirecting the militarism/tourism bind through the lens of play, the *Far Cry* games mark the militourist space as one in need of being secured through the pleasures of travel. Like forms of adventure tourism or backpacking, these games promise pleasures that overlap with the risk involved in military acts, the pleasure of discovering "the real thing" by venturing through spaces characterized as "dangerous, unknown, sexual, and unlawful."[27] Amita's challenge, "We don't need tourists," is the first of many challenges that entice the player to "go native," a challenge met with compounding rewards that level up the player to cross further into the Asiatic. Meanwhile, the game erases all evidences of Western foreign empire, marking the space of humanitarian crisis as premodern or embroiled in warfare (we see remnants of Japanese military bunkers rather than American military bases). In these works, feminism, postcolonial critique, and diaspora all work in conjunction to give players a militouristic experience without consequence, encouraging them to identify with a redemptive narrative that marks their acts of killing as pleasurable since they are necessary to rescue their fellow brown brethren. Indeed, as a mixed Filipino/Chinese/white player with ties to Hawai'i, I was constantly reminded of my own homeland debts by the various rebel leaders who pressured and pleaded for me to avenge my family against the overseas imperialist. Yet, like clockwork, there I was again, killing brown men and women with my newly obtained weapons and skills.

Pleasure and Violence, or "Why Do I Keep Killing People Who Look like Me?"

Story in a game is like a story in a porn movie. It's expected to be there, but it's not that important.
—John D. Carmack, co-creator of *Wolfenstein*, *Doom*, and *Quake*, quoted in David Kushner's *Masters of Doom: How Two Guys Created an Empire and Transformed Pop Culture*

Thus far, the pleasures of militourism that *Far Cry* games achieve could be (and routinely are) excused as mere content, a part of the narrative or the story, irrelevant to the game itself and the real pleasures we receive—the pleasures of the loop. This argument, a ghost from the ludology versus narratology debate of early game studies, has a long and tired heritage within art criticism, where it presumes a natural separation of style from content. In Susan Sontag's own efforts to create an "erotics of art," style and content are not separated as autonomous elements in a work of art but as differences produced through discourses that seek to interpret art. Even so, because the style/content dualism is so pervasive, artists play with this designation in a form of "creative mistreatment" that Sontag terms "stylization": when an artist makes style and content distinguishable and visible by "play[ing] them off against each other."[28] Camus's *The Stranger*, for example, is written in a "white style"—impersonal, expository, lucid, flat—that calls attention to itself because it reflects Meursault's absurdist view of the world. "Stylization" toys with the audience, making them aware that, like the act of reading or listening, interaction, too, is a way of experiencing the artist's vision, of rendering an obscure, rather than transparent, reality. In revealing the artificiality of a style once felt as smooth, easy, and pleasurable, stylization refuses to provide distance, making the story—as well as its politics—all encompassing. Even in its erotic sensations, the political orientation of the work "exercises a total or absolute claim on us."[29]

There is no better example of how art can be made "stylistic" through forms of erotic pleasure than in pornography (Sontag does not include pornography as a form of art except in rare literary instances, but we are far past such pretensions here).[30] Pornography is stylization in full form, for pornography seeks to encompass the audience fully, body and mind, while also keeping a distance from the seriousness of the content. Pornography makes conscious the extremity for a singular intentioned effect, fusing form and content by rejecting layers of meaning to seek a singular erotic sensation. This is why, for the pornography connoisseur, content and style are not separate, nor are they apolitical. To receive pleasure, it matters that an actor is represented not as "person" or "body," but as white, as man, as stepfather, as boss, as Asian woman, as pathetic cuckhold, as bratty bottom, etc. When it comes to erotic pleasure, the political associations of content become indistinguishable from form—music (jazzy or Asian classical), cinematography (point of view), style. The political and social subtext is crucial to erotic sensation, to masturbatory pleasure.

So it is with the game loop. Game loops put the player into an erotic engagement that depends on the political associations within the game, akin to the erotic pleasure of masturbation. Most game researchers use the term "flow" to describe this sensation. As coined by Mihayli Csikszentmihalyi, flow occurs when athletes, dancers, or gamers report feeling "in the zone," where things reach an easy drift granted by their skill and rhythmic repetition.[31] As Steve Swink writes, designers see flow as an achievement of matching a game's challenge to a player's skill, so players never get bored so long as their ability matches the challenge.[32] Challenges are aspirational, promising the player that "through repetition we might arrive at graceful mastery."[33] Characterizations of flow remain in the realm of style and form, or in gamespeak, "mechanics" and "ludology."

Obscuring the way games comment upon US imperialism, many video game critics and designers use concepts like "flow" to resuscitate the mythical separation of style and content, though practically every other media, literary, and art discourse has left this dualism behind. Protagonists who appear as ruthless killers within a racist imperial system are glossed over to focus on how game systems promise the endless flow of risk and reward. Nevertheless, these very game systems, seen as mere "mechanics," provide a useful framework to apprehend imperial violence as constituted through bodily sensations, as an erotics that floats far below the surface of public discourse. As the gaming scholar Amanda Phillips has argued, games provide a glimpse at sensations that are only revealed in real combat situations as scandals.[34] Indeed, the casual distancing of militaristic acts from the pleasures of domination is particularly relevant in contemporary warfare, where, like the open world game, a distanced third world provides a stage for American military prowess to deliver obscene amounts of power onto others. Games help us grasp how pleasure can act to motivate real imperial power, wherein goal-oriented narratives of rescue and liberation facilitate the pleasure one might receive from a violent act—where seeing a man hanged would produce no pleasure, but then, identifying that same man as a terrorist who plotted to kill thousands may give us forms of revenge-oriented pleasure, made possible through the narrative of justice and our recognition of real violence (the corpse).

To refuse the isolation of gameplay from political and social attitudes, I turn to Roland Barthes's sense of "pleasure," an erotic form of flow that is imbricated and conveyed within the political. In *The Pleasure of the Text*, Barthes theorizes how pleasure can place readers into a seamless "form of drift" where they are "driven about by language's illusions, seductions, and intimidations, like a cork on the waves."[35] Barthes calls these texts that form the reader's identity and social world texts of "pleasure," which "contents, fills, [and] grants euphoria; the text that comes from culture and does not break with it."[36] Though Barthes is foremost concerned with literary texts, pleasure itself has been a crucial concept in game studies, and Barthes's multidimensional definition of pleasure can fill in the gap between the pleasurable feelings of absorbing a text and the wider ideological social functions that sustain the player's worldview. Using Barthes's definition, we can see many "pleasureful" video games as providing pleasure-inducing stimulants to seduce gamers not into imperial ideologies per se but into stable forms of identity, secure within the norms of imperial violence. As Barthes writes, the concept of pleasure comes primarily from the need to categorize texts that bring "euphoria, fulfillment, [and] comfort,"[37] yet to limit pleasure to a single mechanical form (like a loop) depoliticizes the pleasure one feels from acts of killing, as if killing can feel the same in *Far Cry 3* and *4* (where one is killing brown Asians) as in *Far Cry 1* and *2* (where one is killing mostly white and European mercenaries in Africa and Asia). Though game theorists have long seen pleasure as central to the play experience, it has mostly been seen as a psychological, philosophical (existential), or ontological category, rather than an aesthetic, political, social, or erotic one. For Barthes, pleasure ("*plaisir*") stimulates both socially and sexually, reproducing (with slight variations) one's very identity and social world.

Pleasure is not necessarily about buying into propaganda or ideology but about the feeling of drifting in a secure space. Thus, we can see a game like *America's Army*, which has been labeled "military propaganda" or "military porn," as *un*pleasurable to gamers who hope for a narrative with at least enough political complexity not to disturb their fun. Barthes thus contrasted the text of pleasure that promotes a "comfortable practice of reading" with the text of bliss, which "imposes a state of loss, the text that discomforts (perhaps to the point of a certain boredom), unsettles the reader's historical, cultural, psychological assumptions, the consistency of his tastes, values, memories, brings to a crisis his relation with language."[38] As game scholar Georg Lauteren has argued, Barthes's notion of bliss (jouissance or ecstasy) expresses the habitual bodily functions of video game interaction. But unlike pleasure, this comes not in the form of a drift but of bodily aggravation, stress, and discomfort.[39] Socially, bliss contrasts the pleasures of stable social norms by invoking a crisis of dissolution, of losing oneself within the intensity of the experience, even if that experience is simply tedious. In commodifying the pleasures of militarism and tourism, the *Far Cry* series portrays imperialist violence as ultimately about the social, aesthetic, and erotic dimensions of pleasure. How can games induce pleasures that secures players' identity and social world as well as the bliss that unsettles them to such an extent that it causes them to reassess their relations to third-world space?

Looping Liberal War

The shooter is not a stand-in for activity. It is activity.
—Alexander Galloway, *Gaming: Essays on Algorithmic Culture*

In Dave Grossman's infamous book *On Killing*, Grossman, a retired lieutenant colonel in the United States Army, provides substantial evidence to show that the psychological techniques employed in military training increased soldier fire rates from less than 50 percent during World War II to over 90 percent in the Vietnam War.[40] Another of Grossman's claims in *On Killing* relies upon very little evidence: that the shift toward greater violence inside and outside the United States is due to media depictions of violence, especially "interactive video games," which cause "violence in our streets."[41] As Grossman writes, video games are "superb at teaching violence—violence packaged in the same format that has more than quadrupled the firing rate of modern soldiers."[42] In paranoid fashion, Grossman then associates any scholarly reports that oppose this point of view with unethical research practices, comparing scholars who defend video games (perhaps myself) with having "the same moral and scientific ground as scientists in the service of cigarette manufacturers."[43] And yet numerous studies have shown no correlation with violence and violent video games, and most studies cited to promote this myth merely prove "that aggressive people like aggressive entertainment."[44]

Due to the dearth of scholarly evidence backing up the games/ violence argument, Grossman's main piece of evidence is his own experience in the US military. For him, the first-person shooter shares similarities with real military training, where cadets are trained to aim and fire at man-shaped silhouettes in a training course that habituates the soldier into a repetitive loop—*aim, shoot, squat, reload.* After so many successful iterations of this loop, the soldier is rewarded with a badge or some form of masculine reinforcement. Eventually this habitual looping produces the soldier as a killing machine, creating "an automatic, conditioned response . . . and the soldier then becomes conditioned to respond to the appropriate stimulus in the desired manner."[45] For Grossman, this repetitive looping technique was effective in increasing firing rates in the Vietnam War and can thus be seen as evidence of a causal relationship between violent video games and real-world violence. Indeed, this training simulation model is similar to how it feels to kill in a video game—automatic, unthinking, the pleasure of the loop. Games teach us not only to kill but to enjoy killing as "vicarious pleasure rather than revulsion," where killing the distanced/dehumanized other becomes fun.[46] So far so true for many video games, and it is no wonder then that Grossman peddles the myth of video games as a form of military conditioning. Yet, as Henry Jenkins has rightfully pointed out, Grossman's model "assumes almost no conscious cognitive activity on the part of the gamers, who have all of the self-consciousness of Pavlov's dogs," and instead "reverts to a behaviorist model of education that has long been discredited among schooling experts."[47] As tempting as it might be to make a causal connection between games and violence, the context for gameplay is so entirely different as to warrant such comparisons comical: gamers play sitting down, not running through a course; gamers play in a "magic circle," never expecting to use these "skills"; and—most importantly—military training simulators feature real guns, while gamers merely push buttons on a controller. Though we can easily dismiss Grossman's paranoia concerning represented violence causing real violence, we can also extend his inquiry into more complex and critical questions concerning how the player's body enacts automation through loops and controls. To start off, how is the pleasure we receive from violent video games separate from that received in militaristic training?

The core mechanics of gameplay help recognize how games offer the pleasure of killing in the form of an automatic, unthinking drift. Developers have termed this core "atom" of gameplay the *game loop*, defined as "the collective set of actions that the player will be doing over a specific time frame."[48] The core loop is the most rudimentary repetitive action, which in military shooters is the *jump, run, aim, shoot* loop. The reward for such repetition arrives in surviving for the next loop as well as new weapons and skills. Then there are secondary loops, which establish higher-order goals that can be achieved through repeating the main loop. In taking a military outpost in *Far Cry 4*, for example, a secondary loop can look like: *sneak inside, kill enemies, shut off alarms, capture outpost*, or, when accomplishing side missions, *expand the map, hunt, loot, craft*. Whereas the core loop takes seconds to execute, the secondary loop can take minutes, demanding higher rewards for achievement: better weapons/vehicles and more progress in the narrative. Finally, there are tertiary loops, which can take hours to fulfill and depend upon the player's emotional investment in the game's characters and story. In open world games, tertiary loops look like: *capture outpost, capture radio tower, complete side quest, complete story mission*. After completion of this loop, the player is given the game's most important rewards: acquiring new skills, running faster, riding elephants, being able to stab two enemies at once, all of which add variations on the core loop of *jump, run, aim, shoot*. Games also offer story-driven rewards through the ethical and moral progression of the hero as he grows from child to man, or in the case of *Far Cry* games, from naive tourist to Asiatic security force. These loops then understand the pleasure of games not as merely repeating the same "training" over and over but in the rewards and the promise of progress, where new settings and challenges await. It is not through mere repetition but in nuanced differences and aspirations that players experience a secure and reassuring form of pleasure.

For some game studies scholars, loops, gamepads, and control schemes are regarded with distinct suspicion, as they signify processes of persuasion that habituate the player into mindless repetition in order to increase efficiency within a capitalist or militarist system.[49] These scholars see looping as a mere mechanical operation akin to the process of repetitive assembly and data-entry work. They also continue to presume the division of form and content, or in this case, hardware and software.

Yet, when players see "the controls," they do not see a bland piece of machinery but a gateway into the world of play, where "gameplay can be as simple as what happens when you realize there's a controller in your hands."[50] Game controllers are not like pages to a novel—mere material media—but like instruments to making music, in that the video game itself only becomes legible "through a learned literacy of the fingers at the input device."[51] The controls linking the player to the game remain a hidden text(ure) meant to make the play experience seamless. With every game the player must learn new habits concerning muscle memory and repetition. For Graeme Kirkpatrick, these features make gameplay loops far closer to the field of dance than routine office work, as they involve "expressive movement of the body" that are innately transient and resist meaning as well as easy incorporation.[52] The act of repeating gameplay loops will be nearly identical in every shooter, with similar button sequencing and joystick titling, but with nuanced variations: the joystick and mouse respond to different tension and pressure; the acts of jumping, running, and shooting will be slightly faster, slightly more impactful, slightly more strained.[53] While many game scholars tend to see "the controls" as outdated or as merely mechanical,[54] it is this joystick moving and mouse clicking that inculcates the player into the material text(ure) of the game, permitting a dance with the gameworld that entails not agency and freedom but the erotics of remaining in a "suspended agency," of habituating to a very limited apparatus.[55]

As a genre, first-person shooters like those in the *Far Cry* series are mapped onto keyboards in nearly uniform ways, as movement always occurs through the WASD keys, ctrl to crouch, shift to run, space to jump, mouse to view, and left-click to fire. The repetition of rapidly tapped keystroke combinations becomes an intuitive gesture, so that recurring control schemes operate like fundamental dance moves (locking, popping, weaving), provoking the player to develop new combinations and techniques based on each game's universe. To bring this analogy further: one could get impatient watching a player navigate the same hallways of a mansion and killing zombies, just as a viewer may feel the same watching a dancer repeat the same gestures over and over. The sheer repetition can feel endless for the viewer, but for the player, repetitive movements can be filled with pleasure and self-expression.[56] For this reason, games rarely call attention to their own style, seeking to use exaggerated and explicitly political stories as their main selling point. Like the dancer forced to reconsider every step, being too conscious of the style or the "controls" for the player often results in a loss of pleasure. The notion that one had power within an open world environment is quickly dismantled by the fact that there are only a few possible actions one can *physically* take. Just as musicians have only thirteen notes at their disposal, or the textile artist, for Sedgwick, is grounded by "the ways that paper, fabric, thread, and other supplies press back so reliably, so palpably, against my efforts to shape them," so, too, does the player only have a small finite number of buttons to push, with one mouse or joystick to drag.[57] The limitless open world becomes constrained by the material text(ure), yet like for the textile artist, these materials resist delusions of agency, as the "fantasy of omnipotence has no opportunity to arise."[58] To call attention to style, controls, or hardware can suspend one's sense of agency, returning one to the limited operations and patterns made available in palpable materials, musical notes in a sequence, or buttons in rapid motions.

The material text(ure) of game loops as limited, repetitive finger dances compels us to read games beyond the scope of ideological coding and encoding. The emphasis on erotic pleasure in game loops shifts the meaning of violence from an act that must be legitimated to a distinctly goal-driven interaction that warrants the pleasure of loops with the promise of more variations in the loops to come. As Ian Bogost reminds us, the meaning construed from games does not come from "a re-creation of the world" but from how the player interacts with the virtual world in respect to the game's "representational goals."[59] In exotic open world games, the player has the opportunity to use nonlethal means or to reduce the number of casualties, yet excessive violence almost always becomes the norm, as the habitual dance of the loop is always easier to perform. Violence is thus shaped through a logic of "liberal war" that sees violence as merely incidental, which gives rise to "the computational concept of collateral damage."[60] One could also call liberal war "gamified war," where warfare consists of humanitarian interventions that only "incidentally" produce violence. In Chandan Reddy's terms, once this warfare's violent methods are exposed, it is then characterized as a form of "legitimate violence" due to its good intentions as well as its backing by the authority of the liberal democratic state.[61] In games this violence-as-incident often takes the form of self-defense: the player activates a mine, leaving a full-on attack as the only option, or the nonplayable characters (NPCs) discover the player, forcing him to defend himself. Or worse, an alarm is triggered, bringing truckloads of new enemies on-site, who are pinned easily onto the entrance for the player to slaughter. "Violence by incident" shapes imperial violence as benevolent through the intentions of the liberal democratic player rather than its outcome, as the player's intent may always be the less lethal way (indeed, awards and skills are granted through less lethal means), yet inevitably the player will, time and again, end up using the more violent methods that the game has "trained" them in (as if the player did not really want to partake in violent acts). A habituated and normalized violence, once exposed as scandal, becomes excused as self-defense and accident.

Though Grossman was wrong about a *causal* relationship between games and violence, his work has helped us pin down an *erotic* one. Exposure can shock, debilitate, irrevocably wound, grieve, tighten, transform. *Repeated* exposure, however, can transfix, merely bemuse, fatigue, anesthetize, numb, normalize. This habituated dance-like pleasure of violence is in no way limited to the buttons of a game controller—one does not even need to stand up to shift violence from the gameworld to the real world. One merely needs to open a web browser and make an investment in military weapons or leave a pro-war status update on social media. While the private button dance of video games can be called a violent act, the acts that empower and invest in real-world violence are mere routine, a casual acceptance of liberal war. But all these acts, we must admit, speak to our habituated and aspirational pleasures, as violence and politics are transmuted into erotic thresholds that push us into the next loop. Seen as text(ure), the *Far Cry* series forces us to face the pleasures of the loop through virtual representations of real-world violences in Asia—the poppy trade, the Chinese Cultural Revolution, dictators who are foreign educated. Granted superhuman abilities, users play the role of a normalized "legitimate violence," a network to themselves, whose primary mode of benevolent intervention requires the pleasure-inducing accidents of militarized violence.

Far Cry's White Hero Knights

"Have you ever refused to sell weapons to anybody?"
"I'm a humanist, I don't judge."
—Oluwagembi and the Jackal, Far Cry 2

Though first-person shooters and open world games are the least Asiatic of game genres, a fair amount of them employ Asiatic settings, which are never taken to be "real" or "authentic" but are merely inspired by or influenced from "real Asia." Ubisoft's other successful open world series, Assassin's Creed, strives for authenticity with historic markers and archives, yet none of the major Assassin's Creed games take place in "Asia" as imagined in video games (the original Assassin's Creed takes place in the Holy Lands during the Crusades, the rest in Europe, America, or Egypt). Yet Ubisoft's Far Cry series, which strives for no authenticity whatsoever, is mostly set in South or Southeast Asia (Far Cry 1, 3, and 4). In seeking to represent not Asia but merely the Asiatic, Far Cry games are able to exclude US imperial histories in Southeast Asia, offering the player an idealistic travel experience by merging all the interests of the international community into that of the player, who, as superhuman one-man army, is also a one-man tourist industry, a one-man humanitarian organization, and a one-man development NGO. The series is known for providing Asiatic tourist fantasies that include having sex with local women, participating in water sports, and collecting ancient artifacts. Such tourist practices invite players to admire the local culture while also shooting, bombing, and stabbing the very locals who inhabit it. For the human rights scholar Anne Orford, texts about interventions like the Far Cry series share elements within a hero narrative genre, which "create a powerful sense of self for those who identify with the hero of the story, be that the international community, the Security Council, NATO or the United States."[62] In rereading Orford's work, Bobby Benedicto considers how this hero narrative casts local and state actors as "entities riven by premodern tribalism, ethnic tensions, [and] religious factionalism."[63] In turn, the hero is depicted as a white knight who must intervene within a humanitarian crisis that exists independent of the international community itself, thus erasing and obscuring the international community's complicity in "the production of the conditions that led to the outbreaks of conflict."[64] The heroic narrative codes violent interventions as "benign or even humanitarian" by invoking the white knight savior, whose innocence and ignorance of historical events casts responsibility for atrocity at the feet of local governments and cultures.[65] For both Benedicto and Orford, the main appeal of this figure is in the pleasure that audiences experience in identifying with the protagonist, who functions as a symbol of the international community. The *Far Cry* series takes part in this form but does so by deploying minority, postcolonial, human rights, and feminist discourses in order to mark the white knight interventionist as an honorary native who becomes more and more "Asiatic" as the game progresses.

The first *Far Cry* (2004) takes elements of the military shooter and combines it with an exotic open world setting, giving players multiple points of entry to invade military bases. The game has avoided being labeled "military propaganda" through its cheesy dialogue, campy style, and its complete absence of local (brown) characters. As Jack Carver, a former United States Army Special Forces soldier, players wield both a military backpack and a Hawaiian shirt as they traverse ancient temples and Japanese colonial-era outposts (see Figure 5.3). Since the success of *Far Cry*, which resulted in a 2008 movie adaptation, the *Far Cry* series has continued to weld the pleasures of militarism and tourism together by depicting the hero's journey as a means of obtaining greater access to Asiatic spaces and cultures. Players neither secure resources for an imperial army nor are they simply touring the land. Rather, as lone heroes they intervene on behalf of the locals who have welcomed them into their paradise but who lack the skills and knowledge (rather than the resources) to rescue themselves. With every reward, the player absorbs more local authenticity, whether he is rewarded with "tataus" (warrior tattoos representing new skills) or with more enticing views of local women. The intervention narrative in the *Far Cry* series is redolent of nationalist human rights discourses that have seen Asia as a series of crises in need of repair, where the "Asian lack of basic freedoms and civil liberties" serves as a reminder "of what the United States is proud to export."[66] Like the figure of the "console cowboy" who tames and navigates Asiatic technology, the *Far Cry* series shapes the player into a multicultural and humanitarian global leader who helps secure Asiatic space and acts in the interests of both the locals

Figure 5.3. *Far Cry*. Jack Carver. Screenshot by author.

and humanitarian intervention regimes. The game's narrative leads players from naive tourist to Asiatic revolutionary by rewarding them with knowledge of the other: cultural knowledge, historical knowledge, political knowledge, militaristic knowledge, and the erotic knowledge of brown women's bodies.[67]

For 2008's *Far Cry 2*, the game's director, Clint Hocking, sought to give greater political complexity to the series by depicting a hyperrealist setting of an unnamed central African country. To get this complexity right, Hocking sent research teams to Africa and based story elements on literary works by Joseph Conrad and Frederick Forsyth. Hocking's determination made *Far Cry 2* an unprecedentedly complex and ambitious open world game, one with a narrative that explicitly critiqued human rights discourse by representing international actors as pleasure-seeking diamond hoarders and war criminals. While critics admired *Far Cry 2* almost universally, many designers like Jeffrey Yohalem, who would be the lead writer of *Far Cry 3* (2012), found the game too aggravating to play. As Yohalem claimed, "I didn't have fun playing it, although I found the ideas really, really interesting."[68] In response, Yohalem sought to make *Far Cry 3* a far less realistic game, with none of the same "problems."

In *Far Cry 3*, the first game in the series to top sales charts, the player controls a privileged white traveler from Southern California, Jason Brody. After refusing to pay for prostitutes in a Bangkok night club, Jason and his similarly gullible white friends are persuaded to parachute over a tropical island near Thailand, where they are captured by pirates whose local Malay leader inexplicably speaks with a Hispanic accent.[69] Throughout the game, every completion of a tertiary loop begins with a new shocking human rights atrocity, from setting alight a man in a box, to sex trafficking and rape, to forced army recruitment of children, all challenging the player to complete the loop by rescuing some locals while killing massive amounts of Asiatic others. The player's rewards are "tataus" (new skills), better weapons, and the affections of the feminized figure of local authenticity, Citra, a local "warrior goddess." At first Citra sees Jason as merely a tourist, uncommitted to "the path of the warrior," challenging the player to complete loops to gain Citra's trust. To reward the player, Citra reveals legends of the island and puts the player into hallucinatory fantasies while she rides him topless. As such a hyper-sexual representation dominates tourist cultures in the Asia Pacific, we can read this act of touristic pleasure as converging with the militaristic pleasure of securing a feminized paradise. The game's representational goals here align with the act of providing rescue to brown women, doing away with the narrative complexity of the previous installment.

While *Far Cry 3* tripled the sales of its predecessor, fans also began to see it as a form of blatant military propaganda, particularly in its white hero fantasy. Yohalem responded to criticisms by claiming that the game was actually a satire. As a former intern for *The Daily Show with Jon Stewart*, Yohalem claimed he sought to create a satirical game that questioned the uneasy relationship between violence and pleasure; as Yohalem said in an interview, "This game is about entertainment, and about how far will you go in these loops."[70] The representation of violence and Asian feminine hypersexuality thus appears, in Yohalem's view, as a means of exposing how these killing loops themselves provide an unthinking, uncritical pleasure. Indeed, one could even read the player's avatar, Jason Brody, as a parody of the white tourist who enjoys narcotics and believes he can become a local warrior. In the end Jason's power fantasy deflates when he is killed by Citra, the "tribal woman" who successfully used Jason's own white masculinity to manipulate him.

Despite these satirical elements, the ideological split between narrative and gameplay keeps many players from noticing any self-awareness, as game journalist John Walker admits, *Far Cry 3* is "unquestionably one of my favourite games in a good long time, but not because of the story, and perhaps even despite it."[71] It would be difficult to find such a statement in a film or novel critique, but in playing a game, players are led to expect rewards more through progress rather than political or ethical meaning, and so long as their characters continue to level up or the plot moves forward, they'll continue to see pleasure within the next loop.[72] As Megan Condis has argued, even if the narrative of *Far Cry 3* is meant to be satirical, it offers so little difference from other first-person shooter narratives that gamers would see the repetitive killing of brown bodies not "as a reversal of colonialist discourse; [but] a repetition of it."[73]

In *Far Cry 3* the player is set on an endless run of white savior loops repeating destruction and massacre committed in the name of "the locals," yet one's pleasures from the game result just as much from repeating the loop and discovering what variations lie farther down the road. The desire to fulfill the game loop as if it is unconnected to the narrative speaks to a particularly cynical consideration of human rights intervention in general: How far are intervening actors willing to go to fulfill their mission, to receive that "ultimate gaming emotion" of achievement, fiero? Here, goal-oriented progression marks the act of killing as simply accidental or incidental. The death of the locals, drug dealers, pirates, and others may be regrettable, but they are rationalized in the greater humanitarian purpose that the player represents. Such games shape the experience of imperial intervention within goal-oriented loops, dismissing its "unintended" effects—the exploitation of new factories, the dismantling of state welfare institutions, the vast increase in sex work and STIs—as incidental. Despite the diverse contexts and histories at play, the loop remains the formal "atom" of the structure begging to be repeated ad infinitum.

Far Cry 4's *Stylistic Pleasure*

The failure of games like *Far Cry 3* to avoid charges of racism has challenged developers to create entertaining shooters without alienating segments of their audience.[74] As the average gamer drifts past the age of thirty, and the "young white male" gamer becomes a less dominating target audience, open world shooters have sought new ways to ideologically suture the contradictions that come in trying to separate the pleasures of domination and killing with its real-world parallels.[75] While *Far Cry 1* and *3* feature typical white heroes, in *Far Cry 4*, the player controls Ajay Ghale, an Asian American returned son who arrives in Kyrat (Nepal) to bury his mother's ashes but is led to help rebels vanquish a despot from Hong Kong. *Far Cry 4's* attempt to flip the typical exotic open world narrative provides a different form of pleasure, one less about domination and more akin to forms of empire operating today, where discourses of US diversity and feminism are deployed to legitimate militaristic violence. If *Far Cry 3* fails in its attempts to perform as satire, its successor, *Far Cry 4*, tries a different tactic, employing Asian American and postcolonial themes by turning the player himself into an Asian diasporic hero. Yet even as critics celebrated *Far Cry 4* for its inclusive politics, the act of killing remained just as commonplace as in previous installments.[76] The militouristic narrative form, too, stayed the same—the player is both tourist and "Rambo"—while the identities and content of the narrative were shuffled about, welcoming the player to wreak havoc, assured that their ethical quandaries were safe in developer hands.

Far Cry 4's in-game missions are fraught with diasporic clichés, from the push by rebel leaders on Ghale to make his father proud to side quests where Ghale discovers his roots in temples, myths, and fighting arenas. As the lead director Alex Hutchinson explains, the story "is really about [Ghale] discovering his own relationship with the country. His family name, how people know him, what his parents were involved with, and then choosing what to do with the fate of Kyrat."[77] As the son of a deceased rebel leader, Ghale returns to Kyrat for the first time since he was a child to bury his mother's ashes, which he carries with him throughout the entire game, occasionally talking to her through the urn. Ghale also carries the traits of a naive Asian American with little knowledge of his homeland, and his voice sounds very "neutral"—or very American. He calls himself "A. J. Gale," while locals call him "Ah-jay Gha-lay," and he never seems to speak in the local language, though he can understand it. Rather than train Ghale in warfare, most of the game's missions reward the player with "diasporic rewards," where Ghale takes possession of his father's homestead, reads redacted CIA files about his parents' relationship, and is accorded the supernatural power to travel to Shangri-la and witness the founding myths of the Kyrati people.

The invitation to play as an Asian diasporic hero rescuing their homeland reflects more contemporary narratives of imperialism by taking the ethical capital of the local into the project of security itself. As Jodi Kim and Jodi Melamed have pointed out, such a deployment of Asian American identity has helped extend imperialist projects through diasporic networks, marking third-world spaces—rather than third-world peoples—as the sites in need of rescue.[78] *Far Cry 4*'s violence is not committed by a direct member of the empire but as a part of its diasporic *subempire*, incorporated into the imperial structure as a dependent.[79] The game thus traces the limits of anti-imperialist critique by rejecting the "return to the old anticolonial nationalist and nativist positions" and instead investing in an imperialism that exercises power "not simply through an imposition of force from the outside, but also from within."[80] As Chen Kuan-Hsing has argued, anti-imperial critique meets its bare limitations when confronted by the local agents who knowingly advocate imperial force. Revealing the imperial violence of an entity like the United States does little in facing subimperial agents, for whom imperial inclusion is preferable considering its alternatives (in the case of Taiwan, advocating for US imperial domination rather than mainland Chinese imperial domination). Indeed, *Far Cry 4*'s representation of the Nepalese Civil War as the story's main backdrop expresses a similar instance of imperialism. Tasked to rescue Kyrat from a Hong Kongese despot, Ghale must choose to side with either the male rebel leader Sabal, who persuades Ghale with the debt of the father, or the female leader Amita, who persuades him with the debt of the mother. If he chooses Sabal, the player witnesses the (unsophisticated) excesses of anticolonial discourse as he helps resurrect forms of traditional patriarchy (including child marriage) and will help execute all "corrupted" villagers to fulfill Sabal's ultimatum that "there must be a cleansing before we can move forward." If the player chooses Amita, he witnesses the (unsophisticated) excesses of anticolonial Marxism as Amita brings about a new cultural revolution, destroying temples, growing poppies for the drug market, and forcing children to enlist in her new army. If much of a game's meaning comes from the representational goals and its system of rewards, one could find potential anti-imperial critique in these multiple endings, which change depending on who the player aligns with. Unlike almost any other open world game of its kind, *Far Cry 4* contains no "happy ending"; each choice ends in certain tragedy for Ghale's homeland. The cynicism of the story's three endings with Kyrat being ruled by either the Hong Kong despot, the patriarchal man, or the revolutionary woman all correspond to states of Asian nations seemingly in need of international intervention (Myanmar, the People's Republic of China, Cambodia, Laos, Indonesia).

While the narrative of *Far Cry 4* appears difficult to evaluate due to its hyperawareness and merging of Asian political realities, the game's most revelatory moments occur in its game loops, which refuse to call attention to themselves or appear "stylistic." *Far Cry 4* relies entirely upon subject matter to make its point, refusing to provide any distance or self-reflection upon the audience by asking them to change the way they play the game. The same brutality remains in ruthlessly slaughtering brown-skinned Asian locals, whether the killer is a white mercenary (*Far Cry 1*), a naive tourist (*Far Cry 3*), or Asian himself (*Far Cry 4*). The absence of any stylistic ruptures in a narrative relying heavily on shock creates what game theorists call "ludo-narrative dissonance," a term coined by the creator of *Far Cry 2*, Clint Hocking, where the gameplay deeply contrasts the values and meanings of its narrative.[81] In *Far Cry 4*, this dissonance produces a gulf between the diasporic hero narrative and the easing drift of the gameplay loops, which remain unimpeded.[82]

For Susan Sontag and Roland Barthes, calling the separation of style and content a case of "ludo-narrative dissonance" would already be limiting the text's meanings by imposing the politics outside of it (while also re-creating faulty presumptions of style and content). Just because the game is not "stylized" does not mean that the pleasure and ease of the game loops in no way represent the contemporary imperial violence of its narrative. In fact, the pleasurable ease of *jump, run, aim, shoot* in *Far Cry 4* only seems like an instance of ludo-narrative dissonance because we make certain assumptions about the act of killing itself: that it does not give pleasure; that it is not easy to do; that if we were responsible for the death of another, we would refuse to continue, we would be too ashamed to even feel pleasure. Even as every US taxpayer becomes indirectly responsible for brutal military actions overseas as well as the toleration of human rights atrocities committed by allies like Saudi Arabia and others, we critics can only imagine violence as a traumatic and life-changing act and thus expect games to follow through on this presumption.

Seen as a text(ure) where style and form remain indistinguishable, *Far Cry 4*'s smoothness, ease, and fun are not dissonant with the act of killing but are productive toward our understanding of imperial violence as pleasurable flow. For Barthes, such "flow" brings pleasure through an unquestioning drift; as Barthes writes, "[d]rifting occurs whenever *I do not respect the whole*."[83] One feels the pleasing drift of constant movement, though there is actually no movement at all. Caught in the drift or flow of pleasure, one is in fact "intractable," within a realm of "stupidity," because one is unable to see the larger picture (drifting within a bathtub rather than upon a river). In *Far Cry 4*, drift emerges through liberal notions of progress that merge with literal progression through more complex and challenging loops. Ajay Ghale, the returned son, does not progress by learning the skills of Asiatic revolutionary warriors—as an Asian, he's a natural—but through information about his culture, parents, and the politics of Kyrat. The player is given "diasporic rewards" for ritualistic slaughter, which do not seem dissonant but a reflection of how empire works for many Asian Americans, whose knowledge of their own homeland is routed through imperialist media like *Apocalypse Now* and is often weaponized for US military ventures (as discussed in Chapter 3). Indeed, the game's white CIA agent, Willis, makes this association clear when he tells Ghale, "Look at you, American in the inside and useful on the outside. You're the perfect wolf in sheepherder's clothing, way better than that SoCal douchebag I had to babysit in my last op. You're both patriots though." The disgruntled CIA agent makes the bind between a drift-like pleasure and acts of imperial violence explicit. By virtue of race and family history, the Asian American returnee becomes easily incorporated into the imperial apparatus, though this incorporation will always feel like a form of progress, a pleasurable drift further into an empowered identity. And yet, in a broader view, nothing has really changed. The "white knight" of intervention has merely swapped with the Asian American returnee, who represents both the "wolf in sheepherder's clothing" and the imperial "imposition of force . . . from within."[84] While we drift, empire remains intractable.

Reading *Far Cry 4* as a text of pleasure understands how the game's text(ure) forms our very selves, not as diasporic heroes but as players trained into a particular style so habitually that we take it to be natural or transparent (the "social jargon," in Barthes terms). On one hand this style is the game loop, which is similar in every first-person shooter and so engrained that for designers to deviate from it would be financially unsound. But in the sense of style as stylization and erotic pleasure, *Far Cry 4*'s truly transparent element is its depiction of Asia as an Asiatic mixture of extreme beauty and extreme violence, one that can be readily accepted within a militouristic fantasy. Once we parse through our own pleasure, the ease of accepting this once transparent element begins to dissolve into style and artifice. We take for granted that Ghale's home-town of Kyrat is invested in the real politics of Nepal, yet, like other settings in the *Far Cry* series, Nepal was chosen not for its political history but for its top-down environment, to "give players verticality" for acts like sky-diving or driving a mini-helicopter as well as providing "a variety of unique animals" for the player to hunt.[85] Similarly, the first *Far Cry* game took place in an exotic Southeast Asian backdrop not to inform the player about Asian history or humanitarian intervention but to showcase Crytek studio's new game engine (CryEngine), which specialized in players seeing far distances without new loading times and in keeping the entire gameworld alive in real time. As with previous installments, *Far Cry 4*'s third-world backdrops take advantage of the "Asiatic" fantasy formed by video games to facilitate a drifting, easy pleasure. The setting, which seemingly provides knowledge about a fictionalized Asia, is merely a stage to "leverage all the toys we were going to put in the game."[86]

What's intriguing about *Far Cry 4* is not so much its reproduction of imperial attitudes about the Global South, but the game's efforts to present empire as a pure drifting pleasure. While the narrative asks the player to act upon political knowledge, the loops deaden conscience. The game thus plays upon our own easiness in accepting military intervention, our own means of drifting into the pleasures of dominating others. As Amanda Phillips writes, a game's emphasis on providing libidinal pleasures can be understood as a crude juxtaposition of "fun and seriousness," which can pressure players to brood upon their own desire to dominate others and how easily that desire can be weaponized.

Pleasure sees imperial violence as repetitive loops that necessitate new and better political orientations in order to maintain its pleasing drift. Meanwhile, the violences our loops create remain mere incidental complications, a collateral damage that will surely not arise in the next loop.

Far Cry 2: *The Ecstasy of Death Loops*

A peace agreement! What a joke. A comedy act. You think these men wanted peace? They wanted privacy, is what they wanted. They wanted the world to stop paying attention to them, so they could go on with their raping and pillaging—in peace, you see.
—The Jackal, *Far Cry 2*

Far Cry 4's lack of stylization, with its transparent easy drift, marks our own ambivalent relation to imperial power. Yet to perceive the game's text(ure) as speaking to the ease of everyday imperial violence depends heavily upon the player's critical interpretation of repetitive loops. In most cases, players inhabit the loops merely out of pleasure, for technological mastery, for the dance of the fingers, for the desire to dominate Asian bodies, for the desire to become Asiatic, for aesthetic appreciation of landscape, or for a mixture of these reasons. Here emerge the difficulties of open world games—the player's "suspended agency" translates not to a desire for power but to a constant struggle with the text(ure) of postures, control schemes, and loops. Like *Fry Cry 4*, Ubisoft's next installment of the *Far Cry* series, *Far Cry 5*, similarly sought to bring a progressive politics into its game by setting the player against an apocalyptic right-wing cult in the heart of America ("Hope County," Montana). Yet, as Ethan Gach of *Kotaku* observed upon the game's release, "all of the game's allusions to real American problems . . . are at odds with the majority of what you see, hear and do in the game," which feels like a "gonzo camping trip."[87] Though the designers intended to merely reproduce the same loops of *Far Cry 4* (and thus remain transparent), in doing so the game appeared stylized even by gamers inhabited to the loop, as its ludo-narrative dissonance was so outrageous as to call attention to itself—its loops noted an excessive self-parody. In a narrative critical of gun-toting, America-loving Christian fundamentalists, the pleasurable drift of the game loops remained such a blatant formulaic copy of *Far Cry 3* and *4*, of uninterrupted jumping, running, aiming, shooting, that for many players, "pleasure" became a difficult drift to maintain.

Though stylization has the effect of pausing one's pleasurable drift, it does not necessarily keep the player from enjoyment (*Far Cry 5* was still the highest selling of its series). Instead, stylization can offer pleasures of a different form. Of all the games in the *Far Cry* series, only *Far Cry 2* consciously attempts stylization, as its designers ambitiously sought to jar the identity-churns of pleasure at the "atom" level of core bodily interactions, pushing players to perceive the erotics of everyday empire.[88] Even so, as a first-person shooter, *Far Cry 2*'s anti-imperial dimensions have been lost in its mere representation of killing. The 2009 human rights report by TRIAL and Pro Juventute list *Far Cry 2* as a specific example of how games irresponsibly represent human rights abuse, citing a scene where a military junta attacks the player inside of a church, a human rights abuse of "neutral grounds" that goes "unpunished." In simply tracking violations, the report ignores the game's larger context, which explores the displacement of refugees by a civil war run by Western mercenaries, international aid organizations, and NGOs, who all become increasingly more violent as the trade in blood diamonds begins to dry. The report's plangent denunciation of *Far Cry 2* not only misreads games as an interactive, experimental experience but also lacks in taking the game seriously, where in fact *Far Cry 2* explicitly critiques human rights discourse in its representation of international actors as pleasure-seeking diamond hoarders. Once one faction in the civil war begins to dominate the others, such international actors take it upon themselves to "jiggle the pot" to keep the war going.

That the humanitarian crises in *Far Cry 2* go "unpunished" is exactly the point of the game, which seeks to criticize the malevolent effects of human rights regimes (perhaps TRIAL and Pro Juventute themselves) through the player's mission to kill the notorious American arms dealer, the Jackal. As the journalist Oluwagembi tells the player:

> I have covered sixteen wars across Africa. Sixteen. And every time, he has been there. Selling his weapons and making a fortune while millions of people suffer and die. He thinks he can continue to do his work in secret.

But not this time. These stories, they are going to come out. The Jackal's. And the warlords'. The soldiers', and the boy soldiers', even the NGOs'. I intend to expose the whole sordid mess.

When the player contracts malaria in the game's beginning, the Jackal reveals himself, chastising the player's unnamed clients who hired the player to assassinate him. The Jackal ridicules their human rights language that calls him a "destabilizing influence" because he is "in clear violation of the Joint Signatory Framework." The Jackal's attitude emerges as a critique of foreign intervention itself.[89] "It's not sick to arm people," he says. "It's sick to bombard their crooks and dictators in protection of our interests, and they call it 'international justice' . . . The drone is the oppressor. The AK-47 is the great equalizer. I empower these people." Rather than place the player on a game loop to become "manly" or to "save locals," the main goals of *Far Cry 2* are to kill the Jackal for money and escape the war-torn country. This assassination narrative is not told through cut scenes but through interactivity, so that the realism of the story corresponds strikingly to the action of the game. As game journalist Tom Bissell has written, the act of killing in *Far Cry 2* does not give one pleasure, but guilt, remorse, and disappointment. After Bissell listens to the terrifying screams of a man he set aflame with a Molotov cocktail, he feels "a kind of horridly unreciprocated intimacy with the man I had just burned to death."[90] He concludes that *Far Cry 2* is "virtually alone amongst shooters," as the game "may reward your murderous actions but you never feel as though it approves of them, and it reminds you again and again that you are no better than the people you kill. In fact, you may be much worse."[91] While the story shows increasingly complex characters who chastise international intervention, the gameplay itself explores "the behavioral and emotional consequences of being exposed to relentless violence."[92] Since the player of *Far Cry 2* is not by default American, the Jackal represents the most American presence in the game, an unlikely "hero" who criticizes the international lack of force by providing force himself.[93]

I conclude this chapter exploring *Far Cry 2* as stylized text(ure) that calls attention to itself by constantly disrupting the player's pleasure with ambivalence and distance that keep the player situated within its world of relentless violence. I thus treat the game as what Barthes terms a "text of bliss" that "imposes a state of loss" by fundamentally unsettling notions of human rights intervention and makes the militouristic delights of the open world game seem frightening, aggravating, and most assuredly unpleasurable.[94] In comparison to the other *Far Cry* games, the player takes part in almost no tourist experiences: no skinning game, no predators to hunt, no helicopters or jet skis, no feminized locals to become infatuated with. The loops in *Far Cry 2* that feature repeated killings are also not pleasurable or easy, but they are disrupted repeatedly by the game's realist style. During any loop of *jump, run, aim, shoot*, players may be interrupted by symptoms of malaria (blurred vision), they might get dizzy from running (impaired motor functions), their weapons may jam, or the skirmish may lead into the forests, forbidding lines of sight. These realist mechanics led to the game's reputation as difficult and unrewarding. While critics admire *Far Cry 2* almost universally, many players and designers, like the lead writer of *Far Cry 3*, have found the game too aggravating to play.[95] Game scholars like Olli Tapio Leino have seen such problems, "which the player might perceive as unpleasant and the designer as faulty," as part of the gameplay experience itself.[96] For Leino, one way to pursue the experience of such problems is in the ultimate disruption of the game loop: the "death loop," where the game saves players' progress just before their death, when they are cornered by enemies, have low health, or are weakened by poison. The *dis*pleasure of playing *Far Cry 2* emerges through this death loop, since nearly every save point in the game seems to represent a new repetition of death. After saving, the player is tasked to drive across the "free" and "open" gameworld where military outposts threaten them at every turn, making every minute feel like a gamble against death. This makes the game not merely challenging but *unfair*. In every return from death the player may yearn to reiterate the jump, run, aim, shoot loop but instead gets stuck, condemned to repeat the death loop again and again so that the "hedonistic project" (or pleasure project) of gameplay is dismantled by an aggravating, seemingly unfair problem. These disruptions of the game loop provide not a pleasurable drift but a bliss that unsettles the security of the imagined exotic open world. Bliss reinterprets perceived "problems" like the death loop as a means of confronting the assumptions behind gameplay itself—namely, that it be a pleasurable experience.

When compared to the game's narrative, the bliss of *Far Cry 2* produces not merely the inward-looking self-shattering of jouissance but also the outward-looking future imaginings of ecstasy. As Sontag writes, the distancing effect of stylization is not "just a movement away from the world, but toward the world."[97] Bliss arrives in an ecstasy that changes the players' views of themselves as well as their relations with others. As Jose Muñoz writes in *Cruising Utopia*, ecstasy (like the taking of the drug) steps outside the self and outside a time (straight time) that is "saturated with violence both visceral and emotional," and "go[es] beyond the single shattering that a version of jouissance suggests."[98] Like the religious experience of ecstasy, feelings of ecstasy do not self-enclose but open to become conscious with others. This is because ecstasy is not necessarily a split from reality but from the social norms of a drifting, secure pleasure. So, too, the bliss of *Far Cry 2* jerks players outside their familiar world of pleasure to venture into a realm of play that may better reflect one's own reality (sitting, feeling a game's text(ure), being an imperial subject). The ecstasy of *Far Cry 2*'s blissful gameplay corresponds to the game's narrative that includes having malaria and trying to survive in a wilderness while being hunted by soldiers. Within this frightful narrative, the pleasures of game loops are replaced by the bliss of slowness, sudden disruptions in the loop, and death. Even touristic aspects only harm and aggravate the player: the map is difficult to read as it jumbles in the player's lap as they drive (see Figure 5.4), the player is forced to spend time fixing cars, and the only currency in the game is rough diamonds, which makes buying anything other than guns extremely difficult. The game's ecstatic bliss calls attention to itself, and in so doing calls attention to the reality of militouristic intervention.

As a stylized open world game about intervention, travel, and militarism, *Far Cry 2* enacts the "suspended agency" of game text(ure), making players feel powerless, trapped by a dangerous world where they do not belong, constraining their agency within the unfair interruptions of pleasurable loops. The "bliss" of the game's shocks and displeasures could perhaps be construed as what Bonnie Ruberg calls queer gaming as an affect, "a way of feeling otherly or 'badly' during play" that represents "a rejection of the heteronormative status quo that takes place on the level of the body."[99] Whereas Ruberg relegates the queer into "no fun," the ecstasy enabled through the text(ure) of *Far Cry 2* suggests

Figure 5.4. *Far Cry 2*. Using the in-game map while driving. Screenshot by author.

a more poignant anti-imperial politics. The realism and shock of the game's narrative is inseparable from the aggravation, desperation, and unsettling experience of gameplay. Unlike the narrativized critiques of intervention in other *Far Cry* games, *Far Cry 2* depicts the violence of militourism through the violence of the death loop: the violence of feeling inexplicably powerless within a genre and series that has promised the pleasures of imperials power. In so doing, *Far Cry 2* instead offers ecstatic engagements, a new political pleasure that arrives not through militouristic power fantasies but through the aggravating and seemingly impossible act of stopping an American gun dealer who speaks the truth of what it means to be an American today: "War," he says, "is my home."

The Anachronistic Subject

In concluding this chapter with the unsettling experience of playing *Far Cry 2*, I don't mean to place games within an ideological binary where games like *Far Cry 2* are indexed as "resistant" and games like *Far Cry 3* and 4 are dismissed as ideological. This focus on the entire *Far Cry* series invokes the internal multiplicity of a genre, which "no individual text will ever be able to represent."[100] In this manner we can read *Far Cry 2* as

a significant anomaly that does not "flip" the hero narrative by introducing an empowered ethnic protagonist (as *Far Cry 4* did) but attempts to
reframe the presumptions of the genre toward an anti-imperial project
even while masking itself within that very genre. In so doing it also pro-
vokes questions concerning the player's very self as a "gamer." Whereas
scholars see gamers as interested in heteronormative and empire-
building fun—so that whatever appears "non-fun," "queer," or "serious"
appears as a counternarrative—this focus on the *Far Cry* series adjusts
to the types of gamers who adopt various postures and enjoy loops for
a variety of reasons (the act of killing is one reason among many). In so
doing, the series delineates the position of the subject who plays the *Far
Cry* series and takes pleasure in each game in it, in both the loops that
bring pleasure and the loops that bring frustration. This is the player
who partakes in both texts of pleasure and texts of bliss, who Roland
Barthes called an "anachronistic subject" who "simultaneously and con-
tradictorily participates in the profound hedonism of all culture . . . and
in the destruction of that culture: he enjoys the consistency of his selfhood (that is his pleasure) and seeks its loss (that is his bliss)."[101] To
comprehend how players can switch between such forms (and accept
them within the same game series) means following how games use
sophisticated techniques and employ various discourses in order to fuse
politics and pleasure. It also means inspecting how games speak to the
multiple desires of the gamer: the desire to help others, the desire to
envision American imperial power as benevolent, the desire to tour and
discover other worlds beyond the one bestowed upon us, the desire to
critique and reflect upon the narratives of these games while also shooting some folks who look just like you. That all these desires are casually
employed toward habituated loops of mass killing marks the anachro-
nism of this subject, who desires both the pleasure of these experiences
as well as their unsettling, who experiences meditations upon diasporic
belonging alongside pleasures of domination of the homeland, and who
playfully experiments with these elements in an open world not quite of
their own making.

The *Far Cry* series navigates the tensions between games and militarism, as each game has sought to invoke the pleasures of killing, yet each
game has also sought to disrupt, debunk, and revise previous iterations
in the series to account for the unethical practices of militourism. These

games are not ideological arguments but are artistic objects in the world, and as such they are "both autonomous and exemplary"; they contain their own worlds that singularly handle the ineffable, the unspeakable, the inexpressible, and in their freedom to mean nothing, they set the stage for examination and evaluation—not of the artwork, but of ourselves.[102] The very erotic pleasures we experience through their text(ure) expose our own attachments to the social world around us, a world of normalized violence, a *doxa* as Barthes called it, a nature in itself. The crisis we need to confront is not the humanitarian crisis abroad but the crisis of ourselves: that, coming from a society founded on slavery, massacres and displacement of indigenous peoples, and permanent imperial war, we have grown inured to violence as an easy, drifting pleasure. Video games help us fathom how none of us are mere spectators who can discuss military intervention from the outside. We are participants whose pleasures challenge the very possibility for such discussion. The mutually constitutive relationship between tourism and militarism is felt in these games through interactive loops of pleasure, where violence remains an incidental but necessarily justifiable byproduct. This, says our erotic pleasures, is not about analyzing a video game. It's about us: we imperial anachronistic subjects who want to have our pleasure and critique it too.

6

E-motion

Transpacific \ Virtual / Blur

I think the great goal is in fact to become someone else . . . to
transform oneself from a unitary identity to an identity that
includes the other without suppressing the difference . . .
That would be the notion of writing a historical inventory,
not only to understand oneself, but to understand oneself in
relation to others, and to understand others as if you would
understand yourself.
—Edward Said, "Edward Said on Orientalism"

This final chapter is not about video games or about us. It's a final slip
into the slipstream of our erotic pleasures that leads always to the other—
not the transcendental other, that other of moral virtue and victimhood,
nor the exotic, savage, primal other. Because our slipstream follows the
digital, this other lives between the real and the nonreal, the authentic
and the inauthentic: it is the virtual other. In the sphere of video games,
"the virtual other" is a broader understanding of the Asiatic, a slip further into the stream, knocking off the glasses that promised exactitude.
The virtual other is the "-ic" of Asiatic, the unknowability, the blur.

Mainstream political discourse tells us that the Asia Pacific is already
a blur, something to be heralded, claimed, or disowned. In the days following his 2012 reelection, US President Barack Obama took a transpacific flight to the Association of South East Asian Nations (ASEAN)
summit in Cambodia, where he stated that "the United States is and
always will be a Pacific nation" and made commitments to "restoring
American engagement" with the Asia Pacific as "the fastest-growing region in the world." Obama's remarks jump-started the United States' "Pacific turn" that characterized much of his second term and manifested
in the Trans-Pacific Partnership (the TPP), a trade agreement similar to

NAFTA that had taken seven years of international negotiations among Asian and North and South American countries. Obama presented the agreement with a competitive machismo that claimed economic dominance over Asia, a style of "black cool" inflected with his own Asiatic self-image (as being born and raised in Hawaiʻi and attending school in Indonesia). In his 2016 appearance on *Late Night with Jimmy Fallon*, Obama responded to Fallon's call, "Are you down with the TPP?" with the Naughty by Nature rap lyric: "Yeah you know me."[1] Despite Obama's efforts to sell the TPP to the public, America's claims over Asian economic structures through Obama's own Asiatic identification dissolved in January 2017, two days after Donald Trump's inauguration, when the United States withdrew from the TPP, leaving much of the world wondering how the new "Pacific Century" would proceed without American economic commitments.[2]

While the Asiatic blur has invariably helped sell Asian commitments in political discourse, in the academy, scholars have downplayed the Asiatic blur to produce work construed as authentic, objective, backed by pedigree and expertise. Said's own *Orientalism* sought to expose the blur of Asia as a space of exoticism and primal desire, while Asian American studies and postcolonial studies scholars have traced the preconditions of imperial and minority histories that brought forth "the other" and reinforced divisions of East and West, Orient and Occident. In the early 2010s, the discourse of transpacific studies emerged as a successor to these discourses by responding to the economic discourses of the TPP, presuming that the agreement itself was inevitable. Responding to Obama's own "Pacific turn," transpacific studies became a paradigm for tracing the intersections of multiple discourses across Asia and the Americas. The publication of two anthologies, *The Trans-Pacific Imagination* (2012) and *Transpacific Studies* (2014), attempted to theorize this new field outside US-centered epistemologies and to critically examine the transpacific as a contact zone that conjured ideas of development and imperial fantasy. Indeed, transpacific studies has responded to the "Asiatic blur" that the Obama administration attempted to claim not by denying the blur itself, but by critically examining it, by asking how the anxieties and desires that emerge from the "Pacific turn" have drawn attention away from bombing campaigns using unmanned aerial vehicles (UAVs/drones), which increased substantially under Obama (more bombs were dropped by drones during Obama's first year than during George W. Bush's entire presidency) and were staggeringly inaccurate (during one five-month period, 90 percent of people killed in drone strikes were not their main target).[3] By reading, comparing, and theorizing sites within a wider view of Asia, scholars have sought to excavate the complex transpacific routes that have isolated the logics and procedures of imperial power.

This concluding chapter reflects upon the allowances of interactive media to lay bare our relationship with virtual others through the abstractions of Asiatic virtual worlds. To complete this codex's loop, I return to the questions from chapter 1 that began this inquiry: How do games shape our understandings of the Asiatic other, and under what circumstances do games offer new ways of comprehending the world and our place in it as a violent and imperialist force? To answer these questions, I consider discourses of virtual otherness manifested in transpacific cartography, travel, and virtual worlds. Transpacific studies provides an overview of these discourses, as it has sought to disrupt the presumptions of Pacific Rim, diaspora, and the TPP itself. Yet transpacific studies reaches its epistemological limits when we surface slowly over the Pacific, where islands and seascapes remain inescapably center framed. Though transpacific studies follows the virtual "blur" of Asia, its emergence as a response to the TPP has made it difficult to account for colonial zones that do not resemble economically powerful nation-states. Islands like Jeju, Okinawa, Hong Kong island, Oahu, the Marianas, and Guam often play the role of a colonial outpost, a frontier, or an insular territory subject to the whims of a larger power. In contrast, the playful cartographies of interactive media provide a digitized distance from virtual others without the lure of authenticity or even facticity, opening imaginaries of the transpacific to not only include but to center upon Oceanic peoples and cultures. Thus, I attempt to reimagine the transpacific by following the presence and absence of a variety of maps, from those on book covers, to tourist maps, to the procedurally generated maps of *Civilization V*, to the virtual reality experience of Google Earth. How can such maps let us follow transpacific connections that go beyond the "cold war" and "hot war" geographies to borderlands that do not configure as either? How can imagined maps reveal the structures at play in the manufacturing of wartime material, atomic testing, war games, drone bombing, environmental degradation, military recruitment, and basic health?

By "virtual other" I mean the other produced through recognizing obscurity, silence, and misrecognition. My use of "Asiatic" in this book has been concerned with Asianish games, styles, and practices, and it has differed widely from terms of endearment like "yellow power" or "Asian American," as it references not the ways subjects see themselves but the gaze that looks upon the "untrue" other, the other always in quotation marks—the virtual other. Though some scholars have sought to deracinate the subjects of Asian America by claiming "Asian American" as a political formation (as a "subjectless discourse" or a "heuristic"),[4] the attachment of minority and diasporic peoples from Asia to Asian American identity has persisted unabated. In our erotic view, we can see that this very desire from academics to claim "Asian America" as a method or discourse speaks to anxieties concerning the erotic body, as bodies are never homogenous—it is their plurality that will always stand out, whether we focus on race, sex, class, or even their ethical and political affiliations (of which Asian America, for better or worse, has many). The Asiatic, in turn, is purely heterogenous and does not presume political essence but mixed-up practices that are only tentatively called Asiatic. As I find in Barthes, Foucault, and Sedgwick, this sense of Asiatic as a placeholder for plurality comes from the desire not to classify others but to understand without knowing, to realize without being certain, to dismantle the self. The Asiatic in this sense is not about the excesses of categorization, nor does it shift a demeaning language into something emboldening, but it is rather about the inherent instability of naming, the blurriness of racial thinking, and our experiences within that blur. For this reason, the Asiatic does not translate well into identity politics. But it does offer routes to social transformation by recognizing what it means to relay, through the other, one's own self-destruction.

Thinking through the virtual other slips deeper into these transpacific relations by placing attention not onto this other but onto the gazer who has given up on obtaining a truthful and authentic access to the other and therefore sees them as virtual, somewhere between the real and the fake. The virtual other stands in as the thing obscured by one's own way of seeing, a "something out there" that calls attention to one's own blurred vision. "Virtual" suggests digitized distance but also fakeness, emptiness, a void that the viewer fills with his or her own hunger. Roland Barthes produces this virtual other in *Empire of Signs* as "the country I am calling Japan"[5] and in his *Travels in China* as the obfuscated China seen through a "sideways gaze."[6] Barthes's travel writings comprehend the virtual other as that which reflects blurred vision—in this case, a vision conditioned by Western political values and the hunger for self-confessed authenticity. Within the same decade, Foucault's observations of Hellenistic society reflect the virtual other produced in his own visits to Tokyo and his fascination with Zen Buddhism. While not seeking to say anything characteristic of Japanese society, Foucault speculated upon Eastern forms of *ars erotica* in contrast to the *scientia sexualis* discourses dominant in the West. So, too, Eve Sedgwick's gravitation toward Buddhism and Japanese arts also produces a virtual other, a signifier of the emptiness and meditations upon death that attracted Sedgwick after her diagnosis with a terminal illness.

Whereas the "Asiatic" can unconsciously relegate people and objects into the realm of the Asianish, and thus the player need not see a game as Asiatic to play with it as such, the virtual other is made possible through a conscious desire to de-imperialize the self by shifting how one perceives, giving deeper meaning to feeling, erotic sensation, and realization. The virtual other thus becomes a refuge for illegibility, representing modes of knowledge (or non-knowledge) that counteract the positivistic thinking of the open world empire. In the work of Barthes, Foucault, and Sedgwick, engagements with virtual others understand the Asiatic as remaining productively obscure and able to produce new, playful imaginings. Indeed, we see this also in virtual worlds: an *unknowingness* fundamental to the virtual other, where the theorist, thinker, traveler approach the space and its associated symbols as neither real nor fictive. Since the viewer has no presumption to authority, the virtual other cannot be made into a subject of knowingness, a being whose "secrets" or "truths" can be exposed or confessed. In interactive media, the other is made virtual not merely through digitization but through the presumptions of play and motion. Playing with and against a distant form is far different from the militaristic practices of survey, identification, and mapping that enhance drone warfare. It names not an identity or category but an ineffable presence.

In video games, the virtual other does not generate affective bonding so much as an erotic s(t)imulation that pushes the player upon drifting waves generated by constant movement through a virtual world. The virtual other here does not suggest nation or subjectivity but distance itself, manifest by its flee(t)ing behavior and our own giving chase. Its erotics are attached to slippery interactive motion, or e-motion. In *Atlas of Emotion*, Giuliana Bruno coins the term "(e)motion" to describe "the haptic affect of 'transport' that underwrites the formation of cultural travel."[7] Bruno points out that the Latin root of emotion concerns a moving force, as it stems from *emovere*, "an active verb composed of *movere*, 'to move,' and *e*, 'out.'"[8] In interactive media, this (e)motion appears within the virtual sensescape as "e-motion," where one feels disembodied within an electricity-like movement over a digitized world. In e-motion one feels computerized, drone-like, watching the virtual other from an aerial view. E-motion leads not to feelings of becoming an overseer or God but to the playful openness of erotic mobility: searching, finding, touching, consistent discovery, and unexpected challenges. E-motion, like e-waste, e-communication, and e-business, is produced via the console device and transforms its core concept ("motion") through a presence that is not quite real, not quite fake, but virtual.

The Transpacific

I maaku
The frigate birds fly high above us and I'm afraid of falling
I maaku
—Teresia Teaiwa, "Fear of Flying (in Broken Gilbertese)"

In seeking to capture the blur of routes, missed connections, and fraught discourses from competing imperial projects, transpacific studies inherits the "transatlantic," a term invoking the slave trade and other movements of bodies and commodities within networks of capital and empire.[9] As a critical response to studies of the Pacific Rim, diaspora, and Asian American studies, as well as to political and economic policies concerning the "Pacific Century," transpacific studies has sought to evade the nationalist trappings of past disciplines, which

Lisa Lowe has called "disciplines at the service of a US nationalist epistemology, disciplines that have traditionally produced knowledge for the established centrality of the United States."[10] With the United States' withdrawal from the Trans-Pacific Partnership, the end of the TPP has emboldened scholars to mutate the discourse into something even more critical and imaginative, one that will no longer rely on counteracting economic and nationalist policies but will trace new zones and relations that have thus far been eclipsed by multiple imperial interests.

In its early start, transpacific studies was problematic in the same way that Pacific Rim and "diaspora" privileged mobility, solidified racialized identities, and sought to explore movements *over* rather than *within* Oceania. Huang's *Transpacific Imaginations* (2008) coined the transpacific as a formation wherein "literary and historical imaginations . . . have emerged under the tremendous geopolitical pressure of the Pacific encounters."[11] Huang's use points to the already existing nation-based epistemologies that compete across the transpacific, a semiotic field that reflects competitions based on military, economic, political, and cultural power. In its emergence, transpacific studies invoked a set of competing imperial and social forces rather than the hegemony of a particular colonial power, even as it maintained focus on unequal networks and transnational power formations (what Rick Baldoz has called a "transpacific imperial zone"[12]). But within this discourse the Pacific as a region remained within the aerial view of a transpacific flight, an isolated body only to be traversed (or vacationed in). Indeed, if the TPP included *no* Pacific Islands states, studies responding to it are only remotely more likely to spotlight these locations. Transpacific projects are thus envisioned as dialogues between globalized East Asia ("Global Asias") and Asian America (already presumed global). As Epeli Hau'ofa has written, global paradigms such as these have threatened ways of knowing and seeing that emerged from Pacific Islands cultures. Or, as Teresia Teaiwa wrote in Gilbertese (Kiribati), "I maaku" ("I am afraid") / "The frigate birds fly high above us and I'm afraid of falling / I maaku."[13]

If, as Subramani writes, one of the greatest threats to peoples of Oceania is "the global paradigm," which routes economic and democratic success for some, and for islanders results in "poverty, malnutrition, unemployment, crime, violence, ethnic conflicts, homelessness, and

Figure 6.1. Book jacket for *Transpacific Studies: Framing an Emerging Field.*

cultural and environmental disruptions," then we must inquire under what grounds "transpacific" has also formed "global" reimaginings of Oceania.[14] Janet Hoskins and Viet Thanh Nguyen's 2014 anthology, *Transpacific Studies: Framing an Emerging Field*, defines "transpacific" as "an inherently critical and oftentimes oppositional approach" to political and economic uses of the term.[15] While the TPP imagines the Pacific as "an arena of economic development and imperial fantasy," deploying transpacific *critically* names a contact zone of "critical engagement with and evaluation of such development and fantasy."[16] A transpacific project can be less focused on comparisons and more on overlapping regimes of power that exist under the radar. Its reference points are transnational: industrial capitalism, modes of imperial governance, repressed social and artistic movements. This conception of the transpacific also considers how popular notions of the term have left the Pacific Islands largely absent,[17] an absence rendered cartographically on the map that makes up the anthology's book cover (see Figure 6.1), which accentuates

North America and Asia on its back, while the Pacific itself remains a non-space left for the book's title, subtitle, and editor names. Major island chains like Hawai'i and New Zealand (Aotearoa) are barely visible or are relegated to the crease.[18]

Published the same year as Nguyen and Hoskins's anthology, Erin Suzuki's definition of the transpacific carries greater focus on Oceania, and in particular "the omnipresence of the U.S. military" within island bases.[19] Suzuki's conception broadens the transpacific to the unequal and imperial forms of exchange within islands such as coolie labor, American neocolonial power, tourism, and the use value of English. Suzuki situates "transpacific" as a successor to "Asia Pacific" and "Pacific Rim" that is broader and more diverse, writing that "there is not just one transpacific, but multiple transpacifics that conflict, intersect, and overlap."[20] Similarly, Denise Cruz's breakdown of transpacific in her 2012 book *Transpacific Femininities* sees the term as opening discursive space for peoples and cultures that are too often seen as tangential or merely in transition toward something else. Cruz notes Aihwa Ong's definition of "trans" as a prefix that "denotes both moving through space or across lines, as well as changing the nature of something."[21] For Cruz, transpacific emphasizes "states of transition and change" and sees mobility across (or within) the transpacific as a change of state. The transpacific notes how transnational subjects (like Cruz's "transpacific Filipina") become unknowable, as they cannot be contained in singular types.[22] Without adequate discursive space, such subjects escape definition, and their fluidity allows them to fill in the gaps of national subjectivity. Freed from the TPP as its main discursive target, transpacific studies has begun to reimagine geographical coordinates in ways that spotlight previously unexamined connections among histories, peoples, and objects that are usually dismissed as too mixed, too transient, or too geographically separate to sustain a viable study.[23] As a term that invokes competing discourses separated by language, nation, and race, transpacific can also speak back to North American studies that have depended upon whiteness and American citizen subjectivity as their major constituting force.

Territories and Terripelagos

Until recently, the sea beyond the horizon and the reefs that
skirt our islands was open water that belonged to no one and
everyone . . . As far as ordinary people of Oceania are concerned, there are no national boundaries drawn across the
sea between our countries.
—Epeli Hau'ofa, "The Ocean in Us"

The easy dismissal of Oceania reflects an age where the "rise of Asia"
only recognizes human value through competitive economic and cultural power. It's not merely that island states are neglected, but that their
exclusion from "the global" naturalizes their position as tourist destinations or as isolated military zones suited for military bases, recruitment,
atomic testing, and war games, as well as sources of servitude (imported
service work and domestic labor). Cartographically, the routes and
shared histories of island nations have been difficult to portray in maps
meant to simplify territorial space, wherein, as Doreen Massey writes,
"loose ends and ongoing stories" remain "real challenges to cartography."[24] Maps typically reinforce what Edward Said termed imaginative
geographies, where imperial lenses conceive of space by "dramatizing the
distance and difference between what is close to it and what is far away."[25]
But, as Caren Kaplan observes, the aerial view provided by maps and
cartographic technology also plays the stimulating role of being "seduc-
tively pleasurable and all-empowering," perceiving of the "unseen" and
the "unsensed," the "unruly and random mobile networks [that] keep
moving."[26] The view from above commonly implies distance, official-
ness, militaryness, surveyship, authority, and an unbreakable distinction
between "remote documentation and humanist portraiture."[27] No doubt
new media saturates us so deeply in aerial imagery that "the map pre-
cedes the territory," yet aerial imagery can also stage radical revisions of
ourselves in relation to space, blurring the distinctions between distance
and proximity, survey and understanding, observance and intimacy.

Craig Santos Perez's poems within *from unincorporated territory
[hacha]*[28] produce maps that reimagine the island of Guam (or Guåhan)
in ways that privilege routes over continents and local epistemologies over settler ones. These maps are not all knowing but deliberately

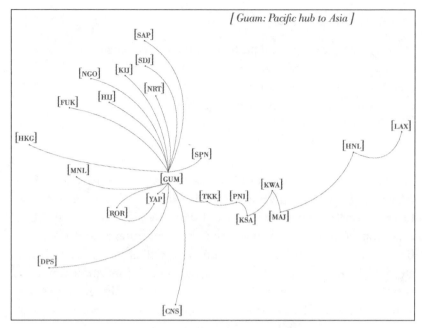

Figure 6.2. "Guam: Pacific hub to Asia" by Craig Santos Perez. Courtesy of the artist. Credit: Tinfish Press and book designer Ben Viwatmanitsakul.

obfuscating, silencing the dominant divisions of islands and seas. His poem "Guam: Pacific hub to Asia" centers Guam within multiple flight paths from destinations identified through their airport codes (see Figure 6.2). The map flattens the importance of each node into economic power centers or capitals (Fukouka is just as prominent as Tokyo). Its flight paths designate island airports that would likely be unknown (Bali's Denpasar [DPS], Palau [ROR], Micronesia's Yap [YAP]) with imperial powers at the edges (Japanese airports and Los Angeles [LAX]). Perez's map re-creates his own experience growing up in Guam and witnessing how American power has hinged upon its strategic positioning within an "imperial archipelago."[29] Perez's inspiration to write poems as maps comes from the Chamorro tradition of "song maps," which "refer to the songs, chants, and oral stories that were created to help seafarers navigate oceanic and archipelagic spaces," and which gave the navigator a literacy to read the oceanic world.[30] In his collection, the poem "Guam: Pacific hub to Asia" immediately follows a poem about nets and fishing, which Perez has described as an attempt "to embody the net in space and in sound."[31] Perez describes many of his poems as both maps and nets, leaving the reader to "pull the net and harvest the meaning."[32] "Guam: Pacific hub to Asia" reimagines the apparatus of "transpacific flights" not as a net meant for survival but as an imperial net spurred by global capital and empire meant to capture, commodify, and militarize.

Perez's poem/map draws us to migrations and diasporas outside Guam, where over half of its Chamorro population resides.[33] Before the TPP there was another acronym that identified the islands, the Trust Territory of the Pacific Islands (TTPI), a post–World War II United Nations–governed territorial formation that gave administrative power over Oceania to the United States. As Vicente M. Diaz points out, the TTPI was one of the first instances of colonial hand-over from Spain, Germany, and Japan to the United States, and though the new micro-states were "Native-driven," "the U.S. was more obsessed with exercising its strategic interests—including nuclear testing—than with permitting such acts of self-determination."[34] In 1986, migrant labor from these islands expanded drastically under the Compact of Free Association (COFA), which gave COFA members in the Pacific the freedom to live permanently or come and go at will in the United States, so that by 2006 one out of every four Micronesians lived in the United States.[35] COFA is also structured to territorialize the islands through its claim of "strategic denial" or exclusive territorial control, granting citizens the right to live permanently in the United States in exchange for the continued use of military sites.[36] Here Perez's poem/map of the "net" of transpacific flights visualizes Guam's relation to the global market within service labor and military recruitment (Micronesia has the highest volunteer rate and casualty rate per capita for the US military; in Guam, one cannot vote in US elections except through military service).

To resist the territorializing efforts that seek to capture Pacific bodies like aquatic denizens, Perez offers the term "terripelago," which "combines territorium and pélago" to foreground how territoriality (or envisioned claims to territory) conjoin "land and sea, islands and continents."[37] "Terripelago" contrasts views of territoriality as claims to land rather than ocean but also broadens the terms of settlement toward a cartographic logic of elimination, including global discourses that have sought to encompass Oceania. To see in forms of terripelago is to approach maps as catalogs of territoriality, as objects produced in what Caren Kaplan calls the "aftermath" of empire: "the undeclared wars that grieve not only the present absences but the absent presents—not so much a matter of ghosts as multiple worlds that a singular worldview cannot accommodate."[38] Kaplan employs "aftermath" within its etymological meaning of the ecological shifts that follow a "math," the mowing of farmland that prepares for a second crop. Implicitly, the mowing of the map that represents the reality of the transpacific is both a temporal and spatial aftermath of multiple empires: the spotlighting of airfields and tourist traps, the arrangement of colonial spaces into the nation of their hosts, the ideological color schemes, the size and scales, the relegation of island space into a book's crease. All of these can be read as the aftermath of empire wherein a territory can be claimed, as it exists spatially within the bounds of imperial aftermath. Maps that express the terripelago not only reveal these aftermaths but attempt to see the unseen and sense the unsensed, providing experiences that unfurl "the unruly or repetitious mode of emotional life."[39]

Digitizing the Map

During an annual family stay at my grandfather's house in Kailua on the Hawaiian island of Oahu, I encountered touristic cartographies of island space when I visited the Polynesian Cultural Center, a cultural theme park owned by the Mormon church and operated by the adjacent Brigham Young University.[40] The park has been widely criticized by scholars and Internal Revenue Service investigators, yet it continues to be one of the highest revenue-earning parks in Hawai'i and rates consistently high on sites like TripAdvisor and Yelp for its supposed ethnic authenticity. Though some have pointed out the site's use of Mormon aesthetics and erasure of Polynesian history, what seemed most disconcerting during my visit was its cartographic erasure of oceanic space as well as its creepy proximity to the Brigham Young campus that neighbored the site.

The Polynesian Cultural Center reproduces imperial notions of territoriality by erasing the oceanic space that Polynesia inhabits, what Epeli Hau'ofa has identified as the main anchor within the common identity of Oceania.[41] The park reproduces, too, the triumphantilism of transpacific

Figure 6.3. Tourist map of the Polynesian Cultural Center at www.polynesia.com. "Purpose and History of Polynesian Cultural Center," *Polynesian Cultural Center*, accessed May 2, 2017, www.polynesia.com.

flights, which see oceanic space as an inconvenience, a no-man's-land to surpass. The Center's tourist map (see Figure 6.3) eliminates oceanic space by compressing Polynesia around a single river to meet the tourist's idyllic dream, squeezing ahistorical cultural "tribes" into buffet form, calling on visitors to "visit authentic villages and mingle with natives from six Pacific cultures as they demonstrate their arts." Native students of Brigham Young University guide tourists through traditional cultural praxis but offer little to no information of the militarized campaigns within these spaces. It is through this zoo-like space that the cultural center claims to speak for all of Polynesia; it even owns the website www. polynesia.com. The park also provides a "Polynesian center" so visitors don't have to physically visit (or ever think about) the other islands or the oceanic space that defines them.[42] In netting "all of Polynesia in one unique place," the park enacts Teresia Teaiwa's sense of "militourism" by reducing a region of vast historical complexity into a single space of enjoined island paradises.[43]

The Polynesian Cultural Center directs our attention to the anthropologic side of militourism that preserves island cultures as warrior cultures in order to legitimate their appropriation by American-mainland entities, whether it be the Church of Latter-Day Saints (LDS), plantation industries, tourist regimes, or the US military. By seeking to offer a comprehensive view of all island life in the Pacific, the Center forecloses present-day realities of these nations and acts as a gateway to the certainty of the aerial gaze. Its call to "visit authentic villages and mingle with natives from six Pacific cultures as they demonstrate their arts," as well as the park's slogan to "Go Native," suggests that visitors

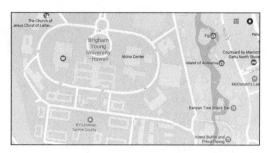

Figure 6.4. The Polynesian Cultural Center and Brigham Young University on Google Maps. Google Maps. "The Polynesian Cultural Center." Accessed March 12, 2017, www.google.com/maps.

can witness a sanctioned re-creation—a force of *cultural* security filtered of any worldviews counter to Christianity or Americanism (traditional "black magic" rituals, animal sacrifice).[44] The villagers' half-nude bodies seem sculpted by the elements, though these workers are in fact Polynesian students at Brigham Young University. Viewed from above using the Geographic Information System (GIS) program Google Maps, the non-space of the tourist map meant for informational text here reveals the Brigham Young Campus and the Church of Latter-Day Saints (see Figure 6.4). By relegating the Brigham Young campus to empty cartographic space, a blotted-out gray zone, the park's map hides the troubling and violent history of Christianity hoisted upon native peoples who were seen as savages and heathens needing to be brought into a common religious fold. As Teaiwa has shown, Christianity has often played a role contiguous with military occupation, as she writes that the inhabitants of Bikini Atoll, when told of the atomic bombs that would be tested on their lands, were guilted into accepting US militarization "by appealing to their sense of Christian duty" that their islands would be used for the good of all mankind. Here the digital map reveals not a knowable present but an uncharted past. It repels the presumptions of the aerial gaze that seek to reaffirm the boundaries among island, sea, park, and campus. This digitized aerial view conjures what Kaplan calls a "world-making propensity" that deviates sharply from the presumptions of territoriality to invoke "the sudden realization of both the vast scope and the vulnerability of the earth as seen from above."[45] The digital maps revealing the Brigham Young campus offer a relationship to the colonial past and present that can only be viewed from above, not within, its walled theme park. In both the Brigham Young campus and the Polynesian Cultural Center, the landscapes of Polynesia remain as absent as its histories and religions. Here militourism operates not only as a relationship between the military and tourism but as a form of cultural resource extraction.[46] The only sea is a river, not an ocean, and the wisdom of wayfinding is replaced with the picturesque pageantry of simplicity and innocence.

As Alice Te Punga Somerville writes, cultural identification for peoples like the Maori can triangulate across different geographical imaginaries: as indigenous to New Zealand (Maori), as part of a larger family of connected islands (Pacific), and as displaced peoples of a lost land (colonial subjects).[47] Maps then can show both one's identity and political worldview (as divided into nations), but when maps are made historically and spatially dynamic, they can speak just as well to our multiplicities. By fiddling with multiple scales of space and time, players can use interactive maps to view colonialism in a de-colonial fashion, to grapple with colonization as a historical aftermath (a form of "re-remembering") rather than erase it outright. Indeed, my use of Google Maps here suggests that GIS systems need not remain within the dominant construct of aerial views, where "elevation yields clarity, an overview garners empowerment, and the view from above is a natural result of human ingenuity and technical achievement."[48] Even as the GIS system here reveals the unspoken relationships between the LDS church and the Polynesian Cultural Center, it does so only by eliminating the naturalized divisions of space for the relational forms of terripelagic mapping that form connections among various categories (sea/island/land, church/university/tourist trap). For Alexander Weheliye, the reliance on comparison found in how we read maps "frequently affirms the given instead of providing avenues for the conjuring of alternate possibilities."[49] A terripelagic reading, in turn, emphasizes notions of space and peoplehood that are not pegged to previous identifications. One could thus wed Perez's sense of terripelago with what Harrod Suarez calls "archipelagic reading," a form of understanding that "intentionally falls into the gaps of our epistemological coordinates, coordinates that have proved to be sufficient for sustaining global empire but insufficient for accounting for all its effects."[50] To read archipelagically spurs one "to glimpse those undercurrents, orienting us differently in the world."[51]

The ubiquitous appearance of mapped aerial views today withholds the aftermath of American empire, while archipelagic forms of reading help recognize the unseen and unsensed silences. Yet the GIS map produced through Google Maps does not reveal the relationship between the LDS church and the Cultural Center as an explicitly imperial relationship. The view from above merely acts as a medium through which dominant narratives of separation and comparison remain intact, masking the relationship between these two spaces as coincidental, random, or as mere proximity. To unravel their neocolonial relationship takes more than the map. It takes movement, motion, reflection, and new heuristics through which such relationships become visible. As critical refugee scholar Yến Lê Espiritu has argued, GIS systems like Google Maps can be critically modified to track historically erased migrant routes such as Vietnamese refugees who were routed through American military bases in the Philippines, Guam, and the American West Coast.[52] As Espiritu says, despite her familiarity with transpacific maps, a moment of cartographic realization only came to her after many years: "Gosh," she says, "I've been doing ethnic studies for 25 years and I didn't recognize the significance of this pattern."[53] Realities invented and reproduced through aerial views here leave migrant and refugee routes undetectable, seemingly accidental and random, rather than calculated forms of imperial aftermath made possible through the post–World War II Pacific garrison, the colonization of the Philippines in 1898, and the settler colonialism of the American West.

To visualize unseen cartographic patterns within the transpacific map, Espiritu charged her graduate student (Ly Nguyễn) to depict these patterns cartographically through the Google Maps GIS (Figure 6.5). The red line shows the US military forces and areas of bombing, while the blue line shows the refugee flight from Vietnam to the United States. Modifying the map allows viewers to understand how American military bases "were the very sites responsible for inducing the refugee displacement in the first place."[54] The island spaces previously ignored or seen as mere tourist traps were integral to the imperial project of dumping and processing refugees. Even as these maps align with imperial logics, they can also allow us to perceive new routes, inspiring players to "graft" as Espiritu describes it: to connect the dots in a way that "offers the promise that even deliberately discarded histories will continue to be

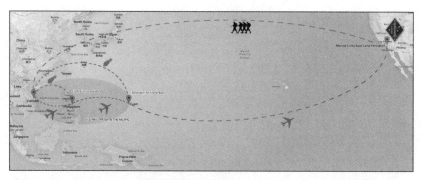

Figure 6.5. Ly Thúy Nguyễn grafts transpacific routes of US military and refugees from Vietnam. Courtesy of the artist, Ly Thúy Nguyễn.

told as they bump against, intersect with, and route through the lives of kin communities."[55] As I will expand upon in the next section, creative remapping through archipelagic reading or grafting can open users to an erotic play that finds pleasure and seduction in discovering what was previously unsensed. Indeed, in urban parlance, to "graft" suggests an erotic register: to persistently flirt, usually through email or social media "until you (eventually/rarely) 'tap that ass.'"[56] Grafting in both the sense of "connecting the dots" on a map and in the sense of digital flirtation presumes seduction through distance. One consults a map as one looks at an attractive profile picture and desires only in the abstract. That is, they desire the blurred, obscured abstraction and the different possibilities of the seductive lure. Like with grafting on a map, to graft as a form of erotic play finds pleasure in distance.

Theorizing the Virtual Other

One certainty: China inspired the first lie I remember telling.
—Susan Sontag, "Project for a Trip to China."

I'm not drunk, you've just gotten blurry.
—a joke

Presumably, elevation offers a militarized gaze that reflects what Keith Feldman has called, in the context of drone warfare, "racialization from above," which recasts "Orientalist imagined geography" along "a vertical vector," and supplements "imperial sovereignty's practices of ubiquitous bordering on the ground."[57] This "racialization from above" reinforces (and is reinforced by) "racialization on the ground,"[58] as it deploys aerial view technology in order to categorize, identify, racialize, and, once a life is determined as "ungrievable,"[59] shoot to kill. Such visual technologies rely upon notions of knowing, the certainty of the racial survey. In contrast, perceiving the spatially rendered other as virtual offers alternatives to the militarizing and territorializing logics of distance.

To sift out how the virtual other is generated through forms of unknowing and erotic attachment, I turn one last time to the writings of Barthes, Foucault, and Sedgwick, whose engagements with Asia not only formed much of their later methods concerning the body and erotics but also brought to the forefront a means of engaging with the "virtual other," the imagined nation, space, and spiritualities attached to the East. In their confrontations with Asia, each theorist sought to comprehend erotic and sensational feelings of discovery and recognition while also remaining aware of their emotions, pleasures, and desires within the discourses partially responsible for producing them. Each theorist was thus concerned with particular Asiatic sites and themes: Barthes's ventures to Japan in *Empire of Signs* and to China in *Travels in China*; Foucault's lectures in Japan and his interviews with Zen Buddhist monks; Sedgwick's engagements with forms of Buddhism in *Touching Feeling*, with Japanese poetry and textile, and her own travels in Nepal, Korea, Japan, and Thailand. Each of these examples exhibits attempts to glean new forms of understanding through confronting Asiatic culture and space as a virtual other—taken as imagined but not unreal, recognizable but not identifiable, always obfuscated and obscured.

Barthes and the Mirage

Barthes's *Empire of Signs* provides a mystical and surreal description of "that country I am calling Japan," cautiously aware of how he invents Japan with his own gaze. Japan's strangeness remains seductive, an entire country seemingly "untouched" by Western colonization during the Sakoku (鎖国, "closed country") period from 1633–1853.[60] The Japan of Barthes's text contains the bliss of the new, and then the memory of that bliss: "Here every discovery is intense and fragile, it can be repeated or recovered only by memory of the trace it has left in you."[61] By displacing "that country I am calling Japan" into the flashes of discovery that remain only in memory (for one cannot rediscover), Barthes searches "not for other symbols but the very fissure of the symbolic,"[62] a means to subvert the discourses placed upon Japan with the shock of exceeding their limitations. The Japanese character Barthes uses to typify this shock of discovery is *mu* 無, "emptiness," a notion that has influenced the Western interest in Zen Buddhism and nonbeing. As Sedgwick herself would later write, Western interest in Buddhism has emphasized this term "mu" to encapsulate Zen Buddhism as an individualist, nonreligious, and adaptable philosophy. Barthes instead remains playful with the term, seeing it as the loss of meaning that stages reevaluation. As Carol Mavor has pointed out, Barthes's conception of Buddhism helps him consider not the subject or the observed object but the act of observing itself as an act expressing loss, emptiness, and the potential creation of something new.[63] Similarly, Trinh T. Min-ha argues that Barthes is not concerned with Japan but "with the approach itself, with the discourse produced." My own familiarity with Mandarin Chinese also stages a playful rereading of mu 無, as in Mandarin the more common traditional character for emptiness reads *Xū* 虚, which could mean "fake," "meaningless," or "empty," but is also commonly used to refer to new technology as *virtual* (*xūcún* [虚存] meaning "virtual memory," or *xūnǐ shìjiè* [虚拟世界] meaning "virtual world").

Barthes's confrontation with Japan as an Asiatic virtual other means presuming to know nothing, replacing the certainty of Orientalist attitudes with silence. In the eyes of some analysts, like Carol Mavor, these attempts ultimately fail, as Barthes's desire for non-knowing means regarding himself as childlike, boyish, and thus uninterested in Japan's real history and living language, writing that Barthes claims Japan as "his 'empire of signs,' and then makes no apologies for wearing the emperor's crown."[64] Seeing Barthes's innocence as a boyish attempt to evade criticism, Mavor also faults Asian and postcolonial critics influenced by Barthes, particularly Trinh T. Minh-ha, who Mavor believes has sided with an Orientalist thinker. However, Minh-ha herself has argued that her appreciation for Barthes emerged through his search for ways of listening to the spaces around him while including the vast plurality of other ways of engaging with that space. For Minh-ha, Barthes's projects helped form "ways of thinking [that] do not *exclude* and therefore appeal more to non-Western thinking."[65] This appeal is evident in how Barthes conceives of "the void," which is not really the void of Japan (the country called Japan) but the void of the subject who gazes. In other words, in constructing the virtual other, Barthes simultaneously deconstructs the self as a "consistent agent," focusing attention onto the acts of gazing, observing, doing, writing, playing, and searching.

The virtual other appears again in Barthes's *Travels in China*, notes from Barthes's 1974 travels at the wane of the cultural revolution. During this trip, Barthes joined a delegation from the French literary review *Tel Quel*, which included the novelist Philippe Sollers, the poet Marcelin Pleynet, the philosopher François Wahl, and the feminist semiotician Julia Kristeva, whose book *About Chinese Women* (1977)[66] was based on the same trip but was widely criticized by postcolonial theorists like Gayatri Spivak as Orientalist.[67] Barthes takes the opposite tactic of not writing about Chinese women, men, or China at all. His only commentary on the "real China," as he later wrote, must be "no comment":

> By producing a subdued mirage of China as something placed outside of the domain of brilliant colors, strong flavors and brutal meanings (all of these having some connection with the everlasting parade of the Phallus), I wanted to bind in a single gesture the feminine (maternal?) infiniteness of the object itself . . . and the right to a special discourse, a discourse which drifts slightly, or which speaks the desire for silence . . . This is not a gratuitous hallucination: it seeks to respond to the way that many Westerners produce their own hallucinations of the People's Republic of China: in a dogmatic, violently affirmative/negative, or falsely liberal mode.[68]

Barthes frames his production of the virtual other ("a subdued mirage of China") as a response to the Western desires and orthodoxies that shape China as a "domain of brilliant colors, strong flavors." Likewise, he seeks to disengage from the politically "negative" China as well as the "falsely liberal" China that many intellectuals in France (like Sollers) had propagated through their alliance with Maoism. The distance in both space and time of the virtual other does not read Asia but allows the audience to read the author in the act of reading Asia.[69] Though he took copious notes, Barthes still felt, according to Minh-ha, "difficulty in saying anything about China," instead making an "attempt to suspend utterance," to "neither affirm nor negate," and to refuse "to speak about the other."[70] In an aside, Barthes takes a moment of frustration with yet another Maoist slogan (a "brick," as he calls it) to reflect on the yearning for "stereotypical language," a "non-language," that comes from both sides: the Chinese officials who seek to present a modern China and the French tourists seeking Marxist wisdom (Sollers) or research subjects (Kristeva).[71] "Quite different," Barthes writes, referring to himself, "is the case of the intellectual who needs to dispossess himself of a previous language."[72]

Upon arrival in Beijing, Barthes observes the local Chinese observing him and feels his own body's reactions to being watched, to being named the Occidental exotic. China, meanwhile, remains unknowable surface, opaque, "bricked" by party lines repeated in migraine-inducing volume by officials, instructors, and tour guides. Watching others watch himself watch China, Barthes travels with an *ars erotica* of the body, his attention spurred from one object to another, feeding off eye candy and finding the pleasure of discovering nuanced differences in China's uniformity. Once immersed in the space of the virtual other, Barthes begins to understand the space's rules and boundaries as he engages less with its signs and more with its pluralistic world, present within the various stages of flirtation that provide rare sparks of pleasure: "The attractive one smiles to me, but what can I say?"[73] All the while Barthes has "the worst migraine of my life—insomnia and nausea."[74] Barthes's headache manifests, in his own opinion, as a reaction to the radical pluralization of China (in its refusal to stereotypes), on the one hand, and in the surface "bricks" of dogmatic Maoist adages that reinstate the stereotype. Barthes describes himself "vomiting out the Stereotype, the Doxa."[75] Physically ill, he must unburden himself with the "real," nonvirtual China, a violent and painful process.

Barthes's engagement with China and Japan attempts to fathom the "blurred vision" that makes the other impossible to comprehend without resorting to "doxa" and "stereotypes."[76] For the foreign theorist, these stereotypes and presumptions cannot merely be tossed away. To remove them takes physical illness, vomiting, and panic, but also a constant awareness of one's pleasures and erotic attachments. As Minh-ha and Stanley Gray argue, Barthes writes of Japan and China "not to decipher Asia, but rather to assess his own position vis-a-vis exoticism, ethnocentrism and, above all, to assess his own hermeneutic posture, his role as decoder."[77] Barthes's engagement with the virtual other attempts to see variety and difference that resists the tourist's and the local's attempts to present uniformity. In looking for the "possibility of difference," Barthes confronts an unknown that "is neither Japan nor China but his own language, and through it, that of all the West."[78] Pleasure emerges in discovering how one fits (and doesn't fit) into the self, one's own particularity in the face of the other's plurality, complexity, and virtual distance.

Foucault and Silence

What is philosophy today—philosophical activity, I mean—if it is not the critical work that thought brings to bear on it? In what does it consist, if not in the endeavor to know how and to what extent it might be possible to think differently, instead of legitimating what is already known . . . to explore what might be changed, in its own thought, through the practice of a knowledge that is foreign to it.
—Michel Foucault, *The Use of Pleasure*, Vol. 2 in *The History of Sexuality*

The "foreign" for Foucault was a realm of possibility and alterity. Foucault's philosophical history of the Hellenistic Greeks and Romans in volumes 2 and 3 of *The History of Sexuality* confronts an other far removed historically but still subject to the gaze of "the foreign" manufactured by historians and state narratives. His attempt to free himself from these discourses in volumes 2 and 3 was met with disdain by experts like Martha Nussbaum, who in her review of volume 2 for the *New York Times* called it a "disappointment" and accused Foucault of using the excuse of conducting "a philosophical exercise" to evade true historical research and to remain "doomed to rely on the vagaries of translators."[79] Nussbaum's critique centers on the presumption that volume 2 was "a prisoner of its own haste in the face of death." Death here appears as an obstacle that Foucault was unable to overcome, one severely limiting his life's project, as it brought on "a retreat from the principles that defined his career."

For us, less interested in Foucault's legacy and more in his methods for encountering otherness, Nussbaum's mournful critique for a Foucault who had, after his diagnosis, appeared to betray himself, is a productive moment to consider otherness in moments when the centrality of the self begins to eclipse. Foucault himself writes that his turn in volume 2 was informed by deeper reflections on life and its alternative possibilities: "The object was to learn to what extent the effort to think one's own history can free thought from what it silently thinks, and so enable it to think differently."[80] Similarly, Eve Sedgwick, after her diagnosis with cancer, turned to questions of otherness, deciphering the "blurs" that constructed the virtual other of Buddhism, Japan, and Asia as a dynamic yet highly fraught realm. Like Barthes, both theorists turned to an *ars erotica* influenced by their confrontation with the virtual other, propelled by their desire, before death, to reach toward more open possibilities.

Not long after the publication of volume 1, Foucault's *History of Sexuality* project began to shift from its interest in sixteenth-century Christianity to a much broader genealogy that began with the Hellenistic teachers of ancient Greece and Rome, who represented an alternative form of living with sexuality, an *ars erotica*. Yet, as Mark Jordan and many others have observed, before volume 2, *ars erotica* was characterized not as Hellenistic so much as Eastern and Asian, as volume 1 contrasted "a Western science of sex with an Eastern art of the erotic, a contrast that begs for qualifications and counter-examples."[81] Indeed, we can locate a crucial turning point in Foucault's ideas during his second visit to Japan in 1978 (his first was in 1970), where he presented his project within the *ars erotica* of virtual Japan and spoke with Zen Buddhist monks to better comprehend alternative forms of sexuality and spirituality.[82] It was in Japan that Foucault "reframed the project of the History of Sexuality" with greater attention onto non-Christian forms of sex, such as those found in Asia and in ancient Greece.[83]

It is clear from Foucault's views of the East that China and Japan deeply informed his notion of *ars erotica*.[84] His view of Asia as a stage for alternative modes of thought also appeared earlier, in his 1970 book *The Order of Things*, where he examined a Borges tale featuring a

Chinese encyclopedia that exposed "the exotic charm of another system of thought . . . the limitation of our own, the stark impossibility of thinking *that*."[85] Indeed, Foucault's imaginary of Asian culture often mingled with his imaginary of the ancient Greeks, as he said in a 1982 interview titled "The Minimalist Self,"

> We don't have a culture of silence; we don't have a culture of suicide either. The Japanese do, I think. Young Romans or young Greeks were taught to keep silent in very different ways according to the people with whom they were interacting. Silence was then a specific form of experiencing a relationship with others.[86]

Foucault frequently wavered from discussing Japan within a touristic orientalizing gaze that reduced its heterogeneity to "a culture of silence" to admitting that he understood next to nothing about Japan and only carried a superficial interest in it as "a problem that we can't avoid, and . . . an illustration of this problem."[87] Foucault's interview with a Zen Buddhist monk comes closest to revealing his conception of Japan as a virtual other able to reveal "new relationships between the mind and the body, and between the body and the outside world."[88] Against the impulse of the positivistic *scientifica*, Foucault sought not to uncover the obscurity that Japan represented but to delve into the obscurity itself.

Foucault's 1978 lecture in Tokyo on the phenomenon of over-knowledge ("*sur-savoir*") notes his interest in Asia as a speculation carved out from the Eurocentric limits of his own project. In theorizing sexuality as *ars erotica*, Foucault grouped Japan alongside India and ancient Greece and Rome, saying "I believe that we have two types of analysis, two types of research, two completely different types of discourse, and that they will be found in two equally different kinds of society."[89] Foucault's reliance on East/West binaries in this lecture is softened in his published work, yet their appearance in Japan is telling for how *ars erotica* was conceived as an alternative to Western ways of life. On one hand, to see *ars erotica* as partially produced through the European gaze tracks a clear Orientalist subtext in all of Foucault's work, yet it also apprehends how his crucial conceptions and analyses were formed through virtual otherness, towing the line between the appreciation for cultural difference and idealist caricature. Indeed, one could very well imagine that the pushback Foucault received for his history of the Greeks in volume 2 would have increased tenfold had he instead explored contemporary Asia (and well deserved it would have been, as claiming expertise would have erased the "virtual" of the virtual other). His instinct not to publish these comparisons was both strategic and due to his own wariness that they were faulty, as he casually admits in the lecture that he had not done enough research and did not consider himself an expert on Asia or Japan except as they problematized the West. His admittedly "blurred vision" was productive in understanding the problems that had produced that very vision and in visualizing possible alternatives. Thus, Foucault's confrontation with Asia reveals a pedagogical role diverting from positivistic and scientific thinking to problematizing the self.

Sedgwick and Transpacific Pedagogy

Both Foucault and Sedgwick spent their last decades interested in forms of self-help from cultures radically distinct from their own. Sedgwick's devotion to spiritual growth, after her diagnosis, informs any reading of her essays on Buddhism, yet her scholarly investment in Buddhism also produced a virtual other that had to be felt and touched rather than categorized or identified. As with Foucault and Barthes, the virtual other in Sedgwick charges a pedagogical scene that collapses co-constituting binaries (even the relationship of teacher/student). This gesture, read as "naive," "childish," or "Orientalist," is easy to malign, partially because it poses a challenge to the tenants of "big theory" in general as conceptualizing frameworks for seeing structures and abstract comparisons. As Sedgwick writes, her turn toward Buddhism rested upon a "respect for realization as both process and practice" at odds with Western critical theory, with its "x-ray gaze of the paranoid impulse," and its "moralizing Marxist insistence that someone else is evading a true recognition of materiality."[90] For Sedgwick, Buddhism presented a way of not merely challenging but "undoing a whole series of dualisms that normally seem inextricable from language itself," though she also writes that Buddhism's real power to unsettle language would always be lost to her as an outsider and non-expert.[91] Sedgwick could never feel "the complete exclusion of language" because "the Buddhist mantras aren't available for these purposes to me in the same way they are to people really steeped in Buddhist traditions."[92]

As with Barthes and Foucault, Sedgwick's insistence on the virtual other as a path to *unknowing* came as an attempt to unmoor theory from its faith in exposure and knowing (by oversimplification).[93] Her reflections are written less as a travelogue and more as a discursive "weeding out" of the various discourses of Buddhism, where a "trans-Pacific pedagogy" emerged but remained difficult to recognize.[94] The goal was not merely to examine Buddhism but to fathom why Buddhism had become so meaningful for many Westerners, herself included, who carried such deep desires to adapt and incorporate it. Tracing the history of a "hypostasized Buddhism" in *Touching Feeling*, Sedgwick considered how thinkers like Carl Jung sought to examine the "exotic oriental psyche," desiring to speak for the exoticized other. Years later, Sedgwick became more interested in how her favorite critics, like herself, turned to Buddhist thought, even when doing so explicitly risked congealing their past work with histories of Orientalism and religiosity that held barely any relation to Buddhist practices "in the Chinatowns and other Asian immigrant communities."[95] Counting herself among these scholars, Sedgwick made little attempt to characterize Asian culture, religion, or people, but sought to understand her own desire to embrace Buddhism while under the shadow of a fatal disease.[96] Her mode of seeing Buddhism contrasted Western "adaptations" of Buddhism that sought to take the "useful" parts of Buddhist teachings and discard the superstitious, the untranslatable, the obscure. For Sedgwick such adaptations dismissed the challenge and confrontations of Buddhism and instead proposed a method of realization that was not deterred by obscurity but through it became "interpellated into a rich yet dissolvent relationality of pedagogy itself."[97] This "dissolvent" symbolizes an evaporating relationship that requires distance, mystery, and opacity in order to manifest as a pedagogical scene.

Sedgwick's refusal to offer Buddhism within a politics of comparison or as a practice that can offer adaptable knowledge extends Barthes's and Foucault's fascination with the virtual other as staging a pedagogical scene to better understand the self, while also attempting to recognize the relations that require change. Sedgwick's most powerful insights concerning the transpacific pedagogy of Buddhism are not in rejecting the dualism of the Orientalist with the non-dualism of the Buddhist, but to recognize the pluralistic conception of space, where people and things are not compared but merely "besides" each other.[98] Perhaps Sedgwick's most compelling

conception of "besides" is in her writings on camp as a "variety of reparative practices" that do justice to its "many defining elements"[99]:

> the startling, juicy displays of excess erudition . . . the passionate, often hi-
> larious antiquarianism, the prodigal production of alternative historiog-
> raphies; the "over"-attachment to fragmentary, marginal, waste or leftover
> products; the rich, highly interruptive affective variety; the irrepressible
> fascination with ventriloquistic experimentation; the disorienting juxta-
> positions of present with past, and popular with high culture.[100]

In order to imagine these many forms of camp, one must let go of a
structure or binary and take on a spatial, aerial view, where the complex
"variety of reparative practices" are relational to each other but sit upon
no logical or linear hierarchy.[101] Here the presumptions of the map's
aerial view meets its opposite: an aerial view that provides uncertainty
rather than certainty, untetheredness rather than a fixed gaze, a spatial
construct not of "and" or "or" but of "besides," which leaves the self "lib-
erated by both possibility and impossibility, and especially by the relative
untetheredness to self."[102]

We can see the heuristic enabled by "besides" within perhaps the most
binary (and nonbinary) type of map: the yin-yang symbol (or the *tàijítú*
[太極圖]). Taoist explanations of the yin-yang often read the image as a
map of a valley and a mountain, where light and darkness cross paths as
the sun drags across the sky (see Figure 6.6). Interpreted as a map, the yin-
yang exaggerates the dualism of the transpacific, where comparisons of
East/West seem unnatural or artificial "blurs" of black and white. As a historical and religious symbol, the tàijítú has been adapted into a blueprint
for the creativity of information technology, whose most glorified figure,
Steve Jobs, was influenced heavily by Eastern spirituality (the philosophy
of "Be Here Now") and the philosophies of the East in his numerous travels to India and Japan. But to offer the yin-yang, with all its troublesome
misreadings and adaptations, as virtual other radically shifts the symbol
from one of industrial innovation to a pedagogical scene for understanding our relations to others. What if these two parts (black/white) are not
contrasting intellectually but embracing sexually (the nipples and scrotum
are too easy to detect)? As virtual other, the yin-yang invites play—it can
be flipped on its side to emphasize global South/North relations, turned

Figure 6.6. The yin-yang or *tàijítú* [太極圖]. Wikimedia commons. Converted to SVG by Gregory Maxwell.

to its diagonal to emphasize capture of the Pacific Islands, and is always deconstructionist or nonbinary, with pieces of the other inside. As virtual other grafted upon the transpacific, the yin-yang does not reinforce binary thinking so much as taunt its excesses, opening to pedagogical relations through constant shifting and imaginative play. The yin-yang, with its two dots, also exemplifies undeniable and unavoidable interpenetration, a concept in Buddhism, Christianity, video games, and sex. As virtual other, one does not perceive these playful imaginings through the yin-yang's versatility so much as through our own brazen misunderstandings (watching ourselves watch Asia). The yin-yang as virtual other does not critique but reduces the structure to mere plaything, inverting its power to a virtual object that we can shape anew.

Cartographic Simulations

It's hard to keep track of you
falling through the sky
—The National, "Fake Empire"

Our long-winded detour into the Asiatic influences of Barthes, Foucault, and Sedgwick archives the virtual other not as mere digitized presence but as an erotic blur that yields pedagogical opportunities. Video games, too, provide this virtual other through virtual worlds that provide aerial views and "e-motion"—the disembodied and disorienting rush of movement. As Caren Kaplan describes it, the aerial view provides experiences of disembodiment and disorientation when one is untethered or within a panorama and must locate one's own body (feel for one's body) by situating oneself not through identity and characterization but through feeling, touch, and point of view. The dominant discourses of travel in the way space is remembered (mapped, reintroducing binaries and otherisms) diverge from the way mobility is directly experienced (as heterogeneous, antibinary because of the loss of the self). The authoritative stature of the map dissolves through the bodily import of spatial e-motion. In other words, one is subject to a continually shifting and changing time and an untethered, unlocatable position within space. Here the virtual map—dynamic, imagined, nonauthoritative—brings the experience of disorientation into the way otherness is conceived.

Feelings of disembodiment when faced with an aerial view remain integrated into the mechanics of many video games, the most well known of the bunch being the *Civilization* series, lauded as one of the most mechanically perfect games ever made. The *Civilization* games are an ambitious simulation of histories of empire, beginning from the destruction of barbarian tribes, to the capitalist routes that see better armaments, to colonizations, to imperial dominations, and finally to the space race. This historical simulation of global empire is only made possible by the disembodied player, who sees the world not as a "god" but as the military technology of a single civilization: the drone, the air balloon, the fighter jet, the satellite image. The pleasure of the game emerges from claiming space and traveling through it, while the space itself remains abstracted, simplified (ground containing gold or wood is seen merely within these terms). Just as Foucault saw the Western obsession with identity and sexual facticity as offering some erotic pleasures (the pleasures of discovering facts and identities[103]), so, too, does *Civilization* expose the pleasures of mapping that go far beyond its pragmatic and militaristic uses: the pleasures of organizing, managing, seeing, naming, reducing, categorizing. This is the pleasure of *Tetris* blocks being put into pristine order, the pleasure of knowing, of control. These are the traveler's pleasures of claiming territorial ownership by merely moving through a space ("surviving" a place as tourist T-shirts say). But in the erotic play of e-motion, the untethered aerial view gazes upon virtual others whose abstractions only reveal the viewer's own blurred vision.

Civilization's virtual others run the gamut from French empires to the Aztec and Iroquois, and in each iteration the game makes little attempt to appear realistic. Every civilization is led by a glib cartoonish head of state and is characterized by particular bonuses and unique units that balance near perfectly when competing against each other. As a video game simulation, details are dismissed for abstractions—a form perfectly suited for maps, which also are a form of oversimplification, even as they create certainty. Often this takes the form of surreal play—a "realistic" map of Eastern Asia feels stunningly inaccurate when confronted with the game's mechanics, where archers and canons can fire from Jeju island to Busan (a distance of 302 kilometers). Out of the five starting maps in *Civilization V*, only one attempts to mirror Earth, and its thirty optional maps include randomly generated maps or speculative maps (donut-shaped worlds, worlds without oceans). Due to its pragmatic abstraction, the playable map is never entirely fictive nor entirely real but generates a virtual otherness that enables the player to grasp our open world empire's spatial distortions.

Let's examine the virtual other in the *Civilization V* expansion pack focusing on the Pacific Islands, whose civilization ("Polynesians") is given the bonus of "can embark and move over oceans immediately" and the unique unit of "Maori Warrior." Here the traditionally barbarian peoples of past civilizing projects are turned into colonizers themselves through their abilities for oceanic travel and "warrior" strength. As if to mimic a tourists' history of Polynesian peoples, the player's best chance for survival is to settle across island spaces as early in the game as possible, then focus on their civilizations' faith and culture (by discovering monuments and natural wonders) to guide the Polynesian empire through inevitable attacks from the outside. The "Paradise Found" scenario sees the player adopting one of four Polynesian civilizations (Hiva, Tonga, Samoa, Tahiti) on a map of the Pacific as they quest "for new islands to colonize" in order to "dominate the mighty Pacific." For many game scholars,[104] the way *Civilization* treats ethnic difference as oversimplification mirrors touristic gazes, yet its depiction of Polynesia also reimagines Oceania not as isolated territories belonging to mainland empires but as a dynamic space of competing cultures, where the ocean represents not a void but mobility and history. The four leading heroes of each civilization are campy, Asiatic imaginings of fearless warriors but with a strange twist—that while three are known for their imperialism and violence, one, Malietoa Savea of the Samoans, was known for civil disobedience, and his representation in the game is an exact replica of Mahatma Gandhi. This in-game joke, analogizing Savea as Ghandi, makes history seem like a repetition of the imperial dynasties of the past, where technologies of sailing and settlement belonged to islanders far before European powers.

The virtual other in *Civilization*, observed through the game's abstraction of space and compression of time, sees the globe in terms of aftermaths, where the contemporary dismissal of the Pacific remains the aftermath of American Empire. Similarly, the presumption that the islands of Hawai'i once underwent a "unification" rather than a bloody massacre is to live within the aftermath of King Kamehameha. *Civilization* thus stages a pedagogical scene that pushes us to understand our own reality produced by mapping as well as global paradigms promising greater critique through abstraction. *Civilization* sees history as predictable, culture as quantifiable, and gradually unspools a spatial story, the "drama of a map changing over time" that can only remain abstract, obscure, and virtual.[105] In playing the game, one also plays upon military technologies of abstraction: the labels of "terrorist," "civilian," "pacification," "collateral damage," and the distance of drone warfare. Stuck within the aerial view, one does not see with a "god view" because god could always zoom in. One is then stuck with abstraction, with teleology, with survival only through domination. By simulating this distance, the game renders how violence and distance are embedded into any narrative of civilization and progress. In refusing to see beyond the limits of empire, the game reveals empire's own blurred vision. Its stereotypes of Gandhi and barbarians needing to be tamed follows precisely the logic of American empire, simulating, too, how it has proceeded from its roots into an indefinitely violent future.

The E-motion of Google VR

A map of the world that does not include utopia is not worth
even glancing at.
—Oscar Wilde, *The Soul of Man*

Forms of virtual travel remain a felt experience invoking sensation, stimulation, and erotics. Whereas the imaginary geography of Google Maps allows users to read across categorical forms of spatial distinctions (such as witnessing the proximity of tourist spaces with military and religious spaces), in the *Civilization* franchise, the representation of cartographic space traces the historical routes and violent turns present within empire's blurred vision. More recently, in the 2010s, visual technologies have featured more advanced graphics than those of Google Maps and *Civilization*, and they have been embedded with high-resolution satellite photos as well as configured through virtual reality consoles. Teased into information technology's promise of the ultimate reveal, viewers can now not only see and interact with virtual cartography but can lose themselves within its simulation in experiences of disembodiment and disorientation.[106] Virtual reality cartographies do not merely represent given space but shift the epistemological presumptions of what is perceived as "the map," simulating the player's presence within the territory in relation to the virtual otherness of the represented space. Rather than operate as a "guide" or a means of categorizing space, virtual reality simulations offer a variety of vantage points through which space can be reconceived.

One of the most popular virtual reality simulations is the easy-to-use GIS program Google Earth,[107] which has punctured into the gaming community and has consistently been listed as one of the top reasons to own a virtual reality headset. Originally released in 2006 and used by over one hundred million people that year, the three-dimensional GIS software lent itself easily to being played as a video game, with its seamless viewing and its real-time exploration of spatial data.[108] Though other GIS programs have remained in use (NASA's World Wind and ESRI's ArcGis Explorer), Google Earth's simplicity and intended lack of information about the space one is traversing makes the simulation feel more "authentic," as if one is really floating over Earth. While disembodied flow through a virtual map provides pleasure for the players of *Civilization, Google Earth VR* propels these e-motions into erotic sensations. Confronted with the sublime possibilities of infinite space, the player could spend hours finding a view that is "picturesque." Their play is in constant movement, in losing themselves in the blur of e-motion. In virtual reality, Google Earth does not merely represent the Earth but simulates it within an easily traversed virtual world that lets viewers whisk about the landscape with a dreamlike speed.

If remote sensing, as Kaplan writes, relies on detailed geographical information, Google Earth curtails the desire for information, presenting "Earth" as a frozen landscape. Whereas both Google Maps and the desktop version of Google Earth have a particularly pragmatic use that peripheralizes places without roads, attractions, and monuments, *Google Earth VR* rewards meandering into the peripheral and the oceanic through which no clear routes exist. One cannot "spy" but only gaze upon a broad panorama. In the shared mapmaking of Google Maps, users are encouraged to label, route, and review spaces on their own. Similarly, the original software version of Google Earth has been plagued with occasional political bouts of territorialization, such as its indifference to pleads for Taiwan to not be included within the People's Republic of China. In *Google Earth VR*, however, countries are not marked by color, islands are not marked by countries, and roads do not offer any clear routes on how to get from point A to point B. This is why Google Earth appeals to video game players and amateurs more than professionals, as it provides only basic measuring and manipulation tools, and independent programmers have created games using Google Earth software (*Geoguessr, Pursuit, Smarty Pins, Map Race*).[109] Players browse through the Earth like migratory birds, reenacting the awe and beauty of a still world. They are not bombarded with zombies or enemies but with a bewildering desire to explore an unadorned landscape. The software's interface also makes keyboard use and note-taking awkward and slow, disrupting the player's urge to catalog. The landscape does not appear as a map one annotates but as a vantage point one experiences. The pictures one can take, upon view, feel flat and glaringly absent of the feeling of being overpowered by mountains, sea, and air.

Virtual reality hardware makes it difficult for players to disengage from the world: they must shift up tight goggles, take off headphones, and reassess their place within their given world. It is easier to just remain in the virtual ambiance. Claudio Fogu calls this effect "hypermediacy," the ability of games "to make us forget the medium."[110] Virtual reality apparatuses go a step further by placing the player within a sensory experience that forgets not merely the medium but also the self, as one's body becomes undetectable, one's own sounds unhearable. Within the map the player must remap their own sensory input/outputs, creating a disorientation that Steve Swink terms "virtual proprioception," when one's sensations are amplified by tactile feedback (moving the neck also moves the camera), but one's mind is perplexed by the need to remap (moving forward is not accomplished by leaning forward or walking but by moving a joystick the player cannot see).[111] One's sensations are amplified, as players learn to swoop over mountains and glide over oceans without the inconvenience of weather elements like clouds, thunder, hurricanes, typhoons, rain, sunlight. The earth is presented as idyllic, paradisiacal, open for travel, but never fully decipherable, as the territories that might offer a space to conquer remain stuck in the abstraction of a latent landscape. Straightjacketed into the virtual reality apparatus, players find it too difficult to annotate, journal, label, cartograph, review, or survey (other GIS systems would be preferable for that). They merely bounce to the rhythm of e-motion.

On my first play of *Google Earth VR*, I searched out places of established meaning—the Eiffel tower, Mount Everest, my own home in Hong Kong. But after an initial period of reaffirming the known came a period of fathoming the unknown, searching out the vast amount of space without meaning, spaces that appeared as voids containing an ineffable presence, an emptiness of language. Finding myself with few narratives for these places, I began to form cartographic imaginaries for places not yet imagined as I lost myself in the archipelagic landmasses that pepper the Pacific Ocean (see Figure 6.7). Played as a game, *Google Earth VR* reminds us that our Earth is primarily oceanic, a boundless seascape littered with more islands than continents. It pushes us to perceive of islands not as islands, since "no island was ever an island to begin with" but are only thought so "by people from that other land form called continents."[112] For most users, maps encourage quick glances over oceanic areas, yet in *Google Earth VR*, the plodding aerial movement through oceanic space rethinks islands, positioned from the disembodied and disoriented self. Wandering the Pacific makes island spaces appear in relation to each other rather than their given colonial mainland, as little seems Chilean about Easter Island or American about the Marianas. Each island remains an isolated outlier within the vast ocean space, requiring the player to spend effort (cartographical and motion-control skills) and time (to arrive at each island destination). *Google Earth VR*'s gameplay is enhanced and made pleasurable within the loops of journeying, looking, and discovering. Given the game's mechanics and stunning oceanic visuals, islands play the part of landscape rewards that players discover like pieces of a body slowly disrobing, heightened also

Figure 6.7. Easter Island viewed in *Google Earth VR*. Screenshot by author.

by the absence of island narratives and the efforts to disguise single island chains (like Hawai'i) as representative of the whole.

Erotic play emerges in *Google Earth VR*'s feelings of untetheredness,
where one confronts the blurred virtual other within holistic views of
terrain but is unable to focus on anything except what war's aftermath
has deemed "seeable." In constant movement, one never finds a true
focal point but rather points of interest, like a mountainside to latch
on to before propelling toward the next vista. The presumption that an
elevated view brings enlightened comprehension dissolves in the swift
and overwhelming e-motion of *Google Earth VR*: the emptiness and
loneliness of being disembodied, alone in the sky, and made small by
the obscure, the unknowable, the infinite and incomprehensible. In the
disembodiment of virtual reality, one could yawp at a vista's beauty without hearing one's own voice. Loneliness settles. One has no mouth to
communicate, no hands to type; one is merely spirit, flying in e-motion.
A panoramic view can never cohere into a gaze, as the player's view
has no beginning or end. Instead, one finds many objects to be drawn
to, zoomed in upon, made meaningful. The map is not comprehensive
but sensational. One does not mathematically survey a cartography but
learns to see infinity—the pedagogy not of linear hierarchies but of a
pluralistic "besides."

Cartographic S(t)imulations

In video games, the e-motion of virtual worlds is not hard to find:
the endless wandering through *Second Life*, the galactic explorations
of *Eve Online*, the procedurally generated worlds of *Minecraft*. Such
confrontations with the virtual other leaves one rapturous, delirious,

or like Barthes, physically ill and needing to vomit away one's own preconceptions. Virtual maps reward exploration of unknown areas, pushing players to wander with the scopophilic pleasure of a strip-tease. As Kingsbury and Jones point out, playing Google Earth can feel like excavating a "digital peep-box" that tempts viewers to explore "an uncertain orb spangled with vertiginous paranoia, frenzied navigation, jubilatory dissolution, and intoxicating giddiness."[113] Kingsbury and Jones focus on exotic or violent phenomena such as naked sunbathers or crashed helicopters, but here we can see the "digital peep-box" as operating more as a burlesque striptease, a style that video games have mastered well. The open world game *The Legend of Zelda: The Wind Waker* takes place primarily on archipelagos, providing a world with a flat horizon where users can spot barely visible islands that invite exploration (see Figure 6.8). Distance here offers an erotic seduction that makes explicit our own carnal desires for the unknowable. Such games offer players a radical reimagining of oceanic space through feelings of wonder and traversal. The ability to fly over a virtual envi-ronment has the feeling of a romantic individualist overtaking new environments (the experience can only be undertaken alone), but it can also produce an intimate connection to the sea and islands, which come with no dominating narrative. One finds herself floating above a landmass she has never heard of, an island that rarely even appears on a map, and yet here it stands, just one of a million unknown monu-ments within a vast ocean.

It is within this striptease of slowly unraveling nature that the land-scapes censored from the viewer become maddening. While playing *Google Earth VR*, players will often come across an unmarked landmass that is grayed out or merely flattened and lacking in any detail. Some-times these spaces (similar to Brigham Young University) are adjacent to tourist spaces surrounded by large hotels and white-sand beaches. While these tourist spaces are well detailed, the gray and flat spaces ap-pear like apparitions haunting the tourist destinations. Just like their visible landmass, no narrative is present to explain them. The obscu-rity of these spaces can be infuriating because they exist contrary to the promises of GIS technology—the promise to deliver the Earth "as it is," to stay politically neutral, to show everything. Just as with the rest of the map, these obscured spaces express no national ties. Thus, one's wayward

Figure 6.8. *The Legend of Zelda: The Wind Waker*. Screenshot by D-e-f-. [D-e-f-. "New Zelda Wind Waker HD Videos." *NeoGAF: Believe (Gaming)*, September 4, 2013, www.neogaf.com.]

exploration inevitably confronts the militarized spatial violence that can be visible through mapped colonial settlement. Players with little knowledge of these violences find themselves in a pedagogical scene, suddenly prompted to discover the truth within these spaces—not the truth of the map but the truth of history, of empire, and of real still-living peoples. In the *Google Earth VR* apparatus, censored spaces are lacking in detail but are not invisible. They are remade into a convenient place-marker of flat satellite imagery through which the player notices and registers signs of censorship. The blots read as a direct attempt to hide at any cost the violences present within that space; they spark a techno-paranoia that presumes the worst and admits to understanding the least. The flat space against a colorful idyllic landscape signifies a darkness restricted to the open world, a violence adjacent to the tourist space that only moments ago was a distinct pleasure to discover. These obscured zones, within open world gameplay, encompass the player with the desire to uncover the striptease of exotic landmass, that piece of fabric that cannot be removed because it hides something off limits.

Through the medium of virtual reality consoles, *Google Earth VR* provides a landscape where people figure within tourist spaces, hotels, houses, and skyscrapers. *Google Earth VR* shifts the racialized cartography of island space from one of cultural exoticism and warrior bodies to tourist buildings, indigenous neighborhoods, and grayed-out military outposts. One's vantage point changes from the deck of a hotel, feet up, sun on the horizon, to a vertical view of the tops and sides of hotel buildings and mountains. This racialized landscape appears intertwined with the racist projects of militourism that function as its vested interests. Its normative dimension shifts with the direction of the gaze, seeing the surveillance state even in its censored form. *Google Earth VR* presents the world as aftermath of war—as always within the "math" (the sectioned growth) of American empire, through what remains visible and seen (American spaces, Paris) and what remains unseen (Afghanistan, gray sites, black sites, military bases). Yet, through the e-motion of erotic play, *Google Earth VR* also makes visible the spaces in between, the spaces that are neither seen nor unseen but are merely on the periphery, blurred out, unfocused, virtual. These are the island states, the oceans, the spaces that become meaningful through the vast striptease of a dotted horizon. Here one finds not anti-empire but the sites of its colonial leftovers.[114]

The cartographic imaginaries in Google Maps, *Civilization V*, and *Google Earth VR* flip the authority of the aerial view into the pleasures of erotic play, where elevation does not yield clarity or empowerment but desire, seduction, and a new understanding of one's self within an unexpected pedagogical scene. Virtual cartographies lend a stage to fathom the competing epistemologies within the Pacific, and the depictions of island space can read island chains in conjunction with places like South Korea's Jeju island, Okinawa, Taiwan, and my current island, the island of Hong Kong. The structural violence that occurs on these Pacific islands, such as militaristic and touristic occupations of space, high rates of diabetes, environmental degradation, and forced migration, rarely registers as a form of colonial oppression, as the islands function as imperial province zones that reap the benefits of mainland stewardship. Pacific islands don't feature as "hot" or "cold" war spaces, yet their roles as centers for refugees, war games, military recruitment, and tourist imaginings are integral to how war has been conducted and strategized within the garrison state of the Pacific Islands.

Coda

Anyway, I dunno . . . the moral is, you're a total bitch.
—Handsome Jack, *Borderlands 2*

In focusing on the virtual other, the final chapter has uncomfortably brought us to the virtual other's other: us, one of our many selves, this one disoriented and confused by the other's virtual bitch slap. The virtual other's topping of us reflects how we have been made bottom by Asiatic technology. To keep ourselves from this truth, we have constructed the open world empire, that more acquisitive piece of ourselves whose main pleasures come from a total accumulation of transparent and easily accessible information. In 1936, Walter Benjamin wrote that the function of film was to adjust the audience's perceptions to better inhabit a totalizing form of capitalism (mechanical reproduction).[1] Likewise, games train us as citizens of the open world empire: to quantify, to tabulate, to enjoy certainty, to be well adjusted to violence, to comprehend the world as a global game. But the playful anarchy and erotic interactions within video games also game us, tease us, throttle us about, push us to perceive the virtual other, and in so doing, perceive ourselves as its total bitch.

The virtual other plays upon viewer expectations, enticing them to intuit the complexity behind the simplicity, to see what the map does not show by covering it with names, colors, or text, or by censoring it directly. Desire plays a key role: the desire to territorialize and tame, the desire to use objective and authentic representations of others to convince us that no crime has been committed and that all violence is either of the past or totally incidental. And yet even in the historical obscurity there remains the capacity to inspire new curiosities concerning others, not as provincial toward us (a mere locality) but as structuring our very present, where militarization, colonization, factory assembly, and ecological ruin have become integral to facilitating our everyday pleasures.

If the war machine sees all technology as made for it and it alone, this book has dared not take the same view. Games, played for the frivolous reason of mere pleasure, can provide what Kaplan calls "an affective stew of indistinguishable sublime sensations."[2] Seeking "stew," this book has plunged into the slipstream that follows erotic pleasure: the ineffable, the indistinguishable, the broader pedagogical scene. Games help realize this scene by wedding the scientific with the aesthetic, the logical with the obscure, the procedural with the anarchic, the militaristic with the e-motional. New technologies do not "become" militarized but are "simultaneously both of and also not only of the military and the environment of war."[3] Efforts to understand how information technology and communications undergird militarism means confronting the omnivorous capacities of empire to curate the reality that best serves its interests. Because games do not aim to teach but to merely give pleasure, their spaces of play enact confrontations with ourselves as imperial subjects and with the spaces around us as imperial aftermath.

Interactive media's greatest potential is in offering the virtual as a space of eros and play, threatening the authoritative power of technologies presumed as militaristic (aerial views, virtual reality, shooter games) and technologies presumed as real (race, gender, nation). Virtual renditions of otherness merge militaristic technologies with aesthetics of landscape art, surrealist abstraction, and e-motion, and they stick these seemingly contradictory depictions into an arena of playful divergences and fluctuations. They loop the self, forcing us to confront our own contradictions as subjects who enjoy "the consistency of his selfhood and its collapse."[4] There is no better example of the contradictory subject than the video game player, who understands the casual depictions of new technology as dystopic and utopic and still decides to play with it—to derive intimacy and erotic pleasure from this seemingly cold and scientific apparatus. Play, as Sedgwick writes with Adam Frank, derives from "the wealth of mutually nontransparent possibilities for being wrong about an object—and, implicatively, about oneself." The game's erotic play has the power to collapse us and to shape this collapse as itself a pedagogical scene, a moment to learn about the self and to confront the mechanisms in place that formed us into the perverse, militarized monsters we were far before video games ever entered our lives.

ACKNOWLEDGMENTS

I began this project in graduate school, when video games operated as a brief salve for the fatigue that had left me numb and anxious. Thanks to Edmond Chang and members of the Critical Gaming Project at the Simpson Center for the Humanities, who brought me into the fold of game studies. Thanks to my advisers at the University of Washington, formal and informal, for entertaining my fringe interests and encouraging me to pursue my passions even within the restrictive atmosphere of disciplined academic writing: Alys Weinbaum, Chandan Reddy, Francisco Benitez, Priti Ramamurthy, Steve Sumida, Carolyn Allen, and Vicente Rafael. Much thanks to the Asian American groups I belonged to and helped organize, who step-by-step disabused me of many perceived truths: the Asian American Studies Research Collective, the Seattle Asian American Film Festival, and the Critical Filipino/Filipina Studies Collective. Special thanks to Vanessa Au, Su-Ching Wang, Martin Tran, Robyn Rodriguez, Michael Viola, and Valerie Francisco-Menchavez.

This project grew while I lived in Nanjing, China, and I met students who played games differently—erotically still, but as conduits of language, wisdom, and understanding. Thanks to Xue Leng (Snow) for guiding me through game centers and arcades and to friends and colleagues who helped me keep my head above water: Beverly Butcher, Anya Hamrick, Douglas Van Wieren, Sonali Chandel, Sophie Scott, Summer Xia, and the late David Oliver.

I nurtured this project for years before I moved to Hong Kong in 2015, where it came together into a book project thanks to two funding sources: a postdoctoral fellowship in the Centre for Cultural Studies at the Chinese University of Hong Kong and a faculty research grant at Hong Kong Baptist University. Being in Hong Kong with close proximity to the Pearl River Delta was sharply instructive for understanding just how deeply inflected information technology has become with colonial projects, bounding real communities to its labor, waste, and fantasies.

I'd like to thank colleagues at the Chinese University of Hong Kong who provided space, time, and resources: Song Hwee Lim, Laikwan Pang, Ka Ming Wu, and Peichi Chung. Thanks to my colleagues at Hong Kong Baptist University for their generosity and wisdom: Dorothy Tse, James Shea, Kwai Cheung Lo, Lucetta Kam, Daisy Tam, Yiu Fai Chow, Tammy Ho Lai-Ming, Jason Polley, Tong Yui, Gladys Chong, and Louis Ho. Special thanks to our faithful and hardworking program chair, John Nguyet Erni, a true inspiration. Thanks finally to my research assistants in Hong Kong who helped with translation and editing, providing me time to work on the book's main concepts: Yicen Liu, Jeff Chow Jung Sing, Kayla Cadenas, Rosinka Babashkina, Pamela Wong, and Patricia Choi.

Fortune has granted me groups of friends and mentors who gather within the circles of Asian, Asian American, and transpacific studies. I'm thankful to everyone in our Trans-Pacific-Rim Confab reading group in Hong Kong, who showed me the joy of reading playfully: Tan Jia, Anjeline de Dios, Elmo Gonzaga, Jeffrey Mather, Jason Coe, Kenneth Huynh, Collier Nogues, Grace Wang, and Elizabeth Ho. Thanks to members of transpacific groups in Canada who have helped me artfully dodge my way across the Pacific: the Asian Canadian & Asian Migration Studies program at the University of British Columbia, the Institute for Transpacific Research at Simon Fraser University, and the Pacific Exchanges group in Toronto. Special thanks to Christopher Lee, Christine Kim, Helen Hok-Sze Leung, Thy Phu, Nadine Attewell, and Vinh Nguyen. Forever thanks to the late Donald Goellnicht, who showed me how to live erotically, playfully, and ethically, within multiple families and homes.

Thanks to my colleagues at the University of British Columbia, who provide camaraderie and purpose whenever the loops of everyday life begin to wear thin: Denise Ferreira da Silva, Minelle Mahtani, and John Paul Catungal. Thanks to LeiLani Nishime and Vernadette Gonzalez, who gave publishing advice and convinced me that my love for writing about games was important. Thanks to the game designers Robert Yang and Minh Le, who improved my meager grasp of the shy gaming industry by sharing their experiences as developers. Heartfelt gratitude to Tara Fickle, who gave feedback on nearly every section of this book and who has helped me think through how Asian American cultures and video games have always been provocatively intertwined.

Every chapter of this book was incited by a conference, workshop, or symposium. Thanks to the organizers who provided a space to tease out these ideas, and thanks to the itinerant conference companions who gave intermittent feedback on this and other projects: Simeon Man, Jan Padios, Lily Wong, Leanne Day, Yến Lê Espiritu, Mila Zuo, Takeo Rivera, Alvy Wong, Catherine Fung, Valerie Soe, Tzu-hui Celina Hung, Oscar Campomanes, Eric Tang, Wendy Hui Kyong Chun, Cathy Schlund-Vials, Martin Joseph Ponce, and Fedinand Lopez. Thanks to creative artists and mentors who have helped push me as a writer and artist: Madeleine Thien, Peter Bacho, R. Zamora Linmark, David Chariandry, and Ken Liu. Thanks to the folks at NYU Press, especially Eric Zinner, Dolma Ombadykow, Karen Tongson, and Henry Jenkins, for their invaluable encouragement and advice. Thanks to the reviewers of this manuscript and to the editors and readers who helped turn a scattershot book of ideas into a focused yet flexible text.

Portions of this book were previously published in different forms, though they have been revised and reframed here. Small sections of chapter 2 come from my article "Asian Americans and Digital Games" in *Oxford Encyclopedia of Asian American Literature and Culture*. Parts of chapter 3 come from my chapter "Making Whales out of Peacocks: Virtual Fashion, Factory Work, and the Logic of Distance" in *Global Asian American Popular Cultures* and from my article "Role-Playing the Multiculturalist Umpire: Loyalty and War in BioWare's Mass Effect Series," in *Games and Culture: A Journal of Interactive Media*. About half of chapter 5 comes from my article "Heroes of the Open (Third) World: Killing as Pleasure in Ubisoft's *Far Cry* Series" in *American Quarterly*.

Mad thanks to all my game companions throughout the years, whose animated love for games was present while writing this manuscript: Josh Jenkins, Kristy Gomez and the Gomez family, Nolan Metcalf, Justin Kelly, Matthew Rinesh, and Christopher Martin. Special thanks to Michael James Drake, game expert extraordinaire, who gave feedback on a late draft of this manuscript. Wholehearted thanks to my twin brother, Cameron Patterson, for the lifetime of playing along in strange bodies and new worlds.

Thanks to my families—biological, chosen, and erratic. Thanks to my parents, Dion Guillermo Glenn and Samuel Patterson, for limiting my game time to two hours a day and thus teaching me that my time with games was to be treasured. To the Guillermos: my sister, Chanel, and nephew, Jacob, in San Antonio, and my uncles, aunties, and cousins in Hawaiʻi, who continue to remind me that knowledge means little without the semblance of understanding. Thanks to Hazel Ann Danao in Hong Kong, whose childcare labor and generosity made much of the revision process possible. Abundant thanks to my ever-faithful and invaluable support network in Vancouver: Mary Tsoi, Phanuel Antwi, Danielle Wong, and Heung and Yok Troeung. Finally, thank you to my soulmate Y-Dang Troeung and our son, Kai Basilio Troeung, who nourish my spirit every single day. There have been no better companions, nor anyone more fun to play with.

NOTES

INTRODUCTION

1 McDonald, "The Global Games Market."

2 See Milburn, *Respawn*; Parra, "Congo"; and Smith, "Tantalus in the Digital Age."

3 See Chan, "The Politics of Global Production"; George, "iPhone, Wii U Manufacturer."

4 Nguyen, *The Gift of Freedom*, xi.

5 Ibid., 28, italics in original.

6 Simone Browne defines racializing surveillance as "when enactments of surveillance reify boundaries along racial lines, thereby reifying race, and where the outcome of this is often discriminatory and violent treatment." Browne, *Dark Matters*, 8.

7 Chun, "Race and/as Technology," 7.

8 Lothian and Phillips, "Can Digital Humanities?"

9 For more on these techno-Orientalist associations, see the collection *Techno-Orientalism: Imagining Asia in Speculative Fiction, History, and Media*, especially the introduction and chapters by Seo-Young Chu, Steve Choe, and Se Young Kim, and Tzarina T. Prater and Catherine Fung.

10 *The Stanley Parable*, Galactic Cafe.

11 Foucault, *The Use of Pleasure*, 159.

12 Chen, *Asia as Method*, 6.

13 Sutton-Smith, *The Ambiguity of Play*, 9.

14 Halberstam, *The Queer Art of Failure*, 3.

15 Entertainment Software Association, "2017 Essential Facts About the Computer and Video Game Industry," *Theesa.com*, 2017, www.theesa.com.

16 For exceptions, see Peuter and Dyer-Witheford, *Games of Empire*; Huntemann and Payne, *Joystick Soldiers*; and Colin Milburn, *Respawn*.

17 Espen Aarseth troublingly wrote about the purity of games as nontextual and chastised "elitist" humanities scholars for embarking upon a "smothering form of generic criticism" that he likened to "academic colonialism." Aarseth, "Genre Trouble," 2004.

18 Eskelinen, "The Gaming Situation."

19 For more on the importance of representation in games, see Nakamura, *Cybertypes*; Everett, *Digital Diaspora*; Leonard, "Not a Hater;" Malkowski and Russworm, *Gaming Representation*; and Shaw, *Gaming at the Edge*.

20 Alfie Bown argues that games can *only* be understood "via the analysis of French psychoanalyst Jacques Lacan . . . or else the [video game] dreamworld will fall into the hands of the corporations and the state." Bown, *The Playstation Dreamworld*, 3.

21 Dyer, *Only Entertainment*, 168. Quoted in Adrriene Shaw, *Gaming at the Edge*, 225.

22 Galloway, "Playing the Code," 33.

23 As Soraya Murray aptly wrote in 2018, "Game studies is in a molten state of turmoil and transition. At the time of this writing, it is neither a codified 'field' with agreed-upon core texts, nor has it been assimilated into a disciplinary formation that occupies a fixed location in the academic setting." Murray, *On Video Games*, 8.

24 Anthropy, *Rise of the Videogame Zinesters*, 10.

25 For similar player-focused refusals of these discourses, see Shaw, *Gaming at the Edge*; Gray, *Race, Gender, and Deviance in Xbox Live*; and Sundén and Sveningsson, *Gender and Sexuality in Online Gaming Cultures*.

26 Halberstam defines low theory as a "theoretical model that flies below the radar, that is assembled from eccentric texts and examples and that refuses to confirm the hierarchies of knowing that maintain the high in high theory." Halberstam, *The Queer Art of Failure*, 15.

27 Jodi Byrd writes that game studies "grapples with the semiotics of machinic language, software, and code as the hard-wired domain of serious and legitimate scholars as opposed to the low theory cultural dabblers who read games as texts." Byrd, "Beast of America," 606.

28 "Playbour" in games is credited to Julian Kücklich, who uses it to discuss the hybrid form of play and labor in modding communities. Kücklich, "Precarious Playbour," 2005. Dyer-Witheford and Peuter revisit this term to encompass machinima, gold farming, management of online servers, and leadership within in-game communities. Dyer-Witheford and de Peuter, *Games of Empire*, 23.

29 Jenkins, *Fans, Bloggers, and Gamers*, loc 3615.

30 Anthropy, *Rise of the Videogame Zinesters*, 35.

31 Anthropy writes, "There is always a scene called World 1–2, although each performance of World 1–2 will be different." Anthropy, *Rise of the Videogame Zinesters*, 52.

32 Keogh, *A Play of Bodies*, loc 310.

33 Berlant, *The Queen of America*, 12.

34 Halberstam, *The Queer Art of Failure*, 20–21.

35 Shaw, "What Is Video Game Culture?" 404.

36 Murray, *Hamlet on the Holodeck*, 19.

37 Ibid., 57.

38 For more on immersion and Murray's detractors, see chapter 4.

39 So often one finds oneself in a game akin to what Murray calls the postmodern "indeterminate text" that affirms "the reader's freedom of interpretation." Murray, *Hamlet on the Holodeck*, 128.

40 Ibid., 148.

41 For more critiques of player agency, see Nakamura, *Cybertypes*; Murray, *On Video Games*; and Keogh, *A Play of Bodies*.

42 Suits, *The Grasshopper*, 83.

43 Salen and Zimmerman provided an early counterpoint when they argued in 2004 that pleasure was "the experience most intrinsic to games," and included "all kinds of pleasure," including constraint, delayed gratification, and seduction. Salen and Zimmerman, *Rules of Play*, 2.

44 Gallagher, "No Sex Please," 400.

45 Harviainen, Brown, and Suominen, "Three Waves of Awkwardness."

46 In February 2010, Apple deleted over 5,000 iPhone games from its digital store overnight for being too sexual (quoted in Anthropy, *Rise of the Videogame Zinesters*, 31); original article: Grannell, "Apple's Stance."

47 Lorde, "The Uses of the Erotic," 340.

48 Condis, *Gaming Masculinity*, 5.

49 Ibid.

50 Foucault, *The History of Sexuality*. Vol. 1.

51 Phillips, "Welcome to My Fantasy Zone."

52 See also on queerness and play: Ruberg, "Queerness and Video Games."

53 Keogh, *A Play of Bodies*, loc 402, italics in original.

54 I agree with and echo Adrienne Shaw's insight that "sexuality is present and relevant in every single video game made, regardless of the sexual identities or relationships (or lack thereof) of the characters." Shaw, *Gaming at the Edge*, 205.

55 Lorde, "The Uses of the Erotic," 341.

56 Halberstam, *The Queer Art of Failure*, 3.

57 Murray, *Hamlet on the Holodeck*, 128.

58 Here I agree with Henry Jenkins, who argues that game studies scholars should "emphasize the knowledge and competencies possessed by game players, starting with their mastery over the aesthetic conventions that distinguish games from real-world experience." Jenkins, *Fans, Bloggers, and Gamers*, loc 3987.

59 Quoted in Bissell, *Extra Lives*, 92–93.

60 Bogost, *Persuasive Games*, ix.

61 Ibid., 43.

62 As Hall writes, "the voluntary associations" of "gender, sexual and ethnic identities," as well as institutions of "the family, churches and religious life" were, for Gramsci, "the permanent fortifications of the front in the war of position." Hall, "Gramsci's Relevance," 18.

63 Hall, "Cultural Identity and Diaspora," 237.

64 As Aubrey Anable writes in *Playing with Feelings*, many games about identity, like Anna Anthropy's *Dys4ia* and Merritt Kopas's *LIM*, do so through modes of affect and feeling.

65 For book-length studies on affect and feelings in games, see Swink, *Game Feel*; Sundén and Sveningsson, *Gender and Sexuality*; Isbister, *How Games Move Us*; Anable, *Playing with Feelings*; Keogh, *A Play of Bodies*.

66 Brian Sutton-Smith noted that often adults play "with each other in innumerable ways, painting each other's bodies, eating food off of each other, playing hide the thimble with bodily crevices, communicating in public with their own esoteric vocabulary, and, in general teasing and testing each other with playful impropriety." Sutton-Smith, *The Ambiguity of Play*, 3.

67 Ruberg and Shaw, *Queer Game Studies.*

68 See Bonnie Ruberg's *Video Games Have Always Been Queer*, Christopher A. Paul's *The Toxic Meritocracy of Video Games*, and Megan Condis's *Gaming Masculinity*.

69 Muñoz, *Cruising Utopia*, 11.

70 Reddy, *Freedom with Violence*, 20.

71 One important exception to this tendency is Emma McDonald's anthology *Digital Love: Romance and Sexuality in Games*, which includes chapters devoted to Asian genres of romance games and Asian perceptions of gender and sexuality.

72 Sedgwick, *Tendencies*, 8.

73 De Villiers, *Opacity and the Closet*, 15.

74 Robyn Wiegman argues that the antinormativity aspirations of queer theory are often impeded when their "move against identity was tacitly confirmed by the authority that identity confers." Wiegman, "Eve, At a Distance," 161.

75 Berlant writes, "A relation of cruel optimism exists when something you desire is actually an obstacle to your flourishing." Berlant, *Cruel Optimism*, 1.

76 Foucault, *The Use of Pleasure*, 4–8.

77 Foucault, *The Care of the Self*, 71.

78 Similarly, Amy Brandzel points out that "there is a joy and a pleasure in righteous critique." Brandzel, *Against Citizenship*, loc 39.

79 Dean, "The Biopolitics of Pleasure," 486.

80 Foucault, *The Use of Pleasure*, 8.

81 This phrase is often revisited as "the soft-spoken queen of gay studies." Hu, "Between Us."

82 Spivak, "Can the Subaltern Speak?"

83 Siegel, "The Madness Outside Gender."

84 "It is perhaps more accurate to say that both Barthes and Warhol have been closeted, rather than that they were closeted." De Villiers, *Opacity and the Closet*, 118.

85 The pleasures of erotics are not only sensational but also, as Susan Sontag has argued, the "poignant longing for beauty, for an end to probing below the surface, for a redemption and celebration of the body of the world." Sontag, *On Photography*, 18.

86 Musser, *Sensational Flesh*, 11.

87 See Richard Miller's foreword to Barthes, *The Pleasure of the Text*, viii.

88 Ibid., 14.

89 Sedgwick, *Touching Feeling*, 21.

90 Barthes, *Empire of Signs*, 29.

91 Massumi, "The Autonomy of Affect."

92 Aubrey Anable similarly rationalizes her focus on affect in games by removing sensation from the subjective realm of erotics: "Identifying a video game as an affective system means resisting locating properties like texture, tone, and feelings in a purely subjective experience of reception." Anable, *Playing with Feelings*, loc 169.

93 De Villiers, *Opacity and the Closet*.

94 Barthes, *Image, Music, Text*, 142.

95 Barthes, *Empire of Signs*, 3.

96 Ungar, *Roland Barthes*, xii.

97 Jordan, *Convulsing Bodies*, 5.

98 See Chapter 6 for a more detailed analysis of this lecture.

99 According to Tim Dean, Foucault's turn from concepts of ideology and "the Althusserian notion of interpellation" were an attempt to understand politics outside of identification, which maintained "the illusion of the human body as a unity, when it is instead through its disunity, at the 'subindividual' level, that power takes hold." Dean, "The Biopolitics of Pleasure," 489.

100 Foucault's second volume, *The Use of Pleasure*, conceived Western sexuality as undermined by "austere, self-denuding pleasures" that expose the self to alterity and inhibit logics of identity-based consumption. Dean, "The Biopolitics of Pleasure," 486.

101 Foucault, *History of Sexuality*. Vol. 1, 57–58.

102 Russo, "The Reeducation."

103 Sedgwick considered herself a Jew and "a sexual pervert" who had intimate friendships with gay men, several of whom died of HIV-related illness. "But why write about men, rather than lesbians?" she was also repeatedly asked. Similarly, for Robyn Wiegman, Sedgwick's refusal to identify as lesbian also gave respect to "what others needed when they asked her to define herself in their terms." Wiegman, "Eve, At a Distance," 159.

104 Muñoz, "Race, Sex, and the Incommensurate," 108.

105 Sedgwick, *Touching Feeling*, 149.

106 Wiegman, "Eve's Triangles," 54.

107 Sedgwick, *Touching Feeling*, 166–67.

108 Nakamura, *Cybertypes*, 4.

109 As Soraya Murray writes in reference to "serious" and "non-serious" games, "The perception that some games are about the politics of identity, while others are not, needs to be dismantled." Murray, *On Video Games*, 46.

110 Roh, Huang, and Niu, "Technologizing Orientalism," 2.

111 Fickle, *The Race Card*.

112 See Consalvo, "Visiting the Floating World," 737; Carlson and Corliss, "Imagined Commodities."

113 Kinder, *Playing with Power*, 4.

114 Winnicott, *Playing and Reality*, 47.

115 Wolin, *The Wind from the East*.

116 Althusser, *For Marx.*

117 In 1977, Noam Chomsky wrote an article in *The Nation* defending the Khmer Rouge and pleading for more suspicion of refugees' stories of atrocities. Chomsky and Herman. "Distortions at Fourth Hand."

118 These theorists' orientations to Asia perceived of Asia during and after the Cold War outside of Marxist reductions ("the working class," "the bourgeois,"); these methods, too, were conceived in light of the incalculable loss of human life that occurred—"falsely" or "truly"—in the name of Marxist revolution.

119 Dean, "The Biopolitics of Pleasure," 483.

120 Barthes, *Empire of Signs*, 27.

121 Ibid., 28–29.

122 Ibid.

123 Wiseman, *The Ecstasies of Roland Barthes.*

124 Foucault and Trombadori, *Remarks on Marx*, 40–41.

125 Sontag, *Against Interpretation*, loc 307.

126 After Sontag's death in 2004, Ellen Willis summarized her career as a retreat from erotics. For Willis, Sontag's "prime concern was no longer achieving an erotics of art, but parsing the morality of art. Or rather, the erotics of art—the pleasure we derived from it—became something to be questioned and inspected for its darker, often sadomasochistic aspects." Willis, "Three Elegies for Susan Sontag," 118. I do not see the shift from "erotics" to "morality" as a reversal, but as further explorations of erotic thinking, shifted by Sontag's later context of writing after a repressed Civil Rights Movement and the war in Vietnam.

127 Holland, *The Erotic Life of Racism*, 9.

128 See Milburn on *Portal 2* and *Final Fantasy VII* and Keogh on *Hotline Miami.*

129 Foucault defines "games of truth" as "the games of truth and error through which being is historically constituted as experience; that is, as something that can and must be thought." Foucault, *The Use of Pleasure*, 6–7.

130 I am using the normative as Robyn Wiegman suggests when speaking of the achievement in normalizing AIDS as a goal of the early LGBT movement. Wiegman, "Eve's Triangles," 49.

CHAPTER 1. GLOBAL GAME

1 Activision Blizzard, "Our Company."

2 Murray, *On Video Games*, 61.

3 This disclaimer was changed in *Assassin's Creed: Syndicate* to add gender and sexuality.

4 Jagoda writes, "If cinema flourished in the local theater, we might say that the twenty-first-century videogame adopts the space and time of the transnational Internet." Jagoda, *Network Aesthetics*, 145.

5 Shaw, *Gaming at the Edge*, 214.

6 As Song Hwee Lim writes, *Memoirs of a Geisha* demonstrates that "a transnational production may precisely provide the timely fodder for a reinstatement of

national(istic) sentiments . . . solidifying rather than challenging notions of ethnic identities that are defined against a vilified Other." Lim, Song Hwee. "Is the Trans- in Transnational," 48.

7   Race can be seen in games that are ostensibly racist (*America's Army*, *Ethnic Cleansing*), antiracist (*September 12th*), or inclusive (*Sleeping Dogs*).

8   Nakamura, *Cybertypes*, 42.

9   As Nakamura has written, "Identity tourism resembled off-line tourism because it gave users a false notion of cultural and racial understanding based on an episodic, highly mediated experience of travel." Nakamura, *Cybertypes*, 129.

10 Chan, "Playing with Race."

11 Leonard, "High Tech Blackface."

12 Shaw, *Gaming at the Edge*, 95.

13 Everett, *Digital Diaspora*, 146.

14 As Shaw writes, academics "focus almost exclusively on dedicated video game fans," who, unlike cultures of literature or the cinema, do not question the ho- mophobia, racism, or sexism rampant in the video games. Shaw, "What is Video Game Culture?" 409.

15 Malkowski and Russworm, "Introduction," 2.

16 Shaw writes: "Wanting representation, the act of desiring it, is different from critiquing portrayals that exist. The market-logic argument for representation glosses over this nuance . . . The reason representation mattered to some inter- viewees was that they saw the under- or misrepresentation of certain groups as unrealistic. This might lead, they hypothesized, to negative effects in the world at large. It was not, however, because they needed to see people 'like them.'" Shaw, *Gaming at the Edge*, 165–66.

17 Nakamura, *Cybertypes*, 22.

18 Sontag, *Against Interpretation*, loc 5439.

19 Ibid., loc 5474.

20 Ibid., loc 5655.

21 Barthes, *Empire of Signs*, 7.

22 Upton cofounded Red Storm Entertainment and was the lead designer for *Rain- bow Six* and *Ghost Recon*, both games based on Tom Clancy novels that valorize counterterrorist special forces.

23 Upton, *The Aesthetic of Play*, loc 161.

24 Ibid., loc 171.

25 Ibid.

26 Roh, Huang, and Niu define techno-Orientalism as "the phenomenon of imagining Asia and Asians in hypo- or hypertechnological terms in cultural productions and political discourse." Roh, Huang, and Niu. "Technologizing Orientalism," 2.

27 This strategy was used most famously by Zeng Guofan, who defeated the Taiping Rebellion by encircling their celestial capital.

28 Boorman, *The Protracted Game*.

29 We must also take into account that these idealizations of play as non-national, as non-historical, and as something "transcendent," are partially due to the fact that game studies itself valorizes video games as an industry, and thus allows developers and game designers themselves to structure the very terms through which games are understood. Upton, for example, chides game studies scholar Bernard Suits for being "a philosopher and not a game designer, [who] fails to grasp the systematically structured nature of a well-functioning playfield, which leads him astray as he tries to explain why overcoming some obstacles doesn't feel playful." Upton, *The Aesthetic of Play*, 300.

30 Upton, *The Aesthetic of Play*, 345.

31 Huizinga, *Homo Ludens*, 10.

32 Castronova, *Synthetic Worlds*, 159.

33 Salen and Zimmerman, *Rules of Play*, 95.

34 Huizinga, *Homo Ludens*, 8.

35 Stenros, "In Defence of a Magic Circle."

36 Shaw, *Gaming at the Edge*, 162.

37 Balibar and Wallerstein, *Race, Nation, Class*, 22.

38 Chun, "Introduction: Race and/as Technology," 38.

39 Chun writes, "Focusing on race as a technology, as mediation, thus allows us to see the continuing function of race, regardless of its 'essence.' It also highlights the fact that race has never been simply biological or cultural, but rather a means by which both are established and negotiated." Chun, "Race and/as Technology," 44.

40 Ibid., 39.

41 As Fickle argues, "the concepts of strategic play and gaming are crucial to understanding broader questions in Asian American literature about identity, authenticity, and national belonging—and to recognizing, furthermore, the fundamentally gamelike attributes that inhere in the [Japanese] internment as a site of historical memory." Fickle, "No-No Boy's Dilemma," 741.

42 Clough faults Chun's theory for seeing "no need to specify which technology is being referenced." Clough, *The User Unconscious*, 131.

43 Ibid.

44 See Yee, Nick. *The Proteus Paradox*; Nakamura, "Don't Hate the Player."

45 Nakamura, "Don't Hate the Player," 142.

46 Ahmed, *The Promise of Happiness*, 45.

47 Ibid., 41.

48 Tolerance, as Ahmed writes, bolsters spaces of happiness as spaces of freedom, since diverse bodies cohabit the same sphere, making the world appear "open to you, as if you can do what you want in the world that you are in." Ahmed, *The Promise of Happiness*, 157.

49 Huizinga, *Homo Ludens*, 11.

50 Ibid.

51 For more on the overlap between playability and racial representation, see Soraya Murray's take on "playable representations," which she calls "a way of acknowl-

edging the dual elements of action and representation at work in the visual culture of games." Murray, *On Video Games*, 25.

52 Cheney-Lippold, *We Are Data*, 10.

53 Ibid.

54 Sontag writes, "the Camp sensibility is one that is alive to a double sense in which some things can be taken. But this is not the familiar split-level construction of a literal meaning, on the one hand, and a symbolic meaning, on the other. It is the difference, rather, between the thing as meaning something, anything, and the thing as pure artifice." Sontag, *Against Interpretation*, loc 5507.

55 Many have faulted Sontag's "Notes on Camp" for its questionable historical presentation of camp (Miller, David A. "Sontag's Urbanity"), as well as her obscure style (which floats inconsistencies) and its epigrams that, according to Mark Booth, are "of an almost oriental inscrutability." Booth, Mark. "Campe-toi!" 67. Yet "Notes on Camp" comes far after her stated intention to write an erotics of art, and it plays with "the serious" by refusing clarity and consistency, delving instead into the obscure so as to "[feel] her way around largely unknown territory" (Ibid.). In so doing, Sontag relies on erotics to perceive a style of camp, making the meanings of camp appear inconsistent, inaccurate, or just plain hubristic (implying that she invented the term, that she can analyze it more fully than those who share in its "given sensibility"). As Sasha Torres writes, "Sontag's de-gaying of camp itself *performs* what it most crucially fails to *explain*. Even as she enacts the straight appropriation of camp . . . she renders invisible the most interesting and elusive thing about camp: its placement at the borderlines of gay and non-gay taste." Torres, "The Caped Crusader of Camp," 337. This borderline we can appropriately call a queer erotic that attends to the sensibilities of camp aesthetics from a slanted (rather than outsider) point of view. Sontag herself claimed to be bisexual, and that she had fallen in love over her life with "Five Women, Four Men." Mackenzie, "Finding Fact from Fiction."

56 Sontag, *Against Interpretation*, loc 5656.

57 Murray, *On Video Games*, 82.

58 Sontag, *Against Interpretation*, loc 5392.

59 Sedgwick, *Touching Feeling*, 149.

60 Ibid.

61 Ngai, *Ugly Feelings*, 32.

62 Halperin, *How to Be Gay*, 191.

63 See uses of camp in the Avital Ronnell case: Wiener, "Avital and Nimrod"; Colucci, "No, Avital Ronell."

64 Sontag, Boyers, and Bernstein. "Women, The Arts," 40.

65 The far-right celebrity Milo Yiannopoulos has been called "Mother Camp." Colucci, "Yes, Mary."

66 Dyer, *The Culture of Queers*.

67 Cleto, "Introduction: Queering the Camp," 204.

68 Ibid.

69 Barthes defines myth in various ways, but politically speaking it is "language," meaning the *styles* of discourses (rather than their consistent content), that allows the bourgeois and "the right" to "keep reality without keeping the appearances." Barthes, *Mythologies*, 150.

70 Wolfe, *Traces of History*.

71 See Chua, *Battle Hymn of the Tiger Mother*; and Chua, "Why Chinese Mothers Are Superior."

72 Wolfe's treatise on race finds the diverse presence of racial skin color itself as a means of obscuring historically produced differences in racial structures (in the case of the bodily labor exploitation of slaves and the territorial dispossession of indigenous or natives). The self-correcting tendency of imperial societies to tolerate or assimilate racialized others, as I have shown in prior work, operates as a pluralist governmentality so that diversity (in skin color) no longer signifies unequal relationships but their transcendence. In *Transitive Cultures: Anglophone Literature of the Transpacific*, I define pluralist governmentality as "an art of government that expects individuals to visibly express their difference via given group identities, and in doing so, to represent imperial state power as neutral, universal, or benevolent." Patterson, *Transitive Cultures*, 15.

73 Wolfe, *Traces of History*, loc 230.

74 Gallagher, "From Camp to Kitsch," 40.

75 See Clough, "Sexualization, Shirtlessness," and Ganzon, "Female Power."

76 Clough, "Sexualization, Shirtlessness," 22.

77 Goto-Jones, "Playing with Being," 39–40.

78 Martin, "Race, Colonial History," 3.

79 Dean Chan has written of video games as performing superflat artistic forms and enacting a "ludic superflatness." Chan, "The Cultural Economy."

80 Murakami, "Earth in My Window."

81 Sawaragi, "On the Battlefield," 204.

82 Murakami, "Earth in My Window," 132.

83 Ibid., 107.

84 Iwabuchi, *Recentering Globalization*, 53.

85 Ibid., 54.

86 Iwabuchi and Takezawa, "Rethinking Race," 2.

87 Iwabuchi, *Recentering Globalization*, 27.

88 Ibid., 27–28.

89 Iwabuchi, "Lost in TransNation," 548.

90 Iwabuchi, *Recentering Globalization*, 27–28.

91 The *Street Fighter* franchise has spawned eight different series, each with updated editions that refined game mechanics (*Street Fighter II* alone had six subsequent editions), and it has led to various animation series in Japan, South Korea, and America as well as three feature films.

92 Gray, *Race, Gender, and Deviance*, 27.

93 Sontag, *Against Interpretation*, loc 5552.

94 As Iwabuchi has pointed out, in the aftermath of Japan's defeat in World War II, racial constructs were revised not with Japanese on top but as "betwixt and between" blackness and the whiteness that signified Euro-American supremacy, positing a new hierarchy of racial otherness where "its own position tenuously mediated color boundaries while maintaining Western centrality." Iwabuchi, *Recentering Globalization*, 6.

95 Despite the fact that they are called "skins," these cannot change race/skin color.

96 As TreaAndrea Russworm writes of digital black minstrelsy in the game *Afro Samurai*, stock or stereotypical characters in games can make use of parody and other rhetorical conventions that "destabilize as much as confirm dominant cultural associations of blackness." Russworm, "The Hype Man," 171.

97 Gallagher, "From Camp to Kitsch," 41.

98 Barthes, *Empire of Signs*, 79.

99 Ibid., 74.

100 Ibid., 70.

101 Especially in traditions like the haiku, which Barthes found so liberatingly empty that, "to speak of the haiku would be purely and simply to repeat it." Barthes, *Empire of Signs*, 71.

102 Ibid., 9.

103 Ibid., 10.

104 Ibid., 26.

105 Barthes calls the body that which "has been known, savored, received, and which has displayed (to no real purpose) its own narrative, its own text." Barthes, *Empire of Signs*, 10.

106 Ibid., 3.

107 Cheng, *Ornamentalism*, x.

108 James, *The Art of Criticism*, 142.

109 Sterne, *The Life and Opinions of Tristram Shandy*, 81.

110 Lye, *America's Asia*, 9.

111 Halberstam, *Trans**, 5.

112 Obama, "President Obama's Speech."

113 Sheer, "Player Tally."

114 *League of Legends*'s biggest teams are almost uniformly Asian teams (The Taipei Assassins (TPA) of Taiwan, Azubu Frost of South Korea, SK Telecom T1 of South Korea, Royal Club of China). Teams from countries outside of Asia are rife with Asian minorities or are dominated by them (SoloMid from North America, Giants Gaming from Spain, g2esports from "worldwide").

115 Anunpattana, Khalid, Yusof, and Iida, "Analysis of Realm of Valor."

116 Marks, "Arena of Valor."

117 From 2012 to 2015, each competition has seen more e-sport teams from China than any other country. Despite the fact that the People's Republic of China had banned video game consoles from 2000 to 2014 for American games depicting violence and drug use, Chinese players, too, have emerged as "naturals" at e-sports.

118 Sutton-Smith, *The Ambiguity of Play*, 86.

119 Guttmann considers how "the political, economic, or cultural powers of the great nations are said to have caused the weaker powers dependent on them to adopt their sports forms." Guttmann, *Games and Empires*, 94.

120 Ludic identity, as Jos de Mul describes it, tends "toward an increase of openness" in how one identifies with histories, institutions, and communities; rather than settle on a single racial, ethnic, or national identity, ludic identities "search for new possibilities" and operate against "the threat of closure" that is repeatedly presented within identity-based discourses. De Mul, "The Game of Life," 260–61.

121 As Toshiya Ueno writes, "If the Orient was invented by the West, then the Techno-Orient also was invented by the world of information capitalism." Ueno, "Japanimation and Techno-Orientalism," 228.

122 Sohn, "Introduction," 8.

123 In reference to the death of Asian gamers from game addiction, Choe and Kim write: "Compared to the healthy body of the white gamer, the Asian player plays ostensibly in order to compensate for his physical impotence." Choe and Kim, "Never Stop Playing," 114.

124 Sontag, *Styles of Radical Will*, loc 756.

125 Somerandomusernameth, "Overwatch Wasn't Supposed."

126 Clark and Kopas, "Queering Human-Game Relations."

127 Shaw, *Gaming at the Edge*, 67.

128 Ibid., 63.

129 A closed search on YouTube of the line "The world could always use more heroes!" results in over sixty videos with the phrase in the title. Many of these videos are of gameplay (previously broadcast on Twitch.tv) where the player merely repeats the phrase to their teammates ad nauseam.

130 Urban Dictionary defines maining as: "In video games, the selecting of the character(s) that one uses the most (i.e., their "main" character)." TheKoW, "Maining."

131 As Michael Cronin writes, a powerful ally in the "utilitarian view of translation in the digital age is the ideology of transparency: What You See Is What You (always) See, and once you see it, you get it." Cronin, *Translation in the Digital Age*, 4.

132 I am inspired here by Vicente Rafael's notion of linguistic insurgency, which he calls "acts of translation that register the untranslatability of language" that "allow us to reckon with ideologies that reduce translation and languages into mere instruments of conversion, colonial conquest, and social control." Rafael, *Motherless Tongues*, 8. These playful insurgencies emerge in literary forms like poetry and critical theory but also in forms of digitized information, such as networks of smartphone texting (such as during the *EDSA II* protests and Occupy movements).

133 On the unpaid and creative work of modders and fans in translating games, see Anthopy, *Rise of the Videogame Zinesters*, 59.

134 As Rafael points out, in conflicts like the Iraq War, American military forces have weaponized translation so that "the work of translation was geared to go in only one direction: toward the transformation of the foreign into an aspect of the domestic." Rafael, Vicente. *Motherless Tongues*, 102.

135 Mei's expression "Hang in there!" appears in Chinese as "zài nà-er tǎng zhe ba," [在那儿躺着吧], "lying there," and in Taiwanese as "biè fàngqì ó" [别放弃哦], "don't give up."

136 Rafael, *Motherless Tongues*, 188.

137 Ibid., 189.

138 Shaw, *Gaming at the Edge*, 36.

139 Nakamura, *Cybertypes*, 60.

140 Milburn, *Respawn*, 3.

CHAPTER 2. LUDOPHILE

1 Chang, "Call for Art."

2 Donlan, "Spelunky 2?"

3 International Game Developers Association, "Game Developer Demographics."

4 Nguyen, *Nothing Ever Dies*, loc 3035.

5 Guillermo, "Robert Yang."

6 See chapter 5, where I consider these characters as Asian avatars that permit gamers to kill at whim.

7 Faith was created by Rhianna Pratchett, daughter of the fantasy writer Terry Pratchett.

8 Bogost, *Persuasive Games*.

9 Even the Game Developers Choice Awards hesitates to name developers in its main awards and only does so for its "Special Awards" section.

10 Smith, "One, Two, Three."

11 Bloom, *Video Invaders*, 114.

12 Ibid., 118.

13 Ibid., 48.

14 Ibid.

15 Ibid., xix.

16 Ibid., 49.

17 Ibid., 75.

18 Brian Reynolds is credited as the primary designer behind *Sid Meier's Civilization II*, *Sid Meier's Alpha Centauri*, and *Sid Meier's Colonization*. Schreier, "Sid Meier."

19 Powe, *Marshall McLuhan and Northrop Frye*, 93.

20 Browning, *David Cronenberg*, 205.

21 Ruberg, "Clint Hocking Speaks Out."

22 Morran, "EA Makes Worst Company."

23 Biggs, "Famed Designer Hideo Kojima."

24 Bloom, *Video Invaders*, 42.

25 Atari was named after the Japanese word "atari," a move in the game Go meaning something like "strike."

26 Bloom, *Video Invaders*, xvii.

27 Ibid.

28 Ibid., 40.

29 Ibid., 81.

30 For the many "father figures" on this list, their games come as prototypical for their genre, not necessarily the first or "urtext." In the case of *Resident Evil*, the main inspiration was the survival horror game *Left Alone in the Dark* (1992).

31 Tetsuya Nomura of Square Enix, Capcom's Shinji Mikami (*Resident Evil*), and Koei Tecmo's Tomonobu Itagaki (*Ninja Gaiden*) and Keiji Inafune (*Mega Man*) are no longer with their parent companies. Other deserters include Castlevania chief Koji Igarashi, who left Konami, as well as Tomonobu Itagaki and Hironobu Sakaguchi (*Final Fantasy, Parasite Eve*).

32 For a book-length study of how Japanese designers pushed games into "art," see Kohler, *Power-Up*.

33 Elsaesser, "Cinephilia," 31.

34 Donaldson, "Suda 51 Wants to Make."

35 Suda 51, *The Art of Grasshopper Manufacture*.

36 Miguel Penabella refers to Suda when defending the use of auteur theory in games, using Suda's background as an undertaker to read the trope of death in his games (even though Suda himself has claimed to "get no inspiration from his time as an undertaker"). Penabella, "Opened World."

37 In their review of *Flower, Sun, and Rain*, *Eurogamer* called it "like the man himself." Welsh, "Flower, Sun and Rain."

38 Boyes, "Q&A: SUDA-51."

39 Iwabuchi, "Lost in TransNation," 546.

40 Ibid.

41 Kazan, *Kazan on Directing*, 322.

42 As Steven Ungar writes, "Removed from the illusion of mastery associated with his earlier critical projects, Barthes sets his writing into the very text of discourse . . . the use of language rather than its mere forms." Ungar, *Roland Barthes*, 78.

43 Barthes, *A Lover's Discourse*, 4.

44 Ibid., 83.

45 Ibid., 192–93, italics in original.

46 Ungar: "The loved one present in the amorous discourse is neither figure nor fetish, but the product of a discursive force." Ungar, *Roland Barthes*, 83.

47 Barthes, *A Lover's Discourse*, 83.

48 Ibid., 134.

49 Waypoint, "Why 'Flower, Sun, and Rain,'" italics mine.

50 In October 2013, Twitch.tv attracted 45 million unique viewers, watching on average 100 minutes a day. See Ewalt, "The ESPN of Video Games."

51 ScottishDuck17, "Let's Play Shenmue 2—Part 60."

52 Like Suda, Suzuki has been known as a niche auteur developer who has had to turn to his loyal fan base and Kickstarter to fund his projects.

53 Alexander Galloway fit Shenmue into an oedipal temporality, referring to the game as "Suzuki's *Shenmue*" and comparing it to "the films of Yasujiro Ozu." Galloway, Alexander. *Gaming*, 10.

54 For more on the white man/brown boy colonial dyad, see Lim, *Brown Boys and Rice Queens*.

55 For more on walking simulators, see Cross, "How 'Walking Simulators.'"

56 Barthes, *A Lover's Discourse*, 11.

57 Ibid., 155.

58 Rivera, "Do Asians Dream," 69.

59 Galloway, *Gaming*, 10.

60 Barthes, *A Lover's Discourse*, 104; Rob Gallagher has similarly pointed out that gameplay desires are often experienced as moments of delayed gratification. Gallagher, "No Sex Please," 404.

61 Ibid., 69.

62 ScottishDuck17, "Let's Play," 3:05.

63 Barthes, *A Lover's Discourse*, 54.

64 Ibid., 55.

65 ScottishDuck17, "Let's Play," 5:40.

66 Ibid. As DoubleO88 writes, "lol i love little things like hang on in random unexpected places its why i love shenmue . . . i've never seen that b4 that was amazing this game is outstanding after 10 years and recently replaying it and theres still countless stuff hidden in it just WOW!"

67 Barthes, *A Lover's Discourse*, 105.

68 Nielsen, "Game Addiction," 233.

69 Chow elsewhere adds that this tendency reinstates a form of coercive mimicry: "Asian Americans are perhaps the paradigmatic case of a coercive mimeticism that physically keeps them in their place—that keeps them, in Balibar's terms, in their genealogy and, I would add, in their genre of speaking/writing as nothing but generic Asian Americans." Chow, *The Protestant Ethnic*, 125.

70 Irene Chien has examined *Journey* as a piece of art that seeks to "universalize" games while still deploying racialized backdrops like unpopulated deserts—what Chien calls "techno-primitive" representation. Others, like Patrick Jagoda, see the game as expressing the common experience of relationships "defined and made possible by strangerhood." See Chien, "Journey," 2017; Jagoda, *Network Aesthetics*, 176; Patterson, "Asian Americans and Digital Games."

71 Bogost, "A Portrait of the Artist." Chen also advises for Annapurna Interactive, a games publisher that specializes in artistic and independent games.

72 Chen, "Flow in Games."

73 Smith, "A Personal Journey."

74 "Gurus" like the brothers Andy and Dan Dinh, who became known for launching one of the first community-based websites dedicated to learning and teaching *League of Legends.*

75 As Michael Nguyen's studies have shown, games like *Shellshock Nam '67*, a game about the Vietnam War, were routinely played by Vietnamese gamers, who saw these games as a chance to understand their own heritage, even from a bleakly American white hero narrative. Nguyen, "New Vietnam War."

76 Danico and Vo, "'No Lattes Here," 181.

77 As Swink writes, "Minh 'Gooseman' Le . . . was able to craft everything. He not only created the rules and challenges of the game, but also defined how fast players could move, how high they could jump, how accurate their weapons would be and what the values for gravity and friction would be in the game." Swink, *Game Feel*, 16.

78 Guillermo, "Race, Terror and Counter-Strike."

79 In his essays on the creation of de_dust and de_dust 2, level designer David Johnston claims to have drawn inspiration from the architecture of his high school, but he never mentions that his two famous levels conjure the desert iconography of the War on Terror, implying that it was only his level design, not racial elements, that enabled it to succeed. Johnston, "The Making of Dust."

80 Le created an Asian terrorist but decided to trash the character when community members called it "ugly" and thought it looked like Luke Skywalker. See SINFO, "SINFO Conf 2015."

81 Le, "I Am Minh Le."

82 Chan, "Headshot!"

83 Wright, Talmadge, Boria, and Paul Breidenbach claim that "*Counter-Strike* players resemble a youth subculture" that promotes "a refashioning of time and community" through an "acceptance of both disorder and creative player actions." Wright, Boria, and Breidenbach, "Creative Player Actions."

84 Minh Le claimed to have more than one hundred maps submitted every week.

85 Anthropy, *Rise of the Videogame Zinesters*, 29.

86 Nguyen, *Nothing Ever Dies*, 110.

87 Burford, "Why *Modern Warfare*'s."

88 Totilo, "The Designer of Call of Duty's."

89 Burford, "*Modern Warfare 2*."

CHAPTER 3. ARS EROTICA

1 Ong, *Spirits of Resistance*, 103.

2 Chua, *Gold by the Inch*, 93.

3 Chun, *Control and Freedom*, vii.

4 Nakamura, "Indigenous Circuits," 931.

5 See Ruberg and Shaw, *Queer Game Studies*.

6 Gee, *What Video Games Have to Teach Us*, 55.

7 See Isbister, *How Games Move Us*, 29.

8 Salen and Zimmerman, *Rules of Play*, 34.

9 Swink, *Game Feel*, 58.

10 Sundén and Sveningsson, *Gender and Sexuality*, 124.

11 Harviainen, "Sadomasochist Role-Playing."

12 Musser, *Sensational Flesh*, 8.

13 Chan, Pun, and Selden, "The Politics of Global Production."

14 George, "iPhone, Wii U Manufacturer."

15 Tam, "Foxconn Factories."

16 These hardware factories are largely owned or contracted from one of the top ten hardware companies. Lenovo, Dell, Hewlett-Packard, Acer, Apple, and Toshiba dominate the market.

17 According to an undercover investigation by Danish and Chinese Labor watchdogs, "Chinese workers at factories making Dell computers are being forced to work seven day, 74 hour weeks under appalling conditions" and for below minimum wage. Such conditions involved breathing in of toxic fumes, standing up for the entire twelve-hour shifts, and having one toilet for every fifty-five workers. Miller, "Appalling Conditions of Factory Workers."

18 Chun, *Control and Freedom*, 178.

19 Nakamura, "Economies of Digital Production," 8.

20 In *Final Fantasy XII* Cid makes his first appearance as an antagonist, and in *Final Fantasy XIII* he similarly works for the empire. In the series' recent iterations, *FFXIV* and *FFXV*, Cid has become sanitized, working for the player as a mechanic, repairing the player's machines, and he has returned to a wise old sage.

21 Chen, *Asia as Method*.

22 See Gee's *What Video Games Have to Teach Us about Learning and Literacy* and McGonigal's *Reality Is Broken: Why Games Make Us Better and How They Can Change the World*, 2011.

23 Simkins and Steinkuehler, "Critical Ethical Reasoning and Role-Play," 334.

24 Jørgensen, "Game Characters as Narrative Devices," 315.

25 On a global scale, the United States embodies a multiculturalist position by positing itself as "the universal, so that U.S. government and military actions are to be understood as being for a supranational good." Melamed, *Represent and Destroy*, 16.

26 In his essay "Is there a 'Neo-Racism'?" Etienne Balibar feared that the ghettoization of cultural ways of life could lead to a rigid multiculturalism, where culture functions "like a nature, and it can in particular function as a way of looking at individuals and groups a priori into a genealogy, into a determination that is immutable and intangible in origin." Balibar and Wallerstein, *Race, Nation, Class*, 22.

27 Yoneyama, *Cold War Ruins*, loc 4488.

28 See Mamdani, *Good Muslim, Bad Muslim*.

29 "Citadel Council," *Mass Effect Wiki*. This fan-made wiki is a collection of information from *Mass Effect*'s in-game encyclopedias.

30 KaineShepard, "Din Korlack: Interview," 1:45.
31 Though the game does not use race as a sign for one's skill set, *Final Fantasy VII* is also not devoid of racial stereotypes. The game introduced the first playable dark-skinned character, Barret, a figure of controversy as he speaks in Ebonics and is modeled off Mr. T but also shows psychological complexity as a father and environmental protector struggling with guilt.
32 Jørgensen, "Game Characters," 318.
33 Bissell, *Extra Lives*, 118.
34 Youngblood, "When (and What) Queerness Counts."
35 Rafael, *Motherless Tongues*, 98.
36 Tu, "A Laboratory of Skin."
37 During the Vietnam War, black men held many front-lines positions because their skin was seen as impenetrable to dioxin, while Asians and other darker-skinned soldiers were marked as less vulnerable to heat and sweat. Tu, "A Laboratory of Skin," 25.
38 Chun, *Control and Freedom*, viii.
39 Galloway, "Playing the Code," 35.
40 Anna Anthropy argues that these Western role-playing games were influenced by Japanese role-playing forms but shifted focus through an attempt to "[sell] the idea of individuality and ego," by adding much more choice (character creation, player decision-making); Anthropy, *Rise of the Videogame Zinesters*, 51.
41 As Miguel Sicart has pointed out in another BioWare game, *Knights of the Old Republic*, "moral choice no longer implies a reflection upon their actions, but rather a strategy, another token in the world of the game." Sicart, *The Ethics of Computer Games*.
42 Boba1911, "Mass Effect," 0:27.
43 Puar and Rai, "Monster, Terrorist, Fag," 121.
44 Alex, "Wrex and the Art."
45 Bissell, *Extra Lives*, 125.
46 Simkins and Steinkuehler, "Critical Ethical Reasoning," 339.
47 Lazzaro, "Why We Play Games."
48 Ibid.
49 Game designer David Freeman argues that emotions in games are linked primarily to the supporting characters, who "move the player through an interlocking sequence of emotional experiences." Freeman, "Creating Emotion in Games," 8.
50 Jørgensen, "Game Characters," 318.
51 Ibid., 316.
52 As Nakamura writes, the notion "that one group of workers would have labor 'sweated' out of them to create intricate, painstakingly crafted decorative objects to adorn the bodies of a privileged class is far from new," as she finds the working conditions of Victorian seamstresses of the nineteenth century are described "in strikingly similar rhetoric to that of the Foxconn workers laboring over iPhones in China." Nakamura, "Economies of Digital Production," 6.

53 According to Yohei Ishii, the director of business development at CCP games, "as a designer, you can create clothes that you wouldn't be able to in the real world because of physics or economics. As a gamer, you can be whomever you want to be." Moore, "Fashion Diary."

54 Wu, "Virtual Goods."

55 Tassi, "The Ten Commandments."

56 Juul, *A Casual Revolution*, 1.

57 Tassi, "The Ten Commandments."

58 The oft-cited example of this is the massive multiplayer online game, EVE Online, which sold very realistic cosmetic clothing items for characters that "far outstripped the value of what the actual physical item would cost in the real world, from t-shirts to monocles." Tassi, "The Ten Commandments."

59 Wu, "Virtual Goods."

60 Ibid.

61 Yin-Poole, "Someone Bought a Dota 2 Courier."

62 Tassi, "The Ten Commandments."

63 Ibid.

64 Chun, *Control and Freedom*, 177.

65 Brown, *Sexuality in Role-Playing Games*, 20.

66 Shaw, *Gaming at the Edge*, 87.

67 Weiss, *Techniques of Pleasure*, 7.

68 Musser, *Sensational Flesh*, 22.

69 Cruz, *The Color of Kink*, 21.

70 Ibid., 56.

71 Foucault, *History of Sexuality*. Vol. 1, 23.

72 Foucault, *The Use of Pleasure*, 35.

73 Ibid., 43.

74 Ibid., 250.

75 Stoler, *Race and the Education of Desire*, 97.

76 Foucault, *The Use of Pleasure*, 23.

77 Ibid., 27.

78 Ibid., 210.

79 Roach, *Friendship as a Way of Life*, 30.

80 Ibid.

81 Weiss, *Techniques of Pleasure*, ix.

82 Brice, "Play and Be Real about It," 81.

83 Ibid., 79.

84 Afinity, "Geeking."

85 Roach, *Friendship*, 35.

86 I write fiction under the name Kawika Guillermo.

87 Roach, *Friendship*, 36.

88 Ibid.

89 Foucault, *Care of the Self*, 85.

90 Jackson, "I am Become Rihanna."
91 As Patrick Jagoda writes in *Network Aesthetics*, "extimacy offers an appropriate frame for thinking through the paradoxes of network form and networked interaction with another person at a distance . . . This sense of extimacy also finds one of its most common expressions in contemporary social media, which facilitate a performance and display of intimacy in a public setting." Jagoda, *Network Aesthetics*, 164.
92 Brown, *Sexuality*, 5.
93 Roach, *Friendship*, 36.
94 Bee, "I Love My Untouchable Virtual Body."
95 Barthes, *Camera Lucida*, 107.
96 Vang, "Ms. Pac-Man," 490.
97 Ibid., 491.
98 Ibid., 494.
99 Tu, *The Beautiful Generation*.
100 Sundén and Sveningsson, *Gender and Sexuality*, 124.
101 Foucault, *The Use of Pleasure*, 203.
102 Ibid., 47.
103 Foucault, *Care of the Self*, 85.
104 Ibid., 95.
105 Foucault, *The Hermeneutics of the Subject*, 82.
106 Ibid., 83.
107 Ibid.
108 Foucault, *Care of the Self*, 238.
109 Milburn, *Respawn*, 200.
110 Ibid., 207.
111 Ibid., 200.
112 It is entirely possible that Foucault's notions of *aphrodisia* and self-care are more projections of alternative ways of living erotically than real practices found in antiquity (more on this in chapter 6).

[PAUSE]
1 Butler, *Gender Trouble*, 5.
2 Holland, *The Erotic Life of Racism*, 9.
3 Dean, *Unlimited Intimacy*, 32.
4 Nguyen, *Nothing Ever Dies*, loc 1072.
5 Sontag, *Against Interpretation*, loc 596.
6 Ibid., loc 626.

CHAPTER 4. POSTURE
1 Sontag, *Against Interpretation*, loc 215.
2 Galloway, "Playing the Code," 39.
3 Amanda Anderson has grouped late Foucault and late Sedgwick within "therapeutic models" that "try to construct some sort of relation, whether mimetic

or mediated, between primary relations to others and an understanding of, or attitude toward, the system." Anderson, "Therapeutic Criticism," 326.

4 Robbins, "The Other Foucault."

5 Foucault, *The Care of the Self*, 95.

6 I rehearse Foucault's volume 3 to make Foucault's argument here distinct from the "repressive hypothesis" of volume 1. Whereas it's easy to leave volume 1 seeing Foucault argue that all problematizations of sexuality are wrong and part of a medical gaze onto perversity, by the end of volume 3 this argument has flipped on its head, and the main problem is in fact the *failure* to problematize sexuality as an erotic scene that detailed one's intimate relations with others.

7 Qiu, *Goodbye iSlave*.

8 See Zimmerman, "Manifesto for a Ludic Century"; Zimmerman and Chaplin, "Manifesto."

9 Anderson, "Therapeutic Criticism," 326.

10 Sedgwick, *Touching Feeling*, 14.

11 Marks, *Touch*, xiii. For a more nuanced reading of Marks in relation to video game interaction, see chapter 1 of Ruberg's *Video Games Have Always Been Queer*. For a quirkier reading of Marks in relation to trans* being, see Halberstam's *Trans**.

12 Marks, *Touch*, 20.

13 Sedgwick, *Touching Feeling*, 17.

14 Ibid., 14.

15 In *The Weather in Proust*, Sedgwick recalls her theories of texture not to read textiles but to read Proust.

16 Sedgwick, *The Weather in Proust*, 117.

17 Anable, *Playing with Feelings*, loc 169.

18 As Eugénie Shinkle writes, "it's not uncommon for gamers to gesticulate wildly with the controller during gameplay, but standard controllers don't recognize such movements as meaningful, and they have no effect on events in the gameworld." Shinkle, "Video Games, Emotion," 909.

19 Swink, *Game Feel*, xiii. Swink's *Game Feel* is highly influential for understanding affect and games, particularly among designers, as is his use of the terms "game feel" and "proprioception," or "a person's subconscious awareness of the position of his or her own body in space" (26).

20 Sedgwick, *Touching Feeling*, 44.

21 Williams, *Marxism and Literature*.

22 See chapters 3 and 4 of my book *Transitive Cultures*. My earliest publication using affect studies methods in this way was: Patterson, "Cosmopolitanism, Ethnic Belonging, and Affective Labor."

23 Sedgwick, *Touching Feeling*, 6.

24 Chun, "Othering Space," 247.

25 Ibid., 429. See also Benjamin and Eiland, *The Arcades Project*.

26 Milburn, *Respawn*, 21.

27 Sedgwick, *Touching Feeling*, 130.
28 Freeman, "Still After," 498.
29 Brooker, "Poor A-Levels?"
30 "Men Against Fire," *Black Mirror*.
31 Sedgwick, *Touching Feeling*, 130.
32 Sedgwick's most revealing moment in tracing the impact of paranoia as a myopic political form arrives in her critique of the scholar D. A. Miller, who, after two full terms of Reaganism in the United States, wrote in 1988 that he wished to demystify the form of care that liberal society uses to gaze upon those it seeks to heal. Sedgwick responds candidly: "As if! I'm a lot less worried about being pathologized by my therapist than about my vanishing mental health coverage—and that's given the great good luck of having health insurance at all." Sedgwick, *Touching Feeling*, 141. Her colloquial response here punctures academic language to express an uncontainable shock at the disjuncture between paranoid analysis (misdiagnosis) and the already exposed everyday violence (lack of health care).
33 Reddy, *Freedom with Violence*.
34 Sedgwick, *Touching Feeling*, 140.
35 The "crisis" in a sense reinforces what Yến Espiritu has criticized about "refugee crises" in the context of the Vietnam War, where scholars focus on "the refugees' needs and achievements" rather than "in the global historical conditions that produce massive displacements and movements of refugees to the United States and elsewhere." Espiritu, "Militarized Refuge," loc 4242.
36 Kwon, "The Transpacific Cold War," loc 1584.
37 As Elizabeth Weed writes, Sedgwick's essay "is designed to enhance critique, not to dispense with it." Weed, "Gender and the Lure," 159.
38 Sedgwick, *Touching Feeling*, 144.
39 Ibid., 146.
40 Wiegman, "The Times We're in," 11.
41 Sedgwick, *Touching Feeling*, 138.
42 Freeman, *Time Binds*, xiii.
43 "Men Against Fire" also invokes game mechanics in its use of first-person point of view similar to first-person shooters.
44 Phillips, "Shooting to Kill," 4.
45 As one YouTube playthrough artist said, "This Nectar stuff is awesome . . . the biggest mistake they made with this game was they get rid of the whole Nectar thing pretty quick." MrManPacster, "HAZE—Gameplay Walkthrough."
46 Richard Hofstadter wrote this in 1963 (quoted in Sedgwick, *Touching Feeling*, 36). Hofstadter, "The Paranoid Style," 1996.
47 Sedgwick, *Touching Feeling*, 138.
48 Plunkett, "Sega's Most 'Shameful.'"
49 KylePP, "Pure Pwnage."
50 Sedgwick, *Touching Feeling*, 114.
51 Ibid., 115.

52 Murray, *Hamlet on the Holodeck*, 111.

53 Salen and Zimmerman, *Rules of Play*, 43.

54 Keogh, *A Play of Bodies*, loc 789. Keogh coins "co-attentiveness" to indicate how "the player's attention is held by two worlds simultaneously" (loc 1542).

55 Sedgwick, *Touching Feeling*, 114. Sedgwick expands: "Escape from what? The real world? The 'real world,' ostensibly, the 'responsibility' of 'acting' or 'performing' in that world. Yet this reading posture registers as extroversion at least as much as introversion, as public as it does private: all a reader need do to transform this 'innerlife' experience to an audible performance is begin reading aloud" (115).

56 Puar and Rai, "Monster, Terrorist, Fag," 117.

57 A study of forty-five kids ages five to fifteen revealed that subjects "go to full-on slouch in as little as five minutes." Good, "Study of Gamers' Posture," 2010.

58 Sjöblom, "Gaming as a Situated Collaborative Practice."

59 Shaw, *Gaming at the Edge*, 106.

60 Sartre, *Being and Nothingness*, 282.

61 Joan Copjec usefully summarizes Freud's and Lacan's thinking on the subject, writing that "the sensible disturbance," or the thing that interrupts and produces anxiety, is "the subject's own surplus-jouissance, the libidinal knock or beat of the signifier on some part of the body." Copjec, "May '68, the Emotional Month," 102.

62 Taylor, "Gothic Bloodlines in Survival Horror Gaming," 92.

63 In *Silent Hill 2*, the main villain, Pyramid Head, appears as a rapist monster who only attacks the female.

64 The game's lead art designer, Jon McKellan, noted, "We had this rule: If a prop couldn't have been made in '79 with the things that they had around, then we wouldn't make it either." KrisWB, "Alien: Isolation Review."

65 The A.I. is entirely unscripted, as it is actually two A.I.s communicating with each other: a "director-AI" that can see the player and an "alien-AI" that can't. The director-AI gives hints to the alien-A.I. Thompson, "The Perfect Organism."

66 Batchelor, "18 Things We Learned."

67 *The Beast Within*, Dir. Charles de Lauzirika.

68 *Alien Evolution*, Dir. Andrew Abbott and Russell Leven.

69 Gallardo and Smith, *Alien Woman*.

70 See Ngai, *Ugly Feelings*, 213.

71 In *Aliens*, the second installment of the series, Ellen Ripley (Sigourney Weaver) wakes out of cryostasis after fifty-seven years to discover that her daughter Amanda was married, had no kids, and died at the age of sixty-six, two years before Ellen Ripley woke.

72 Kelly, "The Making of Alien: Isolation."

73 Gallardo and Smith, *Alien Woman*, 83.

74 Chatterjee, "On Civil and Political Society."

75 Sarkeesian and Cross, "Your Humanity Is in Another Castle," 108.

76 Indeed, reviews of *Alien: Isolation* spoke to this growing anxiety, as the game received near perfect reviews from outlets like *The Guardian* (5/5) and *Kotaku*

(a noted enemy of #GamerGate minions) but scored low among entrenched game critics at places like *IGN* (5.9/10) and *Gamespot* (6/10).

77 Byrd writes that the #GamerGate "emphasis on design, platform, code, and software reflects and in part draws on the academic turn to new materialisms, the nonhuman, machine-oriented ontologies and the object-oriented programming languages that mediate our access to information, communication, and sociality." Byrd, "Beast of America," 601.

78 Murray, *On Video Games*, 39.

79 Everett, "Forward."

80 Lay goes on to liken the Joes' vocal patterns to "those automated messages you get when you phone a call center—the content of the words are polite and friendly but it's lacking any real sincerity." Aaron Percival, a.k.a. Corporal Hicks, "Interview with Alien: Isolation Writers."

81 Browne, *Dark Matters*.

82 Hernandez, "Alien: Isolation, Without All the Horrifying Parts."

83 Hernandez, "Alien: Isolation Isn't As Scary."

84 Hamilton, "Alien: Isolation: The Kotaku Review."

85 Butler, Gambetti, and Sabsay, "Introduction," 4.

86 Sedgwick, *Weather in Proust*, 183.

87 Ibid., 62.

88 Hamilton, "Alien: Isolation: The Kotaku Review."

89 In *A View from the Bottom*, Tan Hoang Nguyen conceives of bottomhood capaciously, "as a sexual position, a social alliance, an affective bond, and an aesthetic form . . . bottomhood articulates a novel model for coalition politics by affirming an ethical mode of relationality." Nguyen, *A View from the Bottom*, 2.

90 Sedgwick, *Touching Feeling*, 128.

91 Lorde, "The Uses of the Erotic."

CHAPTER 5. LOOP

1 The first-person shooter emerged in the early 1990s from id Software, a studio that originated in America's "heartland," Dallas, Texas. The company produced three games that came to define the first-person shooter, beginning in 1992 with *Wolfenstein*, then popularized with *Doom* in 1993, and made three dimensional with *Quake* in 1996. Though open world games have significant urtexts in Japanese games like *Flower, Sun, and Rain* and the *Shenmue* series, open world games are typically seen as Western, beginning with the smash hit *Grand Theft Auto III* (2001), made by designers in Edinburgh and published by Rockstar in New York. Later iterations of the genre came in the *Saints Row* series, made by designers in Illinois and publishers in Germany, and the *Far Cry* series, made by the French and Canadian company Ubisoft.

2 Kietzmann, "Half-Minute Halo."

3 Barthes, *The Pleasure of the Text*, 15.

4 Ibid.

5 Sedgwick, *The Weather in Proust*, 83.
6 Shaw, *Gaming at the Edge*, 97.
7 David J. Leonard, "Foreward," in Gray, *Race, Gender*, xiii.
8 Jenkins, *Fans, Bloggers, and Gamers*, loc 3690.
9 TRIAL and Pro Juventute. "Playing by the Rules," 3.
10 Ibid.
11 Ibid., 4.
12 To add perhaps even more emphasis on the decontextualizing of these games from their narrative form and medium, the report gives equal weight to shooters taking place in World War II and games "with elements of science fiction such as non-human like beings." TRIAL and Pro Juventute, "Playing by the Rules," 5.
13 Bogost, *Persuasive Games*, 15.
14 See the introduction to *Joystick Soldiers* by Nina B. Huntemann and Matthew Thomas Payne.
15 Galloway, *Gaming*, 71.
16 Singer, *Wired for War*.
17 Halter, *From Sun Tzu to XBox*; Turse, *The Complex*.
18 Schulzke, "Rethinking Military Gaming America's Army."
19 Dyer-Witheford and De Peuter, *Games of Empire*, 8.
20 King and Leonard, "Wargames as a New Frontier."
21 Teaiwa, "Reading Gauguin's," 251.
22 Bello, "Conclusion," 314.
23 Shigematsu and Camacho, "Introduction," xxviii.
24 Crogan, *Gameplay Mode*, 14. Quoted in Bogost, "Pretty Hate Machines."
25 Gonzalez foregrounds "how tourism and militarism's mutual work produces the possibilities for American historical and contemporary dominance in the region." Gonzalez, *Securing Paradise*, 4.
26 Ibid., 5.
27 Leonard, "Live in Your World," 5.
28 Sontag, *Against Interpretation*, loc 392.
29 Ibid., loc 592.
30 Sontag, *Styles of Radical Will*.
31 Csikszentmihaly, *Beyond Boredom and Anxiety*, 36. Quoted in Swink, *Game Feel*, 23.
32 Swink, *Game Feel*, 23.
33 Anable, *Playing with Feelings*, loc 2137.
34 Phillips refers to the pictures from Abu Ghraib prison as an instance where military acts irrespective toward human life have broached public discourse.
35 Barthes, *The Pleasure of the Text*, 18.
36 Ibid., 15.
37 Ibid., 19.
38 Ibid., 14.
39 Lauteren, "The Pleasure of the Playable Text," 221.

40 *On Killing* was credited as the philosophical basis of the *Black Mirror* episode "Men Against Fire," analyzed in the previous chapter.

41 Grossman, *On Killing*, xvi.

42 Ibid., 315.

43 Ibid., xvi.

44 Jenkins, *Fans, Bloggers, and Gamers*, loc 3799.

45 Grossman, *On Killing*, 313. Grossman writes: "In behavioral terms, the man shape popping up in the soldier's field of fire is the 'conditioned stimulus,' the immediate engaging of the target is the 'target behavior.' 'Positive reinforcement' is given in the form of immediate feedback when the target drops if it is hit." Grossman, *On Killing*, 254.

46 Ibid, 311.

47 Jenkins, *Fans, Bloggers, and Gamers*.

48 Askagamedev, "Progression or Skill Tree Systems."

49 Bown, *The Playstation Dreamworld*.

50 Shinkle, "Video Games, Emotion," 909.

51 Keogh, *A Play of Bodies*, loc 2051.

52 Kirkpatrick, *Aesthetic Theory and the Video Game*, 113.

53 Kirkpatrick, "Controller, Hand, Screen," 140.

54 Janet Murray's *Hamlet on the Holodeck* compares the hand gestures of gameplay to dance only, to declare that games contain far greater agency: "When things are going right on the computer, we can be both the dancer and the caller of the dance. This is the feeling of agency" (129). Murray argues that because the gamer can change his visual perception on the screen, he has far more agency than a dancer, even though the dancer can shift his body openly upon a dance floor, can touch others to their choosing (and consent), and can also change his visual perception (turning around). Indeed, Murray invokes dance only to return to projecting agency into an "immersive" game experience, sacrificing the material conditions of gameplay and outright neglecting those gamers and scholars who confuse "the pleasure of agency in electronic environments . . . with the mere ability to move a joystick or click on a mouse" (161). Murray, *Hamlet on the Holodeck*.

55 Sedgwick, *Touching Feeling*, 83.

56 As Kirkpatrick writes, gameplay emerges in the tension between "movement of the hands" and "feelings of exhilaration and of pleasure" where the players/dancers discover their own way through the building blocks of available movement. Kirkpatrick, "Controller, Hand, Screen," 133.

57 Ibid.

58 Ibid.

59 Bogost, *Persuasive Games*, 16.

60 Nguyen, *The Gift of Freedom*, 20.

61 Reddy, *Freedom with Violence*, 38.

62 Orford, "Muscular Humanitarianism," 159.

63 Benedicto, "Reimagining the Intervention Narrative," 105.

64 Ibid., 105.

65 Ibid., 106.

66 Bow, "The Gendered Subject of Human Rights," 38. Walden Bello furthers this argument when he explains that, since 2001, human rights has continued to be given primacy in Asia in order to contrast America's War on Terror with a symbolically human face and thus showing "the leadership necessary to establish and protect a new order." Bello, "Conclusion," 317.

67 As Leslie Bow writes of figures like Aung San Suu Kyi, local Asian women in humanitarian contexts can act as "a means of accessing Asia." Bow, "The Gendered Subject," 40.

68 Walker, "Far Cry 3's Jeffrey Yohalem."

69 Promotional material for the game featured not the main white characters but Vaas, the main antagonist, whose voice actor, Michael Mando, often plays Hispanics in shows like *Better Call Saul*. Vaas seems to be the only native character to speak with such an accent, calling the protagonists "white boys," "California boy," and "hermano."

70 Walker, "Far Cry 3's Jeffrey Yohalem."

71 Ibid.

72 So-called "serious games" like *September 12th* explore this same issue of asking how much traumatic content the player will endure for the sake of repeating game loops.

73 Condis, *Gaming Masculinity*, 42.

74 As Dyer-Witheford and de Peuter have argued, gamers will practice forms of "digital dissent" toward games that are explicitly imperial or pro-military, like *America's Army*. Dyer-Witheford and de Peuter, *Games of Empire*, xiv.

75 Jesper Juul's *A Casual Revolution* marks this shift from the gamer as white, young, and male to casual gamers, who are older and majority female.

76 As Viet Thanh Nguyen writes, in war machines, the bristling armaments are on display, but more important are the ideas, ideologies, fantasies, and words that justify war, the sacrifices of our side, and the death of others. Nguyen, *Nothing Ever Dies*, loc 1562.

77 Edney, "Talking About Far Cry Four."

78 See Kim, *Ends of Empire* and Melamed, *Represent and Destroy*.

79 As Chen Kuan-Hsing writes, "I use the word 'subempire' to refer to a lower-level empire that is dependent on an empire at a higher level in the imperialist hierarchy." Chen, *Asia as Method*, 18.

80 Ibid.

81 Hocking, "Ludonarrative Dissonance in Bioshock."

82 For the game scholar Jesper Juul, actions in games carry "double meanings," where "we move a piece around a board, but this also means invading Scandinavia with our troops." In military shooters, one can both click a mouse and kill an enemy in the same action, yet precisely how these dual actions correspond speak to how the game forms player subjectivities. Juul, *Half-Real*, 141.

83 Barthes, *The Pleasure of the Text*, 19.

84 Chen, *Asia as Method*, 18.

85 Reeves, "To Nepal and Back."

86 Ibid.

87 Gach, "Far Cry 5: The Kotaku Review."

88 I see *Far Cry 2* alongside games like *Spec Ops: The Line*, *Bioshock*, and *Haze* as part of what Brendan Keogh calls "second wave" shooters: "After so many years of shooters that don't think twice about the excessive violences they ask their players to participate in, the shooter genre is set for a 'second wave' of games that, much like the Western film genre, turn the gaze back onto themselves. These shooters won't necessarily be trying to determine if shooters are 'good' or 'bad,' but will simply want to create shooters that poke at the genre, interrogate it, unsettle it." Keogh, *Killing is Harmless*, loc 81.

89 The player finds the Jackal's opinions in interview tapes made by Oluwagembi.

90 Bissell, *Extra Lives*, 143.

91 Ibid.

92 Ibid., 145.

93 The player can select from a number of mercenary protagonists, from the Sikh Mauritian, Quarbani Singh, to the Algerian ex-real estate broker, Hakim Echebbi.

94 Barthes, *The Pleasure of the Text*, 14.

95 See Yohalem's distaste for *Far Cry 2*'s mechanics in Walker, "Far Cry 3's Jeffrey Yohalem."

96 Leino, "Death Loop as a Feature."

97 Sontag, *Against Interpretation*, loc 653.

98 Muñoz, *Cruising Utopia*, 189.

99 Ruberg, "No Fun," 110.

100 Moretti, "Graphs, Maps, Trees-3," 52.

101 Barthes, *The Pleasure of the Text*, 14.

102 Sontag, *Against Interpretation*, loc 781.

CHAPTER 6. E-MOTION

1 *The Tonight Show Starring Jimmy Fallon*, "'Slow Jam the News' with President Obama."

2 By excluding China, the TPP was implicitly meant to combat China's growing influence in the region by securing the hegemony of American business interests. The TPP's replacement agreement, the Regional Comprehensive Economic Partnership, led by China, excluded North and South American countries entirely, leaving the idealisms and critiques of the transpacific in limbo.

3 Scahill, "The Assassination Complex."

4 Prior work that attempts to reframe Asian America away from mere identity category has been influential to this book as well as my previous work. See Omatsu, "The 'Four Prisons'"; Chuh, *Imagine Otherwise*; Kim, *Ends of Empire*; Patterson, *Transitive Cultures*.

5 Barthes, *Empire of Signs*, 28.

6 Barthes, *Travels in China*, 177.

7 Bruno, *Atlas of Emotion*, 7.

8 Ibid., 6.

9 Gilroy, *The Black Atlantic*.

10 Lowe, "The Trans-Pacific Migrant and Area Studies," 65.

11 Huang, *Transpacific Imaginations*, 2.

12 Baldoz, *The Third Asiatic Invasion*.

13 Teaiwa, "Fear of Flying (in Broken Gilbertese)," 378.

14 Subramani, "The Oceanic Imaginary," 160.

15 Hoskins and Nguyen, "Introduction," 3.

16 Ibid.

17 The Pacific Islands are nearly entirely absent in the first transpacific anthology. Sakai and Yoo, *The Trans-Pacific Imagination*.

18 As the editors write, "The complexities of the Pacific Islands are not sufficiently reflected in the coverage that is present, and the voices of Pacific Islanders are not represented." Hoskins and Nguyen, *Transpacific Studies*, loc 776.

19 Suzuki, "Transpacific," 359.

20 Ibid.

21 Cruz, *Transpacific Femininities*, 8.

22 Ibid.

23 In my previous book *Transitive Cultures: Anglophone Literature of the Transpacific*, I used "transpacific" to archive works deemed "inauthentic" to both nationalist literatures and to American ethnic literatures. Patterson, *Transitive Cultures*, 21.

24 Massey, *For Space*, 107.

25 Said, *Orientalism*, 55.

26 Kaplan, *Aerial Aftermaths*, loc 211.

27 Ibid., loc 283.

28 Perez, *From Unincorporated Territory [Hacha]*.

29 Lanny, *Imperial Archipelago*.

30 Perez and Amich, "Moving Islands."

31 Perez and Washburn, "No Page Is Ever Truly Blank," 7.

32 Perez and Amich, "Moving Islands."

33 Perez, "Transterritorial Currents."

34 Diaz, "To 'P' or Not to 'P'?" 193.

35 Hezel and Samuel, "Micronesians Abroad."

36 Letman, "Micronesians in Hawaii Face Uncertain Future."

37 "Territoriality" for Perez signifies "a behavioral, social, cultural, historical, political, and economic phenomenon." Perez, "Transterritorial Currents," 620.

38 Kaplan, *Aerial Aftermaths*, loc 512.

39 Kaplan calls the unsensed legacies of traumas and ongoing wars "the past [that] refuses to remain neatly contained and may roam around in the present or hail

the future, folding different times and spaces into an unruly or repetitious mode of emotional life." Kaplan, *Aerial Aftermaths*, loc 512.

40 Stanton, "The Polynesian Cultural Center."

41 Hau'ofa, "The Ocean in Us."

42 The website claims that the area of the park was "originally desolate and uninhabitable," and that the campus helped transform it into "a beautiful center of spirituality, education and ethnic harmony." "Purpose and History of Polynesian Cultural Center," Polynesian Cultural Center.

43 See chapter 5 for a deeper fleshing out of the term "militourism." Teaiwa, "Reading Gauguin's," 251.

44 Webb, "Highly Structured Tourist Art," 67.

45 Kaplan, *Aerial Aftermaths*, loc 388.

46 As Webb writes, the cultural lectures within each tribal setting "omit many details of traditional Polynesian life and religion that would conflict with Mormonism or detract from the carefree aura of island life." Webb, "Highly Structured Tourist Art," 67.

47 Somerville, *Once Were Pacific*, xix.

48 Kaplan, *Aerial Aftermaths*, loc 388.

49 Weheliye, *Habeas Viscus*, 14.

50 Suarez, *The Work of Mothering*, 16.

51 Ibid.

52 Espiritu, "Vietnam, the Philippines, Guam and California."

53 Ibid., 8.

54 Ibid., 9.

55 Espiritu, *Body Counts*, 181.

56 "Grafting," *The Urban Dictionary*.

57 Feldman, "Empire's Verticality," 329.

58 Ibid., 329.

59 Butler, *Frames of War*.

60 Barthes, *Empire of Signs*, 28–29.

61 Ibid., 36.

62 Ibid., 4.

63 Mavor, *Reading Boyishly*.

64 Ibid., 47–48.

65 Minh-ha, *Framer Framed*, 233, italics in original.

66 Kristeva, *About Chinese Women*.

67 Spivak pointed to "the completely ungrounded way in which [Kristeva] writes about two thousand years of a culture she is unfamiliar with." Quoted in Almond, *The New Orientalists*, 2007. 154.

68 Barthes, *Alors la Chine?*, 14; quoted in Minh-ha, *Framer Framed*, 45.

69 Barthes literally analyzes himself analyzing Asia in his memoir, where he writes of himself in the third person that, "he was not 'choosing' China (too much

was missing for him to shed light on such a choice) but *acquiescing* in silence." Barthes, *Roland Barthes by Roland Barthes*, 48, italics in original.

70 Minh-ha, *Framer Framed*, 233.

71 Barthes writes that this language "gives comfort, security, justification to the subject who speaks, and who in this case ('masses') becomes its subject without usurpation." Barthes, Herschberg-Pierrot, and Brown, *Travels in China*, 126.

72 Barthes, Herschberg-Pierrot, and Brown, *Travels in China*, 126.

73 Ibid., 106.

74 Ibid., 14.

75 Ibid.

76 Even the "bricks" of party lines and orthodox Maoism, Barthes admits, are only characteristic of the virtual other produced through the limits of translation, since "the person often has a loquacious discourse that makes them laugh, but it's reduced to a brick, a signified, by the time it comes out translated." Barthes, Herschberg-Pierrot, and Brown, *Travels in China*, 164.

77 Minh-ha and Gray, "The Plural Void," 48.

78 Ibid.

79 Nussbaum, "Affections of the Greeks."

80 Foucault, *The Use of Pleasure*, 8–9.

81 Jordan, *Convulsing Bodies*, 124.

82 Jeremy Carrette sees Foucault's 1978 visit to Tokyo as recentering the *History of Sexuality* project on arguments that "would form the underlying force of the second and third volumes of his History of Sexuality and . . . [shape] the study of the Greco-Roman world around his earlier understanding of Christianity." Carrette, "Prologue to a Confession," 41.

83 Jordan, *Convulsing Bodies*, 122.

84 Barthes, too, saw Japan within the realm of *ars erotica*, where sexuality remained outside of the sex act itself. As Barthes wrote in reference to Japan, "Sexuality is in sex, not elsewhere; in the United States, it is the contrary; sex is everywhere, except in sexuality." Barthes, *Empire of Signs*, 29.

85 Foucault, *The Order of Things*, xv.

86 Foucault, "The Minimalist Self," 4.

87 Foucault, *Religion and Culture*, 111.

88 Ibid., 113.

89 Ibid., 119.

90 Sedgwick, *Weather in Proust*, 212.

91 Ibid., 110.

92 Ibid.

93 Weigman, "Eve's Triangles," 55.

94 Sedgwick, *Touching Feeling*, 155.

95 Sedgwick, *Weather in Proust*, 206.

96 Sedgwick, *Touching Feeling*, 155.

97   Ibid., 160.

98   Sedgwick writes, "even to invoke nondualism, as plenty of Buddhist sutras point out, is to tumble right into a dualistic trap." Sedgwick, *Touching Feeling*, 2.

99   Sedgwick, *Touching Feeling*, 149.

100 Ibid., 150.

101 One could indeed still enforce dualistic principles upon such a map by comparing those of "camp" with the self, that is, unless one was oneself a subject of the gaze as Barthes described it while in China, a feeling of being abstracted and "dispossessed of my body." Barthes, Herschberg-Pierrot, and Brown, *Travels in China*, 119.

102 Sedgwick, *Touching Feeling*, 179.

103 Foucault writes of "the pleasure of knowing that truth, of discovering and expos-ing it, the fascination of seeing it and telling it, of captivating and capturing others by it, of confiding it in secret, of luring it out in the open—the specific pleasure of the true discourse on pleasure." Foucault, *The History of Sexuality*, 71.

104 See Galloway, "Playing the Code,"; Bogost, *Persuasive Games*; Mukherjee, "Playing Subaltern."

105 Friedman, "Civilization and Its Discontents," 139.

106 I agree here with Aubrey Anable's argument that disorientation in games can cre-ate a "productive confusion between present and past, self and other, and inside and outside that both video games and affect theory might perform." Anable, *Playing with Feelings*, 2018, 524.

107 Google Earth. Google.

108 Sheppard and Cizek, "The Ethics of Google Earth."

109 In the most popular Google Earth game, *Geoguessr*, players are thrown into a random spot of Google Earth and asked to guess where they are. Anton Wallén, *Geoguessr*.

110 Fogu, "Digitalizing Historical Consciousness," 105.

111 Steve Swink, *Game Feel*, 28.

112 Diaz, "To 'P' or not to 'P,'" 90–91.

113 Kingsbury and Jones, "Walter Benjamin's Dionysian Adventures."

114 As Kaplan says about aerial photos, they need not always be about waging war but can be "confounding, disturbing, overwhelming." Kaplan, *Aerial Aftermaths*, loc 765.

CODA

1   Benjamin writes that film's function is "*to train human beings in the appercep-tions and reactions needed to deal with a vast apparatus whose role in their lives is expanding almost daily.*" Benjamin, *The Work of Art in the Age of its Technological Reproducibility*, 26, italics in original.

2   Kaplan, *Aerial Aftermaths*, loc 2898.

3   Ibid., loc 2177.

4   Barthes, *The Pleasure of the Text*, 21.

REFERENCES

Aarseth, Espen. "Genre Trouble." *Electronic Book Review* 3 (2004): 1–7.

Abbott, Andrew and Russell Leven, dirs. *Alien Evolution*. Gruyères: *Channel 4*, 2003.

Activision Blizzard. "Our Company." Activision Blizzard. www.activisionblizzard.com, accessed on November 25, 2018.

Afinity. "Geeking." Apple App Store, Vers. 0.181.12, January 29, 2016. https://itunes.apple.com, accessed on May 8, 2017.

Ahmed, Sara. *The Promise of Happiness*. Durham, NC: Duke University Press, 2010.

Alex. "Wrex and the Art of the Privilege Check." *The Border House*, December 2, 2009. https://whilenotfinished.wordpress.com.

Alien: Isolation. Creative Assembly. Sega of America, 2014. Multiplatform.

Almond, Ian. *The New Orientalists: Postmodern Representations of Islam from Foucault to Baudrillard*. New York; London: IB Tauris, 2007.

Althusser, Louis. *For Marx*. London: Verso, 2005.

America's Army. United States Army. United States Army, 2002. Personal Computer.

Anable, Aubrey. *Playing with Feelings: Video Games and Affect*. Minneapolis: University of Minnesota Press, 2018.

Anderson, Amanda. "Therapeutic Criticism." *Novel: A Forum on Fiction* 50, no. 3 (2017): 321–28.

Anthropy, Anna. *Rise of the Videogame Zinesters: How Freaks, Normals, Amateurs, Artists, Dreamers, Drop-outs, Queers, Housewives, and People Like You Are Taking Back an Art Form*. New York: Seven Stories Press, 2012.

Anunpattana, Punyawee, Mohd Nor Akmal Khalid, Umi Kalsom Yusof, and Hiroyuki Iida. "Analysis of Realm of Valor and Its Business Model on PC and Mobile Platform Comparison." *Asia-Pacific Journal of Information Technology and Multimedia* 7, no. 2.2 (2018): 1–11.

Askagamedev, "Progression or Skill Tree Systems, the Type You . . ." *Ask a Game Dev*, Tumblr, November 14, 2014, http://askagamedev.tumblr.com.

Assassin's Creed. Ubisoft Montreal. Ubisoft, 2007. Multiplatform.

Baldoz, Rick. *The Third Asiatic Invasion: Empire and Migration in Filipino America, 1898–1946*. New York: New York University Press, 2015.

Balibar, Etienne, and Immanuel Maurice Wallerstein. *Race, Nation, Class: Ambiguous Identities*. New York; London: Verso, 1991.

Barthes, Roland. *Alors la Chine?* Paris: Christian Bourgois, 1975.

———. *Camera Lucida: Reflections on Photography*. London: Macmillan, 1981.

———. *Empire of Signs*. New York: Hill and Wang, 1982.

————. *Image, Music, Text*. New York: Hill and Wang, 1977.

————. *A Lover's Discourse: Fragments*. New York: Farrar, Straus and Girous, 1978.

————. *Mythologies*. New York: Hill and Wang, 1972.

————. "'Preface' to Renaud Camus, Tricks." In *The Rustle of Language*, edited by Roland Barthes and Richard Howard, 291–95. New York: Hill and Wang, 1986.

————. *The Pleasure of the Text*. New York: Hill and Wang, 1975.

————. *Roland Barthes by Roland Barthes*. London: Palgrave Macmillan, 2010.

Barthes, Roland, Anne Herschberg-Pierrot, and Andrew Brown. *Travels in China*. Cambridge, UK: Polity Press, 2012.

Batchelor, James. "18 Things We Learned about Alien: Isolation Last Night." *Develop*, February 13, 2014, https://mcvuk.com/.

Bayonetta. PlatinumGames. Sega of America, 2009. Multiplatform.

Bee, Aevee. "I Love My Untouchable Virtual Body." *Boing Boing*, May 6, 2015, https://boingboing.net.

Bello, Walden. "Conclusion: From American Lake to a People's Pacific in the Twenty-First Century." In *Militarized Currents: Toward a Decolonized Future in Asia and the Pacific*, edited by Keith L. Camacho and Setsu Shigematsu, 309–22. Minneapolis: University of Minnesota Press, 2010.

Benedicto, Bobby. "Reimagining the Intervention Narrative: Complicity, Globalization, and Humanitarian Discourse." *Budhi: A Journal of Ideas and Culture* 9, no. 1 (2005): 105–17.

Benjamin, Walter. *The Work of Art in the Age of Its Technological Reproducibility, and Other Writings on Media*. Cambridge, MA: Harvard University Press, 2008.

Benjamin, Walter and Howard Eiland. *The Arcades Project*. Cambridge, MA: The Belknap Press of Harvard University Press, 2003.

Berlant, Lauren Gail. *Cruel Optimism*. Durham, NC: Duke University Press, 2011.

————. *The Queen of America Goes to Washington City: Essays on Sex and Citizenship*. Durham, NC: Duke University Press, 1997.

Biggs, Tim. "Famed Designer Hideo Kojima on Auteur Video Games and Going Independent." *Sydney Morning Herald*, February 2, 2017, www.smh.com.au.

Bissell, Tom. *Extra Lives: Why Video Games Matter*. New York: Vintage, 2011.

Bloom, Steve. *Video Invaders*. New York: Arco Publishing, 1982.

Boba1911. "Mass Effect—Ashley Williams kills Wrex," video, August 16, 2009, www.youtube.com/watch?v=lHLhvRXhlDE.

Bogost, Ian. *Persuasive Games: The Expressive Power of Videogames*. Cambridge, MA: MIT Press, 2007.

————. "A Portrait of the Artist as a Game Studio." *Atlantic*, March 15, 2012, www.theatlantic.com.

————. "Pretty Hate Machines: A review of gameplay mode." *Game Studies* 12, no. 1 (September 2012), http://gamestudies.org.

Boorman, Scott A. *The Protracted Game: A Wei-ch'i Interpretation of Maoist Revolutionary Strategy*. New York: Oxford University Press, 1969.

Booth, Mark. "Campe-toi! On the Origins and Definitions of Camp." In *Camp: Queer Aesthetics and the Performing Subject: A Reader*, edited by Fabio Cleto, 66–79. Edinburgh, UK: Edinburgh University Press, 2008.

Bow, Leslie. "The Gendered Subject of Human Rights: Asian American Literature as Postcolonial Intervention." *Cultural Critique* 41 (1999): 37–78.

Bown, Alfie. *The Playstation Dreamworld*. Cambridge, UK; Malden, MA: Polity Press, 2018.

Boyes, Emma. "Q&A: SUDA-51 on No More Heroes." *Gamespot*, January 18, 2008, www.gamespot.com.

Brandzel, Amy L. *Against Citizenship: The Violence of the Normative*. Urbana: University of Illinois Press, 2016.

Brice, Mattie. "Play and Be Real about It: What Games Could Learn from Kink." In *Queer Game Studies*, edited by Bonnie Ruberg and Adrienne Shaw, 77–82. Minneapolis: University of Minnesota Press, 2014.

Brooker, Charlie. "Poor A-Levels? Don't Despair. Just Lie on Job Application Forms." *Guardian*, August 21, 2011, www.theguardian.com.

Brown, Ashley ML. *Sexuality in Role-Playing Games*. New York: Routledge, 2015.

Browne, Simone. *Dark Matters: On the Surveillance of Blackness*. Durham, NC: Duke University Press, 2015.

Browning, Mark. *David Cronenberg: Author or Film-maker?* Bristol, UK: Intellect Books, 2007.

Bruno, Giuliana. *Atlas of Emotion: Journeys in Art, Architecture, and Film*. London: Verso, 2018.

Burford, G.B. "Modern Warfare 2 Deserves More Credit." *Kotaku*, May 27, 2015, https://kotaku.com.

———. "Why Modern Warfare's 'All Ghillied Up' Is One of Gaming's Best Levels." *Kotaku*, October 23, 2014, https://kotaku.com.

Butler, Judith. *Frames of War: When Is Life Grievable?* New York; London: Verso, 2009.

———. *Gender Trouble: Feminism and the Subversion of Identity*. New York: Routledge, 2011.

Butler, Judith, Zeynep Gambetti, and Leticia Sabsay. "Introduction." In *Vulnerability in Resistance*, edited by Judith Butler, Zeynep Gambetti, and Leticia Sabsay, 1–11. Durham, NC: Duke University Press, 2016.

Byrd, Jodi. "Beast of America: Sovereignty and the Wildness of Objects," *South Atlantic Quarterly* 117, no. 3 (2018): 599–615.

Call of Duty 4: Modern Warfare. Infinity Ward. Activision, 2007. Multiplatform.

Call of Duty 4: Modern Warfare 2. Infinity Ward. Activision, 2009. Multiplatform.

Carlson, Rebecca, and Jonathan Corliss. "Imagined Commodities: Video Game Localization and Mythologies of Cultural Difference." *Games and Culture* 6, no. 1 (2011): 61–82.

Carrette, Jeremy R. "Prologue to a Confession of the Flesh." In *Religion and Culture: Michel Foucault*, edited by Jeremy R Carrette, 1–47. Manchester, UK: Manchester University Press, 1999.

Castronova, Edward. *Synthetic Worlds: The Business and Culture of Online Worlds.* Chicago: University of Chicago Press, 2005.

Chan, Albert. "Headshot!: An In-Depth Analysis of the Success of Counter-Strike as a Team-oriented First Person Shooter and its Effects on Video Game Culture Around the World." *Stanford University*, 2012, accessed 30 Mar 2017, http://web.stanford.edu.

Chan, Dean. "The Cultural Economy of Ludic Superflatness." Paper presented at *DiGRA International Conference: Situated Play*, Tokyo, Japan, September 24–28, 2007, www.digra.org.

———. "Playing with Race: The Ethics of Racialized Representations in E-Games." *International Review of Information Ethics* 4, no. 12 (2005): 24–30.

Chan, Jenny, Ngai Pun, and Mark Selden. "The Politics of Global Production: Apple, Foxconn and China's New Working Class." *New Technology, Work and Employment* 28, no. 2 (2013): 100–15.

Chang, Edmund. "Call for Art: 'Asian American Arcade, the Art of Video Games,' Wing Luke Museum." *Critical Gaming Project*, August 17, 2011, https://depts.washington.edu.

Chatterjee, Partha. "On Civil and Political Society in Post-Colonial Democracies." In *Civil Society: History and Possibilities*, edited by Sudipta Kaviraj and Sunil Khilnani, 165–78. New Delhi, India: Foundation Books, 2001.

Chen, Jenova. "Flow in Games: A Jenova Chen MFA Thesis." University of Southern California, 2006, accessed February 2, 2016, www.jenovachen.com.

Chen, Kuan-Hsing. *Asia as Method: Toward Deimperialization.* Durham, NC: Duke University Press, 2010.

Cheney-Lippold, John. *We Are Data: Algorithms and the Making of our Digital Selves.* New York: New York University Press, 2018.

Cheng, Anne Anlin. *Ornamentalism.* New York: Oxford University Press, 2019.

Chien, Irene. "Journey into the Techno-Primitive Desert." *Gaming Representation: Race, Gender, and Sexuality in Video Games*, edited by Jennifer Malkowski and TreaAndrea M. Russworm, 129–46. Bloomington: Indiana University Press, 2017.

Choe, Steve, and Se Young Kim. "Never Stop Playing: *Starcraft* and Asian Gamer Death." In *Techno-Orientalism: Imagining Asia in Speculative Fiction, History, and Media*, edited by David S. Roh, Betsy Huang, and Greta A. Niu, 112–24. New Brunswick, NJ: Rutgers University Press, 2015.

Chomsky, Noam and Edward S. Herman. "Distortions at Fourth Hand." *Nation*, June 6, 1977, https://chomsky.info.

Chow, Rey. *The Protestant Ethnic and the Spirit of Capitalism.* New York: Columbia University Press, 2002.

Chua, Amy. *Battle Hymn of the Tiger Mother.* New York: Bloomsbury Publishing, 2011.

———. "Why Chinese Mothers Are Superior." *Wall Street Journal* 8, January 8, 2011, www.wsj.com.

Chua, Lawrence. *Gold by the Inch.* New York: Grove Press, 1999.

Chuh, Kandice. *Imagine Otherwise: On Asian Americanist Critique.* Durham, NC: Duke University Press, 2003.

Chun, Wendy Hui Kyong. "Introduction: Race and/as Technology; or, How to Do Things to Race." *Camera Obscura: Feminism, Culture, and Media Studies* 24.1, no. 70 (2009): 7–35.

———. *Control and Freedom: Power and Paranoia in the Age of Fiber Optics.* Cambridge, MA: MIT Press, 2008.

———. "Othering Space." In *The Visual Culture Reader,* edited by Nicholas Mirzoeff, 241–54. New York: Routledge, 2002.

———. "Race and/as Technology, or How to do Things to Race." In *Race After the Internet,* edited by Lisa Nakamura and Peter Chow-White, 44–66. Minneapolis: University of Minnesota Press, 2008.

"Citadel Council." *Mass Effect Wiki* (Fandom: Powered by Wikia), 2012, accessed 5 June 2013, http://masseffect.wikia.com.

Civilization V. Firaxis Games. 2K Games, 2010. Personal Computer.

Clark, Naomi, and Merritt Kopas. "Queering Human-Game Relations: Exploring Queer Mechanics and Play." *First Person Scholar,* February 18, 2015, www.firstpersonscholar.com.

Cleto, Fabio. "Introduction: Queering the Camp." In *Camp: Queer Aesthetics and the Performing Subject: A Reader,* edited by Fabio Cleto, 1–42. Edinburgh, UK: Edinburgh University Press, 2008.

Clough, Michelle. "Sexualization, Shirtlessness, and Smoldering Gazes: Desire and the Male Character." In *Digital Love: Romance and Sexuality in Games,* edited by Heidi McDonald, 3–36. Boca Raton, FL: CRC Press, 2017.

Clough, Patricia Ticineto. *The User Unconscious: On Affect, Media, and Measure.* Minneapolis: University of Minnesota Press, 2018.

Colucci, Emily. "No, Avital Ronell and Her Defenders, Sexual Harassment Is Not Camp: A Filthy Dreams Rant." *Filthy Dreams,* August 21, 2018, https://filthydreams.org.

———. "Yes, Mary, There Is Still Camp, But It's Just Conservative Camp." *Filthy Dreams,* March 19, 2017, https://filthydreams.org.

Condis, Megan. *Gaming Masculinity: Trolls, Fake Geeks, and the Gendered Battle for Online Culture.* Iowa City: University of Iowa Press, 2018.

Consalvo, Mia. "Visiting the Floating World: Tracing a Cultural History of Games through Japan and America." Paper presented at *DiGRA International Conference: Situated Play,* Tokyo, Japan, September 24–28, 2007, www.digra.org.

Copjec, Joan. "May '68, the Emotional Month." In *Lacan: The Silent Partners,* edited by Slavoj Žižek, 90–114. London: Verso, 2006.

Counter-Strike. Valve. Valve Corporation, 2009. Personal Computer.

Crogan, Patrick. *Gameplay Mode: War, Simulation, and Technoculture.* Minneapolis: University of Minnesota Press, 2011.

Cronin, Michael. *Translation in the Digital Age.* New York: Routledge, 2012.

Cross, Katherine. "How 'Walking Simulators' Allow Us to Touch Other Worlds." *Gamasutra,* August 14, 2015, www.gamasutra.com.

Cruz, Ariane. *The Color of Kink: Black Women, BDSM, and Pornography.* New York: New York University Press, 2016.

Cruz, Denise. *Transpacific Femininities: The Making of the Modern Filipina*. Durham, NC: Duke University Press, 2012.

Crysis. Crytek. Electronic Arts, 2007. Personal Computer.

Csikszentmihaly, Mihaly. *Beyond Boredom and Anxiety*. San Francisco: Jossey-Bass, 1975.

Danico, Mary Yu, and Linda Trinh Vo. "'No Lattes Here': Asian American Youth and the Cyber Café Obsession." In *Asian American Youth: Culture, Identity, and Ethnicity*, edited by Jennifer Lee and Min Zhou, 177–89. New York: Routledge, 2004.

de Lauzirika, Charles, dir. *The Beast Within: The Making of Alien*. Los Angeles: 20th Century Fox, 2003.

D-e-f-. "New Zelda Wind Waker HD Videos." *NeoGAF: Believe (Gaming)*, September 4, 2013, www.neogaf.com.

Dead Island. Techland. Deep Silver, 2011. Multiplatform.

Dead or Alive. Team Ninja. Tecmo, 1996. Arcade.

Dean, Tim. "The Biopolitics of Pleasure." *South Atlantic Quarterly* 111, no. 3 (2012): 477–96.

———. *Unlimited Intimacy: Reflections on the subculture of barebacking*. Chicago: University of Chicago Press, 2009.

Diaz, Vicente M. "'To 'P' or Not to 'P'?': Marking the Territory between Pacific Islander and Asian American Studies." *Journal of Asian American Studies* 7, no. 3 (2004): 183–208.

Donaldson, Alex. "Suda 51 Wants to Make a Game as Distinctive as *No More Heroes* for Nintendo's Switch." *VG247*, January 9, 2017, www.vg247.com.

Donlan, Christian. "Spelunky 2? In the Age of Nex Machina Anything is Possible." *Eurogamer*, October 31, 2017, www.eurogamer.net.

Dota 2. Valve. Valve Corporation, 2013. Personal Computer.

Dragon Age: Origins. BioWare. Electronic Arts, 2009. Multiplatform.

Dyer, Richard. *The Culture of Queers*, New York: Routledge, 2005.

———. *Only Entertainment*. London: Routledge, 2005.

Dyer-Witheford, Nick, and Greig de Peuter. *Games of Empire: Global Capitalism and Video Games*. Minneapolis: University of Minnesota Press, 2009.

Edney, Andrew. "Talking About Far Cry Four with Creative Director Alex Hutchinson." *Huffington Post UK*, October 16, 2014, www.huffingtonpost.co.uk.

Elsaesser, Thomas. "Cinephilia or the Uses of Disenchantment." In *Cinephilia: Movies, Love and Memory*, edited by Malte Hagener and Marijke de Valck, 27–43. Amsterdam, Netherlands: Amsterdam University Press, 2005.

Eskelinen, Markku. "The Gaming Situation." *Game Studies* 1, no. 1 (2001), http://gamestudies.org.

Espiritu, Yến Lê. *Body Counts: The Vietnam War and Militarized Refugees*. Oakland: University of California Press, 2014.

———. "Militarized Refuge: A Critical Rereading of Vietnamese Flight to the United States." In *Transpacific Studies: Framing an Emerging Field*, edited by Janet Hoskins and Viet Thanh Nguyen, 201–24. Honolulu: University of Hawaii Press, 2014, Kindle Edition.

————. "Vietnam, the Philippines, Guam and California: Connecting the Dots of US military Empire." *Asia Colloquia Papers* 6, no. 2 (2016): 1–17.

Everett, Anna. *Digital Diaspora: A Race for Cyberspace.* Albany: SUNY Press, 2009.

————. "Forward." In *Gaming Representation: Race, Gender, and Sexuality in Video Games,* edited by Jennifer Malkowski and TreaAndrea M. Russworm, ix-xvii. Bloomington: Indiana University Press, 2017.

Ewalt, David M. "The ESPN of Video Games." *Forbes*, November 13, 2013, www.forbes .com.

Far Cry. Crytek. Ubisoft, 2004. Personal Computer.

Far Cry 2. Ubisoft Montreal. Ubisoft, 2008. Multiplatform.

Far Cry 3. Ubisoft Montreal. Ubisoft, 2012. Multiplatform.

Far Cry 4. Ubisoft Montreal. Ubisoft, 2014. Multiplatform.

Far Cry 5. Ubisoft Montreal and Ubisoft Toronto. Ubisoft, 2018. Multiplatform.

Feldman, Keith P. "Empire's Verticality: The Af/Pak Frontier, Visual Culture, and Racialization from Above." *Comparative American Studies: An International Journal* 9, no. 4 (2011): 325–41.

Fickle, Tara. "No-No Boy's Dilemma: Game Theory and Japanese American Tnternment Literature." *MFS Modern Fiction Studies* 60, no. 4 (2014): 740–66.

————. *The Race Card: From Gaming Technologies to Model Minorities.* New York: New York University Press, 2019.

Final Fantasy VII. Square. Sony Computer Entertainment, 1997. PlayStation.

Flower, Sun, and Rain. Grasshopper Manufacture. Marvelous Entertainment, 2001. PlayStation 2.

Fogu, Claudio. "Digitalizing Historical Consciousness." *History and Theory* 48, no. 2 (2009): 103–21.

Foucault, Michel. *The Hermeneutics of the Subject: Lectures at the Collège de France, 1981–1982.* New York: Picador, 2006.

————. *The History of Sexuality.* Vol. 1, *An Introduction.* New York: Vintage, 1990.

————. *The History of Sexuality.* Vol. 2, *The Use of Pleasure.* New York: Vintage, 2012.

————. *The History of Sexuality.* Vol. 3, *The Care of the Self.* London: Penguin Books, 1990.

————. "The Minimalist Self." In *Michel Foucault: Politics, Philosophy, Culture, Interviews and Other Writings,* edited by Lawrence D. Kritzman, 3–16. New York: Routledge, 1988 (1977).

————. *The Order of Things: An Archaeology of the Human Sciences.* London; New York: Routledge, 2002.

————. *Religion and Culture,* edited by Jeremy Carrette. New York: Routledge, 2013.

Foucault, Michel, and Duccio Trombadori. *Remarks on Marx: Conversations with Duccio Trombadori.* New York: Semiotext (e), 1991.

Freeman, David. "Creating Emotion in Games: The Craft and Art of Emotioneering." *Computers in Entertainment (CIE)* 2, no. 3 (2004): 1–11.

Freeman, Elizabeth. "Still After." *South Atlantic Quarterly* 106, no. 3 (2007): 495–500.

———. *Time Binds: Queer Temporalities, Queer Histories*. Durham, NC: Duke University Press, 2010.

Friedman, Ted. "Civilization and Its Discontents: Simulation, Subjectivity, and Space." In *On a Silver Platter: CD-ROMs and the Promise of a New Technology*, edited by Greg Smith, 132–250. New York: New York University Press, 2005.

Full Playthroughs. "Haze | PS3 | Full Gameplay/Playthrough | No Commentary," video, March 11, 2016, www.youtube.com/watch?v=0NI34Me7seY.

Gach, Ethan. "Far Cry 5: The Kotaku Review." *Kotaku*, March 26, 2018, https://kotaku.com.

Gallagher, Rob. "From Camp to Kitsch: A Queer Eye on Console Fandom." *G| A| M| E Games as Art, Media, Entertainment* 1, no. 3 (2014): 39–50.

———. "No Sex Please, We Are Finite State Machines: On the Melancholy Sexlessness of the Video Game." *Games and Culture* 7, no. 6 (2012): 399–418.

Gallardo, Ximena and Jason Smith. *Alien Woman: The Making of Lt. Ellen Ripley*. New York: Continuum, 2004.

Galloway, Alexander. *Gaming: Essays on Algorithmic Culture*. Minneapolis: University of Minnesota Press, 2010.

———. "Playing the Code: Allegories of Control in Civilization." *Radical Philosophy* 128 (2004): 33–40.

Ganzon, Sarah Christina. "Female Power and the Emotional Labor of Peace in Code: Realize—the Guardian of Rebirth and Princess Arthur." In *Digital Love: Romance and Sexuality in Games*, edited by Heidi McDonald, 37–58. Boca Raton, FL: CRC Press, 2017.

Gee, James Paul. *What Video Games Have to Teach Us about Learning and Literacy*. New York: Palgrave Macmillan, 2004.

Geoguessr. Anton Wallén, May 9, 2013, https://geoguessr.com. Personal Computer.

George, Richard. "iPhone, Wii U Manufacturer Admits to Employing Children." *IGN Entertainment*, October 17, 2012, https://ign.com.

Gilroy, Paul. *The Black Atlantic: Modernity and Double Consciousness*. Cambridge, MA: Harvard University Press, 1993.

Gonzalez, Vernadette Vicuña. *Securing Paradise: Tourism and Militarism in Hawai'i and the Philippines*. Durham, NC: Duke University Press, 2013.

Good, Owen. "Study of Gamers' Posture Returns Predictable Results." *Kotaku*, June 1, 2010. http://kotaku.com.

"Google Earth," Google, 2005, accessed October 5, 2018, https://earth.google.com.

Google Earth VR, 1.1 (Google, 2016), Personal Computer.

Google Maps. "The Polynesian Cultural Center." Accessed March 12, 2017, www.google.com/maps.

Goto-Jones, Chris. "Playing with Being in Digital Asia: Gamic Orientalism and the Virtual Dōjō." *Asiascape: Digital Asia* 2, no. 1–2 (2015): 20–56.

"Grafting." *The Urban Dictionary*, January 18, 2010, www.urbandictionary.com.

Grannell, Craig. "Apple's Stance on 'Adult' Apps Is Indefensible." *TechRadar*, February 23, 2010, www.techradar.com.

Grand Theft Auto III. DMA Design. Rockstar Games, 2001. PlayStation 2.

Gray, Kishonna L. *Race, Gender, and Deviance in Xbox Live: Theoretical Perspectives from the Virtual Margins*. London: Routledge, 2014.

Grossman, David. *On Killing: The Psychological Cost of Learning to Kill in War and Society*. Boston: Little, Brown and Company, 1996.

Guild Wars 2. Areanet. NCSOFT, 2012. Personal Computer.

Guillermo, Kawika. "Race, Terror and Counter-Strike: Interview with Minh Le (Gooseman), Co-creator of Counter-Strike." *Anomaly Magazine*, April 14, 2017, https://medium.com/anomalyblog.

———. "Robert Yang: 'the car in Stick Shift is gay, by the way.'" *Anomaly*, September 4, 2017, https://medium.com/anomalyblog.

Guttmann, Allen. *Games and Empires: Modern Sports and Cultural Imperialism*. New York: Columbia University Press, 1994, 94.

Halberstam, Jack. *The Queer Art of Failure*. Durham, NC: Duke University Press, 2011.

———. *Trans**: A Quick and Quirky Account of Gender Variability*, Oakland: University of California Press, 2017.

Hall, Stuart. "Cultural Identity and Diaspora." In *Diaspora and Visual Culture*, edited by Nicholas Mirzoeff, 222–37. London: Routledge, 2014.

———. "Gramsci's Relevance for the Study of Race and Ethnicity." *Journal of Communication Inquiry* 10, no. 2 (1986): 5–27.

Halperin, David M. *How to Be Gay*. Cambridge, MA: Belknap Press of Harvard University Press, 2012.

Halter, Ed. *From Sun Tzu to XBox: War and Video Games*. New York: Thunder's Mouth Press, 2006.

Hamilton, Kirk. "Alien: Isolation: The Kotaku Review." *Kotaku*, October 7, 2014, https://kotaku.com.

Harviainen, J. Tuomas. "Sadomasochist Role-Playing as Live-Action Role-Playing: A Trait-Descriptive Analysis." *International Journal of Role-Playing* 2 (2011): 59–70.

Harviainen, J. Tuomas, Ashley ML Brown, and Jaakko Suominen. "Three Waves of Awkwardness: A Meta-Analysis of Sex in Game Studies." *Games and Culture* 13, no. 6 (2016): 605–23.

Hau'ofa, Epeli. "The Ocean in Us." In *Culture and Sustainable Development in the Pacific*, edited by Anthony Hooper, 32–43. Canberra: Australian National University Press, 2005.

Haze. Free Radical Design. Ubisoft, 2008. PlayStation 3.

Hernandez, Patricia. "Alien: Isolation Isn't As Scary When The Alien Glitches Out." *Kotaku*, October 8, 2014, https://kotaku.com.

———. "Alien: Isolation, Without All The Horrifying Parts." *Kotaku*, October 14, 2014, https://kotaku.com.

Hezel, Francis X., and S. Eugenia Samuel. "Micronesians Abroad." *Micronesian Seminar* 64, December 2006, http://new.micsem.org/.

Hocking, Clint. "Ludonarrative Dissonance in Bioshock." *Click Nothing*, October 7, 2007, http://clicknothing.typepad.com.

Hofstadter, Richard. "The Paranoid Style in American Politics, (1964)." In *The Paranoid Style in American Politics and Other Essays*, edited by Richard Hofstadter, 3–40. Cambridge, MA: Harvard University Press, 1996.

Holland, Sharon Patricia. *The Erotic Life of Racism*. Durham, NC: Duke University Press, 2012.

Hoskins, Janet, and Viet Thanh Nguyen. "Introduction: Transpacific studies: Critical Perspectives on an Emerging Field." In *Transpacific Studies: Framing an Emerging Field*, edited by Janet Hoskins and Viet Thanh Nguyen, 1–38. Honolulu: University of Hawaii Press, 2014.

Hotline Miami. Dennaton Games. Devolver Digital, 2014. Multiplatform.

Hu, Jane. "Between Us: A Queer Theorist's Devoted Husband and Enduring Legacy." *New Yorker*, December 9, 2015, www.newyorker.com.

Huang, Yunte. *Transpacific Imaginations: History, Literature, Counterpoetics*. Cambridge, MA: Harvard University Press, 2008.

Huizinga, Johan. *Homo Ludens: A Study of the Play-Element in Culture*. Boston: Beacon Press, 1955.

Huntemann, Nina B., and Matthew Thomas Payne, eds. *Joystick Soldiers: The Politics of Play in Military Video Games*. New York: Routledge, 2009.

International Game Developers Association. "Game Developer Demographics: An Exploration of Workforce Diversity." October 2005, https://gamesindustryskills. files.wordpress.com.

Isbister, Katherine. *How Games Move Us: Emotion by Design*. Cambridge, MA: MIT Press, 2016.

Iwabuchi, Koichi. "Lost in TransNation: Tokyo and the Urban Imaginary in the Era of Globalization." *Inter-Asia Cultural Studies* 9, no. 4 (2008): 543–56.

———. *Recentering Globalization: Popular Culture and Japanese Transnationalism*. Durham, NC: Duke University Press, 2002.

Iwabuchi, Koichi, and Yasuko Takezawa. "Rethinking Race and Racism in and from Japan." *Japanese Studies* 35 (2015): 1–3.

Jackson, Gita. "I am Become Rihanna, the Destroyer of Worlds." *Paste Magazine*, September 22, 2015, www.pastemagazine.com.

Jagoda, Patrick. *Network Aesthetics*. Chicago: University of Chicago Press, 2016.

James, Henry. *The Art of Criticism: Henry James on the Theory and the Practice of Fiction*. Chicago: University of Chicago Press, 1986.

Jenkins, Henry. *Fans, Bloggers, and Gamers: Exploring Participatory Culture*. New York: New York University Press, 2006.

Johnston, David. "The Making of Dust: Architecture and the Art of Level Design." In *The State of Play: Creators and Critics on Video Game Culture*, edited by Daniel Goldberg and Linus Larsson, 169–82. New York: Seven Stories Press, 2015.

Jordan, Mark D. *Convulsing Bodies: Religion and Resistance in Foucault*. Stanford, CA: Stanford University Press, 2014.

Jørgensen, Kristine. "Game Characters as Narrative Devices: A Comparative Analysis of Dragon Age: Origins and Mass Effect 2." *Eludamos, Journal for Computer Game Culture* 4, no. 2 (2010): 315–31.

Journey. Thatgamecompany. Sony Computer Entertainment, 2012. PlayStation 3.

Just Cause 2. Avalanche Studios. Eidos Interactive and Square Enix, 2010. Multiplatform.

Juul, Jesper. *A Casual Revolution: Reinventing Video Games and Their Players*. Cambridge, MA: MIT Press, 2010.

———. *Half-Real: Video Games Between Real Rules and Fictional Worlds*. Cambridge, MA: MIT Press, 2005.

KaineShepard. "Din Korlack: Interview—Mass Effect 1—FULL HD," video, May 8, 2012, www.youtube.com/watch?v=nYk9e2Vr2Ik.

Kaplan, Caren. *Aerial Aftermaths: Wartime from Above*. Durham, NC: Duke University Press, 2017.

Kazan, Elia. *Kazan on Directing*. New York: Vintage, 2010.

Kelly, Andy. "The Making of Alien: Isolation." *PC Gamer*, January 29, 2015, www.pcgamer.com.

Keogh, Brendan. *Killing is Harmless: A Critical Reading of Spec Ops: The Line*. Marden, Australia: Stolen Projects, 2013.

———. *A Play of Bodies: How We Perceive Videogames*. Cambridge, MA: MIT Press, 2018.

Kietzmann, Ludwig. "Half-Minute Halo: An Interview with Jaime Griesemer." *Engadget*, July 14, 2011, www.engadget.com.

Kim, Jodi. *Ends of Empire: Asian American Critique and the Cold War*. Minneapolis: University of Minnesota Press, 2010.

Kinder, Marsha. *Playing with Power in Movies, Television, and Video Games: From Muppet Babies to Teenage Mutant Ninja Turtles*. Berkeley: University of California Press, 1991.

King, C. Richard, and David J. Leonard, "Wargames as a New Frontier: Securing American Empire in Virtual Space." In *Joystick Soldiers: The Politics of Play in Military Video Games*, edited by B. Huntemann Nina, 107–21. New York: Routledge, 2009.

Kingsbury, Paul, and John Paul Jones. "Walter Benjamin's Dionysian Adventures on Google Earth." *Geoforum* 40, no. 4 (2009): 502–13.

Kirkpatrick, Graeme. *Aesthetic Theory and the Video Game*. Manchester, UK: Manchester University Press, 2011.

———. "Controller, Hand, Screen." *Games and Culture* 4, no. 2 (2009): 127–43.

Kohler, Chris. *Power-Up: How Japanese Video Games Gave the World an Extra Life*. Mineola, NY: Dover Publications, 2016.

Kristeva, Julia. *About Chinese Women*. London: Marion Boyars, 1977.

KrisWB. "Alien: Isolation Review." *ThisIsXbox*, November 8, 2014, www.thisisxbox.com.

Kücklich, Julian. "Precarious Playbour: Modders and the Digital Games Industry." *Fibreculture* 5, no. 1 (2005).

Kwon, Heonik. "The Transpacific Cold War." In *Transpacific Studies: Framing an Emerging Field*, edited by Janet Hoskins and Viet Thanh Nguyen, 64–84. Honolulu: University of Hawaii Press, 2014.

KylePP. "Pure Pwnage—FPS Doug CS:S," video, July 6, 2006, www.youtube.com /watch?v=a9qXbgrx9rg.

Lanny, Thompson. *Imperial Archipelago: Representation and Rule in the Insular Territories under US Dominion after 1898*. Honolulu: University of Hawaii Press, 2010.

Lauteren, Georg. "The Pleasure of the Playable Text: Towards an Aesthetic Theory of Computer Games." Paper presented at *Computer Games and Digital Cultures Conference*, Tampere, Finland, June 6–8, 2002, www.digra.org.

Lazzaro, Nicole. "Why We Play Games: Four Keys to More Emotion without Story." Paper presented at *Game Developers Conference*, Oakland, CA, January 1, 2004, www.xeodesign.com.

Le, Minh. "I Am Minh Le, aka. Gooseman, Co-Creator of the Original Counter-Strike and now Tactical Intervention, AMA!" *Reddit*, May 2, 2013, www.reddit.com.

League of Legends. Riot Games. Riot Games, 2009. Personal Computer.

The Legend of Zelda: The Wind Waker. Nintendo EAD. Nintendo of America, 2002. GameCube.

Leino, Olli Tapio. "Death Loop as a Feature." *Game Studies* 12, no. 2 (December 2012), http://gamestudies.org.

Leonard, David. "High Tech Blackface: Race, Sports, Video Games and Becoming the Other." *Intelligent Agent*, vol. 4, no. 4.2 (2004): 1.

———. "Live in Your World, Play in Ours: Race, Video Games, and Consuming the Other." *Studies in Media & Information Literacy Education* 3, no. 4 (2003): 1–9.

———. "Not a Hater, Just Keepin' It Real: The Importance of Race- and Gender-based Game Studies." *Games and Culture* 1, no. 1 (2006): 83–88.

Lim, Eng-Beng. *Brown Boys and Rice Queens: Spellbinding Performance in the Asias*. New York: New York University Press, 2014.

Lim, Song Hwee. "Is the Trans- in Transnational the Trans- in Transgender?" *New Cinemas: Journal of Contemporary Film* 5, no. 1 (2007): 39–52.

Lorde, Audre. "The Uses of the Erotic: The Erotic as Power." In *The Lesbian and Gay Studies Reader*, edited by Henry Abelove, Michèle Aina Barale, and David M Halperin, 339–43. Abingdon, UK: Taylor & Francis, 1993.

Lothian, Alexis and Amanda Phillips. "Can Digital Humanities Mean Transformative Critique?" *Journal of E-Media Studies* 3, no. 1 (2013): 1–25.

Lowe, Lisa. "The Trans-Pacific Migrant and Area Studies." In *The Trans-Pacific Imagination: Rethinking Boundary, Culture and Society*, edited by Naoki Sakai and Hyon J. Yoo, 61–74. Singapore: World Scientific, 2012.

Lye, Colleen. *America's Asia: Racial Form and American Literature, 1893–1945*. Princeton, NJ: Princeton University Press, 2009.

Mackenzie, Suzie. "Finding Fact from Fiction." *Guardian*, May 27, 2000, www.the guardian.com.

Malkowski, Jennifer, and TreaAndrea M. Russworm. "Introduction: Identity, Representation, and Video Game Studies beyond the Politics of the Image." In *Gaming Representation: Race, Gender, and Sexuality in Video Games*, edited by Jennifer

Malkowski and TreaAndrea M. Russworm, 1–16. Bloomington: Indiana University Press, 2017.

Mamdani, Mahmood. *Good Muslim, Bad Muslim: America, the Cold War, and the Roots of Terror.* New York: Pantheon Books, 2004.

Marks, Laura U. *Touch: Sensuous Theory and Multisensory Media.* Minneapolis: University of Minnesota Press, 2002.

Marks, Tom. "Arena of Valor: The Most Popular Game in the World is Coming to North America Tomorrow." *IGN Entertainment*, December 16, 2017, https://ign .com.

Martin, Paul. "Race, Colonial History and National Identity: *Resident Evil 5* as a Japanese Game." *Games and Culture* 13, no. 6 (2016): 568–86.

Mass Effect. BioWare. Microsoft Game Studios, 2007. Multiplatform.

Mass Effect 2. BioWare. Electronic Arts, 2010. Multiplatform.

Mass Effect 3. BioWare. Electronic Arts, 2010. Multiplatform.

Massey, Doreen B. *For Space.* London: Sage, 2005.

Massumi, Brian. "The Autonomy of Affect." *Cultural Critique* 31 (1995): 83–109.

Mavor, Carol. *Reading Boyishly: Roland Barthes, J. M. Barrie, Jacques Henri Lartigue, Marcel Proust, and D. W. Winnicott.* Durham, NC: Duke University Press, 2007.

McDonald, Emma. "The Global Games Market Will Reach $108.9 Billion in 2017 With Mobile Taking 42%." *Newzoo* 20, April 20, 2017, https://newzoo.com.

McDonald, Heidi, ed. *Digital Love: Romance and Sexuality in Games.* Boca Raton, FL: CRC Press/Taylor & Francis Group, 2018.

McGonigal, Jane. *Reality Is Broken: Why Games Make Us Better and How They Can Change the World.* London: Penguin, 2011.

Melamed, Jodi. *Represent and Destroy: Rationalizing Violence in the New Racial Capitalism.* Minneapolis: University of Minnesota Press, 2011.

"Men Against Fire." *Black Mirror*, written by Charlie Brooker, directed by Jakob Verbruggen, Netflix, October 21, 2016.

Mighty Jill Off. Anna Anthropy. *Deesgeega*, 2008. Personal Computer.

Milburn, Colin. *Respawn: Gamers, Hackers, and Technogenic Life.* Durham, NC: Duke University Press, 2018.

Miller, Daniel. "Appalling Conditions of Factory Workers Who Make Dell Computers Who Are Forced to Work Seven-Day, 74-Hour Weeks and Live in Dorms with No Hot Water." *Daily Mail*, November 8, 2013, www.dailymail.co.uk.

Miller, David A. "Sontag's Urbanity." In *The Lesbian and Gay Studies Reader*, edited by Henry Abelove, Michèle Aina Barale, and David M. Halperin, 212–20. Abingdon, UK: Taylor & Frencis, 1993.

Minh-ha, Trinh T. *Framer Framed: Film Scripts and Interviews.* London; New York: Routledge, 2012.

Minh-ha, Trinh T., and Stanley Gray. "The Plural Void: Barthes and Asia." *SubStance* 11, no. 3 (1982): 41–50.

Moore, Booth. "Fashion Diary: Designers Look to the Virtual World." *Los Angeles Times*, September 18, 2011, www.latimes.com.

Moretti, Franco. "Graphs, Maps, Trees-3." *New Left Review* 28 (2004): 43–63.

Morran, Chris. "EA Makes Worst Company In America History, Wins Title For Second Year In A Row!" *Consumerist*, April 9, 2013, https://consumerist.com.

Mortal Kombat. Midway Games. Midway Home Entertainment, 1992. Arcade.

MrManPacster. "HAZE—Gameplay Walkthrough—Part 2—Using Nector [HD]," video, August 24, 2012, www.youtube.com/watch?v=s6xaFe2xD4E.

Mukherjee, Souvik. "Playing Subaltern: Video Games and Postcolonialism." *Games and Culture* 13, no. 5 (2018): 504–20.

De Mul, Jos. "The Game of Life: Narrative and Ludic Identity Formation in Computer Games." In *Representations of Internarrative Identity*, edited by Lori Way, 159–87. New York: Palgrave Macmillan, 2015.

Muñoz, José Esteban. *Cruising Utopia: The Then and There of Queer Futurity*. New York: New York University Press, 2009.

———. "Race, Sex, and the Incommensurate: Gary Fisher with Eve Kosofsky Sedgwick." In *Queer Futures: Reconsidering Ethics, Activism, and the Political*, edited by Beatrice Michaelis, Eveline Kilian, and Elahe Haschemi Yekani, 103–15. Farnham, UK: Ashgate Publishing Group, 2013.

Murakami, Takashi. "Earth in My Window." In *Little Boy: The Arts of Japan's Exploding Subculture*, edited by Takashi Murakami, 99–149. New York: Japan Society, 2005.

Murray, Janet Horowitz. *Hamlet on the Holodeck: The Future of Narrative in Cyberspace*. Cambridge, MA: MIT Press, 2017.

Murray, Soraya. *On Video Games: The Visual Politics of Race, Gender and Space*. London: IB Tauris, 2017.

Musser, Amber Jamilla. *Sensational Flesh: Race, Power, and Masochism*, New York: New York University Press, 2014.

Nakamura, Lisa. *Cybertypes: Race, Ethnicity, and Identity on the Internet*. New York: Routledge, 2013.

———. "Don't Hate the Player, Hate the Game: The Racialization of Labor in World of Warcraft." *Critical Studies in Media Communication* 26, no. 2 (2009): 128–44.

———. "Economies of Digital Production in East Asia: iPhone Girls and the Transnational Circuits of Cool." *Media Fields Journal* 2 (2011): 1–10.

———. "Indigenous Circuits: Navajo Women and the Racialization of Early Electronic Manufacture." *American Quarterly* 66, no. 4 (2014): 919–41.

Ngai, Sianne. *Ugly Feelings*. Cambridge, MA: Harvard University Press, 2005.

Nguyen, Michael. "New Vietnam War Video Game Sparks Controversy." *Viet Weekly* [Online Reprint], September 5, 2004, http://news.pacificnews.org/.

Nguyen, Mimi Thi. *The Gift of Freedom: War, Debt, and Other Refugee Passages*. Durham, NC: Duke University Press, 2012.

Nguyen, Tan Hoang. *A View from the Bottom: Asian American Masculinity and Sexual Representation*. Durham, NC: Duke University Press, 2014.

Nguyen, Viet Thanh. *Nothing Ever Dies*. Cambridge, MA: Harvard University Press, 2016.

Nielsen, Rune Kristian Lundedal. "Game Addiction in a Framework of Love: A Ludophilic Investigation." In *Game Love: Essays on Play and Affection*, edited by Jessica Enevold and Esther MacCallum-Stewart, 231–52. Jefferson, NC: McFarland & Company, 2015.

Night Trap. Digital Pictures. Sega, 1993. Sega CD.

Nussbaum, Martha. "Affections of the Greeks." *New York Times*, November 10, 1985, http://movies2.nytimes.com.

Obama, Barack. "President Obama's Speech to the NAACP Centennial Convention." *U.S. News and World Report*, July 17, 2009, www.usnews.com.

Omatsu, Glenn. "The 'Four Prisons' and the Movements of Liberation." In *Contemporary Asian America: a multidisciplinary reader*, edited by Min Zhou and Anthony C. Ocampo, 60–98. New York: New York University Press, 2000.

Ong, Aihwa. *Spirits of Resistance and Capitalist Discipline: Factory Women in Malaysia*. Albany: SUNY Press, 2010.

Orford, Anne. "Muscular Humanitarianism: Reading the Narratives of the New Interventionism." *European Journal of International Law* 10, no. 4 (1999): 679–711.

Overwatch. Blizzard Entertainment. Activision Blizzard, 2016. Multiplatform.

Parra, Juliana Rincón. "Congo: The Coltan Conflict Is in Our Hands (and Cellphones)." *Global Voices*, February 20, 2010, https://globalvoices.org.

Patterson, Christopher B. "Asian Americans and Digital Games." In *Oxford Research Encyclopedia of Asian American Literature and Culture*, edited by Josephine Lee, Floyd Cheung, Jennifer Ho, Anita Mannur, and Cathy Schlund-Vials, 1–24. New York: Oxford University Press, 2018.

———. "Cosmopolitanism, Ethnic Belonging, and Affective Labor: Han Ong's Fixer Chao and The Disinherited." *WorkingUSA* 15, no. 1 (2012): 87–102.

———. *Transitive Cultures: Anglophone Literature of the Transpacific*. New Brunswick, NJ: Rutgers University Press, 2018.

Paul, Christopher A. *The Toxic Meritocracy of Video Games: Why Gaming Culture is the Worst*. Minneapolis: University of Minnesota Press, 2018.

Penabella, Miguel. "Opened World: A Living Out of Dying." *Haywire Magazine*, July 19, 2017, www.haywiremag.com.

Percival, Aaron, a.k.a. Corporal Hicks. "Interview with Alien: Isolation Writers Will Porter and Dion Lay." *AvPGalaxy*, February 3, 2013, www.avpgalaxy.net.

Perez, Craig Santos. *from unincorporated territory [hacha]*. Kaneohe, HI: Tinfish, 2008.

———. "Transterritorial Currents and the Imperial Terripelago." *American Quarterly* 67, no. 3 (2015): 619–24.

Perez, Craig Santos, and Candice Amich. "'Moving Islands': An interview with Craig Santos Perez." *Waxwing* 6, Summer 2015, http://waxwingmag.org.

Perez, Craig Santos, and Kathleen Washburn. "'No Page Is Ever Truly Blank': An Interview with Craig Santos Perez." *Postcolonial Text* 10, no. 1 (2015): 1–13.

Phillips, Amanda. "Shooting to Kill: Headshots, Twitch Reflexes, and the Mechropolitics of Video Games." *Games and Culture* 13, no. 2 (2015): 136–52.

———. "Welcome to My Fantasy Zone: Bayonetta and Queer Femme Disturbance." In *Queer Game Studies*, edited by Bonnie Ruberg and Adrienne Shaw, 104–24. Minneapolis: University of Minnesota Press, 2017.

Plunkett, Luke. "Sega's Most 'Shameful,' 'Sick' and 'Disgusting' Video Game." *Kotaku*, March 11, 2011, https://kotaku.com.

Powe, Bruce W. *Marshall McLuhan and Northrop Frye: Apocalypse and Alchemy*. Toronto: University of Toronto Press, 2014.

Puar, Jasbir K., and Amit Rai. "Monster, Terrorist, Fag: The War on Terrorism and the Production of Docile Patriots." *Social Text* 20, no. 3 (2002): 117–48.

"Purpose and History of Polynesian Cultural Center." *Polynesian Cultural Center*, accessed May 2, 2017, www.polynesia.com.

Qiu, Jack Linchuan. *Goodbye iSlave: A Manifesto for Digital Abolition*. Urbana: University of Illinois Press, 2017.

Rafael, Vicente L. *Motherless Tongues: The Insurgency of Language Amid Wars of Translation*. Durham, NC: Duke University Press, 2016.

Reddy, Chandan. *Freedom with Violence: Race, Sexuality, and the US State*. Durham, NC: Duke University Press, 2011.

Reeves, Ben. "To Nepal and Back: How Ubisoft Montreal created a new country for Far Cry 4." *GameInformer*, June 18, 2014, www.gameinformer.com.

Rivera, Takeo. "Do Asians Dream of Electric Shrieks?: Techno-Orientalism and Erotohistoriographic Masochism in Eidos Montreal's Deus Ex: Human Revolution." *Amerasia Journal* 40, no. 2 (2014): 67–86.

Roach, Tom. *Friendship as a Way of Life: Foucault, Aids, and the Politics of Shared Estrangement*. Albany: SUNY Press, 2012.

Robbins, Bruce. "The Other Foucault: What Led the French Theorist of Madness and Sexuality to Politics?" *Nation*, November 2, 2017, www.thenation.com.

Roh, David S., Betsy Huang, and Greta A. Niu, "Technologizing Orientalism: An introduction." In *Techno-Orientalism: Imagining Asia in Speculative Fiction, History, and Media*, edited by David S. Roh, Betsy Huang, and Greta A. Niu, 1–19. New Brunswick, NJ: Rutgers University Press, 2015.

Ruberg, Bonnie. "Clint Hocking Speaks Out on the Virtues of Exploration." *Gamasutra*, May 14, 2017, www.gamasutra.com.

———. "Queerness and Video Games: Queer Game Studies and New Perspectives through Play." *GLQ: A Journal of Lesbian and Gay Studies* 24, no. 4 (2018): 543–55.

———. "No Fun: The Queer Potential of Video Games That Annoy, Anger, Disappoint, Sadden, and Hurt." *QED: A Journal in GLBTQ Worldmaking* 2, no. 2 (2015): 108–24.

———. *Video Games Have Always Been Queer*. New York: New York University Press, 2019.

Ruberg, Bonnie, and Adrienne Shaw, eds. *Queer Game Studies*. Minneapolis: University of Minnesota Press, 2017.

Russo, Maria. "The Reeducation of a Queer Theorist." *Salon Magazine*, September 27, 1999, www.salon.com.

Russworm, TreaAndrea. "The Hype Man as Racial Stereotype, Parody, and Ghost in Afro Samurai." In *Game On, Hollywood!: Essays on the Intersections of Video Games and Cinema*, edited by Gretchen Papazian and Joseph Michael Sommers, 169–82. Jefferson, NC: McFarland & Company, 2013.

Said, Edward. *Orientalism*. New York: Vintage 1994 (1979).

Sakai, Naoki, and Hyon J. Yoo, eds. *The Trans-Pacific Imagination: Rethinking Boundary, Culture and Society*. Singapore: World Scientific, 2012.

Salen, Katie, and Eric Zimmerman. *Rules of Play: Game Design Fundamentals*. Cambridge, MA: MIT Press, 2003.

Sarkeesian, Anita, and Katherine Cross. "Your Humanity Is in Another Castle: Terror Dreams and the Harassment of Women." *The State of Play: Creators and Critics on Video Game Culture*, edited by Daniel Goldberg and Linus Larsson, 103–26. New York: Seven Stories Press, 2015.

Sartre, Jean-Paul. *Being and Nothingness: An Essay on Phenomenological Ontology*. New York: Routledge, 2003.

Sawaragi, Noi. "On the Battlefield of 'Superflat': Subculture and Art in Postwar Japan." In *Little Boy: The Arts of Japan's Exploding Subculture*, edited by Takashi Murakami, 187–207. New York: Japan Society, 2005.

Scahill, Jeremy. "The Assassination Complex: Secret Military Documents Expose the Inner Workings of Obama's Drone Wars." *Intercept*, October 15, 2015, https://theintercept.com.

Schreier, Jason. "Sid Meier: The Father of Civilization." *Kotaku*, June 26, 2013, https://kotaku.com/.

Schulzke, Marcus. "Rethinking Military Gaming America's Army and Its Critics." *Games and Culture* 8, no. 2 (February 2013): 59–76.

ScottishDuck17. "Let's Play Shenmue 2—Part 60—HANG ON!" video, February 9, 2009, www.youtube.com/watch?v=ZLZetsitTd8.

———. "My Top 20 Dreamcast Game (10 to 1)," video, June 20, 2017, www.youtube.com/watch?v=PF2MbaVZgQ8.

Sedgwick, Eve Kosofsky. *Epistemology of the Closet*. Berkeley: University of California Press, 1990.

———. *Touching Feeling: Affect, Pedagogy, Performativity*. Durham, NC: Duke University Press, 2003.

———. *The Weather in Proust*. Durham, NC: Duke University Press, 2011.

September 12. Newsgaming. Games for Change, 2010. Personal Computer.

Shaw, Adrienne. *Gaming at the Edge: Sexuality and Gender at the Margins of Gamer Culture*. Minneapolis: University of Minnesota Press, 2015.

———. "What Is Video Game Culture? Cultural Studies and Game Studies." *Games and Culture* 5, no. 4 (2010): 403–24.

Sheer, Ian. "Player Tally for 'League of Legends' Surges." *Wall Street Journal*, January 27, 2014, https://blogs.wsj.com.

Shenmue. Sega AM2. Sega, 1999. Dreamcast.

Shenmue II. Sega AM2. Sega, 2001. Dreamcast.

Sheppard, Stephen RJ, and Petr Cizek, "The Ethics of Google Earth: Crossing Thresholds from Spatial Data to Landscape Visualization." *Journal of Environmental Management* 90, no. 6 (2009): 2102–17.

Shigematsu, Setsu, and Keith L. Camacho. "Introduction: Militarized Currents, Decolonizing Futures." In *Militarized Currents: Toward a Decolonized Future in Asia and the Pacific,* edited by Setsu Shigematsu and Keith L. Camacho, xv–xlviii. Minneapolis: University of Minnesota Press, 2010.

Shinkle, Eugénie. "Video Games, Emotion, and the Six Senses." *Media Culture and Society* 30, no. 6 (2008): 907–16.

Sicart, Miguel. *The Ethics of Computer Games.* Cambridge, MA: MIT Press, 2011.

Siegel, Carol. "The Madness Outside Gender: Travels with Don Quixote and Saint Foucault." *Rhizomes* 1 (2000): 1–18.

Silent Hill 2. Konami Computer Entertainment Tokyo. Konami, 2001. Multiplatform.

Simkins, David W. and Constance Steinkuehler. "Critical Ethical Reasoning and Role-Play." *Games and Culture* 3, no. 3–4 (2008): 333–55.

SINFO. "SINFO Conf 2015—Minh Le (Counter-Strike)," video, March 21, 2015, www.youtube.com/watch?v=-yDM9XRK2lU.

Singer, Peter Warren. *Wired for War: The Robotics Revolution and Conflict in the Twenty-First Century.* New York: Penguin Press, 2009.

Sjöblom, Björn. "Gaming as a Situated Collaborative Practice." *Human IT* 9, no. 3 (2008): 128–65.

Sleeping Dogs. United Front Games. Square Enix, 2012. Multiplatform.

Smith, Alexander. "One, Two, Three, Four I Declare a Space War." *Videogamehistorian,* February 2, 2017, https://videogamehistorian.wordpress.com.

Smith, Ed. "A Personal Journey: Jenova Chen's Goals for Games." *Gamasutra,* May 2012, www.gamasutra.com.

Smith, James H. "Tantalus in the Digital Age: Coltan Ore, Temporal Dispossession, and "Movement" in the Eastern Democratic Republic of the Congo." *American Ethnologist* 38, no. 1 (2011): 17–35.

Sohn, Stephen Hong. "Introduction: Alien/Asian: Imagining the Racialized Future." *Melus* 33, no. 4 (2008): 5–22.

Somerandomusernameth. "Overwatch Wasn't Supposed This Depressing [x-post from r/overwatch]." *Reddit,* May 14, 2006, www.reddit.com.

Somerville, Alice Te Punga. *Once Were Pacific: Māori Connections to Oceania.* Minneapolis: University of Minnesota Press, 2012.

Sontag, Susan. *Against Interpretation: and Other Essays.* London: Penguin, 2013.

———. *On Photography.* New York: Farrar, Strauss and Giroux, 1977.

———. *Styles of Radical Will.* London: Penguin, 2013.

Sontag, Susan, Robert Boyers, and Maxine Bernstein. "Women, the Arts, & the Politics of Culture: An Interview with Susan Sontag." *Salmagundi* 31/32 (1975): 29–48.

Spec Ops: The Line. Yager Development. 2K Games, 2012. Multiplatform.

Spivak, Gayatri Chakravorty. "Can the Subaltern Speak?" In *Can the Subaltern Speak? Reflections on the History of an Idea*, edited by Rosalind Morris, 21–78. New York: Columbia University Press, 2010.

The Stanley Parable. Galactic Cafe. Galactic Cafe, 2013. Personal Computer.

Stanton, Max E. "The Polynesian Cultural Center: A Multi-Ethnic Model of Seven Pacific Cultures." In *Hosts and Guests: The Anthropology of Tourism*, edited by Valene Smith, 247–62. Philadelphia: University of Pennsylvania Press, 2012.

Stenros, Jaakko. "In Defence of a Magic Circle: The social, Mental and Cultural Boundaries of Play." *Transactions of the Digital Games Research Association* 1, no. 2 (2014): 147–85.

Sterne, Laurence. *The Life and Opinions of Tristram Shandy, Gentleman*. Leipzig: B. Tauchnitz, 1849.

Stoler, Ann Laura. *Race and the Education of Desire: Foucault's History of Sexuality and the Colonial Order of Things*. Durham, NC: Duke University Press, 1995.

Street Fighter II: The World Warrior. Capcom. Capcom, 1991. Arcade.

Suarez, Harrod J. *The Work of Mothering: Globalization and the Filipino Diaspora*. Urbana: University of Illinois Press, 2017.

Subramani. "The Oceanic Imaginary." *Contemporary Pacific* 13, no. 1 (2001): 149–62.

Swink, Steve. *Game Feel: A Game Designer's Guide to Virtual Sensation*. Boca Raton, FL: CRC Press, 2008.

Suda 51. *The Art of Grasshopper Manufacture: Complete Collection of Suda51*. Tokyo: PIE International, 2015.

Suits, Bernard. *The Grasshopper: Games, Life and Utopia*. Peterborough, Canada: Broadview Press, 2014.

Sundén, Jenny, and Malin Sveningsson. *Gender and Sexuality in Online Game Cultures: Passionate Play*. New York: Routledge, 2012.

Sutton-Smith, Brian. *The Ambiguity of Play*. Cambridge, MA: Harvard University Press, 1997.

Suzuki, Erin. "Transpacific." In *The Routledge Companion to Asian American and Pacific Islander Literature*, edited by Rachel Lee, 352–64. New York: Routledge, 2014.

Tam, Fiona. "Foxconn Factories Are Labour Camps: Report." *South China Morning Post*, October 11, 2010, www.scmp.com.

Tassi, Paul. "The Ten Commandments of Microtransactions." *Forbes*, November 25, 2013, www.forbes.com.

Taylor, Laurie N. "Gothic Bloodlines in Survival Horror Gaming." In *Horror Video Games: Essays on the Fusion of Fear and Play*, edited by Bernard Perron, 46–61. Jefferson, NC: McFarland, 2009.

Teaiwa, Teresia. "Fear of Flying (in Broken Gilbertese)." *Poetry (Chicago)* 208, no. 4 (2016): 378.

———. "Reading Paul Gauguin's Noa Noa with Epeli Hau'ofa's Kisses in the Nederends: Militourism, Feminism, and the 'Polynesian' Gody." In *Inside Out: Literature,*

Cultural Politics and Identity in the New Pacific, edited by Vilsoni Hereniko and Rob Wilson, 249–69. Lanham, MD: Rowman & Littlefield, 1999.

TheKoW. "Maining." *Urban Dictionary*, March 19, 2008, www.urbandictionary.com.

Thompson, Tommy. "The Perfect Organism: The AI of Alien: Isolation." *Gamasutra*, October 31, 2017, www.gamasutra.com.

The Tonight Show Starring Jimmy Fallon. "'Slow Jam the News' with President Obama," video, June 9, 2016, www.youtube.com/watch?v=ziwYbVx_-qg.

Torres, Sasha. "The Caped Crusader of Camp: Pop, Camp, and the Batman Television Series." In *Camp: Queer Aesthetics and the Performing Subject: A Reader*, edited by Fabio Cleto, 330–43. Edinburgh, UK: Edinburgh University Press, 2008.

Totilo, Stephen. "The Designer of Call of Duty's 'No Russian' Massacre Wanted You to Feel Something." *Kotaku*, August 2, 2012, https://kotaku.com.

TRIAL and Pro Juventute. "Playing by the Rules: Applying International Humanitarian Law to Video and Computer Games." *TRIAL*, October 2009, https://trialinternational.org.

Tu, Thuy Linh Nguyen. *The Beautiful Generation: Asian Americans and the Cultural Economy of Fashion*. Durham, NC: Duke University Press, 2011.

———. "A Laboratory of Skin: Medicine, Military, and U.S. Race-Making in the Mekong Delta." Paper presented at *Imagining Asia in the Era of Trump*, Hong Kong University, Hong Kong, April 2017.

Turse, Nick. *The Complex: How the Military Invades Our Everyday Lives*. New York: Metropolitan Books, 2008.

Ueno, Tosyhia. "Japanimation and Techno-Orientalism: Japan as the Sub-Empire of Signs." In *The Uncanny: Experiments in Cyborg Culture*, edited by Bruce Grenville, 223–31. Vancouver: Arsenal Pulp Press, 2001.

Ungar, Steven. *Roland Barthes, the Professor of Desire*. Lincoln: University of Nebraska Press, 1984.

Upton, Brian. *The Aesthetic of Play*. Cambridge, MA: MIT Press, 2015.

Vang, Ka. "Ms. Pac-Man Ruined My Gang Life." In *Charlie Chan Is Dead 2: At Home in the World: An Anthology of Contemporary Asian American Fiction*, edited by Jessica Tarahata Hagedorn, 488–94. London: Penguin Books, 2004.

De Villiers, Nicholas. *Opacity and the Closet: Queer Tactics in Foucault, Barthes, and Warhol*. Minneapolis: University of Minnesota Press, 2012.

Walker, John. "Far Cry 3's Jeffrey Yohalem On Racism, Torture and Satire." *Rock Paper Shotgun*, December 19, 2012, www.rockpapershotgun.com.

Waypoint. "Why 'Flower, Sun, and Rain' Represents Video Game Punk Rock," video, April 25, 2017, www.youtube.com/watch?v=h6Cx8x6Noyg.

Webb, Terry D. "Highly Structured Tourist Art: Form and Meaning of the Polynesian Cultural Center." *Contemporary Pacific* 6, no. 1 (1994): 59–86.

Weed, Elizabeth. "Gender and the Lure of the Postcritical." *differences* 27, no. 2 (2016): 153–77.

Weheliye, Alexander G. *Habeas Viscus: Racializing Assemblages, Biopolitics, and Black Feminist Theories of the Human*. Durham, NC: Duke University Press, 2014.

Weiss, Margot. *Techniques of Pleasure: BDSM and the Circuits of Sexuality*. Durham, NC: Duke University Press, 2011.

Welsh, Oli. "Flower, Sun and Rain: The Dating Game." *Eurogamer*, November 5, 2008, www.eurogamer.net.

Wiegman, Robyn. "Eve, At a Distance." *Trans-Scripts: An Interdisciplinary Online Journal in the Humanities and Social Sciences* 2 (2012): 157–75.

———. "Eve's Triangles, or Queer Studies beside Itself." *differences* 26, no. 1 (2015): 48–73.

———. "The Times We're In: Queer Feminist Criticism and the Reparative 'Turn.'" *Feminist Theory* 15, no. 1 (2014): 4–25.

Wiener, Jon. "Avital and Nimrod: Sexual Harassment and 'Campy Communications' at NYU." *Los Angeles Review of Books*, August 20, 2018, http://blog.lareviewofbooks.org.

Williams, Raymond. *Marxism and Literature*. Oxford: Oxford University Press, 1977.

Willis, Ellen. "Three Elegies for Susan Sontag." *New Politics* 10, no. 3 (Summer 2005), https://newpol.org/.

Winnicott, Donald Woods. *Playing and Reality*. London: Routledge, 2012.

Wiseman, Mary Bittner. *The Ecstasies of Roland Barthes*. London; New York: Routledge, 1989.

Wolfe, Patrick. *Traces of History: Elementary Structures of Race*. London: Verso, 2016.

Wolin, Richard. *The Wind from the East: French Intellectuals, the Cultural Revolution, and the Legacy of the 1960s*. Princeton, NJ: Princeton University Press, 2010.

Wright, Talmadge, Eric Boria, and Paul Breidenbach. "Creative Player Actions in FPS Online Video Games: Playing Counter-Strike." *Game Studies* 2, no. 2 (2002): 103–23.

Wu, Susan. "Virtual Goods: The Next Big Business Model." *TechCrunch*, June 21, 2007, https://techcrunch.com.

Yee, Nick. *The Proteus Paradox: How Online Games and Virtual Worlds Change Us-And How They Don't*. New Haven, CT: Yale University Press, 2014.

Yin-Poole, Wesley. "Someone Bought a Dota 2 Courier for $38,000." *Eurogamer*, June 11, 2013, www.eurogamer.net.

Yoneyama, Lisa. *Cold War Ruins: Transpacific Critique of American Justice and Japanese War Crimes*. Durham, NC: Duke University Press, 2016.

Youngblood, Jordan. "When (and What) Queerness Counts: Homonationalism and Militarism in the Mass Effect Series." *Game Studies* 18, no. 3 (2018), http://gamestudies.org.

Zimmerman, Eric. "Manifesto for a Ludic Century." In *The Gameful World: Approaches, Issues, Applications*, edited by Steffen P. Walz and Sebastian Deterding, 19–22. Cambridge, MA: MIT Press, 2015.

Zimmerman, Eric and Heather Chaplin. "Manifesto: The 21st Century Will Be Defined By Games." *Kotaku*, September 9, 2013, https://kotaku.com.

INDEX

AAA games, 3, 31

Aarseth, Espen, 277n17

About Chinese Women (Kristeva), 252

Abu Ghraib scandal, 2

action role-playing games, 87

Activision, 83

adolescent rebellion, 6

The Adventures of the Galaxy Rangers (television show), 102

aerial bombings, 2

Aerith (fictional character), 122, 128

aesthetics, 19, 45, 49, 54–55, 100, 140, 207, 285n55; appreciation, 88, 224; discourses of, 91; of fighting games, 64; forms of, 60, 61; Japan and, 50–51, 61; kawaii, 56; of landscape art, 272; Mormon, 244; national, 38; "odorless," 58; racial, 47

affect, 18, 158, 191, 192, 228, 237, 281n92, 297n19; binding powers of, 29; positive, 162, 163, 170, 174, 175, 180; psychological, 128; studies, 160; theory, 23

Afghanistan war, 102

Africa, 7, 151

Afro Samurai (video game), 287n96

Against Interpretation: And Other Essays (Sontag), 32, 157

Ahmed, Sara, 46

air, Barthes concept of, 144

Ajay Ghale (fictional character), 195, *195,* 219–22

Akira (manga), 52

Alavi, Mohammed, 105–6, 107, 109

Alien (film series), 185, 187, 299n71

Alien Evolution (2001), 184

Alien: Isolation (video game), 32, 76, 163, 180–85, 187–88, 190–93

Amanda Ripley (fictional character), 182, 187, 188, 192

American exceptionalism, 119–20

American studies, 6

America's Army (video game), 207

America's Asia (Lye), 60

Amita (fictional character), 194, 204, 220

amorous discourse, 103, 110

amorous objects, 111

Anable, Aubrey, 162, 281n92

anachronistic subjects, 230, 231

Anderson, Amanda, 296n3

anonymity, 138, 139, 142

Anthropy, Anna, 10, 11, 31, 105, 294n40

anti-imperial critique, 220

Aonuma, Eiji, 87

aphrodisia, 23, 138, 145, 150, 296n112; attributes of, 143; exercises of, 140; focused upon self, 147; Foucault and, 136, 137; *The History of Sexuality* and, 146; technologies of, 148

Apocalypse Now (1979), 171

Apple, 14, 99, 113, 116

arcade games, 78

arcades, 83

archipelagic reading, 247, 249

Arena of Valor (video game), 62

ars erotica (arts of erotics), 18, 21, 25, 150, 157, 253; contemporary, 28; Foucault on, 135; Greek society and, 149;

ABOUT THE AUTHOR

Christopher B. Patterson is Assistant Professor in the Social Justice Institute at the University of British Columbia. His previous books include *Transitive Cultures: Anglophone Literature of the Transpacific* and *Stamped: An Anti-Travel Novel,* written under his pen name, Kawika Guillermo.